# The Business of Europe is Politics

# The Business of Europe is Politics

Business Opportunity, Economic Nationalism and the Decaying Atlantic Alliance

DIMITRIS N. CHORAFAS

Routledge
Taylor & Francis Group

LONDON AND NEW YORK

First published in paperback 2024

First published 2010 by Gower Publishing

Published 2016
by Routledge
4 Park Square, Milton Park, Abingdon, Oxon OX14 4RN

and by Routledge
605 Third Avenue, New York, NY 10158

*Routledge is an imprint of the Taylor & Francis Group, an informa business*

© 2010, 2016, 2024 Dimitris N. Chorafas

The right of Dimitris N. Chorafas to be identified as author of this work has been asserted in accordance with sections 77 and 78 of the Copyright, Designs and Patents Act 1988.

Publisher's Note
The publisher has gone to great lengths to ensure the quality of this reprint but points out that some imperfections in the original copies may be apparent.

**Gower Applied Business Research**
Our programme provides leaders, practitioners, scholars and researchers with thought provoking, cutting edge books that combine conceptual insights, interdisciplinary rigour and practical relevance in key areas of business and management.

**British Library Cataloguing in Publication Data**
Chorafas, Dimitris N.
  The business of Europe is politics : business opportunity,
  economic nationalism and the decaying Atlantic alliance.
  1. Business and politics--European Union countries.
  2. European Union countries--Foreign economic relations.
  3. European Union countries--Commercial policy.
  4. Nationalism--Economic aspects--European Union countries.

  322.3'094-dc22

**Library of Congress Cataloging-in-Publication Data**
Chorafas, Dimitris N.
  The business of Europe is politics : business opportunity, economic nationalism and the decaying Atlantic Alliance / by Dimitris N. Chorafas.
    p. cm.
  Includes index.
  ISBN 978-0-566-09151-3 (hbk.)
  1. European Union countries--Economic policy. 2. European Union countries--Commercial policy. 3. European Union. I. Title.
  HC240.C4845 2009
  337.1'42--dc22

                                                              2009024528

ISBN: 978-0-566-09151-3 (hbk)
ISBN: 978-1-03-292011-5 (pbk)
ISBN: 978-1-315-61425-0 (ebk)

DOI: 10.4324/9781315614250

# Contents

# List of Tables

# Preface

In his definition of human society that held well for nearly 24 centuries, Aristotle said that *man is a political animal*. Human beings are truly human only in society and more precisely in a community (*polis*) where social order has been created by humans and for humans. From the early small work teams of farmers, artisans and traders to the modern corporation, a *business enterprise* is also an expression of communal living.

The same is true of laboratory work and, in a larger perspective, of science. While the laws of science, however, are universal, from *polis* to *polis* the laws of men are different. L.P. Hartley began his novel *The Go-between* with the words 'The past is a foreign country: they do things differently there' – in fact, not only the past but also the present and the future. Leadership makes the difference.

'We never do anything bold,' Walter Bedell-Smith, Eisenhower's Chief of Staff during World War II, complained in a conference. 'There are at least 17 people to be dealt with, so [we] must compromise, and compromise is never bold.'[1] If 17 are a hindrance to bold decisions, think about having to deal with 26 individualistic chiefs of state in NATO; and, even worse, 27 autocrats in the European Union. It is not for nothing that, as another proverb has it, growth for growth's sake is the philosophy of the cancer cell.

****

Written primarily for the academic and professional audience, this book focuses on the present and future of the *European Union* (EU) and, by extension, of the *North Atlantic Treaty Organization* (NATO). To a very significant extent the EU and NATO share the same membership, albeit with some exceptions, and they also suffer from very similar ills, mismanagement being one of the most deeply rooted. Moreover,

---

1   Cited in Max Hastings, *Armageddon. The Battle for Germany 1944–45*, Pan Books, London, 2004.

- the fact that their business model belongs to a time which is resolutely past and is unreformable is widespread and worrisome; and

- they also suffer from a crisis best described as *déclinisme*, a state of malaise and lack of confidence because of the bankruptcy of the EU's political and business system and cracks in NATO's security shield.

These were the opinions of a lot of cognizant people with whom I consulted in preparation for writing this book. One of the things that struck me during the 2008 and 2009 meetings is that some of the experts I was talking to are no more at ease at expressing an opinion, if that opinion is contrary to the mainstream or is likely to upset 'social peace' (whatever that is supposed to mean).

For those of us who fought at the side of freedom in World War II, this is very bad news – as if we are back again in the 1930s, with their turbulence, their bias and their scares. To a growing number of people capitulation to the Frankenstein of the day seems the better alternative than the cry freedom or death.[2]

'*Death is no event in life because we don't live in order to die,*' wrote Ludwig Wittgenstein, the mathematician and philosopher.[3] '*But freedom of thought and expression is the juice of life, cornerstone of progress and cradle of civilization.*'

I would also add that a life of fear and slavery, including mental slavery, is not worth living. Upon such principles of the Dark Ages, the most momentous consequences hang. Freedom, or lack of it, affects the destiny not only of individuals, but of nations and civilizations. Other dreams, too, made in the bleak days of the world war years have been deceived.

For the young generation of the immediate post-World War II years a European Union was a dream, which proved to be inconsistent and unreal. As for NATO, its model might have been right for fighting twentieth century

---

2    For instance, when they expressed critical views of events, some people asked not to be identified. The reader should also note that certain references (including approximate statistical estimates) are based on discussions made, or papers presented, in conferences and symposia. Therefore, when not identified through footnotes, numbers expressed are in order of magnitude rather than exact statistics (which, in a number of cases, are simply not available).

3    Ludwig Wittgenstein, *Tractatus Logico-Philosophicus*, Cosimo Books, New York, 2007 (first published in 1922).

wars, but not twenty-first century insurgencies which include fundamentalist passions and terrorist actions.

Is there a hope left that tomorrow will be more glorious? If yes, what are the preconditions that would allow the EU to be put back on track towards a future of greater prosperity and how could NATO revamp and restructure itself to become effective? These are the main themes this book aims to answer, after first identifying what has gone wrong and why – as well as what should not be repeated, an example being economic nationalism.

'If you know the plumbing you know who is running the water,' says a popular proverb. In business and in politics the plumbing is the network of decisions which see to it that goals are met, plans are kept dynamic, schedules are maintained and those in charge are responsible for their deliverables. Or, alternatively, that nothing is done because the arteries of the organization are clogged and there is no longer anyone in charge.

The book is divided into four parts. Part 1 starts with a snapshot of the original European Economic Community and brings to the reader's attention that the deepest reason why it was born in 1957 was the need for Franco-German rapprochement, which seemed to succeed for nearly four decades but then started to fall apart.

The business of America may be business, but the business of Europe is primarily politics, and politics have got in the way. *Déclinisme* did not help because it institutionalized a pervasive belief that the state would take care of everything, which has never been the case in any society in the medium to longer term.

Part 2 brings to the reader's attention that the EU, its citizens and its leaders are confronted by conflicting aims and inadequate business practices. Much of this has to do with inadequate management standards, violations of governance principles and the heavy hand of a growing bureaucracy collectively known as 'Brussels'. It features 37,000 managers and employees as well as 15,000 lobbyists.

'Brussels' is by no means a democratic outfit. Its bosses are appointed, not elected. This has created the preconditions for disorientation among the EU electorate where resentment exceeds common feelings. A rather intense sense of political stagnation has led to the French, Dutch and Irish 'No!' votes to constitutional referendums, along with a business environment of mounting debt promoted by left-leaning governments.

The only thing that seems to be truly growing in the EU is its membership, and this has a curious parallel with NATO. The more they grow in number of members, and therefore in incompatibilities and differences of opinion, the weaker becomes the unity of command of either and both organizations, while the structure as a whole shows clear signs of stress and strain.

Too many EU politicians resort to higher public spending as an easy option to buy off dissatisfied voters. Very few care about cutting their country's (or 'Brussels') suffocating bureaucracy and spending burdens. Hardly any venture to do away with obsolete labour laws by introducing labour market reforms, but a growing number are keen to protect national champions.

This growing economic patriotism and what it means for business is the theme of Part 3. It is also one of the reasons why, in the EU, wealth creation has taken a back seat. While the economy of the so-called BRICS (Brazil, Russia, India, China) is rapidly growing, that of the PIIGS (Portugal, Ireland, Italy, Greece, Spain) is stagnant at best or outright declining.

Clearly enough, globalization has winners and losers, and so does an economic union. But is industrial patriotism and economic nationalism the best policy for the future? Plenty of case studies included in this book suggest that this is far from being the case, no matter if a past president of France once denounced liberalism as the new communism. Economic nationalism has strained relations among European Union members and has been a hindrance, not just a nuisance, to the creation of strong pan-European companies.

Part 4 brings to the reader's attention the fact that, as far as NATO is concerned, a similar unenviable legacy of blunders and mismanagement is found to prevail. Afghanistan, where NATO attempted to act in unison (admittedly far away from its birth place, the North Atlantic), proved to be incredibly booby-trapped and what followed provided evidence that multinational forces composed of small contingents are, to say the least, totally ineffective.

Looked at from this perspective, one is justified in asking: 'Does NATO know what it wants?' Documented through facts, figures and the losing battle in Afghanistan, a snap answer is: 'No!' In the twenty-first century NATO's results have been dismal and a similar statement is valid about the EU's results. That's what the facts say, but bureaucrats and second-class politicians have probably not read Aldous Huxley, who once stated that facts don't cease to exist because they are ignored.

****

According to an old proverb, nothing succeeds like success. To their misfortune, however, neither the European Union nor present-day NATO are success stories by any stretch of the imagination. In the one as in the other case, the founding fathers have been followed by people with no civil courage, admittedly the sort of courage which is most rarely found. Moreover, in both cases:

- many member states have played the system; and

- plenty of time has been lost in nationalisms, friction and horse-trading.

One of the experts who contributed ideas for this book said that the people who ran the old continent's fortunes were completely ignored until they became presidents or prime ministers, and then they fell into obscurity again after leaving office. Jacques Chirac of France, Tony Blair of Britain, George W. Bush of America and plenty of others fit that reference. All they did while in power was to apply some distorted, outdated solutions to a modern society's twenty-first-century problems. Therefore, it is time to expose the myth that:

- the West has responsible and accountable political leaders, and

- the decisions which they make have only one goal: the common good.

The reasons for the decay of the Atlantic Alliance are only partly those that brought the European Union towards irrelevance as a political entity; still, as documented by facts and figures in the 13 chapters of this book, there are many similarities characterizing the two entities' decay. At the top of the list can be found:

- poor leadership

- loss from sight of original goals

- uncontrollable expansion of membership

- nationalistic revival and

- general apathy regarding the 'common cause'.

Behind all that lies the fact that EU and NATO members, the nation-states, no longer agree on worthy objectives which could motivate them and make them work in synergy. Centrifugal forces pull what remains of the European Union and of the Atlantic Alliance apart, and, as generations of politicians change, new bonds show up which, in their turn, underpin the importance of the German–Russian energy axis.

****

I am indebted to a long list of knowledgeable people, and of organizations, for their contribution to the research which made this book feasible. Also to several senior executives and experts for constructive criticism during the preparation of the manuscript: Dr Heinrich Steinmann and Dr Nelson Mohler have been among the most important contributors.

Let me take this opportunity to thank Martin West for suggesting this project, Gillian Steadman for seeing it all the way to publication and Pat FitzGerald for editing the manuscript. To Eva-Maria Binder goes the credit for compiling the research results, typing the text, compiling the index and making valuable suggestions.

Dr Dimitris N. Chorafas
Valmer and Vitznau

# PART 1

# The EU's Cocktail of Business and Politics

# 1

# Beyond the European Union's Fiftieth Birthday

## 1. The European Economic Community

Better known as Common Market, the *European Economic Community* (EEC) has been in existence since its original six founding members signed its charter, the Treaty of Rome, on 25 March 1957.[1] This was preceded by a 1955 meeting of the six countries – Belgium, France, Germany, Holland, Italy and tiny Luxembourg – in Messina, Italy, which confirmed their desire not only to join forces, but also avoid a third European civil war. Euratom, the European Atomic Energy Committee, was also established in Rome on the same day as the EEC.

The European Economic Community was by no means the only supranational organization in Europe, after the end of World War II. In 1959, two years down the line from the Treaty of Rome, the rival European Free-Trade Association (EFTA) came into being, aggregating seven countries: Austria, Britain, Denmark, Norway, Portugal, Sweden and Switzerland.

- 'Six and seven' was how some newspapers greeted the two trading blocks.

- The sum, however, does not make 13 because, at least on paper, the goals of the two blocks were different.

While, as its name implied, EFTA was essentially a free trade area, the EEC's concept was much more ambitious. Incorrectly labelled 'federalists', those who saw the Treaty of Rome as beginning of an age of a fully integrated European

---

1   The ceremony took place in Rome's Capitoline museum, and behind the political leaders one could see two seventeenth-century frescoes depicting ancient Rome's bloody history; suitable semantics and reminders of Europe's own civil wars.

continent yearned to build a unitary state; one that they had hoped for from the time of the European Coal and Steel Community set up by Jean Monnet (who was also the intellectual force behind the EEC) in 1951.

It did not happen that way, nor did it help that the Treaty of Rome had come hard on the heels of two other not so positive events. One of them was the French National Assembly's rejection of the proposed European Defence Community (EDC) dating back to 1954 (section 2). The other was the Suez Crisis of 1956 which turned the tables on transatlantic links, (more on this in section 2).

In addition, several years later, five of the seven EFTA members, along with many other states which belonged to neither of the original blocs, eventually joined the EEC, which was rebaptized the *European Union* (EU). The task was challenging, because member states had to confront an economic reality consisting of a combination of changing demography and rising costs of huge entitlement programmes: social security, medical care, unemployment benefits and more which:

- created big deficits

- inflated the national debt and

- over several decades, put practically every one of the EEC's members under stress.

To this cocktail has been added a rising nationalism in some EEC states (Part 3) and the rule of *mediocracy*, leading the EEC's critics to predict with some confidence that the outcome would resemble a classical Greek tragedy: the principal character – in this case Monnet's concept of a United Europe – would rise by dint of talent and energy to the pinnacle, and then would be brought crashing down by inner flaws or demons he cannot control.

Not only have political forces combined against the preconditions necessary for a truly united Europe,[2] but also, since then, lesser men than the founding fathers have taken over the reins of the common goals of the EEC's member states. As a result, in the five decades of its existence, the Community has been characterized by:

- confused ideas

---

2    As opposed to today's misnomer of a 'European Union'.

- petty nationalism and

- low achievements.

More than 50 years of low-level deliverables have far from fulfilled the European public's dreams and expectations. Because of the politicians' mistakes and infighting, Europe has lost its coherence while its economy has been kept in a state of relative hibernation. Half a century has been sacrificed to political incompetence, and we still are not at the end of the tunnel. Yet, the principle of good governance is simple:

- the EU's politicians should worry about the citizen, not about how to outmanoeuvre one another; and

- they should be listening to the arguments made, and priorities set, by educated men and women – a fast-growing breed of European citizen.

An increasing number of EU citizens are now saying that the seeds of disunity were planted at the beginning because, at the time it was signed in March 1957, the Treaty represented nothing more than an expression of goodwill by six nations who had gone through the devastating experience of two world wars and did not want to see this happening again. The virus was in the cocoon, because:

- the Treaty of Rome set only general guidelines;

- but, as experience teaches, the devil is in the detail.

There is no doubt that the EU is in crisis partly due to its unstoppable enlargement (Chapter 7) and partly because of the second-raters who have been unable to fulfil the EEC's premises. Membership seems to be the only thing that is growing. Jacques Delors, who was president of the European Commission from 1985 through 1994, says that the present crisis is the worst in the project's history – worse than the period of:

- Charles de Gaulle's 'empty chair' (in 1965); and

- Margaret Thatcher's persistent demands for 'my money back' (1979 to 1984).

In Western Europe in particular there has been popular disenchantment with the EU project. There is no common vision that strikes a chord with today's European citizens, in the way the end of the European civil war did 64 years ago. Most of today's leaders devote their time inwards to different nationalisms (including economic – see Chapter 9), mistrusting not just the Union and the Brussels bureaucracy (Chapter 5), but also one another.

On the rare occasions that common citizens have been given the right to express their opinions, they said what they thought of the current EU leadership in a dramatic way. French and Dutch voters did so when they rejected the EU Constitution in 2005 and Irish voters gave the same message when they rejected the so-called mini-Treaty in June 2008.

These rejections have not been accidental; they are a reflection of the fact that the EU is characterized by *déclinisme* (Chapter 3) and by a severe democratic deficit, as if absolute monarchy had come back with a vengeance (Chapter 6). Democracy requires the informed consent of the governed and will not last if citizens are not given the chance to choose among options connected to major themes – the EU Constitution and EU enlargement being examples.

Biasing or short-circuiting the democratic tradition leads to wider public indifference, leaving the European Union's institutions vulnerable to popular indignation. This leads to more bias by unscrupulous politicians because no institution or constitution ever defined the longer term. A better tomorrow can only be assured through the continuing interest, support and work of the public.

The first to emerge from the Constitutional Conventions after the American War of Independence, Benjamin Franklin, when asked by citizens anxious to know about the country's future which was the chosen regime, answered: 'Democracy, if you can keep it.' For his part, at end of World War I George Clemençeau, the then French Prime Minister, made the famous statement: 'The Treaty (of Versailles) will be what you make of it.'[3] What was made of the Treaty of Rome is not so brilliant:

- the removal of internal tariffs by creating a wider Common Market has been achieved;

---

3   Cited in David Stevenson, *1914–1918. The History of the First World War*, Penguin Books, London, 2004.

- but the concept of political union is one of the skeletons in the EU cupboard; and

- the structure to sustain a pragmatic European integration, represented by the EU Commission and European Parliament, is unstable at best (more on this in Chapter 5).

Shortly after signing the Treaty, a regime change in France demonstrated that the original goodwill of the founding fathers can be easily twisted by those who hold the reins of national governments. According to the pros, this assessment is too pessimistic, but their argument forgets that, as the saying goes, 'a pessimist is an optimist whose opinion is enriched through experience'.

## 2. Paradigm Shift

In the physical sciences a theory, any theory, is always provisional. In the large majority of cases it can never be proven, and new fact(s) which contradict it and its predictions can tear it to pieces. The same is true of political initiatives which seem to convey some definite advantage but cross over established interests whose negative response makes the project vulnerable. The European defence force provides an example.

In 1950 René Pleven, then French head of state, proposed the creation of a European Defence Community (EDC). That plan pleased the post-Roosevelt United States, which was at that time fully committed to building up Europe as an ally against the Soviet Union – but also to taming France and preventing Germany from becoming a challenger again.

- The EDC treaty, which included Britain, was signed in 1952.

- But it never went into effect because in Paris the Gaullist-dominated parliament refused to ratify it in 1954.[4]

Pointing to a reassertion of nation states in post-World War II Europe, the EDC's rejection became a turning point. Within two years came another watershed event: Suez and the frustration it created. In Britain the Suez adventure ended with the fall of Anthony Eden's government; but in France the

---

4    Considering it to be a threat to France's sovereignty.

after-effect was deep anger against the United States and reassertion of French identity – indeed, a paradigm shift.

A different way of making this statement is that the first blow to the Atlantic Alliance did not come from de Gaulle in the early 1960s, as is generally thought, but from the Suez Crisis of 1956. As a brief reminder, after Gamal Abdel Nasser[5] nationalized the Suez Canal, the French and British made an ill-fated invasion of Egypt, starting at Port Said and going nowhere.

- This cast doubt on their resolve and ability; and

- the doubt grew as neither government paid attention to the fact that once authority is lost it is nearly impossible to regain.

At the time, there was a rumour that the Dulles brothers, John Foster and Allen, had not only tacitly given their accord for the Suez operation, but had also set a one-week limit for it to succeed. Poor planning and abysmal execution by both the French and British saw to it that that week was exceeded without obtaining any tangible results. The rest is history; but also part of this history is the fact that Suez's psychological aftermath is still present, even if more than half a century has passed.

The rising anti-Americanism of France, essentially a wave of negative public sentiment fed by the media and the government, started as a result of President Eisenhower's intervention to end the Suez operation, which was going very badly. This was largely an American initiative. Nikita Khrushchev played a role in Suez just to be in the news, though he eventually managed to get a foothold in Nasser's Egypt. It is quite interesting that, after recognizing how big the problem was, the two Suez operators had diametrically opposed reactions.

- Since then, British policy has paralleled that of America in the English-speaking countries.

- By contrast, in France the (then in power) socialist government stayed put, and the popular rage against the American intervention gained momentum.

---

5   Nasser was an Egyptian nationalist, not an Islamist. Early on, as chief of state, he prosecuted the jihadists; most particularly, the Moslem Brotherhood, which originated in Egypt and (in modern times) is the first fundamentalist organization on record.

This has been a true paradigm shift, the change that takes place when one dominant idea is overtaken by another. Suez led France to conclude that a supranational European community was not in its vital interest. Supranationalism would have effectively required doing away with national sovereignty (section 4), and many politicians opposed it. Within a short span of time another event intervened to steer the EEC away from the Atlantic Alliance (Part 4) and from a United Europe: the return to power of Charles de Gaulle.

Clouds of nationalism (economic and otherwise) gathered over the European continent, and they are still covering the sky. In 2007, 50 years after the birth of the EEC, Europe's leaders locked horns on the question of what to write on a grandiose birthday card intended to commemorate the European Union's anniversary. Debate on the contents of the so-called 'Berlin declaration' was a proxy for wider debate and disagreement about:

- the very future of Europe;

- what to do with the stalled EU constitutional treaty; and

- whether the circus of EU's enlargement should continue or finally be stopped.

Angela Merkel, the German Chancellor, wanted the declaration (to be unveiled in the German capital on 25 March 2007) to kick-start the debate on reviving the constitution. She hoped to produce a text summing up the EU's 'achievements' and its future tasks. France wanted it to give high priority to social policies; Britain insisted on playing down references to the euro; Poland pressed for mentioning Eastern Europe's past communist oppression; and other EU countries had *their* pet themes that they wanted to see displayed in the communiqué.

A number of EU member states, including the Czech Republic, Britain[6] and Poland, have been anxious that nothing appears in the text which commits the EU to rushing ahead with a new or ambitious constitutional treaty. There was as well a lyrical part. According to rumours, some EU members intended to bring in an author or journalist to give the EU's birthday declaration a sentimental flavour, on the premise that every treaty is a ceremony.

---

6    True enough, Britain, a commonly-used abbreviation of 'Great Britain', only covers England, Scotland and Wales, and does not include Northern Ireland and should, correctly. In this book, however, Britain is used interchangeably with 'the UK', as this is how it is used colloquially.

It is an interesting hindsight that in the end the 'Berlin declaration' marking the EU's fiftieth birthday was written in secret and signed only by the European Union's top brass: Merkel as holder of the EU's rotating presidency and the heads of the European Commission and Parliament. Some EU watchers have commented that it is most likely that any revised constitutional treaty will also be cooked up in secret with the aim of ratification by national parliaments, which are easier to handle than referendums, where popular opinion may go the opposite way to the one politicians and oligarchs have chosen.

## 3. The Ceremony of French–German Rapprochement

André Malraux, the French author, has written that 'every civilization is a ceremony' and 'there is no other way for winning over the latent barbarity in the heart of people, than chain them with rules'.[7] (André Maurois, another French (and greater) author, might have added that at the heart of every ceremony is religion, and therefore politics.) Not only ceremonies but also the love and hate surrounding a civilization save it from *public apathy*, which Arnold Toynbee, the British historian, has defined as the penultimate stage of decadence. Toynbee said that civilizations proceed:

- from *bondage* to spiritual faith;

- from spiritual faith to courage;

- from courage to liberty;

- from liberty to abundance;

- from abundance to selfishness; and

- from selfishness to *apathy*, which is precisely the state of the EU today.

There has not been much bondage between France and Germany, save at the time of Charlemagne (Karl der Grosse), when both countries shared the same ruler. There was, however, plenty of French involvement in the politics and military fortunes of German states during the years of Louis XIV,[8] and an

---

7    André Maurois, *Cinq Visages de l'Amour*, Messeiller, Neufchatel, 1942.
8    See also section 4.

enmity between them which started in Bismarck's time and led to two world wars.

People promoting the ceremonial role of the EU point out that, propelled by continuing Franco-German *rapprochement* and helped by a personal relationship between de Gaulle and Adenauer, the EEC made progress towards the target of establishing common market bonds. The removal of internal tariffs and quotas started under the first president of the European Commission, Dr Walter Hallstein. Critics respond that compared to the EEC's original goals of political unity:

- the removal of tariffs was no more than an intermediate step, and even that has been a slow process completed only in July 1968;[9]

- by contrast, the big goal of political and social integration, was put onto the back-burner by de Gaulle and from there into a time capsule.

The critics have a point. Existing evidence suggests that foremost in the minds of Robert Schuman, the French-Alsatian, Konrad Adenauer, the German, and Alcide De Gaspari, the Italian who started his political career in the parliament of Vienna, was to avoid a World War III due to renewed Franco-German friction, while creating a world-power through Franco-German integration.

- *If* this was really the aim, as many historians believe,

- *then* the answer is that the 'EEC of independent states' has totally failed in reaching the main goal of the Treaty of Rome.

It did not help that by the early 1960s Robert Schuman was gone from the political scene; De Gaspari was consumed with political troubles in Italy; and Adenauer was more interested in building bridges with de Gaulle than in pressing for European integration. Moreover, the lack of open public debate on European political union saw to it that the public was apathetic about how far cross-border integration could go among countries who, over the centuries, had fought with one another.

---

9    Accompanied by the erection of a common external tariff.

Some hope, however, did persist. In 1970, a year after de Gaulle quit the French presidency, came the Davignon Plan of integration and operation – but it soon found its way to oblivion. Then, in 1974/75 the Regional Development Fund was set up to close the gap between prosperous and less prosperous regions of the EEC.[10] Over the years this has been highly overexploited by member states, most particularly Spain which, while being a rich country, continues to receive a poor country's financial support.[11]

The record of ineffectual EEC ceremonial duties continued. In 1979, through the joint efforts of Helmut Schmidt, the West German chancellor, Valéry Giscard d'Estaing, the French president, and Roy Jenkins, President of the European Commission, the European Monetary System (EMS) was founded, with an exchange rate mechanism designed to limit currency fluctuations. The trick was linking member currencies to a newly devised European Currency Unit (ECU) which was proclaimed as the pivot.

The headwinds confronting this initiative originated from the fact that the EEC heads of state miscalculated the member countries' financial powers. The EMS's central value became not the ECU but the Deutsche mark. In addition, a second objective, that of establishing a Community-style IMF to be known as the European Monetary Fund (EMF), failed to materialize. Its goal would have been to:

- pool together member states foreign exchange reserves; and

- provide loans to EEC countries facing balance of payment difficulties.

The silver lining of that failure was that, by all the evidence, the EMF would have had a bleak future. In the early Mitterrand years the French government had tried and failed on three successive occasions to jump-start the economy by spending lots of public money. This led to three devaluations of the franc in the early to mid-1980s.

In the mid-1980s came another ritual. Margaret Thatcher wanted 'her money back', meaning Britain's contribution to the common coffer, which she

---

10  The EEC fulfilled in the most questionable way the Treaty's provision for a Common Agricultural Policy (CAP). CAP has been a failure.

11  Spain was and is the largest single beneficiary of EU regional funds. Up to November 2008 it had received a total of €186 billion, most of which was spent on improving roads and railways.

considered to be unacceptably high. At the Fontainebleau summit of 1984 this led to a compromise involving a rebate to Britain of 66 per cent of the difference between its VAT contributions to EEC funds and its share of benefits. In fact, with the exception of Germany, all EU countries have tried to get out of the common purse every penny they put in – which is admittedly a ridiculous practice.

At the beginning of 1985 Jacques Delors, former minister of finance of the first Mitterrand government and newly appointed boss of the EU Commission, made a tour of European capitals to sound out opinions on ways of moving matters closer to the founders' goals. These included two revivals: (i) defence union and (ii) monetary union; as well as a new goal: reform of the EEC's institutional structure. In its general lines, Delors' proposal for structural changes appealed to the different country leaders. Difficulties began when he argued that:

- a rigorous approach to internal market integration involved a mass of new legislation; and

- the Treaty of Rome not only had to be amended, but also enriched with details which would strengthen the way it works.

Jacques Delors' concept was right. The cornerstone of an effective European Economic Community was harmonization of rules and regulations among its member states. The obstacle was (and continues to be) that no member state wanted to give up its ongoing practices in the name of wider interest; and no supranational rules and regulations were acceptable to the second-raters who, by the 1980s, ran the EU members.

The contradiction between national ceremonial standards and common policy became known as the *Cassis de Dijon*, after a celebrated 1979 case at the European Court of Justice. A West German firm was prevented from importing Cassis de Dijon because it allegedly did not conform to exacting West German standards for liqueurs. The Court ruled that Bonn could only prevent the import of an EU drink if it could prove that the liquid was harmful to the health of its citizens.

In the twenty-first century the Cassis de Dijon was tested in the case of Moslem terrorists who, according to EU supranational laws, had to be extradited to the country in which they had committed crimes to face justice. In the case of Germany, the lawyer for Islamic terrorists appealed to the Supreme Court in Karlsruhe, which found that *according to German law* – written by the Allies when World War II ended – the terrorists had to be set free. Supranational EU law and national law collided, with the result that:

- it's all right to drink cassis made in France;

- but it's wrong to protect German and other European citizens from terrorist bombs and bullets.

The collision of European Economic Community regulations with corresponding national laws and regulations has been, and will continue to be, a major problem. On one hand, lack of political union does not permit streamlining laws; and on the other, *Brussels*[12] bureaucracy tends to over-regulate the trivia while leaving important issues as gaping holes. Over and above that has come the unravelling of French–German relations.

## 4. From Richelieu to Aristide Briand

Roman law established that you have to accept agreements once you have signed them. The loophole is that – though the concept that economic *and* political union as the only effective way to avoid another major civil war in Europe is in the background of the Treaty of Rome – nothing is written in black and white of the fact that France and Germany have to work hand-in-hand.

- The force pulling in this direction is common interests.

- The centrifugal forces are the remnants of nationalism and of political ideology.

The origins of the divide between the two countries which share the Rhine as a common border date back to the early to mid-seventeenth century, the time just before and during the reign of Louis XIV. The conflict known as the Thirty Years War[13] between Protestants and Catholics began in the Holy Roman

---

12  'Brussels' is a short-cut label for Brussels-based EU commissions, its agencies, directorates, 37,000 bureaucrats and 15,000 lobbyists.

13  Ironically, World War I, which started in 1914, and World War II, which ended in 1945, also make, between them, a 30-year war. The Peleponnesian War which destroyed Ancient Greece was also a 30-year war.

Empire and gradually developed into a general political war involving most of Europe.

It was the deliberate decision of Cardinal Richelieu that Catholic France joined the otherwise Protestant side of the war, which theoretically had to do with the religion of the fragmented collection of states in the Holy Roman Empire, but practically was concerned with the sovereignty of three monarchies: the House of Habsburg in Austria, the Spanish monarchy and the House of Bourbon in France.

- The conflict brought to light Spain's political and military decline; and

- with Spain weakened, France became the dominant power in Europe.

The Peace of Westphalia, which settled the Thirty Years War, also laid the foundations of the sovereign nation state, established fixed territorial boundaries for many of the countries involved in the prolonged conflict and changed the relationship between rulers and their subjects. Previously, people had overlapping loyalties. Thereafter, citizens were subjected to the whims of their king, the secular and religious laws of their government and the nationalisms these bred.

Westphalia also ushered in the age of national armies.[14] The armies of France made the law in northern Italy and central Europe, at least until the battle of Blenheim. For their part, absolute monarchies survived as venerable institutions, though they started to crumble with the French Revolution and fell to ruin at end of World War I.

After the first global war ended, in 1918, Germany's Weimar Republic veered towards liberalism and, following the interim of the Nazi years, after World War II German liberalism was reinforced. The reasons may well be historical. The roots of modern liberalism date back to the seventeenth and eighteenth centuries when, as a response to the strict rules of Westphalia:

- politicians tried to limit the arbitrary power of kings and churches; and

---

14  Though universal conscription had to wait Napoleon's years.

- this led to a political movement whose after-effect has been the growth of liberal democracy.[15]

Liberalism, of course, is far from being the only alternative regime with which society has experimented since the mid-nineteenth century. Others were socialism, fascism, Nazism, communism, authoritarianism, populism and dirigisme. These have shared the common root of the rule of the state: 'The government knows always "better", and that it has the statutory right to be a steady interventionist' (the French model).

Liberalism and interventionism provide a more accurate description of political and social philosophy than the more classical and increasingly meaningless dichotomy between the political right, centre and left. As an example, contrary to those in modern Germany, post-World War II regimes in France have tended to be dirigist and interventionist – whether they came from the centre-left or the centre-right.

Governments come and go, and regimes change, but the remnants of a political ideology (and associated state structure) impact in a material way on the longer-term relations between nations – for instance, between France and Germany within the EU. To appreciate this issue better one has to think of the European Union not as a political monolith but as an entity falling between two views which have dominated its five decades of history (and where Britain had a critical role; see also Chapter 2).[16]

- The EU was supposed to be a cathedral, where member states leave their sovereignty (and nationalisms) at the door.

- But de Gaulle's hand, steady enlargements and nationalism have kept it at the status of a free trade area, with governments connected mainly by commercial links.

A serious study of the recent past would document that in the longer term only the first option should be viable. Political leaders would have learned lessons from past failures. Prior to 1914 and therefore World War I, far-sighted individuals had urged the need for pan-European institutions, though there

---

15  As well as of liberal economic ideas.
16  Although in the liberalism vs dirigisme debate Britain has steadily been on the side of liberalism – in a way not unlike the Catholic France of Louis XIV, which sided with the Protestants – the country has sided with the dirigist state(s).

had been no organized movement in favour of them. In the aftermath, that initiative for peace in the European continent[17] was overtaken by the warriors.

A few years after World War I, in the 1920s, prompted by the memory of millions of people who died for nothing in the trenches, a movement emerged which comprised several people and groups lobbying for a European customs union and a *Pan-Europa* organization. Aristide Briand, a notable French prime minister and foreign minister, became the president of this organization, and Richard Couldenhove-Kalergi the motor. Both called for greater political unity among European nations, persuading businessmen, intellectuals and politicians that:

- the states of the continent needed much closer ties; and

- political integration was the best way to reduce the dangers of revolution and war.

Another commendable initiative was the Kellogg-Briand Pact of 1928 (between America and France), with the main powers undertaking not to go to war except in self-defence. The Pact led nowhere, and history books state that this was anyway too little for Aristide Briand, who had hoped for more concrete American commitment, but the 1920s was a time of US isolationism and nothing else could be obtained. (Little had Briand foreseen that his countrymen would turn anti-American a dozen years after being liberated by the American army in World War II.)

Aristide Briand, however, was not discouraged. Instead, he turned towards his own countrymen, the Germans and other European countries' citizens with a plea for a union. Legitimately considered as the current EU's predecessor, Briand's 1929–1930 proposal for a *European Union* was based on:

- a permanent consultative assembly;

- a continent-wide network of Locarno-style arbitration treaties; and

- a common market, betting on the likelihood that commercial interests would provide strong financial and cultural bonds.

---

17  Jean Jaurès, the great French humanist and political leader, played a major role in the movement for peace, but was assassinated before he had a chance to complete his work.

Another major twentieth-century political figure who believed in a European federation was Ireland's Eámon de Valéra. In 1932, as president of the Council of the League of Nations, he encouraged his colleagues to accept the Briand plan, but to no avail. De Valéra also believed that some surrender of national sovereignty was essential in order to resolve disputes through the machinery of international law.[18] The tournaments among chiefs of state in the EU provide evidence that Briand, Couldenhove-Kalergi and de Valéra were right in their assessment. Any treaty deprived of the political will for deliverables is half-baked, or outright pointless.

## 5. France 'vs' Germany, or France 'and' Germany?

When, in the 1980s, Helmut Kohl, then chancellor of Germany, spoke of a United States of Europe, Margaret Thatcher, then British prime minister, thought that that was dangerous talk. Kohl was in search of a lasting political vision, fearing that later generations of leaders in Europe would not understand the dangers of political frictions, protectionism and nationalism.

- The political union of which so many people before Kohl had dreamed did not happen.

- Monetary union did, but it has not marked a big change in European political culture, nor did it lead towards civil integration (Chapter 8).

Even on the monetary union project, where France and Germany were partners, more often than not they agreed to disagree on the need for monetary stability targets, measures and priorities. This, experts say, is at once petty and perilous. It is perilous because national rivalries can surface and easily get out of hand. And it is petty because financial stability leads to trust – and trust is everything in a partnership.

In German eyes, since the end of World War II several French presidents have managed their states' business badly. To show his socialist credentials François Mitterrand nationalized industries and banks in 1981. Jacques Chirac, his successor, began by watering down the Stability and Growth Pact which had been signed to safeguard the euro's value. Then Nicolas Sarkozy demanded

---

18  European University Institute, *Sources for the History of European Integration*, Florence, 1980.

political control over the European Central Bank (ECB) – and therefore the euro – which would have meant adopting awfully inflationary policies.

The French and German rapprochement and divergence, in short the history of the two countries' relations post-World War II, provide an example of the difficulty with which changes may be happening in Europe. In the years that preceded the 1957 Treaty of Rome, as well as those immediately following it, the French and German governments sought close relations. Political analysts looked favourably on this trend, documented by the relations established between de Gaulle and Adenauer; Giscard d'Estaing and Schmidt; Mitterrand and Kohl; and, to a lesser extent, Chirac and Schröder.

But is the post-World War II Franco-German rapprochement still valid? Rumour has it that Angela Merkel is nervous about the go-get-it policies of Nicolas Sarkozy, the French president, while the latter is uneasy about what he considers to be the complacent attitude of the German Chancellor.[19] According to experts, behind this thinly veiled friction hides not one but a number of issues on which the two heads of state don't see eye-to-eye:

- the expensive euro versus the dollar;[20]

- independence of the European Central Bank;

- Maastricht's criteria and commitment to financial stability;

- co-ownership of EADS, Boeing's competitor;

- AREVA, and nuclear energy expertise;

- power production and distribution;

- common agricultural policy (CAP);

- enlargement of the European Union;

- Turkey's contemplated entry into the EU (Chapter 7), and more.

---

19  In reality, Merkel's policy has been prudent, as it should be, rather than complacent.
20  Whose exchange rate is established by the global market and not by the ECB as some people believe.

This is a growing list of important subjects where French and German interests are diverging, with the after-effect that relations between the two countries are no more what they were a few decades ago. Gone is the talk about the Franco-German 'couple' – an expression heard for many years after the end of World War II.

A recent example of what makes the relationship between Sarkozy and Merkel a matter for concern far beyond France and Germany is provided by the so-called Mediterranean Union. Alarmed that Sarkozy might try to split the EU and divert resources into North African countries, Merkel forced him to agree that the Mediterranean Union:

- would be embedded in the EU's present structure; and

- all EU members would be welcome to participate in it.

But that's only one issue. Sarkozy also has big plans for the environment (to which Italy, Poland and other EU countries object), defence, energy, agriculture and immigration. In Germany there is scepticism and fear that *if* too many projects are started at once, *then* nothing will be achieved beyond filling top jobs, and even that may be compromised.

There are, as well, funny contradictions which impact on a paralysed European governance, tailored by countries such as Britain, which support further EU expansion (for which purpose?) but resist the scrapping of national vetoes. This leaves the European Union in limbo and the splitting of the formerly close post-WWII France-German collaboration does nothing to help things.

As a stratagem to bypass some of the differences by way of third-party advice, Sarkozy wanted the December 2007 EU summit to set up a committee of wise men to address long-term questions. Other EU heads of state thought that this wish was simply a strategy to obtain a recommendation from the 'wise men' that 'this' or 'that' should or should not be done (such as, Turkey should never join the EU).[21]

Optimists say that it is only normal that differences of opinion, even important ones, arise in an alliance. France and Germany are by no means the only EU countries which have found themselves at odds in the last 100

---

21  That would evidently clash with some other EU politicians' *rotten* position – for instance Tony Blair's – that Turkey is a worthy candidate for EU membership.

years. Right after World War I, with Germany beaten, traditional Anglo-French animosity quickly resurfaced as a pervasive influence on the two countries, influencing and twisting the ex-allies' policies.

The way David Stevenson has it, not only were the French seen as colonial rivals by the British, 'but in Europe too, much of the British delegation from Lloyd George downwards suspected them of imperialist ambitions that would undermine a stable peace and might threaten Britain directly. These considerations set Britain against much of the French territorial and security program.'[22]

Some other EU-related incidents, too, are worth noting. Within the EU itself, the treaties of Maastricht and Nice were rejected by Danish and Irish voters (although they were largely implemented later). Many observers see a Machiavellian political plot behind this attitude of agreeing only on some of the issues and disagreeing on many others. Critics are in fact suggesting that several EU leaders have adopted a confrontational policy in the hope that,

- if they do disagree often enough,

- then their electorate will think that its interests are duly protected.

This is only partly true because the citizens themselves have their own minds and they don't always need the politicians to fabricate disagreements. In mid-2008, a fortnight before he started his six-month term as president of the European Union, Nicolas Sarkozy got first-hand experience of the anti-cooperative attitude of EU members through the Irish 'No!' vote to the so-called mini-Treaty which had replaced the EU Constitution.

That's not the first time politicians have misjudged the overwhelming preoccupation of their electorate – the European public. Alive or dead, the mini-Treaty is scant consolation to the millions of British retirees who in 2008 saw the equivalent of $2.8 trillion of their pension money disappear, lost in poor credit-related decisions by the funds which managed it. While a great deal of time is spent in political infighting:

- there is a curious absence of a thoroughly studied plan on how the 2007–2009 banking and credit crunch can best be handled;

---

22  David Stevenson, *1914–1918. The History of the First World War*, Penguin, London, 2004.

- but there is plenty of readiness by governments – in the US and the EU – to throw money at the problem, forgetting about the risk of igniting a Weimar-type hyperinflation which will be a great disaster for pensioners.

There exists plenty of evidence on how easily things can get out of hand. After World War I, in 1922 both France and Germany were badly hit by an economic and financial crisis. The French franc lost half its value. The German mark turned to ashes in the wake of Weimar Republic's hyperinflation. This left deep scars in Germany and had a significant impact on its monetary policies, which continues today.

The evils of inflation on an industrial economy are a twentieth-century curse which should always be kept in perspective. Moreover, the Weimar hyperinflation was not caused only by the defeated nation's monetary policy. Not only Germany but also the victors, France and Britain, went through financial turmoil in the post-World War I years as political and social issues:

- deepened the gulf between the rulers and the ruled; and

- made the results of monetary instability far worse than they might have been otherwise.

The challenges dividing France from Germany today (and both of them from Britain) are no different. They are about financial stability, jobs, standard of living, the inability to restructure antiquated labour laws, economic nationalism, dirigisme versus liberal policies – and egos. But they are many, and as they don't get solved; competing interests feed upon them and the gulf between nation states within the EU becomes wider.

In conclusion, the banking crisis, credit crunch and economic downturn of 2007–2009 have made matters worse. In 2009 the European Union is about many things, but growth is not one of them. Companies cannot contain their level of profits and employment at the same time, nor can they easily diversify into other EU markets, since other firms are already well-established and operating there. This has made each EU government even more conscious of national interests and even less willing to build a United Europe.

## 6. Brussels and the Question of Sovereignty

Whether under its past mantra of EEC or its present as European Union, any critical view of Europe should necessarily include the European Executive in Brussels, the European Parliament in perpetual motion between Brussels and Strasbourg and their lack of authority over member states (Chapter 7). Both are themes of Part 2, but a few words are necessary at this point as they relate to issues treated in the present chapter, most particularly with regard to national sovereignty.

In her book *The Downing Street Years*, Thatcher makes the point that 'ministers can get out of the habit of thinking politically and become cocooned in their departments'.[23] Change the word *departments* to *bureaucracy* and you have the description of what is going on in Brussels – or, if you prefer, in the European Commission.

At the heart of the problem has been the fact that the different EU institutions collectively known as 'Brussels' produced no leaders. Since the start, the EEC's president and commissioners have been mostly passing figures in a larger drama: the failed integration of European states. And, as critics are quick to suggest, few things are more useless than a government that cannot govern.

Brussels has become the epitome of an artificial megastate which has no soul to blame and no body to kick. What it has is a layer of bureaucracy over the already existing layers of bureaucracy of the different nation states (Chapter 5) – but without the powers to cut those other groups' red tape for the common European good. Its more visible characteristics are not statesmanship but:

- some absurd and contradictory regulations;

- pork-barrel policies, particularly in agriculture; and

- plenty of lobbying, providing a good living for its 15,000 practitioners.

The pros point to the customs union, competition policy, single market, abolition of exchange controls, and creation of a single currency managed by an independent central bank which they consider to be supranational. Critics answer that Brussels has failed to modernize Europe's entrenched welfare state

23  Margaret Thatcher, *The Downing Street Years*, HarperCollins, London, 1993.

and, even in those years when the European economy was on an upswing, many countries suffered from high unemployment. (This is particularly true for the young and the unskilled.)

A growing body of Brussels watchers now say that the EU Executive is a creature of its own publicity machine. It has been endowed with no real authority and no control over the different heads of state, who do as they please – including publicly aired attacks against the EU Commission itself and the European Central Bank, in spite of its independent status.

When it is convenient to them, the politicians in charge of EU member states often put on Brussels' back their own inability to solve problems at home. At the time he was president of France, Jacques Chirac frequently used the excuse that he could not do 'this' or 'that' because Brussels would not allow it. This became a policy even on matters where the European Commission had no jurisdiction (Chapter 11).

'The 27-member EU is nothing more than a bird cage packed with squabbling parrots,' said one of the experts who contributed to this book. 'The whole place is about politics, highly paid jobs, travels, dinners and soft-pedalling'. In short, EU citizens are getting fleeced all over the EU – in Brussels and at home.

One of the most severe criticisms of the past five decades is that the appointed managers of the European Union have failed to dismantle the stone walls dividing member countries. This has left the old continent as a conglomerate of different jurisdictions. Even those EU governments which try to be as close as possible to European laws see to it that their own laws come first, which proves that the failure of integration

- is not a problem of finance;

- it is a mixture of politics and of sovereignty.

'We have and will have negotiations within the EU', said one of the better-known politicians, 'but the final decision is not with commissioners or the president of the EU Commission.' EU member countries are ready to accept subsidies but not Brussels rules. Non-member countries feel even more strongly about preserving their sovereignty. Switzerland (not an EU country) presents an example.

'We have a unique type of democracy,' commented an educator in Geneva. 'The people are sovereign. This is not the case in any other country in Europe. There is no referendum anywhere as a consistent policy prior to major decisions and constitutional changes. We have elaborated that over hundreds of years. It's a tradition.' 'It cannot be that European law is higher than Swiss law unless the people and the cantons vote by majority that they agree to it,' said a friend in Zurich. The prevailing spirit in many countries which are EU members is not too different:

- today no nation state would give away its sovereignty;

- but several might have done so in 1958 when Europe was still licking its wounds from World War II.

After their defeat during World War II and the looming loss of the colonies, the politicians who governed France in the 1950s more or less appreciated that a *merger* with another European power would have been the best possible policy. Also, in the 1950s Germany was more or less ready to go along with political integration in the EU, and most particularly with France, but:

- that opportunity was lost; and

- within another decade new strategic priorities were established by a self-assertive Germany.

In a wider EU sense, protectionism has been alive and well within the EU's borders. In the early 1990s, Martin Bangemann, then EU internal market commissioner, dismissed the growing demand for protectionism from some countries regarding industries such as cars and electronics, arguing that European companies should be more confident about free competition. In a reversal of earlier Brussels policies, Bangemann also refused to intervene in a dispute between Britain and Germany over fireproof standards for mattresses, or to set EC standards for free-range chicken.

But, on other occasions under other commissioners, EU 'standards' were established for the curvature of bananas, as the French demanded;[24] and the diameter of condoms, as the Italians wanted. All this manipulation of the EU's existence and preoccupation with trivia tremendously weakened Brussels' prestige

---

24 Intended to keep out Central America's bananas, in favour of West African (ex-colonial) produce.

and the EU's institutions. The policy of protecting one's own turf has been the worst possible scenario in a union of European nations – and in the end it has backfired.

Today, when EU politicians shout loudly that 'changes taking place are extremely significant from a political viewpoint', they simply disseminate false information. Governments are not giving up sovereignty over parts of their economy; and, as real-life events document, nor are they ready to change their legal and social structure. Instead:

- practically all EU governments try to be at the same time 'in' and 'out' of the ill-defined common cause; and

- while they are gaining whatever they can by being 'in', they also feel free to act on their own *as if* they were out of the EU. Economic nationalism is an example (Chapters 9 and 10).

As if to make matters worse in economic terms, little attention is given to crucial issues such as the harmonization of fiscal policies and of taxes. Raising Value Added Tax (VAT) is commonplace. For heads of state, here is some food for thought on taxation. It dates back to the fourteenth century, when the Arab historian Ibn Khaldun made a comment about taxes which continues to be true right up to today:

- at the beginning of the Arab empire, the tax rates were low and revenues were high;

- at the end of the empire, tax rates were high and revenues were low (then came decadence).

It is difficult to find a more accurate description of the beginning and end of an epoch. Let's face it. A public debate which is dramatically necessary to a union of independent states – such as on entitlements, taxes, savings and inflation – is definitely missing; and policy coordination is nowhere to be seen, in spite of 'summits' as well as the multiple, expensive and inefficient layers of bureaucracy in the EU – or because of them.

## 7. Five Freedoms and More EU Treaties

Sovereignty is important, but it is not the only thing that counts. Any solution one adopts has its shadows. 'The splendour of light,' Winston Churchill once wrote, 'cannot exist without the shadows it creates.'[25] The shadows of the EU originate in the congregation of 27 countries, an infinite place where one government's size might be another one's hindrance; one's wish might be another one's curse; or one's truth another one's lie. This is today's European Union. But how did we come there?

The European Coal and Steel Community of 1952 had set very precise goals for itself. The bottom line was business. This was not true for the 1957 Treaty of Rome (Section 1). Yet, there was an example that could have been used as a reference. The Netherlands, Belgium and Luxembourg were already in the process of integrating their economies into one entity: Benelux. This, experts say, provided the background of the founding fathers' guiding policy which emphasized *four freedoms* to be phased in through a jointly agreed timetable:

- movement of goods;

- movement of people;

- movement of services; and

- movement of capital (which in the meantime has been globalized).

It is tempting to add a fifth basic freedom to these four: *the freedom of expression and of choice*, giving citizens a say in how laws are chosen and shaped. This is a fundamental democratic principle which gains its strength from, and at the same time underpins, the freedom of expression. Back in 1762 Jean-Jacques Rousseau and Voltaire maintained that:

- the rights of men must be respected;

- any citizen is permitted to write whatever he wishes about religion; and

- he cannot be condemned without being heard.

Moreover, the trial must be public. Nor has this right been our civilization's accomplishment. In ancient Athens and among the Romans, witnesses were heard publicly in the presence of the accused, who could reply to them and question them himself. But politicians in the EU have found ways to circumvent

---

25  Winston Churchill, *Reflections et Aventures*, Delachaux & Nistlé, Neuchatel, 1944.

this basic freedom, turning the clock back to Europe's age of absolute monarchies.

The proof is that the founding fathers' four basic freedoms and Voltaire's idea are not fully respected, which happens against good sense and in violation of principles taught by experience. An example is the violent reaction to the Bolkestein Directive (named after the Dutch EU Commissioner), which has been most severely criticized, particularly by the French. Yet all it did was to confirm the free movement of people and services in the EU *as originally planned*:

- *if* member states respected these five freedoms; and

- *if* they subsequently enlarged them in their scope;

- *then* there are reasons to believe that this would have led to real integration.

Instead, barriers have been raised by different EU countries to the free movement of people and services (*le plombier polonais*). As one should have expected, the target of these barriers has been 'jobs', because, ironically, as more and more countries joined the formerly exclusive EU club, the cake of the EU economy shrank and the free movement of people and services was no longer welcome.

As for freedom of speech and of choice, had they been living today Voltaire and Rousseau would have wondered if Louis XIV had come back to life. Apart from meetings, dinners and 'summits', which are a dime a dozen these days (all at the taxpayers' expense), nothing has really happened that would promote democracy in the EU. The pros say this statement is wrong, proof being the existence of:

- the EU institutions in Brussels[26] (Chapter 5);

- the European Commission (or do-nothing EU Executive), also in Brussels;

- the European Parliament (in both Strasbourg and Brussels, at double expense to the taxpayer); and

---

26  Which are expensive, impotent and lobbyist-ridden.

- the removal of barriers to trade and similar goodies the Common Market brought over the years.

The pros are wrong, however, because they forget that the bureaucracy in Brussels is a hindrance to democratic rule rather than a help (and a costly one for that matter); the European Parliament has no authority whatsoever; and the aim to create a single, unified market of people and services hit the rocks, having found its nemesis not so much in diverging national interests as in the steady and irrational enlargement of the EU.

Even the removal of barriers to trade proceeded very slowly, because of lack of political will. The Single European Act (SEA) saw the light only in 1987, three decades after the signing of the Treaty of Rome, and with it some things began to move. (Negotiated within an intergovernmental conference (IGC) under the supervision of the European Council, the Single European Act was signed in February 1986 and came into effect on 1 July 1987.) Experts look at the SEA as the first comprehensive revision of the Treaty of Rome.

One of the stated (but not realized) SEA purposes was to make the EU more politically responsive, as a way of avoiding subsequent enlargements creating a sort of sclerosis. This goal is still up in the clouds. Also, part of the Single European Act has been a cooperation procedure requiring that certain legislation undergoes two readings in the European Parliament. Moreover:

- the SEA gave the EU's member states until the last day of 1992 to achieve an *internal market* within which the movement of goods, services, capital and labour would be unrestricted; and

- by not limiting itself only to trade issues, the Single European Act also specified a series of institutional reforms, aimed at improving cooperation between heads of state and governments.

The second bullet proved to be hot air – a dubious measure which mainly led to an avalanche of useless dinners, meetings and summits (in short, *summit tourism*). The EU's next milestone came with the signing of the Treaty on European Union (TEU) in February 1992 in Maastricht.[27] Almost overnight the

---

27  It is interesting to note a historical precedent to the February 1992 Maastricht conference. On 7 December 1994, Eisenhower, Bradley and Montgomery had also met at Maastricht for a planning conference; a meeting that had led nowhere in particular.

name *Maastricht* became synonymous with the overhaul of the Treaty of Rome, because it transformed the EU project by:

- extending the competence of (weak) EU institutions;

- supposedly creating a new framework for the EU;

- establishing objectives which theoretically were integrationist; and

- providing a stimulus for creating a single currency on a firmer basis than the EMS and ECU.

The first of these four goals just created more bureaucracy. The second never materialized in any effective way. The third was put into the time capsule. Only the fourth led to something: the unique currency first for 12, then for 16, Euroland members. In 1997 the TEU was followed by the Treaty of Amsterdam, which did nothing worth recording. After Amsterdam came the Treaty of Nice, in February 2001, organized to deal with what in Amsterdam was called 'leftovers'.

History books record that the European Union's meeting in Nice soon became a platform for horse-trading among the different heads of state: the 15 of the 2001 EU and the 10 of the enlargement (then projected for 2004), each one of them accomplished by a contingent of ministers and advisors. The only result from Nice was weighting of member-state votes under so-called Qualified Majority Voting (QMV), subsequently unilaterally altered by the EU Constitution voted out in 2005.

One thing this plethora of meetings, treaties, travels and other pleasures did accomplish was to extend authority (but not necessarily competence) into new fields such as the EU's social policy (a mare's nest), environmental protection (a one-sided surrender) and foreign policy (a controversial subject, open to all types of discord). In all of these fields, results have been rather substandard and they aren't really worth recording.

The pros say that the 50-year anniversary of the EU and the processes which were put in motion demonstrate that the architects of the 'new Europe' had a collective mind, wanted to do good and laboured to quicken the pace of change. This is the lie of the century. Over the years, the European Union has been drifting, precisely because nobody is in charge.

- Who are these 'architects' to start with?

- Why did they fail to accomplish the European Union's original goal?

- Why did they not respect the five freedoms?

- Why did they lie to the European public that they could transform immovable static economies into a dynamic whole?

- Why did they promise to boost the common cause within a combined economy, and then do everything they could to promote 'national' interests rather than European?

One of the many false statements, and unattainable promises, made over the 50-plus years of the European Union – and repeated like an echo – was that among the main benefits from unifying the European economy has been the elimination of bureaucratic paperwork at the operational level. Exactly the opposite took place as a new layer of bureaucracy was added in Brussels, with the result of slowing development and messing things up rather than finding effective solutions.

# 2

# Britain, America, Russia and the EU

## 1. From William of Orange to Thatcher and Blair

The way political analysts have it, since William of Orange (William III, King of England, Ireland and Scotland), Britain had one main goal in Europe: to bend the curve of French expansion on the continent, and contain the ambitions of French kings and emperors. This was as true with Marlborough and the Battle of Blenheim in Louis XIV's time, as with Wellington, Napoleon's Waterloo and thereafter.

For a long list of reasons, the time of William of Orange, a Dutchman by birth, was a turning point in British history. Among the most important milestones was that the British Crown was no longer subject to French bribery. History books say that Louis XIV paid Charles II of England (who eventually lost his head) a secret pension of £225,000 a year for the duration of the war against the Dutch. Charles' chief minister, the Earl of Sunderland, also pocketed vast sums.[1]

The buck stopped at William of Orange, who also saw that shrewd, meticulous long-range planning was essential if a relatively small country, compared to what was then the might of France, was to achieve anything. This quality of meticulous planning, a very important ingredient of sound governance, held good in the century and a half of the British Empire; indeed it contributed a great deal to its success.

In spite of the twist in the English language where 'that's history' means it's over and done with, this lesson of history has not been lost on British governments even after the empire passed away; and it has guided the hand of

---

1    Charles Spencer, *Blenheim. Battle for Europe*, Weidenfeld and Nicholson, London, 2004.

some of them in the post-World War II years. Available evidence indicates that after the 1957 Treaty of Rome, the British government set two complementary aims in terms of European policy:

- prevent Franco-German domination of continental politics; and

- from the start and at all costs, stop the drive towards European political union.

De Gaulle sensed that design and, though himself no friend of a continental political union, in 1963 he blocked Britain's entry into the EU. Ten years later, Britain joined. Then, as now, many French people saw the event as the worst that might have happened to French plans for European dominance, using their country's privileged alliance with Germany as a Trojan horse.

A turning point came another decade later, in the early 1980s, when Margaret Thatcher redefined and sharpened up the aforementioned British goals. Tony Blair kept the course, but the main contributor to the success of the British plan – dividing France from Germany and from the other EU member states – was Jacques Chirac, the ineffectual French president who stayed at the helm for 12 long years.[2]

As far as keeping the European Union underperforming and mismanaged was concerned, Tony Blair and Jacques Chirac worked together, complementing one another's efforts like the Korean Ying and Yang. No better pair could be found to bury for good the last chances of a European political union – and therefore the EU as conceived by its founding fathers. Gordon Brown soft-pedalled on this policy but, though he confirmed the EU Treaty (Chapter 6) through parliament,[3] he did not rebuild what Thatcher and Blair had demolished.

That partnership-by-default of Chirac and Blair somewhat resembles Laurel and Hardy. Laurel provided the opportunities for Hardy's gaffes; Blair cultivated the opportunities for Chirac's half-measures, mistakes and reverses. General Karl von Clausewitz once said that many assume that half-efforts can

---

2  This does not mean Chirac and Blair were always in accord with one another. A book about the euro's birth records Chirac interrupting British complaints at one of Blair's first summits with the question 'Are we going to keep buggering houseflies for much longer?'
3  In spite of the Labour Party's promise to hold a referendum.

be effective; but they are not. In the background of Clausewitz's remark are the notions that:

- average people are not willing to cross a wide ditch without having crossed first a ditch half as wide; and

- going only a few steps rather than all the way is thought to be easier than doing the whole job – and just as effective – which is evidently an error in judgement.

Leadership cannot be exercised through half-steps or by uncertain measures; for a start, it requires a long view. Even with an EU of six, then of ten member states, crossing the wide ditch of European political integration called for a clear, consistent and flexible approach. This is precisely what Chirac did not have and Blair did not wish to provide.

By persisting in the old, worn-out ways under the cover of their authority, political autocrats don't improve upon a current situation that is wanting; they only make it worse. Moreover, political leaders who lack vision fail to realize that they cannot really micromanage people and events:

- an able head of state forecasts, plans and controls things;[4] and

- leads people to the desired goal because they trust *him or her*, though they may not necessarily trust his or her party or government.

This has not been the case in France since the de Gaulle years. The French vote on the EU Constitution referendum in 2005 confirms the lack of leadership (see Chapter 6). This was a constitution designed in great secrecy by Valéry Giscard d'Estaing, another autocrat and former president of the French Republic. To appreciate the 'No!' vote's background, the reader should keep in perspective that:

- the failed European Constitution did not benefit from public debate among the French public, let alone on an EU-wide basis; and

---

4    The six functions of management are forecasting, planning, organizing, staffing, directing and controlling, with the first two and the last falling to the CEO – while the middle three can be delegated under control.

- it was mortally wounded by Chirac's double talk about Turkey's EU entry, which is anathema to the large majority of the French.

In Germany too, and many other EU countries, the oligarchs who run the government decided for the people – quite often against the will of the people – as if the EU were a political rebirth of the Soviet Union. A senior Italian executive put his thoughts in this way:

- the whole EU project is a failure;

- in order to succeed, a union of countries had to be able to excite the peoples' imagination;

- this could be done through innovation; but in the EU today there is no innovation. It's the old political mentality which runs things.

Unwillingness to learn from lessons taught from history leads to repeating the same mistakes. From William of Orange to Margaret Thatcher and Tony Blair, rulers of Britain capitalized on continental European muddling. Somehow the French, Spanish, Italians, Germans and Poles got it all wrong – a theme of Utopia crystallized in Jan Zielonka's idea that Europe should adopt a 'neo-medieval' way of looking at itself. According to its inventor, this neo-medieval state will be characterized by:

- soft borders, rather than hard ones; and

- multiple overlapping structures, rather than neat tidy ones.[5]

That's a recipe for dividing and ruling continental Europe, as in the time that preceded the Treaty of Westphalia (Chapter 1). William of Orange could not have phrased it in better terms. Soft borders would mean a large number of illegal immigrants coming in unchecked, making the old continent the garbage bin of the world. And multiple overlapping structures would lead to a much greater degree of confusion than what currently prevails in the EU – which is already plenty.

One thing Zielonka got right is that a hill of 25 pebbles, incremented by Bulgaria, Romania and rest of the Balkans, is too big and too disordinate to act

---

5    Jan Zielonka, *Europe as Empire: The Nature of the Enlarged European Union*, Oxford University Press, Oxford and New York, 2006.

like a union, now or ever. Instead of 'fortress Europe', he argues, there will be 'maze Europe'.[6] Up to a point, this matches the prophesy of Jacques Delors, the French president of the European Commission from 1985 to 1995, who had referred to the EU as an 'unidentified political object', while trying to turn it into a union (a hopeless task).

How far Europe is from a 'union' is documented by the latest statistics of British *Euroscepticism*. Gordon Brown's government confirmed the EU's Lisbon Treaty, but avoided putting it to public approval through a referendum. Yet neither the prime minister nor his ministers could claim to be unaware of the fact that, according to the polls, by 2009 the proportion of British people believing membership of the EU to be a good thing had fallen from 43 per cent in the mid-1990s to 31 per cent. Other statistics, too, are startling:

- the share of British citizens who think EU membership is unwise rose from 30 per cent in 1995 to 37 per cent in 2009;

- support for greater integration has dropped, from 33 per cent to just 20 per cent, over the same period; and

- only one-quarter of this '20 per cent' favour a federalist European government – that's half the number inclined toward a federal EU in 1995.

Other statistics, too, tell how much the Labour government of 2009 has become detached from public will. During the last 15 years, public support for *loosening* Britain's EU ties has risen from 36 per cent to 51 per cent, while the number of those who want Britain to withdraw from the European Union almost doubled from 12 per cent to 21 per cent as late as 1995.[7] There has been a downturn in public sentiment.

## 2. The Strategy of Divide and Conquer

In retrospect, Britain has had the same foreign policy objective of raising roadblocks to political union in the EU that it maintained in the times since it fought the expansionism of Louis XIV and of Napoleon. The old principle was that neither France nor Germany, let alone both working together, should

---

6    It's already here.
7    *The Economist*, 30 May 2009.

dominate the continent. In the case of the EU, this strategy's new version is that *the more members* it has:

- the more arguments will be stirred up; and

- the more futile and impotent the old continent will become, as a 'union'.

It does not take a genius to understand that this is the key reason behind Britain's push for Turkey's EU membership and to appreciate that, without a constitution, Europe is broken down politically. As *The Economist* aptly remarked: 'When Jack Straw, the British foreign secretary, claimed to be saddened by the French vote [the "No!" to the EU Constitution], you could almost hear his officials popping champagne corks behind him.'[8] This is by no means a critique of British policy:

- *if* it were to Britain's advantage to break up the EU;

- *then* this is exactly what its politicians should have done, with or without Chirac's assistance.

By and large nowadays, professional politicians tend to be more sophisticated in their moves if they grew up in an environment of parliamentary debate. That is how sociologists explain why Britain has more politicians capable of enveloping their opponents than continental European countries have.

There exist also some legacies. As a political analyst had it, the Germans tend to look for leaders able to exercise greater authority and the French for rather average politicians but with a lot of 'social ideology' about them. By contrast, the same political analysts say, the British see politicians who stick by certain set beliefs, or have a passion for intellectual consistency, as stubborn troublemakers – because they lack flexibility.

According to that point of view, political sophistication and intellectual flexibility correlate because flexibility in one's concepts and beliefs permits adaptation to a changing political environment, local, regional or global. In the twenty-first century EU the political climate is totally different from that prevailing nearly three decades earlier, when Margaret Thatcher feared that,

---

8    *The Economist*, 4 June 2005.

- within the EU, British influence would wane; and

- the country might be slowly but surely drawn into a continental political union.

The best way to avert this was the old strategy of divide and conquer, by splitting France from Germany. As a consummate politician, the then French president François Mitterand most likely saw Thatcher's grand design but either he did not feel like fighting it or chose to stick to his strategy of building up continental Europe without Britain but with Helmut Kohl's Germany.

When it came to the euro, Mitterrand trapped Kohl, with Giulio Andreotti's (Italy's prime minister) assistance. The way David Marsh has it, the plan was conceived over dinner and it did full justice to the two politicians' reputations, as it made the European monetary union inevitable in spite of the German Chancellor's reservations about the common currency's monetary stability.[9] During Maastricht's pre-summit meetings the EU finance ministers had agreed on the need for anti-inflation criteria:

- putting stability above employment in the list of priorities; and

- being in accord regarding the independence of the future European Central Bank from the heavy hand of governments.

But there was something missing in the form of a formal pact. The formula the Mitterrand/Andreotti team devised was what became known as the Stability and Growth Pact, which brought Kohl into the fold. This involved a number of rigorous economic targets – later on diluted on two different occasions by Chirac. Still, some pillars remained:

- the overall public debt had to be limited (or in cases brought down to) 60 per cent of GDP (a target which has been widely breached by Euroland's members); and

- annual budgetary deficits had to be at worst near to, but below, 3 per cent of GDP. (This, too, is no longer on the table: even Germany has exceeded it for a couple of years.)

---

9   David Marsh, *The Bundesbank*, William Heinemann, London, 1992.

Chirac did not have Mitterrand's political savvy in handling the British, Germans or Italians. For instance, by fighting with Britain, he wanted to have his cake and eat it, too. But in the end it was Tony Blair who got the best of it. Two referendums, French and Dutch, let Blair off the hook of holding his own promised referendum on the constitution. The irony has been everywhere.

- After spending long years being reviled as bad Europeans and ready to protect US interests;

- the British were taking satisfaction from all the criticism being made of France; most particularly of Chirac, and of his referendum, which had turned everything on its head.

In the aftermath of the French president's misfortunes, political commentators said that if *luck* favoured the British strategy of turning the tables on the European Union, so did Chirac's *maladresse*. A key factor which contributed to the success of the British strategy in killing the EU's unionist trend has been that both the Germans and French suffered from total lack of strategic vision.[10]

Today, even the future of the European common currency, the euro, which Britain has not joined, is being openly questioned, not so much because of the bombshell of French and Dutch votes against the European Constitution, which is by now old news (or the more recent Irish 'No!') but because the severe banking and economic crisis of 2007–2009 has led to inflationary measures and flagrant violations of the Stability and Growth Pact, including:

- plenty of money put on the table in the vain hope of kick-starting the EU economy;

- massive capital injection and guarantees by EU governments to wounded European big banks; and

- a very large (and unwarranted) transfer of toxic waste in the wounded banks' vaults (practically worthless structured financial instruments) to the European Central Bank (ECB).[11]

---

10  In addition, after the very poorly conceived leveraged buy-out of East Germany, Germany was preoccupied with the (hugely miscalculated) after-effects of unification and the problems it brought with it.

11  D.N. Chorafas, *Financial Boom and Gloom. The Credit and Banking Crisis of 2007–2009 and Beyond,* Palgrave Macmillan, London, 2009.

Structural errors have aggravated the problem. Monetary policy has been entrusted to the ECB, but the supervision of the banking and credit industry has not. Yet, monetary policy and bank supervision cannot be thought of as having a separate existence; to a quite substantial extent they are interwoven both among themselves and with national economic interests. When, in the twenty-first century, bank supervision waned, the banking industry engaged in excesses and from there it went into a tailspin.

This was no longer divide and conquer, but divide and perish. Critics say that one of the tragedies of the European Union is that, at all levels, political leaders of member states look at their careers as an end in themselves. But in the case of controlling superleverage they did not do even that. If the Temple of Delphi, of ancient Greek fame, were still in business, it would have given the EU's (and America's) current leaders an oracle most similar to that which it gave King Croesus of Lydia: crossing a barrier destroys a mighty state and a career that goes with it.

- In King Croesus' time, in the ancient world, this was the Halys river.

- In the modern world it is the destruction of financial staying power.

Bank supervision aside, one of the main reasons why financial staying power is destroyed is that traditional 'political rights' are now mixing with 'social' and 'economic rights' which are much more materialistic, highly subjective in their definition and much more elusive for damage control.

Food, jobs and housing are certainly necessities. But no useful purpose is served by calling them *rights*. The public at large, however, has been conditioned by politicians to think otherwise. Even vacations have become rights. And though critics respond that those keenest to use the language of social and economic rights tend to show least respect for human rights, there is a point to be made that traditional strategies like divide and conquer are waning (section 6).

## 3. George F. Kennan's View of European Union

George F. Kennan of the US State Department, a former ambassador to Tito's Yugoslavia, was the famous author of 'Plan A' of the 1940s. The solution this plan offered in confronting the challenge posed by the Iron Curtain was *containment* of Soviet forces in Europe and internationally. Plan A was based on a clear idea, it was well studied and it worked perfectly.

Another famous Kennan proposition which was not very different to the thesis of Plato, the ancient Greek philosopher, did not fare so well. What government policy, and most particularly foreign policy, needed – said this proposition – was a council of wise men, not elected politicians. This idea hit a wall, because it ran contrary to the fact that, during the Cold War, US foreign policy was already a profoundly elitist affair.

Critics said that basically Kennan was a diplomat and a romantic, not a risk-taker. His *forte* was linking political action to great concepts. An interesting hindsight into his personality and the advice he gave the US government as boss of the State Department's Policy Planning Staff was that of integrating Western Europe into a closely knit political, economic and military entity. Others in Foggy Bottom thought this might run against US interests, even in the presence of a Soviet threat. (More on this in section 4.)

For their part, in the immediate post-World War II years, several European leaders concurred with Kennan's thesis. In the winter and spring of 1949, a number of prominent politicians, including Winston Churchill and Paul-Henri Spaak, then prime minister of Belgium, were pressing for a closer association among European states. Churchill wanted to integrate Europe under British influence. The French objected.

History books suggest that, at the time, the degree of European integration was a hot issue for the US government. The majority opinion focused on the need for common action, but mainly on resurrecting the European economy and on reconstruction – as contrasted to the resurrection of a French or Franco-German power at world status, about which there have been persistent and strong reservations.

This choice of the economy as prime target was animated by a belief that something should be done to *integrate the economies* of European countries not only in the interests of recovery, but also for security reasons. By the late 1940s, several organizations had already been established, or were in the process of establishment, to serve as vehicles for the realization of economic and security interests among European states. The more prominent were the:

- Economic Commission for Europe (ECE), embracing those European countries that were members of United Nations;

- Organization for European Economic Cooperation (OEEC), including European countries associated with the Marshall Plan (forerunner of the OECD);

- North Atlantic Treaty Organization (NATO), just in the process of coming into being, incorporating (at the time) nine European countries but omitting a number of others that were members of the ECE and OEEC;

- Council of Europe, also in the process of establishment, with an original membership similar to that of the European component of the Atlantic Pact; and

- Brussels Union, made up of Britain, France, and the Benelux countries; a group of states that belonged, without exception, to all the preceding organizations.

In view of this plurality of entities with very similar goals, George Kennan raised the issue that such proliferation posed the problem as to how one should be proceeding with doing something effective.[12] The answer was far from being obvious, and the questions Kennan posed made sense:

- Which of these existing organizational forms was more promising?

- What circle of countries was preferable?

- To what degree did merging of sovereignty permit effective facing of common problems?

These were issues which related to Europe's long-term future. Equally important questions, for the US State Department and for some of the European states – particularly France – have been: What sort of policy should be followed towards Germany? Towards the Soviet Union? Towards countries that had by then become Soviet satellites?

Most of the government authorities Kennan is said to have consulted tended to regard the division of Europe by the Iron Curtain as an accomplished fact; something final and unalterable. This proved to be the case for the next four

---

12  George F. Kennan, *Memoirs 1925–1950*, Atlantic Monthly Press, Little Brown, Boston, 1967.

decades, but eventually the Iron Curtain fell and, through the wise diplomacy of John Paul II, Eastern European countries recovered their freedom.

To the question of whether European unification was really necessary as a precondition for economic, financial, industrial and military recovery, Kennan says that the answer which he received was generally 'No!'. By contrast, continental European governments stated that unification *was needed* to provide a framework into which Germany could satisfactorily integrate. This was the thesis of Schuman of France, De Gaspari of Italy and Germany's Adenauer in signing the Treaty of Rome in 1957.

With regard to Germany's future, Kennan pressed the point (also supported by others) that a fragmentation of Germany was unrealistic. At the same time, the general opinion was that to leave a reborn Germany free to continue to realize her national ideals and aspirations, within her own sovereign framework, would not avoid the repetition of events that had followed the Versailles Treaty.

One of the most interesting aspects of Kennan's thinking is that, on all the evidence, he was the first to pose the question of a European Union's policy towards Britain. The trigger was problems presented by Britain's position in world trade and finance, as well as her relations with the Commonwealth – but not, apparently, her special relationship with the United States.

Additionally, according to George Kennan, in the immediate post-World War II years it was Britain, of all European countries, from whom had come many ideas and initiatives towards some sort of European integration. Other available evidence than Kennan's also suggests that Britain had taken the initiative to ask the US government what it thought was:

- the possibility of progress toward a European union within the next five years;

- the future of Germany, and of Germany's relationship to a possible European union; and

- the most desirable form of Britain's association with such a union – in the opinion of the US.

For instance, should the initiative towards European integration imply a third force in the world? What might be its aftermath in the Atlantic community? Should it be something that could be stretched beyond the confines of the Atlantic Ocean? If yes, how far? These were soul-searching questions for political leaders who were trying to put the broken pieces of Europe together, after the ravages of the old continent's second major civil war.

Like the Peloponnesian War of old, which meant the end of Ancient Greece and laid out the welcome mat first for Philip of Macedonia and then for the Romans, the aftermath of World War II cast a heavy shadow over Europe. America from the West and Russia from the East were at the doors, while the badly bleeding Britain and continental European countries weighed up past and current events when trying to judge which way they should choose in the future.

## 4. Henry Kissinger's View of European Union

The answer European governments provided to themselves and to others in connection with the questions raised in section 3 were not necessarily clear-eyed and they were certainly not far-reaching. This is the message read between the lines of Henry Kissinger's book *White House Years*.[13] In Kissinger's opinion, the only issue which left no room for doubt was Britain's privileged position and special relationship with the United States – the kind of policy ancient Athens had followed with Rome.

The former Secretary of State paid no attention to the thesis of a great American, Thomas Paine, who once said that society and government are two bodies which move in contradiction to one another: the one encourages intercourse, the other creates distinction, making coordination tough enough in even one country.

The way Henry Kissinger had it, an economically strong Europe would be more self-reliant. He did not miss the point made by European realists that a price would have to be paid for the EU's success, and that this price would be political union; this, however, created a negative reaction in Kissinger's mind in spite of plenty of signals that, in the end, near-sighted national interests would take the upper ground.

---

13  Henry Kissinger, *White House Years*, Little Brown, Boston, 1979.

The former Secretary of State notes in his book that in the 1960s, the de Gaulle years, the French saw to it that Atlantic relations became controversial. This is true, and it can also be added that they remained controversial up to and including Jacques Chirac's last year in office. Kissinger also emphasizes that, for its part, the American government seems to have taken seriously the economic challenge an integrated EU could provide.

Particularly worrisome to Washington was the notion of an expanded European Union, to include Britain and Norway. Norwegian voters turned down EU membership by a referendum on 26 September 1972. But the British had joined in the early 1970s when the then French president, Georges Pompidou, overruled de Gaulle's veto to British entry. (More on the British entry in Chapter 7.)

American reaction to the nascent European Union is vividly described by Kissinger's statement that the departments of Treasury, Commerce and Agriculture, following the pattern of the Pentagon, had constructed a *worst case* analysis of the consequences of EU enlargement on America. The themes of the scenarios were:

- manufactured products,

- agricultural goods, and

- economic presence in developing countries.

A study by the National Security Council (NSC) pressed the point that, in the longer run, an 'expanded Europe' comprising the Common Market and the then European Free Trade Area (EFTA), as well as former French and British colonies, could account for about half of world trade compared to 15 per cent of the US (in 1970).

In 1970, whoever said 'NSC' meant 'Kissinger' and vice versa. In the opinion of the former NSC boss and Secretary of State, international relations were a matter of economic and military power – a doctrine steadily holding over time. 'Henry Kissinger had a powerful, largely invisible influence on the foreign policy of the [George W.] Bush administration,' says Bob Woodward. 'Kissinger's ego was monumental, but [Dick] Cheney found his hard-line advice useful after 9/11 … Bush, according to Cheney, was a "big fan of Kissinger".'[14]

---

14  Bob Woodward, *State of Denial. Bush at War, Part III*, Simon & Schuster, New York, 2006.

(In the background of this 1970 fear of competition from an integrated European Union was the notion of discriminating trade. It should, however, be noted that there is no such thing as non-discriminatory trade. Whether the North American Free Trade Area (NAFTA), the EFTA, the European Common Market, or any other so-called free trade agreement, it is inherently discriminatory towards outsiders because:

- it is formed by favouring the products and services of its members

- while raising tariffs and other obstacles against imports from the rest of the world.)

Kissinger further states in his book that the US economic agencies disapproved a passage of President Nixon's Foreign Policy Report of February 1970, which welcomed the strengthening of the EU. In my judgement, behind this difference of opinion was the power of prognostication and the political savvy that one party had and the other lacked. Nixon was a mature and shrewd politician who had seen, through his mind's eye, that the EU was a divided house and, as such, posed no material threat to the US.

Not everybody in the US administration welcomed Nixon's liberal opinion. As Kissinger puts it, 'Treasury and other agencies thought that this passage encouraged European economic pressure against us … The economic agencies insisted that we use the forthcoming negotiations for British entry into the Community to conduct the battle.'[15]

- That 'battle' centred around what the Treasury, Commerce and Agriculture thought to be Nixon's *carte blanche* for European economic nationalism; and

- in retrospect, this proved to be an overreaction to the President's welcome message – which was based on lack of fear that there would indeed be a United Europe.

This was not the only miscalculation Kissinger made. The way Margaret MacMillan has it in her recent book,[16] Kissinger was not good at economics or forecasting, a fact clearly shown by his dismissive judgement that 'the maximum amount of bilateral trade possible between us (America and China) even if we

---

15  Henry Kissinger, *White House Years*, Little, Brown, Boston, 1979.
16  Margaret MacMillan, *Seize the Hour: When Nixon Met Mao*, John Murray, London, 2006.

make great efforts, is infinitesimal in terms of our total economy'. Tomorrow's newspaper was read by the former Secretary of State upside down.

The lack of depth and miscalculation of this statement about future trade links between the US and China needs no comment. The trouble is that this was an evaluation made by a senior US official at the time he was negotiating the re-establishment of diplomatic and economic relations between America and what was called at that time Mainland China or Red China – a negotiation whose trade terms proved to be quite unfavourable, if not outright disastrous, to the US.

Kissinger's judgement was also wrong about the EU. As far as the panic in connection to the European Union is concerned, Richard Nixon had seen much further than others in Washington. The killing off of the Common European Army in the mid-1950s and de Gaulle's 11 years in power must have given a consummate politician like Nixon a strong signal that:

- nationalism in Europe was alive;

- truly common endeavours were unlikely; and

- given the size of each individual continental country, none posed a threat to the United States.

Had the aforementioned US government agencies done their homework, they would have found that – whether or not Charles de Gaulle was the catalyst – by 1970 the member states of the European Union were no longer thinking in terms of political unity. Instead, they had decided that economic integration would be pursued for its own sake – but in a low-key way and as a limited mission, which has also failed, as we will see in subsequent chapters. However, quite relevant at this point is the fact that the same mistakes are being committed nowadays in terms of relations between the US and Britain on one side and Russia on the other.


## 5. The European Union and Post-Soviet Russia

In the closing paragraph of his excellent book *Spheres of Influence*, Lloyd C. Gardner describes as follows the division of Europe between East and West: 'When Averell Harriman went to see Stalin to discuss the meaning of Roosevelt's death, Foreign Minister Molotov kept muttering: "Time, time, time!" In the end, that was what spheres of influence was all about.'[17] Decided by Stalin but confirmed by Churchill and Roosevelt, the division of Europe:

- lasted four and a half decades from the end of World War II onward; and

- though highly criticized in the West and for nearly two generations creating tensions which took time to heal, did serve a purpose.

By all evidence, the purpose was to buy time for all concerned until the nearly fatal wounds of World War II had healed and a measure of confidence had returned. Though this meant great hardship for many nations which became Soviet satellites, the silver lining was that each party, in East and West, appreciated that limits existed which it was better not to test; therefore both sides knew where to stop.

Officially, the division of Europe ended on 25 December 1991 when the Soviet flag above the Kremlin was lowered for the last time and Mikhail Gorbachev, the last president of the Soviet Union, made his resignation speech: 'The totalitarian system has been eliminated … free elections … free press, freedom of worship, representative legislatures and a multi-party system have all become reality.'[18] A few hours after Gorbachev's speech, George Bush declared victory in the Cold War. Shortly thereafter, the East and West halves of Europe got together again.

While Gorbachev was still the nominal head of state, the Soviet Union was partitioned through a Boris Yeltsin initiative. Here is how Paul Klebnikov describes that side of the drama: 'In early December (1991), Yeltsin flew to a Belarussian hunting resort called Belovezhskaya Puschcha[19] to meet with the leaders of two other big Slavic republics … Together, on December 8, they decided to abolish the Soviet Union and declare independence.'[20] Made just nine months after a nationwide referendum in which 76 per cent of Soviet citizens voted to keep the union intact, this decision was:

- unconstitutional,

---

17  Lloyd C. Gardner, *Spheres of Influence*, Elephant Paperbacks, Chicago, 1993.
18  *The Economist*, 29 November 2008.
19  Which has since become a tourist attraction.
20  Paul Klebnikov, *Godfather of the Kremlin*, Harcourt, New York, 2000.

- illegal, and

- anti-democratic.

The dissolution was engineered by Boris Yeltsin as his way of getting rid of Soviet President Mikhail Gorbachev, who had assumed his post legally, in accordance with the constitution. The former centralized Russian Empire which the October Revolution had transformed into the Soviet Union dissolved into 15 republics. Many of them were republics only in name, run by old-fashioned autocrats.

With the exception of Russia and possibly the Ukraine, many of these republics were poor, featuring a small gross domestic product. On the map Kazakhstan looks vast and it is believed to be rich in oil. But 17 years after independence its GDP was still $91.5 billion (on 24 November 2008 Kazakhstan decided to spend $18.3 billion to support its economy, representing 20 per cent of its GDP).

For its part, modern Russia became a federation constructed from roughly three-quarters of the population and three-quarters of the land of the former Soviet Union. The political structure it adopted is quite different from that of Soviet times as well as from imperial Russia – which in 1918 had gone down fighting when confronted by the pseudo-communist takeover.

- Yeltsin signalled the change, but his solution was an oligarchy rather than democracy, and

- Vladimir Putin put in place his own political model, a de Gaulle-type presidential regime.

Sharing, as it does, a long frontier with the Russian Federation (even if on the map Belarus and the Ukraine are interposed), the EU cannot ignore Russia as a neighbour and trade partner. If nothing else, it supplies about half of its gas imports.[21] Nor can the EU leaders deny Russia a role as actor in world trouble spots from Iran to North Korea, Kosovo, Georgia (a former Soviet republic) and the Middle East.

---

21  What happens when Russia turns off the gas supply was demonstrated in the week of 5 January 2009, in a *réglement des comptes* with the Ukraine.

What has just been written about the EU is equally valid in regard to America. The failure of the Iraq adventure (and the pending one in Afghanistan, Chapter 11) have given plenty of evidence that Douglas MacArthur was right when, in his last days, he advised President Johnson never to put the feet of American soldiers on mainland Asia.

- Russia has the experience of being well-implanted in Asia; it also has huge energy resources.

- America most urgently needs to share both assets with Russia – doing so in a spirit of friendship and cooperation rather than confrontation.[22]

What kind of chickenshit policy is fighting with Russia over Georgia or the Ukraine? Russia has legitimate national interests in regard to both countries. Differences in opinion, and in approach, should not be permitted to lead to acrimonious discussions between Russia, American and European Union leaders, often taking place in an environment overshadowed by arguments. A representative example is the 'summit' in the week of 13 May 2007 in Samara, on the Volga.

Participants to this on the EU's side were Angela Merkel, the German Chancellor in her role as the (rotating) EU president and José Manuel Barroso, who leads the EU Commission. At a gathering that ended without agreement, or even a joint statement, Merkel and Putin took pains to stress the boom in EU-Russian trade, but they were unable to hide the cracks in the EU–Russian relationship.

The meeting started badly as Merkel challenged Putin about the lack of press freedom and his country's poor human rights record. Both issues might have been good for the communiqué but they were very bad choices if one wanted to reach an agreement.[23] Putin became visibly irritated after being repeatedly asked about human rights.

- Merkel and Barroso expressed 'concern' about law enforcement and freedoms in Russia (not their business) – all the way from detention of activists to Chechnya.

---

22  See also the opinion of an American judge on this issue in Chapter 12.

23  This sort of behaviour is, however, typical of European and American politicians, which is why it is taken in this text as an example.

- Putin hit back, claiming that German police had recently taken similar 'preventative' action against protesters in Hamburg (in connection with the G8 meeting).[24]

For his part, José Manuel Barroso 'warned' that if Russia wanted close cooperation with the EU it was 'very important' to understand that the Union[25] was 'based on principles of solidarity'. In so doing, Barroso probably forgot that while Turkey continues to occupy the northern half of Cyprus – a European Union member – with 30,000 troops, the EU has opened negotiations for membership with Turkey. That's one of the many contradictions between:

- what is said,

- what is done and

- what should be done.

It is no surprise, therefore, that Russian and European leaders ended two days of talks with a tense exchange over human rights, but without an agreement on how to negotiate closer economic links. The differences between the two sides were stark, with the German Chancellor and European Commission President clashing with the Russian President over side issues.

The energy talks were unaffected, at least at the corporate level.[26] A few days after the Samara meeting, Europe's three largest gas companies called for increased business ties with Gazprom, the Russian energy giant, saying that growing tensions between Moscow and the European Union should not be allowed to jeopardize energy security. This blunt assessment came from:

- Gaz de France,

- Eni of Italy, and

- E.ON Ruhrgas of Germany.

The statement was timed to coincide with Vladimir Putin's arrival in Vienna for a state visit shortly after the collapse of the EU–Russia summit. As the EU's

---

24  *Financial Times*, 19/20 May 2007.
25  Which 'union'?
26  Which speaks volumes about the weight of the politicians' blah-blah.

leaders and their Russian counterparts continue to disagree, the bloc's big energy companies have been making their own deals with Russia. 'It is about long term contracts, infrastructure, joint ventures and asset swaps,' said Uwe Fip, senior vice president of E.ON Ruhrgas. Edouard Sauvage, vice president of the supply division of Gaz de France, added that the strategy towards Russia was to have reliable and secure contracts for energy delivery.[27] Businesspeople have more brains than politicians.

(There exist huge differences in the EU countries' energy dependence on Russia.[28] For its part, Russia has a product line exposure. More than 70 per cent of its exports are made up of oil and natural gas. Therefore, Russia cannot be blamed for maximizing the economic benefits of its energy resources and geography. Every country does the same. In response to delays in EU negotiations, it has played a canny game, building cosy bilateral relations with Germany, Italy, Austria, Hungary, Netherlands, Greece and Bulgaria.)

## 6. Georgia, Ukraine and Other Frictions

When relations between the EU and Russia sour, the victim paraded on the newspapers' front page is the Partnership and Cooperation Agreement (PCA), signed by the two parties in 1997. Talks on renewing it are long overdue and they show no sign of starting on the right foot. In 2007 the obstacle was a Polish veto, prompted by a Russian embargo on Polish meat exports. By the time that was resolved, the Lithuanians argued that the previously agreed negotiating position was too soft and too limited.[29]

The former Soviet satellites may have scores to settle with Russia, but this should not be the EU's business. Accusations and counter-accusations are a bad policy. Poland, Lithuania and Estonia may be determined to veto talks on the new partnership agreement, but it is Brussels' indecision about what it really wants from a Russian partnership that has been the bigger flop.

---

27  *International Herald Tribune*, 24 May 2007.

28  This stands at practically 100 per cent for Finland and Slovakia, 95 per cent for Bulgaria, nearly 90 per cent for Lithuania and 75 per cent for Austria and Greece, but 'only' 42 per cent for Germany, 30 per cent for Italy and 20 per cent for France. In terms of share of Russian gas sold to or carried through an EU country, at the top of the list are Germany and Slovakia followed by Poland, the Czech Republic and Austria.

29  Also, Lithuania is too small and too dependent on Western Europe to be a troublemaker.

EU and Russian relations with Georgia and the Ukraine are not simplifying the issues connected to an EU–Russia *entente*. The brief August 2008 war between Russia and Georgia was about many things besides South Ossetia and Abkhazia. It was about Russia's 'near abroad' security and its place in the world, as well as energy.

Whether the West admits it or not, the EU–Russian debate about Georgia and its two breakaway provinces was also about Kosovo's independence from Serbia, and this for two important reasons. First, the frontiers (right or wrong) established by World War II were broken unilaterally by the West's action in support of Kosovo's 'independence' – which was a severe political mistake. Second, and most importantly, either one believes in self-determination of peoples or one does not. Arguments made to justify the independence of Kosovo while denying the same right to South Ossetia and Abkhazia are lightweight and self-serving.

- The basic issue is that minorities do exist within other nations' borders. Do these have the right to choose independence?

- Answering 'Yes, here' but 'No, there' is hypocritical, and giving the right to some but denying that same right to others can only lead to more trouble.

The troubles in Abkhazia and South Ossetia (particularly the latter) have, after all, been Georgia's folly, as it struck first; a folly exploited by Russia. Experts suggest that for this reason not even the United States proposed to take on Russian tanks as they rolled in. On the EU's side, too, talk of sending troops to uphold the ceasefire quickly died away. Instead, civilian EU monitors were sent to do an ill-defined job.

One can only hope that other countries will learn from the reckless Georgian move to retake breakaway South Ossetia by force. The good news is that there has been no new Iron Curtain descending across Europe, and no ideologically-based new Cold War. This being said, two comments made in readers' letters addressed to, and published by, *The Economist* made interesting reading, as they reflect public opinion.[30]

One of the letters stated that Georgia and Ukraine have belonged to Russia's backyard for centuries, and the West is deluded if it thinks Russia will tolerate

---

30  *The Economist*, 30 August 2008.

them joining NATO or the European Union. The other reader's letter underlined its author's disappointment that the obvious parallel between Russia's invasion of Georgia and America's invasion of Iraq was not drawn by the magazine. In the reader's opinion, it was a lust for oil that drove the actions of both countries, though they gave altruistic, and unfounded, reasons for their wars.

This August 2008 mini-war also had its funny side, as reported by *Le Canard Enchaîné*, the French weekly, quoting some internauts' correspondence. One message read: 'I live in Georgia[31] but nowhere do I see Russians. I don't even hear them. The news however is there are tanks in the street. Should I be worried?' The other internaut expressed astonishment that the US allowed Russia to invade Georgia, a state of the Union, asking: 'Are the Russians near Atlanta?'[32]

According to at least some experts, the situation in the Ukraine is quite different because its government, unlike Georgia's, controls all of its own territory and harbours, with no disputed enclaves and exclaves. This argument is half-baked at best. Ukraine's independence was a unilateral act by Yeltsin on his way to reign in Russia (section 5) and it was never accepted psychologically by the Russians, whose history starts with medieval Kievan Rus. In addition, Ukraine is split between:

- a pro-EU west,[33] and

- a pro-Russian east.

Eight million of the country's 45 million people are ethnic Russians, many of them with Russian passports. And Crimea, a peninsula handed to Ukraine by Nikita Khrushchev (himself Ukrainian) in 1954 when both were parts of the Soviet Union, is not only heavily populated by Russians, but also Sebastopol hosts Russia's Black Sea fleet, under a lease expiring in 2017.

Both the Ukrainian politicians and the public are divided on whether to look towards the EU or towards Russia.

---

31 In south-eastern United States.

32 *Le Canard Enchaîné*, 27 August 2008. For starters, Atlanta is the capital of the state of Georgia in the US.

33 Galicia in the west has Western cultural and religious traditions as it used to be part of the Austro-Hungarian Empire and after World War I was part of Poland, while Ruthenia was part of Czechoslovakia.

The EU, too, is split on what to do about the Ukraine. Countries like Poland and the Baltic States are asking that the Ukraine become another NATO member (see Part 4), which is the unpopular Ukrainian President's line. But other EU countries such as Belgium, the Netherlands and Germany are unwilling at this stage even to hint at candidate status for Ukraine.

This is not unlike other themes connected to EU decision-making at large and issues affecting EU–Russia relations in particular. The 27 member states and their leaders are divided into several overlapping camps. At one end are those who think Russia can and must be engaged as a partner and at the other end are those who think Russia needs containment. As for arguments behind each position:

- on one side, the EU depends heavily on Russian energy; and

- on the other, the EU should use its leverage because it is Russia's biggest market for gas and other exports.

Quite recently, matters have become more complicated because of NATO's missile controversy (Chapter 12). In response to the radar site in the Czech Republic and anti-missile installation in Poland, the Russians threatened to put short-range Iskander missiles in the Kaliningrad territory (former northern half of East Prussia), nearer to the heart of Western Europe.

West Europeans are uneasy. Nicolas Sarkozy, the French president who (from 1 July to 31 December 2008) also presided over the European Union, said on 14 November 2008 that the American plan did nothing to bring security while it complicated things. The Polish and Czechs – who themselves were not sure they wanted the missiles and radar – answered that France signed up to a decision at the NATO summit in April that same year in support of them, and so on and so forth.

It looks as if history is repeating itself. As Arnold Toynbee put it with regard to second-century BC Rome, the external proletarians (barbarians at the empire's frontiers), and internal proletarians (the growing Christian population) had put at risk the Roman Empire, which thought of itself as being universal.[34] Toynbee's dictum fits all three main parties in the controversy – Russia, America and the EU – as well as their stagehands, like a glove. (More on the travails of this three-party relation in Part 4 on the Atlantic Alliance.)

---

34  Cited in Michel Rouché, *Les Empires Universels; IIe-IVe Siècle*, Larousse, Paris, 1968.

## 7. Deglobalization

Even though they sometimes manage to get the headlines, Georgia, Ukraine and other points of friction are minor events for the European Union and its future. This, however, is not true of *deglobalization* because many of the EU member states have been major exporters.

The severe financial crisis of 2007–2009 and the economic meltdown which followed it led to notable retrenchment in trade, with *deglobalization* being an unavoidable after-effect. World trade has plunged, leading to a reversal of the process of global integration of capital, goods and jobs. Unemployment is rapidly rising[35] while poll after poll indicates that the European public:

- trusts companies less and less;

- by a large majority, is keen to see more regulation; and

- believes that it is an aberration to spend trillions to save self-wounded banks from bankruptcy.

Even people who were long-time proponents of free trade and of free movement of capital now believe that this should not continue without regulation, controls and limits.[36] There are plenty of things to be rethought, many economists now say, and this includes not only the banking industry, but the whole current design of the world's economic trade, social and political landscape as well.

'Globalization was the last successful attempt by the ruling class to steal everything,' says Alan Berger, 'This is proven by the growing disparity of salaries and wages in the west which not only left workers behind but also pushed the middle class to catch up in standard of living by increasing its indebtedness to a level clearly unaffordable and unsustainable.'[37] One in five Americans pays an annual interest rate of 25 per cent or more on his or her debt, according to President Obama.

---

35   It hit 8.6 per cent in France in April 2009.
36   D.N. Chorafas, *Globalization's Limits. Conflicting National Interests in Trade and Finance*, Gower, Farnham, 2009.
37   From a discussion in a meeting on 5 June 2009.

Indeed, the term *deglobalization* is not used to describe only the commercial or financial transborder business, but rather the overall effect of a change in international perspective – which goes well beyond banking and trade and reaches into social issues. An example is the effect of the global economic crisis on binational marriages, which were on their way to becoming quite common among high-earning and highly mobile families.

These were largely superficial marriages, the proof being that when the individuals involved lost their big earnings streams their life became tricky and sometimes ugly. Families that used to live on huge bonus incomes suddenly became unable to continue with the commitments they had taken on in the high life. The way an article in *The Economist* had it, an impressive proportion of the once-rich couples now breaking up includes at least one foreign spouse.[38]

For the majority of EU citizens, however, particularly in some countries like France, globalization has been seen for more than a decade as nearly synonymous with the risk of losing one's job – and, ironically, at the same time as the opportunity of low-cost exotic vacations. Of the two versions, jobs hold the high ground. In the summer of 2008 European Union pollsters reported that some 65 per cent of EU citizens were considering globalization as profitable only for large firms, not citizens.[39]

As with everything else, of course, globalization had both its positives and its negatives. For instance, during its high tide, many countries benefited from *foreign direct investments* (FDIs) by private capital, rather than waiting forever for another state's support. But with the global economic crisis FDIs dried up, and this became a widespread phenomenon affecting not only developing countries, but also several states in the EU.

Britain, Italy and Germany have seen FDIs fall between one-third and half. Finland and Ireland have experienced net outflows. By contrast, in developing countries FDIs were still growing in 2008, albeit by only 4 per cent after a rise of 21 per cent in 2007. In large measure, foreign direct investments have been channelled by the banking system, but big banks did not only serve their clients in transborder deals, they also gambled among themselves and they ruined their balance sheets through excesses.

---

38   *The Economist*, 7 February 2009.
39   Correspondingly, in 2002, 78 per cent of Americans thought foreign trade helped the country but by 2007 this figure was only 59 per cent and by early 2009 it was less than 50 per cent.

The West is divided about the best way to control the economic crisis and financial meltdown which brought with it *deglobalization*. In the US, the Bush and Obama administrations opted for further deregulation, even if official statements seem to say exactly the opposite (see also in the Epilogue the double talk at the 2 April 2009 G-20 'summit' and in the same-day accounting standards change).

By contrast, France and Germany maintain that the 2007–2009 descent into the abyss has been largely a balance-sheet-deep recession precipitated by a financial crisis. Therefore, the underlying concept of a new world order should be that, rather than making the taxpayers pay for other people's faults and greed, a speculator-pays principle should be introduced and applied when things go wrong. Big banks, hedge funds, private-equity firms and other parts of the *shadow banking system* should be tightly regulated, along with:

- over-the-counter (OTC) derivatives;

- collateralized debt obligations (CDOs);

- credit default swaps (CDSs);[40] and

- other highly risky structured products.

Clearly thinking industrialists do appreciate that something radical has changed in the world economy. Jeffrey Immelt, General Electric's CEO, said that the crisis will result in the global economy and capitalism being 'reset in several important ways', and that government would become a 'key partner' to business.[41]

Other captains of industry have come to similar conclusions, but most are not sure about where the limits should be. Must the role of the state be confined to prudential but effective supervision or should it be given a free rein in coming up with hefty subsidies? The present international agreements by the World Trade Organization (WTO), as well as bilateral and multilateral agreements, provide no real guidance against domestic subsidies. Therefore, they more or less leave the way open to:

- big-way dumping,

---

40  D.N. Chorafas, *Financial Boom and Gloom. The Credit and Banking Crisis of 2007–2009 and Beyond*, Palgrave Macmillan, London, 2009.
41  *The Economist*, 7 March 2009.

- state interventions and

- other forms of economic nationalism.

Many countries push their currency towards devaluation, or raise tariffs, and they do so despite the resulting disruption to global supply chains. Ironically, *global sourcing* which was hailed as great advance in world trade amplifies the effects of tariff rises and bounces them back.

In good times, global sourcing was seen as a breakthrough because trade grows much faster with it than in a world where commerce is done in only finished goods: semi-manufactured items, components and partly-assembled merchandise have to cross borders several times. Trade figures are also boosted by the practice of measuring the gross value of imports and exports rather than their net value.

All this unravelled with the economic crisis, particularly so as changes in demand in one country affect not just the domestic economy, but also the economies of several other countries and associated trade flows. In late March 2009 the World Trade Organization predicted that the volume of global merchandise commerce would shrink by 9 per cent over that year. Whether by 9 per cent or a similar figure, this will be the first fall in trade flows since 1982.[42]

It comes as no surprise that some countries have been affected much more than others by *deglobalization*. Taiwan's exports dropped by about 50 per cent; Indonesia's, Argentina's, Japan's, China's, Canada's by over 35 per cent; Italy's, Britain's, Mexico's, France's and Germany's by between 30 per cent and 35 per cent. But Australia's exports slightly increased. The aftermath is not unexpected:

- with hefty reductions in export trade, and in domestic consumption, the global economic machine has gone into reverse;

- output has been declining, and the turmoil shook commerce in goods of all sorts bought and sold by rich and poor countries.

---

42  Between 1990 and 2006 trade volumes grew by more than 6 per cent annually, about double the average growth rate of world output, which was about 3 per cent.

The credit crunch added an additional squeeze through an estimated shortfall of $100 billion in trade finance, which lubricates 90 per cent of world trade. At the London 'summit' of 2 April 2009, the G20 tried to ease this constraint by allocating money to trade finance, but no summit can solve the problem that there is no demand for goods to move cross-border. Two of the five countries most concerned by this big drop in global trade are in the European Union:

- Germany, with nearly $1.5 trillion at stake and 9.1 per cent share of world trade;

- China, with over $1.4 trillion and 8.9 per cent;

- the United States, with nearly $1.3 trillion and 8.2 per cent;

- Japan, with $800 billion and 4.9 per cent; and

- The Netherlands, with $600 billion at stake and 3.8 per cent of world trade.

Other EU member states with significant merchandise exports are France, Italy, Belgium and Britain, in that order. Countries that are not at the top of the list of global exporters also suffered greatly through *deglobalization* – for instance, India, whose exports are around 15 per cent of GDP and Brazil where the economy has been hard hit by:

- declining exports and

- falling commodity prices.

The effects of *deglobalization* have been sharpest among East Asia's 'tigers' – Singapore's economy shrank at an annualized rate of 17 per cent in the last three months of 2008. With exports representing over 60 per cent of GDP and caving in, Taiwan's economy shrank in early 2009. (Many of Taiwan's exports went to China, which itself lost a big chunk of its export markets.)

There is, in addition, a correlation between hardship and failure to plan properly for reserves. While several European Union countries and some big emerging markets have built up foreign exchange reserves and cut their external debts, in Eastern Europe reserves have been a chimera, external debts have risen and current-account deficits have grown considerably after they joined the EU. Therefore, as should have been expected, the reversal of globalization has exacerbated other problems that were building up and made these countries run cap-in-hand to Brussels and to the IMF.

# 3

# The Business of Europe is Politics

## 1. The Mentality of Going Downhill

Calvin Coolidge, the US President in the 1920s, is famous for the dictum: 'The business of America is business.' This is not true of the old continent, despite precedents such as Venice and Albion. The business of Europe is politics and war. Both are governed by risk and ambivalence. Up to a point (but only up to a point) the former can be managed; the latter is not – as evidenced by the 30-year Peloponnesian War,[1] those of the Roman Empire, the 30-year central European war (1618–1648)[2] and the 30-year most recent European civil war (1914–1945).[3]

At the root of vicious politics and devastating wars is nationalism. A salient problem faced by the European Union today is the fact that, like Venice in its eighteenth-century decline, its member states have hibernated for too long on the strength of their past glories. Living in the past saw to it that during these years most of the member states of the EU lost a great deal of their economic might. The success of the Treaty of Rome lies in the fact that there has been no war in the European mainland for over five decades.[4]

The rise and fall of Venice offers an interesting parallel to the EU's ongoing decadence (section 2). Since the beginning of the second millennium AD the queen of the Mediterranean had achieved from the Byzantine, and then from the Ottoman Empire, a near-monopoly on trade with the East. That was a lucrative business that easily paid for:

- the standard of living of Venetian citizen; and

---

1  Started by Pericles, of Golden Age of Athens fame.
2  Which followed the Bohemian Defenestration and whose maestro was Wallenberg (1583–1634); see Chapter 1.
3  Started by the German Kaiser and followed up by Hitler.
4  Except the civil war in Bosnia.

- the city-state's beautiful palaces and churches, as well as its naval might.

By analogical thinking, post-World War II Europe could have benefited hugely from a combination of economic factors and the presence of a highly educated workforce. But, over the years, globalization of manufacturing and trade – practised without a plan and without limits[5] – eroded those advantages. Worse still has been the fact that, like Venice in its eighteenth-century decline, France, Germany, Italy and other countries in Europe became infused with:

- the mentality of going downhill; and

- the vice of enjoying the fruits of decadence.

Right after World War II, with the reconstruction effort in full swing, the standard of living in Western Europe rose some 3 per cent per year. As Raymond Aron, the French author and journalist, aptly said in the early 1970s at the time of the first oil shock, this '3 per cent' promoted democracy and kept in check political and social unrest. But:

- it also led to too many handouts in social services, wages, pensions, health care, you name it; and

- distributed entitlements beyond what the European economy could afford in the longer term.

All that is part of late twentieth-century EU history. What did change did so for the worse. The risk of poverty significantly increased and so did the unemployment of the young. About 20 per cent of Germans under 16 now live in households with incomes below the poverty line, as some recent statistics suggest. In other EU countries that ratio is worse, and this is an almost unavoidable result of obstinacy in avoiding:

- social and

- labour reform.

---

5    D.N. Chorafas, *Globalization's Limits. Conflicting National Interests in Trade and Finance*, Gower, Farnham, 2009.

The ruling autocracy has never really explained to the European public that, for the economy to prosper, every citizen must be prepared both to face the new market forces and to contribute an honest day's work. What counts most is wealth creation rather than redistribution of existing wealth. The irony of this is that more and more people in the EU

- are convinced of the need for reform,

- but they want reforms that *do not* affect them, though they may affect their neighbours.

Some of the people who participated in this research asked me: 'Is there one single maxim that could ruin a country?' The answer is 'yes!' The way Confucius, the Chinese teacher and sage, put it: the only pleasure of being a prince is never having to suffer contradiction. If you are right and no one contradicts you, that's fine; but if you are wrong and no one contradicts you – is this not almost a case of 'one single maxim that could ruin a country'?

With the European Parliament perfectly impotent and the EU Commission under the thumb of the heads of state of EU member nations (Chapter 5), that is the fate of the EU and this is another reason why only a *real political union* with a vibrant parliament and the will to develop and sustain contradiction can see through the release of latent forces in the EU. Even if decadence has started, such forces are still considerable: human, cultural, industrial and financial.

This lack of public debate on changes which are necessary and who pays for them condemned the European Union to going the way of General Motors; the worst continues to worsen. Optimists say that the EU is still in diapers and every birth has crises which are inevitable. The same, the optimists maintain, was true of the US.

Realists point out that such an analogy to early America does not hold. Until the late 1960s the US was most successful in moving forward by managing change, while that is far from being true of the EU and (with couple of minor exceptions) its member states. In addition, high use of technology, cash for investments and the ability to master the global markets favour the US, not the EU. Therefore, the realists don't fail to ask some daunting questions:

- What's the sense of the European Union after all?

- What are the motives for *us* to remain members, in spite of half a century of poor deliverables?

- Where are the common goals for the near and further-away future, as well as the values characterizing the daily life of EU citizens?

Answers to those questions are as important for the heartland of old Europe as for its newly acquired periphery of member nations. To work out as a system, the core and edges of a 'Union' must proceed with a *commonly shared idea* of accomplishment. There should also be targets set for the entire community by its citizens – not by autocrats, bureaucrats and lobbyists (Chapter 5). Only a common attitude can produce qualitative changes in people's lives.

## 2. *Déclinisme*. The Spirit of Our Time

The French have invented a buzzword: *déclinisme*.[6] This term, which fully qualifies to enter the English language as so many other French words have done in the past, sums up their country's growing belief that its institutions, as well as state and social structures, are crumbling and unreformable. At a time when audacity is greatly needed to redress past reverses, *déclinisme* is leading to gradual but irreversible loss in status in the world, effacing the might and glory that Europe once represented.

Part, but only part, of *déclinisme* is abandoning previous obsessions with things that nowadays most people are indifferent to, such as the means to uphold and substantiate great power status; and doing so in favour of things people care about, such as secure jobs, good pensions and all-inclusive health services. The roots are, however, deeper because even more important reasons for sliding towards irrelevance are the unwillingness and inability to take risks to restructure worn-out institutions and to reinvent our civilization in ways that:

- excite public imagination,

- promote freedom of expression,

- encourage cultural evolution, and

- get the economy moving again.

---

6    A word coined during the years of the Jacques Chirac presidency. See also Chapter 4.

Exciting public imagination is a two-edged sword. The Spanish *conquistadores* did so, and the same is true of the building of the British Empire. Nowadays, however, public imagination has been excited by the possibility of living much better today than yesterday and truly in more luxury than the neighbours – financing all this by amassing debt which one day will have to be repaid, but who cares?

A friend of mine, a professor at the University of Louven, used to say that living in a society which is in decadence provides greater ease and many more goodies than in an ascending society. The latter requires hard work and offers low pay, as a large amount of money must be channelled into investment. It is therefore no coincidence that the decadent society is *déclinisme*'s homeland.

Exciting public imagination by building a new Europe would have been a great stimulus. A European identity based on common goals and political union might have worked as a catalyst in capturing the public mind. Had they opted for political union, the original six, or first 12, member states of the EU could have started a new era. With 27 members this is no longer possible. Instead, what *déclinisme* has brought to the surface is:

- parochial nationalism – 'my country is better than yours',

- which is now masquerading as economic nationalism (Chapters 9 and 10) in a sea of unstoppable and irrational EU expansion (Chapter 7).

Like growth for growth's sake, expansion without limits (and this includes both EU membership as well as globalization) is the philosophy of the cancer cell which mirrors the body's *déclinisme*. For the EU, the right type of expansion would have been to include Switzerland, but the Swiss don't want to hear of it and for good reason.

- They have nothing to gain from EU membership.

- But they have plenty to lose, all the way from greater exposure to illegal immigration to Brussels *diktat*, and more.

Switzerland is a confederation in which the *people* and not the politicians decide on important matters. This should also have been the case in the EU. In Switzerland the politicians propose and the people vote. Decisions are taken on propositions when 14 out of 26 cantons vote 'yes' and at the same time the majority of the Swiss people give a 'yes' vote.

By contrast, one of the most evident characteristics of the EU is creeping autocracy, Brussels-style. It brings to mind Milton Friedman's aphorism about the US, 'This land is blessed in having to surmount only one tyranny: that of the status quo', which applies all the way to the Brussels phenomenon with only one small change. Instead of 'status quo' read 'new regulations written by bureaucrats in an ivory tower'.

Autocracy and the practice of nationalism correlate. In the late 1980s, in one of her speeches on Europe, Margaret Thatcher poured scorn on the idea of an 'identikit European personality' designed to suppress nationhood. She also pointed out that this would be highly damaging because, in her judgement, 'Europe will be stronger precisely because it has France as France, Spain as Spain, Britain as Britain, each with its own customs, traditions and identity.' A few years later in France, Jacques Chirac said something similar, albeit:

- in vaguer terms and

- mixed with frustration at not being able to shape the EU in his own image.

While acknowledging that national traditions will persist for long time, a staunchly pro-European will look for a new start through real integration. The EU of *déclinisme* and that of a renaissance are two different and incompatible things. But is a renaissance a realistic option when each member state and each citizen wants to take out of the common effort more than it contributed to it?

Economic expansion within the EU would have been a positive indicator about its future, but this requires leadership and foresight – not stonewalling. The EU Commission and heads of member states have done too little to improve the EU's sclerotic economies because (among other reasons) they cannot put themselves together to initiate a serious programme of liberalization and deregulation of the labour market. Moreover, even the few and timid measures being proposed are under attack from economic nationalists.

True leaders would have appreciated that economic expansion through greater competition is exactly what the EU needs. In his book *Godfather of the Kremlin*, Paul Klebnikov quotes Andrei Sakharov, the nuclear scientist, who was once asked about the meaning of life. 'The meaning of life is expansion,' the famous physicist and Soviet-era dissident replied. 'From the moment you start reproducing – I'm talking about the sexual instinct – it's expansion, in a sense. You are replicating yourself. The same with the desire to spread religious or philosophical ideas: that's expansion too.'[7]

One, but only one, of the reasons why economic expansion did not materialize in the EU in more than a barely modest way during the good years was lack of clarity about who is in charge. The Maastricht Treaty was ambivalent on whether heads of state, finance ministers, the European Central Bank, or some other institution should be the responsible party. This meant that benign neglect – another sign of *déclinisme* – became the rule.

During the middle years of the first decade of this century, only German exports seemed to be holding up reasonably well. One of the reasons was that, after years of cost cutting, German industry was in a better position to withstand a sharp euro appreciation versus the dollar, the yen and the yuan.[8] But German exports are not immune to a severe downturn, as the 2008/2009 events demonstrate.

## 3. The European Union's Democratic Deficit

'Rights' sounds like a positive word, and it is a popular one too. There are human rights, women's rights, children's rights, and plenty of other *rights*. But nobody talks much about *responsibilities*, even if the two are twins because one person's rights are another one's responsibilities.

Moreover, it is a mistaken belief that, rights being 'good things', the more of them the better. There is a 'rights' inflation and therefore a rights dilution. Emphasis on a new category of what people now call social and economic rights, for example, has diluted the traditional focus on political rights. It is therefore a much better policy to prioritize the 'rights' we wish to have, as well as to understand that few rights are truly universal. By consequence, what will interest us in this section is the European Union's

- political rights and

---

7    Paul Klebinkov, *Godfather of the Kremlin. Boris Berezovsky*, Harcourt, New York, 2000.
8    During the Group of Eight meetings, the Europeans complained loud and clear to the Americans and Japanese, who in turn ignored whatever the EU had to say.

- growing democratic deficit.

This is written in the sense of 'respecting the people' and not in the populist one of 'serving the people', a Maoist legend. (In dark contrast to this pronouncement, Mao lived like an emperor surrounded by concubines and carried on litters by peasants. He was also placated by everyone while his slogan was 'Serve the people'.) In the EU, as elsewhere, respect for the people has waned because of:

- lack of transparency;

- absence of accountability; and

- remoteness from the citizen.

Irrefutable evidence of the EU's democratic deficit is that the Commission is unelected, though up to perhaps 80 per cent of the laws passed at national level originate in Brussels. With an estimated 15,000 lobbyists around town, corruption certainly exists, while the auditors' habitual qualification of the EU's annual budget relates largely to how the money is spent at national level.

Many of the critics of the current democratic deficit in the EU believe the failure has been that of not making clear to citizens that they have to protect their civil rights by influencing what is going on in Brussels – because, theoretically, that's the job of the Parliament. But, as Chapter 5 will document, the EU Parliament has very limited authority. It is not a parliament that acts as gatekeeper of democratic rule.

What has been the reason for the very low profile and ineffectual attitude of the European Parliament? Is it its limited statutory rights, the inertia of its members, a 'good boy' attitude, or the fact that the EU's continuous enlargement has thrown the parliamentarians off balance? No matter what the cause is, a parliamentary democracy is not created through abdication of responsibilities. Nor does it consist of new steel-and-glass extension to existing buildings, to accommodate the EU's new parliamentarians.

- The cost of extensions across three blocks in Brussels was more than €1 billion ($1.40 billion); and

- the sleepy European Parliament maintains still another vast (and costly) building in Strasbourg, which is used for only one to four days a month.

One might be inclined to say that, silly as they may be, such vast expenses have at least a return on investment because they make EU parliamentarians feel at ease, as they are keen on debating laws, authorizing initiatives and scrutinizing what the EU Commission does or intends to do. Steady scrutiny and challenge would have strengthened their muscles for:

- challenging the Executive's decisions-to-be; and

- auditing and censoring decisions made, as well as deliverables.

But as we will see through practical examples in Chapter 5, this is far from being the case. The European parliamentarians' (MEPs') role is rather limited to warming their seats – which is done *if* and *when* they are present, something that does not happen very often. Such lack of interest in one's duties translates into impotence for parliamentary democracy, and raises the question of to what purpose a do-nothing organization should continue being financed:

- What kind of decisions did the European Parliament take when France, Germany and Italy (among others) repeatedly violated the 3 per cent upper limit of the Euro's Stability and Growth Pact?

- When Tony Blair, Jacques Chirac and Gerhard Schröder tried to steamroll Turkey into the EU, in full violation of the will of European citizen?

- When the International Atomic Energy Authority (IAEA) submitted a report about nuclear risk, 20 years after Chernobyl, with plenty of findings?

- When more and more European citizens talk about the EU's *democratic deficit*, which they want to see corrected, and nothing is done in that regard?

The answer to these and many more queries is: zero point zero. Parliamentarians have always fancied themselves as representatives of the people since, contrary to CEOs and members of the EU Commission, they are elected not appointed. To justify their salaries and fringe benefits, they present the Parliament's action as the answer to longstanding complaints about the EU's democratic deficit. But down to basics:

- the EU Parliament is part of the problem;

- it is by no means part of the solution.

The business of Europe is politics, but this is assigned to the different heads of state, not to MEPs. When people point to lack of connection between European voters and the institutions of the EU, so-called pro-European politicians routinely respond that the answer is to give the European Parliament more powers. This would evidently come from curtailing the powers of national parliaments. And since the EU is no more than a free trade area (rather than 'a union'), the national parliamentarians reject this suggestion.

For their part, the politicians who make up the European Commission, the Union's executive arm, need not bother about elections as they are nominated by national governments for five-year terms. In fact, many commissioners are sent to Brussels as a consolation prize after rejection by voters at home. This makes the rulers of EU's fortunes an undemocratic college – which, however, spends hefty sums on useless projects such as wave after wave of Europe-wide surveys under the 'Eurobarometer' banner.[9]

In a famous 2007 Eurobarometer, for example, the EU Commission trumpeted statistics showing 80 per cent support for the European satellite navigation system, Galileo (Chapter 10) and 63 per cent support for spending billions on it. It was thereafter revealed that only 40 per cent of respondents had heard of Galileo before they were telephoned by the surveyors about their opinion.[10]

Much more serious has been the setback from the June 2009 ruling by Germany's Constitutional Court on the European Union's Lisbon Treaty, which turned the latter on its head. The court said that *the EU is not democratic enough to support more integration*, and it:

9    Each is rumoured to cost about €20 million. The use of polls by Brussels is often political and it is set to become more political still.

10   *The Economist*, 23 February 2008.

- told the German government to call for a pause;

- asked the German parliament to pass a new law to give itself more say over EU affairs; and

- added that even if national legislators become more active, there are limits to the powers that they can cede to Europe.

That the EU is not a democratic outfit and the European Parliament is not a proper legislature is precisely what this book has been saying all along (see also Chapter 7). It comes, therefore, as no surprise that the Constitutional Court ruled that Germany must retain the power to shape its citizens' circumstances of life in the areas of criminal law, taxation, education and religion.

In Bavaria, the Christian Social Union (CSU) has seized the opportunity presented by the Constitutional Court's ruling to demand that major European Union decisions, evidently including the admission of new members, be put to referendums. It also stated that the next European Commission should not include an enlargement commissioner and called for the introduction of a system of *integration control* suggested by the Constitutional Court.

Not only the Eurosceptics, but also the pro-Europeans, have embraced the court's call to assume more responsibility. Germany's liberal Free Democrats think the Bundestag should weigh in not only on transfers of power, but also on directives and the admission of new countries.[11] But on 17August 2008, politicians from the CDU and SPD, the German coalition partners, agreed to rush through parliament legislation which practically changes the constitution rather than having to change their own (wrong) way of thinking.

## 4. The Swedish Syndrome. A Terrifying Shadow of the Nanny State

Ronald Reagan, the former US President, is held to have said, 'The nine most terrifying words in the English language are: "I'm from the government and I'm here to help you".' One of the most flagrant examples of populist policies applying Reagan's dictum is the *nanny state*'s, or more precisely the state supermarket's, deadly embrace supposedly motivated by the wish 'to do good'

---

11 For his part Václav Klaus, the Czech Republic's President, when visiting European parliamentarians attacked his Euroscepticism, compared them to communist-style thought police. *The Economist*, 25 July 2009.

for, and 'be good' to everybody. That's a thinly veiled excuse, because behind the wolf's kind words hides the fact that:

- bureaucrats are generally poor planners and

- they are even worse executors of the socialist credo and other empty promises.

More than one model of socialistic society exists in Europe. With little doubt, the more advanced level (if it can be called that) of the state supermarket can be found in Sweden, the nanny state's paradise. Those who are pro the Swedish model say that their particular solution, which combines the world's highest taxes and most generous social benefits, has delivered:

- strong growth;

- low unemployment;

- a healthy budget; and

- current account surpluses.

Critics answer that these bullets tell lies, and what is generally known as the *Swedish Syndrome* has fed the emigration of society's best performers, particularly to Zug, Switzerland. Also, employment-wise it has kept the private sector in the doldrums, while the number of bureaucrats and other do-nothings has soared.[12] Over the 1950 to 2005 timeframe:

- Sweden created no net private sector jobs,

- but the number of its bureaucrats grew fourfold.

Sweden, in short, provides plenty of documentation for Parkinson's Law. The Swedish Syndrome is the sort of 'standards' to which the French model feels proud to compare itself. True to Parkinson, in the French Ministry of Agriculture, which serves an ever-shrinking population of farmers, the number of staff continues growing while its output shrinks. French farmers say that all this bureaucracy does not provide good value for money.

---

12  A bureaucrat, said a Swedish bureaucrat, is purposely inactive because his or her career depends on not making mistakes, not on successful outcomes.

With the private sector being on guard or downright disconnected, a common characteristic shared by the two state supermarket models, Swedish and French, is lack of employment opportunities. In Sweden, the official unemployment figure has been 6 per cent. But cognizant people comment that until the last election the country's socialist government was a champion at massaging jobless figures, which exclude:

- people forced into early retirement;

- students who would prefer to be working;

- people in government job-creation programmes which produce nothing.

To these forgotten citizens is added Sweden's suspiciously large number of workers on long-term sick leave who, curiously enough, are counted as working and are included in the employment rate. The Swedes, of course, are not alone in this racket. Paying people for not working is a common illness throughout Europe, and the same is true of slimming down unemployment statistics.

In Sweden, people who lose their jobs get as much as 80 per cent of their previous income for three years. To make matters much worse, the Swedish labour market, like that of the French, is wrapped up in red tape. The government has set up a so-called Labour Market Board, which is generally considered to be ineffectual and dictatorial. Informed people add that this anti-labour and anti-markets Board has become a sort of sacred cow which should be slaughtered, but successive governments are too weak to use the axe.

Moreover, quite like the practice in South Italy, in socialist Sweden absenteeism is common and unemployment benefits are high enough to discourage seeking a new job. As for workers on long-term sick leave, the country's sickness benefits account for 16 per cent of public spending, which outrages those whose income is taxed to death.

In the nanny state's paradise, about 1 million people are out of work in a population of 8 million. After accounting for all this unwarranted manipulation of the meaning of employment and of its figures, critics conclude that the 'true' unemployment rate in the Swedish state supermarket is around 15 to 20 per cent. This high unemployment rate puts the country roughly on a par with Spain, which is also socialist.

Like France and Britain, Sweden also faces the challenge of a rapidly growing immigrant population and this is where the shortage of jobs is felt the most. Some immigration policies applied by socialist governments over three decades have seen to it that 10 per cent of the people living in the country, and about 15 per cent of those of working age, are foreign-born. Predominantly Moslem, they have integrated poorly into Swedish society.

Theoretically for humanitarian reasons, the socialist state overprotects the immigrants. In practice, this sort of preferential treatment has negative results. A study of comparable Somali groups in Sweden and Minnesota found that fewer than a third of working-age Somalis in Sweden had jobs; half the share of those in Minnesota. The result of *self-made marginalization* is a worrying phenomenon because it has created a new group of restless and agitated people who fail to integrate into Swedish society.

The only good news about the after-effect of socialism in Sweden is that the government did not become corrupt. In his search for hard data on corrupt economies Jakob Svensson, an economist at Stockholm University, studied the cultural patterns and found that traditionally socialist, as well as recently socialist, regimes show higher levels of corruption than others.[13]

A paradox which is found in France, Sweden and other countries which fell under the socialist *coup de grâce*, is that while small and medium enterprises (SMEs) suffer and entrepreneurial initiative is a rare bird, big companies prosper. Still, the squeeze socialists put on SMEs is counterproductive because more employment is created by small and medium enterprises than by any other sector of the economy.

The globalized AirFrance-KLM, AXA, Carrefour, Lafarge, L'Oréal, LVMH, Michelin, Pernod-Ricard, Renault and many others are French-based, self-reliant and ready to employ people worldwide. Alfa-Laval, ASEA-Brown Bovery, Bofors, Ericsson, Ikea, Scania, SKF and more are based in Sweden, but operate and offer employment around the globe. It is good to have world-status companies. But it is no solution to unemployment blues.

---

13  *The Economist*, 23 December 2006. Some decades ago, in London, a frequently heard opinion was that Labour ministers are prone to corruption scandals, while Conservative ministers are more likely to be involved in sex scandals. A famous scandal which rocked the French Popular Front of 1936 was that of Serge Alexandre, known as Sacha Stavinsky, who was charged with defrauding 500 million francs mainly from small investors (Jean Egen, *Messieurs du Canard*, Stock, Paris, 1973).

Added to all the preceding issues is the fact that, in the Swedish state supermarket, hiring is a dangerous enterprise because the terms of labour contracts are largely set by labour unions which, like their French counterparts, dislike temporary or part-time work. Also, in a way similar to that in France, the prevailing labour regime makes it expensive to sack anybody, which evidently discourages hiring.

Stiff labour markets and the sheer impossibility of having one's ingenuity and hard work translated into career development and wealth lead to another serious problem of the nanny state: brain drain. Since the original brain drain of the 1960s, Sweden more or less covered its losses in knowledgeable people going abroad through brain gain from neighbouring Scandinavian and other countries, but France does not have that luxury.

For the first time ever, during the last ten years young French citizens, particularly university graduates, dissatisfied with their home-grown state supermarket, are going to work in Britain, Canada and the United States. The language barrier which discouraged their elders from doing so has been broken, as men and women who want to make a career learn English.

There is one more question before concluding this section. Where does all that leave the French and Swedish state supermarkets? Georges Pompidou, the late French president, once said that he envisioned France no longer as a great power but as a kind of Sweden by the Mediterranean. University professor and banker by profession, Pompidou was an enlightened man who saw further than his contemporaries.

## 5. Is the EU Divided by Linguistic Nationalism?

In mid-December 2006 Michèle Alliot-Marie, who at the time was the French minister of defence, compared Jacques Chirac to the Eiffel Tower. An editorial in *Nice Matin* pointed out that this parallel is not necessarily a compliment because the top of the Eiffel Tower is often in the mist, its structure moves with the wind and it needs frequent painting otherwise it gets rusty.[14]

Chirac's wheeling and dealing in irrelevance has been a sort of legend. On Thursday 23 March 2006, for example, he stormed out of a meeting associated with a European Union summit, profoundly shocked to hear a

---

14  *Nice Matin*, 18 December 2006.

French industrialist speaking in English. The person who had shown such deep linguistic disrespect was no other than his friend Ernest-Antoine Seillière, head of the European Union's business organization and former president of MEDEF, the French employers association.

The way the media had it, the President of the Republic left the meeting in a hurry and in protest because his French compatriot had spoken (according to Seillière's own words) the language of business. Critics said that this abrupt response to someone who spoke in English was a demonstration of the French President's 'mentalité Maginot',[15] a failure to recognize that times have changed from pre-World War II Europe when the beautiful French language was the *lingua franca* of:

- diplomacy and literature,

- but less so of business.

Seillière had explained the reason for his decision to deliver a speech in English: he was addressing a European business meeting and had decided to speak a language every participant understood. To this should be added the fact that the use of English for business reasons is a usual practice in multinational French companies, among many others.

In the boardroom of Air Liquide, the French industrial gas group, meetings are usually held in English. This is equally true at the media group Thomson, once chaired by Thierry Breton, who was Chirac's finance minister (in London, Breton joined his president in boycotting English-speaking Seillière). At France Telecom, where Breton was also once the CEO, English is commonly used in internal memos.

Meetings at Total, the global oil company, regularly take place in English, even when only French employees are present. English is also the usual language at Thales, the electronics and defence firm and at EADS – the owner of Airbus, Boeing's top competitor (Chapter 11). The French government has large stakes in both of these electronics and aerospace firms.

The argument about using English in meetings and in memos among the better-known French firms is technical. These companies have to compete and survive in the global market. Air France-KLM holds meetings of the strategy

---

15   See also Chapter 9.

management committee in English. Competence in English is compulsory for managerial recruits at Renault, the carmaker. The French government is a major shareholder in both Air France and Renault. Chirac's reaction, however, should not go unnoticed.

- It shows that in the EU, among its member states, nationalism is alive and well even at the linguistic level; and

- this further documents that leaders of member states turn away from common EU interests and towards *their interests*, as a means of promoting their policies.

On the other hand, the language we use forms our minds. Though American educated, the former French president probably did not appreciate that one of the basic reasons why French companies choose English is because they do most business outside the hexagon (their national borders). Another reason is that most of their business partners, suppliers and clients speak English.

The bad news for the EU is that Chirac has not been alone in rearguard action. In March 2006 French courts fined a division of General Electric €580,000 (then $700,000), for failing to translate English documents into French (see also the case of economic nationalism in Chapter 9). I leave it up to the reader to say if this is Palaeolithic nationalism, keeping in mind that:

- rearguard action is the tactic of a retreating army, not of an advancing one; and

- practically all EU members continue this policy of cherishing the past rather than looking to the future.

*If* this does not stop, *then* the EU will be dying before our eyes – and every nationalistic actor will be responsible for it. To bring this linguistic absurdity one step further, given that each of the 27 national governments has equal rights in the EU, if every one follows the same policy, then the European Union meeting will be a Tower of Babel, with 22 different languages[16] that

- are being spoken simultaneously; and

---

16  Given that Britain, Ireland and Malta speak English; Greece and Cyprus, Greek; Germany and Austria, German; and Belgium speaks French and Dutch.

- should be understood by everybody who is present.

Prior to British entry, the then Common Market missed a unique opportunity to adopt English as the *language* all citizens of member states should speak, read and understand.[17] This was the language of none of the original six founding countries; hence it created no national rivalries. An added advantage was that, post-World War II, English had become the most widely spoken language in the world.

Instead of speaking in one language, the Tower of Babel extended to all aspects of working together: different laws, different fiscal policies, different welfare systems and more. 'It could be worse,' said a Swiss executive, pointing out that the current EU politicians are unable to solve the Babel problem because they spend their time with trivia. That's their way of justifying lavish take-home pay without stepping on each other's toes.

(Legal differences which continue to prevail within the EU make things just as messy in both business and civil life. Under Napoleonic law bankruptcy starts at midnight; under English law, at noon. Another interesting difference demonstrated in the McCann case (the missing little girl) was between the English common-law system and Portugal's quite distinct civil-law tradition. According to Anglo-Saxon law, details of an investigation can be reported usually until someone is charged. After that, a virtual blackout is imposed on the press until the case comes to trial. By contrast, in Portugal nothing about a criminal investigation should be reported until charges are brought – a two-step procedure, starting with the naming of official suspects which requires rather little evidence, before progressing to a formal indictment if more conclusive evidence is established.)

Legal and linguistic differences make the EU enterprise dysfunctional. 'The difference between the 27 national governments constituting the European Union and the Brussels based EU Commission, is that these national governments are themselves increasingly becoming *dysfunctional*,' said another cognizant executive who contributed to the research which led to this book, 'By contrast, the EU Commission has been *non-functional* for many years.'

It is, of course, absurd to let this situation continue. Rather than being chronically non-functional by typically turning its wheels in a vacuum, Brussels-

---

17   This is equally true of the United Nations. From the start, English should have been chosen as
     the language of the UN, particularly as at the time there were no contenders.

based EU civil servants should have been working alongside EU governments in closing legal and linguistic gaps and eliminating contradictions, as well as alongside EU businesses helping them to attract, develop and reward top-class human resources from all over the world. They should also have been assisting EU companies to:

- recruit talent across a broad spectrum of disciplines;

- assist the young in gaining valuable real-world experience; and

- be proactive in fields such as *innovation* and the *management of change.*

Another domain where the EU Executive should have shown excellence is in helping member-state firms to implement *cost control,* which has become imperative because of globalization. EU companies cannot set the market price of their products. Therefore, to survive, they must learn how to keep their operating and overhead costs at rock bottom. This makes business sense and, as the title of this book warns the reader, the business of the EU is politics.

## 6. Integration is a Failure, but *Eurabia* is a Fact

Oriana Fallaci, who coined the word *Eurabia* to reflect her concern about immigration from Moslem countries, held the opinion that illegal and uncontrolled immigration, as well as the expansion of non-integratable ethnic minorities, would lead to indigenous populations being overwhelmed by a culture that was foreign to them. Recent events in Italy has provided proof that she was right. In my view, Fallaci was more farsighted than EU politicians and bureaucrats as

- she was able to display the courage to express her concerns about the EU, and

- she was not burdened, as the politicians of today are, by any conflict of interest.

It is indeed most curious that no EU head of state, prime minister, or EU commissioner has yet stated, as Abraham Lincoln did during the American

Civil War: 'I shall try to correct errors when shown to be errors; and I shall adopt new views so fast as they appear to be true views.'[18] Yet there are plenty of reasons for doing so because of plenty of errors are committed daily and there is need for a new departure.

The rapid growth of alien populations in the EU is an example of major and persistent political mistakes, finding their origin in past policies which have been too lax in dealing with illegal immigrants and socialist hopes concerning their assimilation. For several decades after the end of World War II the gates of European countries were wide open to all those who came in as a migrant, without much thought given to:

- what would happen years down the line; and

- whether the people who claimed to be refugees were able to integrate into European society, as well as what would happen if they didn't.

In hindsight it is argued that a plan to achieve integration, and rules to which immigrants must abide, should in some way have been a precursor to significant immigration. There has also been too little focus on controlling it. Too often, immigrants who have entered EU countries illegally have been officially tolerated, and even allowed to benefit from public provision in the form of state benefits.

This 'no questions asked' attitude by the authorities was influenced by the fact that Britain, France, Germany, The Netherlands, Spain and Italy, among others, were confronted not just by alien immigrants who don't want to be assimilated, but also by their own *fellow travellers* and *fifth falange*.[19] Coined in the immediate post-World War II years, the term *fellow traveller* applied to persons ready to be taken for a ride by communists. Today, the terms 'fellow travelers' and 'fifth falange' might be applied to those who are so intent on maintaining their liberal credentials that they run the risk of being soft on immigration issues and, by default or neglect, on illegal immigration and even terrorism.

It is a sad fact indeed that today's ascendant political ideology in the EU is the insistence on *human rights without responsibilities*, a credo advanced by

18  Cited in Harry Hansen, *The Civil War. A History*, Mentor, New York, 1961.
19  A term used by Franco during the Spanish Civil War to mean 'takeover from within'.

fellow travellers who frequently turn out to be protectors of various sorts of malfeasance. This raises institutional questions:

- Can 'human rights' really exist without 'human responsibilities'?

- Is it not true that the doors of rights and responsibilities are adjacent and indistinguishable?

The Moslem fundamentalists who killed thousands of people in the Twin Towers and the Pentagon, the Paris Metro; London Underground and buses; Spanish trains, Indian trains and hotels in Mumbai had no 'right' to do so in the name of anybody. The Mumbai killings, for example, highlighted the responsibilities of governments to deal robustly with terrorist organizations alleged to be sheltering on their territory.

Just the same, in the Madrid, Paris and London cold-blooded murders, the local large Moslem communities had the responsibility to take action against a repetition of atrocities – which they also did not do. Curiously enough, this attitude is not just condoned but also encouraged by the West's fellow travellers, who are quick to accuse the silent majority of being oppressive. Fellow travellers have a record of being blind to what the fifth falange commits, and in this particular case the record includes acceptance of the third-class status to which fundamentalists relegate their own women.

One of many examples of failures committed by the different EU oligarchs, their advisors and agents is the lack of study of possible consequences further down the line-related to serious violations connected to the equality of sexes, which has become a pillar of European and American culture. Moslem cultural norms in favour of the veil are a hallmark of Islam's institutional and doctrinal separation of the sexes.

- This forced discrimination decreed by fundamentalist imams and ayatollahs is in direct contradiction of European norms of equality and human rights.

- Acceptance by European governments that such separation can coexist with equality ignores vital lessons of history country leaders are supposed to have learned.

For instance, the lesson from America's history of racial segregation expressed in the Supreme Court's 1954 decision in *Brown* v. *Board of Education* is that 'separate can never be equal', as Erdal Riza Dervis points out in a letter to *The Economist*.[20] A similar case exists about the need for integration and active assimilation.

Only on 8 December 2006, one of the dime-a-dozen prime ministers had the courage to say that 'the immigrants *have to* integrate'. That was Tony Blair, speaking about Britain. A short while before, a British government minister reacted negatively to veiled Moslem women. Though his comments were about veiled women having an interview with a public person, some commentators pointed out that thoughts about public safety were also present.

In France, no politician has yet found the courage to say something similar. Instead, the trend is to throw more money at the problem – and not just by the socialists. In its 2007 electoral campaign some politicians suggested 'positive discrimination' for unassimilable Moslems – a policy which, as a similar American experience of the 1960s demonstrates, is a total failure.

By a large majority the French people are attached to the separation of church and state, which was achieved with the French Revolution and recognized in the first years of the nineteenth century through acts of parliament. Contrary to this fundamental French cultural characteristic, in the majority of Moslem countries and most particularly among fundamentalists, church and state are one.

Another major error with potentially grave consequences is that all politicians in Europe are, at best, fence-sitting about Turkey's projected entry into the EU. If ever this happens, the problems of integration may increase. The bigger the Moslem community in the European Union becomes:

- the more complex is the governments' effort to go ahead with assimilation; and

- the higher is the cost, poorer the results and the greater the friction which will follow (Chapter 7).

German Turks tell pollsters that they are happy with their host country and that they accept the principle of separation of church and state. But when

---

20   *The Economist*, 9 December 2006.

examined in detail, the polls indicate the opposite: young German-born Turks are growing more fervent in their attachment to Islam. In one survey, 85 per cent said they were rather or *strictly* religious. And the number of those who think that women should cover their heads is rising.

France has a different, but even more severe, problem connected to a population which not only does not want to assimilate with the majority of French people, but has also run out of control. This is best described by the *suburban intifada* which lies behind the riots and car-burnings that exploded in the *banlieues* of Paris and of other French cities in October/November 2005, and on many other occasions by Maghrebian youths who, un-Islamically, have totally escaped parental supervision.

Car burning and looting have become hallmarks. Nearly nine thousand cars were burned in the 2005 uprising, and several shops were looted. Malfeasance did not end there. As car burning turned into a hobby, and some people say into a business, in the first six months of 2006 alone 21,000 vehicles were burned in the so-called 'difficult' suburbs and the trend continued in 2007, 2008 and New Year's Eve 2009.[21]

While the revolt in the 'difficult suburbs' of major French cities, which includes the burning of public buildings and schools as well as cars, has become current currency, it is appropriate to point out that not all young Moslems participate in them. Many have found jobs and work diligently. The youths in constant revolt are largely either *agents provocateurs,* or come from broken families – where the father has abandoned his elder wives and, left alone, the mothers have no control over their children, many of whom are teenagers.

## 7. Mini-Case Studies on Aggression and Malfeasance

Anecdotal evidence has is that the suburban intifada is a mass movement and the result of roaming bands of young hoodlums and insecurity created by small aggressive groups of Moslem teenagers have become additional destabilizers of French society. Their violence leads to a rapidly spreading sense of *personal insecurity*, which magnifies other ills and makes a clash of civilizations more or less inevitable.

---

21  On some occasions, the cars being burned in French cities by young Moslems are 'in support of the Palaestinians'.

Here is a recent example of what the silent majority has to suffer. Since the beginning of the 2006–2007 scholastic year, the students of four colleges in and around Nice – Apollinaire, Masséna, Pasteur and Pierre-Sola – have been the subjects of attacks by wolf packs of four and five young Maghrebians who literally fall on their victims. These are 14- to 15-year-olds – teenagers who prey near their victims' schools.[22]

In Nice, this type of aggression appeared first in 2004, and since then it has progressed unstoppably. Assured of impunity because French law does not allow prosecution of minors, the bands of Maghrebian teenagers multiply, become bolder and get better organized. Personal insecurity reigns supreme as young outcasts attack their victims in broad daylight:

- when they wait for the bus, and

- as they go to or leave school.

The 14- and 15-year-olds usually operate, knife in hand, to take away mobile telephones, money, or other saleable assets that may be carried. Beating is the typical punishment for victims who resist, but the students' parents don't exclude the risk to their children's life, as the situation deteriorates and runs out of control. Similar incidents happen in other French cities.

Even more depressing is the fact that when the police catch the teenaged armed thieves and bring them to justice, the typical court's decision is leniency and, at worst, impunity. 'I want a lawyer,' said Hocine, a young Maghrebian skinhead. 'The case will be delayed,' the president of the court informed him. 'Yes, but I spat from the window of my car, not on the police officers,' insisted the youth.

'The police officers are not present, but according to them there has been this spitting and a rebellion,' observed the president. 'I would like to stay out of prison,' responded Hocine, 'without my salary my mother and brothers cannot make ends meet.' The public attorney thought it over… 'Even though his file includes incidents of violence, I don't ask for provisional detention,' she said.[23] Justice was done.

---

22  *Nice Matin*, 18 December 2006.
23  *Le Canard Enchaîné*, 15 November 2006.

In another case, the president of the court turned towards 29-year-old Ali, who had tried to steal a bag at Gare du Nord, in Paris: 'You have declared: I did it to eat. I just came out of prison.' 'Yes, but unfortunately I am on drugs,' said the Maghrebian. 'Unfortunately you have got 15 convictions. What are we going to do with you?' said the judge.[24]

Teenaged Maghrebians are not French society's only wound. Here is the case of 45-year-old Mohammed. 'You were drunk and fell from your bicycle,' said the president. 'The police helped you and found that you have been banned from the territory [of the French Republic].' 'I did nothing wrong,' answered Mohammed. 'But I see [in your file] theft and sexual exhibition,' responded the president. 'I would like to return to Morocco,' said the Maghrebian. 'But you have 17 identity cards,' said the president. 'Sometimes you say you are Moroccan, in other cases Algerian … We don't know where to send you.'[25]

These are not exceptional cases, but everyday business in French courts. Among them they make a pattern of malfeasance partly due to continuing illegal immigration; and partly due to booming birth rates among polygamous Maghrebians and Sub-Saharans who are paid lavishly by social security for their reproduction practices. As a joke has it, they are paid to reproduce not to educate and control their kids.

Altogether, however, this is not a joke. France has Europe's biggest Moslem population which, since the 1960s, has been increasing in leaps and bounds. Anecdotal evidence puts it at an estimated 5 million or more,[26] which means over 8 per cent of the population. A roughly similar case exists in The Netherlands, with 1 million Moslem immigrants. Some think that the steadily growing social revolt of the Maghrebians and Sub-Saharans in the French Republic is provoked by a toxic concentration of social problems:

- family breakdown;

- lack of parental authority;

- joblessness;

---

24  *Le Canard Enchaîné*, 13 December 2006.
25  Idem.
26  Anecdotal evidence, of course, is not enough for population statistics but when official figures are missing it serves as proxy. In fact, since this anecdotal evidence suggests that the Moslem population in France is between 5 per cent and 10 per cent, writing '5 per cent or more' is the best way to relieve ambiguity.

- poverty;

- drugs;

- organized crime;

- continuing illegal immigration; and

- Islamist indoctrination.

Here is an example of what has become daily business. In 2006, six Maghrebians aged between 15 and 18 took the bus linking Toulon to Hyères in the South of France and started molesting the passengers. The driver told them to stop, but they continued. As the bus entered Hyères, the driver changed course and went straight to the gendarmerie, blowing the horn full power. The policemen arrested the youngsters but, because they were under age, they let them go. The public attorney decided that in spite of their age they would be brought to court, but courts are known to be very lenient with young Moslems.[27]

Experts say that leniency emboldens the insurgent Moslem youths. In late October 2006, on the anniversary of the 2005 uprising, a group of Maghrebian youngsters obliged the driver of a bus to get out at gunpoint, emptied the bus of its passengers and set it on fire. A day later in Marseilles three young *cagoulés* forced their way into a bus and set it on fire, burning along with it a 26-year-old woman.

The French Prime Minister said that this time he would be firm and bring the young Moslem pyromaniacs to justice. However, they were minors, and therefore legally they could not be prosecuted, according to a 1945 law which gives minors *carte blanche*. The law has to be changed, but not everyone in France agrees with stiffening the sentences. Many socialists, communists and other fellow travellers prefer to buy the young insurgents' friendship with money – a policy which has been tried for decades and failed.

Yet France, and Europe at large, owes it to itself to flush out and bring to justice the young hoodlums and terrorists. As the Israeli Chief of Staff said in an interview on 31 July 2006, 'We will fight terror wherever it is, because if we don't fight it it will fight us. And if we don't reach it, it will reach us.' In the

27  *Nice Matin*, 15 September 2006.

EU, we must fight terror no matter what fellow travellers might say, or fifth falangists might do.

Just as ominous is the fact of foreign interference. Saudi Arabia pays lavishly to build new mosques on French soil; it also establishes schools for imams. It's like Bismarck's money and Bismarck's hand in the 1870 siege of Paris. In many private conversations and some official ones whose echoes reached Paris, the German Chancellor had said that the gates of the encircled city would be opened to him by civil war.

# 4

# *Declinismé* in the EU:
# A Case Study on France

## 1. History Has the Nasty Habit of Repeating Itself

In his book, *1914–1918. The History of the First World War*, David Stevenson advances the thesis that Europe's élites started and prolonged World War I. They took the confrontational decisions that caused its outbreak, and after the war began they mobilized men and weapons, rejected peace feelers and concentrated resources on the war fronts.[1] This head-on attitude:

- made the first major European civil war devastating; and

- raised its human cost to between 5 and 6 million young people.

In a way not too dissimilar, these days the oligarchs of the European Union's member states have put in place an incompetent autocracy populated by near-sighted heads of state and prime ministers, whose wrong-way decisions are devastating what is left to Europe, compromising the old continent's future, and squashing the hopes of its young people. Brussels-based management is done in plain disregard of the fact that:

- democracy and autocracy contradict one another; and

- perpetuation of an oligarchy has corrosive effects, swamping change and leading to general *déclinisme* (more on this in section 2).

What is disquieting is not only the parallels to the egocentric events which led to World War I, but also that fact that some of the same mistakes of the 1920s and early 1930s are now being repeated within the shell organization

---

1    David Stevenson, *1914–1918. The History of the First World War*, Penguin Books, London, 2004.

called the EU. History, however, has the nasty habit of repeating itself. As Abraham Lincoln once said, you cannot escape the responsibility of tomorrow by evading it today.

In a way similar to what took place at the end of World War I, after World War II traditional Anglo-French animosity quickly resurfaced as a pervasive influence on French and British policy (see Chapter 7). Mistrust became deep-rooted again. 'Do you know that Nigger starts at Calais?' the president of a major British firm asked me at a research meeting in London on the Knowledge Revolution in 1966.[2]

What is happening today around Europe, as well as in America, is characteristic of an epoch which refuses the image of decay but does nothing to avoid it – in disregard of the fact that the course of events will not change just by denying them. Little is done by way of thinking of the future, much less of planning how to confront its challenges and be ahead of the curve.

> Over the past 20 years, little by little, the French people have divorced themselves from France. An economic crisis ... has broken for many the link of confidence that tied them to society. There is anxiety over unemployment and the risk of exclusion ... It is not a matter of fatigue, nor malaise, but a veritable collective depression.

Summing up what French newspapers wrote at the time, this is what Jacques Chirac heralded to the electorate ahead of his election to the presidency in 1995. After being elected, the candidate who promised to right the balances did precisely nothing. The 12 long years he resided at the Elysée Palace were the 'lost dozen' for the French Republic. No wonder that in an early 2007 poll:

- 54 per cent of respondents said that they considered their country to be in decline; and

- only 12 per cent thought the opposite – a statistic which could be found practically all over the EU and the US of George W. Bush.

One thing Bush of the US, Chirac of France, Brown of Britain and many other politicians of the late twentieth and early twenty-first centuries have in

---

2    Reference made in the course of a personal meeting. D.N. Chorafas, *The Knowledge Revolution*, George Allen and Unwin, London; McGraw-Hill, New York, 1968. Translated and published in 14 languages.

common is that they neither paid anything other than lip service to the need for social renewal, nor did they cut their countries' suffocating bureaucracy and tax burden. Instead, they resorted to higher public spending and debt as an easy option to buy off voters.[3]

As with the saying that Christmas is the time when kids tell Santa Claus what they want and adults pay for it, public deficits are the case when adults tell the government what they want and their kids pay for it.[4] People who know what they are talking about think that some decades down the line there will be a *war of generations* motivated by, among other reasons, the facts that:

- deficits have become unsupportable;

- social costs continue to explode; and

- the nanny state eats up people's earnings for breakfast.

Already in several EU countries, Italy being an example, the national debt has reached stratospheric proportions. Unless the country declares bankruptcy, in one way or another this debt will have to be repaid and the most likely candidate for this task is the young generation, which at the same time is confronted by:

- lack of employment opportunities, and

- increasing scarcity of truly remunerative activities.

'Out of the box' ideas on how to go about this challenge and change the course of events are missing, as governments are run by an old, tired generation characterized by very limited imagination and lack of interest in novel solutions. Italy, France and Greece (in that order) also have a high average age level of deputies in parliament – typically people who look towards the future through the rear-view mirror.

This spells trouble, and it contributes a great deal to *déclinisme*. It is indeed ironic that the aging fellows who today mismanage the future of France belong to the generation of the May 1968 student revolution, precisely the one that was the most critical of the consumer/producer society and whose slogan was: 'Bring imagination to power.'

---

3    Both Jacques Chirac and George W. Bush ended by becoming very unpopular Presidents. The die for Gordon Brown is not yet cast.
4    Attributed to Richard Lamm.

Not only did imagination not respond to the call, but also when this May 1968 generation came to power it abused in the most flagrant way the goods and services provided by the consumer society. It also produced the current politicians who don't care to understand the people and their wishes. Not only France but the whole of Europe is run by a generation of politicians who, critics say, have sacrificed themselves and public interests to the cult of their own re-election.

Let's face it, said one of the contributors to this research, the majority of the EU's member state governments don't represent their people's thoughts and aims. After being elected, the different presidents and prime ministers lose contact with their base. Additionally, many Frenchmen are bitter about the fact that successive governments – socialist and centre-right alike – have failed in:

- preparing the country's future; and

- explaining to the public the realities of the new century.

Time is pressing. In a vivid discussion on 9 December 2006, on Arté, the liberal Franco-German TV station, the interviewed French expert said that if the balances are not put right *now*, in a couple of decades France will be beyond repair. He then suggested that the forthcoming 2007 presidential elections were an excellent opportunity to focus on this issue (more on this in section 3).

The majority of the French electorate, the interviewed expert suggested, does not want only security and jobs but also wants politicians to focus on problem-solving rather than point-scoring. This statement is right. A country's ability to rise up from under greatly depends on putting every issue on the table and having it clarified such that the public can understand what's involved and what will be the price to pay. It is not obvious that this will happen:

- partly because of lack of vision;

- partly because of embedded interests; and

- partly because politicians who are bold and forthcoming find it difficult to get elected.[5]

---

5    In the 1980s in Italy Guido Carli, a former governor of the Bank of Italy, explained in the most lucid manner what was wrong with the economy and what needed to be done to turn it around – but this displeased the people and Carli was not elected.

In the dark alleys not only of France but also of all other EU countries there are plenty of things that have not been (and will never be) clarified, since the policy of politicians is to keep them opaque. That's why in 2005 the majority of French and Dutch voters rejected an autocratic EU Constitution written without explaining, without elaborating options, and without consulting the people (Chapter 6). That's also why in June 2008 the Irish voters did the same.

As we saw in Chapter 1, what the Treaty of Rome did in its time was to establish a roadmap. This grand design, however, helped very little when negotiations between member states came to details, parochial interest gained the high ground over the common good and the nomenclatura put its weight against any major change.

In the infighting which followed, the order of the day was no longer to create new wealth through a United Europe, but to gain the most of what already existed, and to stonewall and bring forward all sorts of disagreements by attacking the other parties' viewpoints. This led to the result that nowadays the fundamental problem of the EU is disunity and disinterest about common objectives.

With the media publicizing discords and adversities, the European public ends up seeing the whole EU enterprise as having been futile. Had there been born leaders among EU politicians, they would have turned this situation around. But, to Europe's misfortune, experienced and forceful politicians have become increasingly rare, if not altogether an extinct species.

## 2. *Déclinisme* of the Fifth Republic

'There is a palpably sour mood in France these days,' said a feature article in *The Economist*. 'As Jacques Chirac enters the twilight months of his 11th and (surely) final year as president, he is the most unpopular occupant of the Elysée Palace in the fifth republic's history ....'[6] On his watch, the country accelerated its decline and reached (hopefully) the bottom of its modern history, dramatized by the fact that the French under his reign invented the buzzword *déclinisme*, summing up the belief that the country is unreformable.

Therein exists a paradox. On the one hand, France is home to some of the world's most successful multinational companies (Chapter 3). But on the other, career opportunities are poor, the public sector is bloated and the tax burden

---

6   *The Economist*, 28 October 2006.

excessive. The public finances are out of control because public spending accounts for half of the country's GDP, and in the past ten years the public debt has increased faster in France than in other major EU countries – except in 2008 when the British Labour government assumed that dubious 'honour'.

In a way quite similar to the *Swedish Syndrome* (Chapter 3), the policy of successive governments has been tax, tax and tax. In December 2006 Johnny Hallyday, a popular aging French rock star, caused a political stir when he said he had moved to Switzerland because he had had enough with French taxes. Hallyday claimed that 68 per cent of his income went into the government's pockets.

Another depressing statistic for the French Republic is that for a dozen years in a row under Chirac the overtaxed economy grew by less than the rich-country OECD average. At current exchange rates, over the past quarter-century the French have dropped from seventh place in the world to seventeenth in terms of GDP per head.[7] This happened in spite of relatively high wages paid to workers and employees. In terms of minimum wages France pays:

- more than double the US rate;

- 2,678 per cent the Indian rate; and

- 8,270 per cent the Chinese rate.[8]

No wonder, then, that France (like every Western country) is flooded with Chinese-made products whose low cost helps in temporarily improving the standard of living, but in a permanent fashion takes away jobs. Critics say that the salient problem facing France is not wages but leadership and therefore they press the point that quality of leadership will determine whether France is reformable.

- Unfortunately, leaders of the stature of Georges Clemençeau and Charles de Gaulle are not on the horizon, though Nicolas Sarkozy may prove to be well above the recent average (section 3).

---

7    And this while the expensive euro promoted a higher GDP ratio.
8    Most evidently, both living standards and the cost of living vary tremendously between these countries. The focal point, however, is the effect in western markets of goods produced in very low wage countries.

- Without effective leadership, the French people found it difficult to decide on change, falling back by default on a world which is past; and

- for decades the country was paralyzed by a sense of terminal decline, with politicians preoccupied by the distribution of wealth, not its creation.

No wonder, therefore, that the typical citizen has been taken over by a belief in their country's decline, seeing themselves as victims of globalization, looking at free markets as a threat and considering corporate profits as being something suspicious. Sensing that the public mood is against change, left-wing politicians stick to the nineteenth-century Socialist Manifesto. In its official programme for the spring of 2007 presidential and parliamentary elections, the Socialist Party pledged to:

- reverse tax cuts;

- renationalize the electricity utility;

- raise minimum wages; and

- enforce the 35-hour week most vigorously.

*If* this is a political programme, *then* it is the programme of the losers. Worse, yet, some of these moves – and most particularly the cries of anti-liberalism and anti-globalization – are shared by both left and right. A particularity of French political life is that economic nationalists exist throughout the political spectrum, ready to fend off what they believe to be 'foreign predators' (Chapters 9 and 10).

Yet there is plenty of evidence that an inward-looking society marks the way to decline. The 2005 United Nations Human Development Index (HDI) ranked France at sixteenth position, down from eighth in 1990; in spite of all the money spent on health care and welfare (or, maybe, because of it). The UN HDI provided proof, if proof were necessary, that the so-called *French model* no longer works. The citizens feel the slippage keenly in the loss of purchasing power, which is one of their top concerns. Clear-eyed French experts say that:

- the country's heavily planned economy has reached its limits; and

- the French *dirigist* policy, which relies on a strong centralized state interference, is totally unfit for this modern age.

The disastrous 35-hour week, also part of the so-called French model, has given dismal results, benefiting the managers rather than the workers. Counted by annual hours worked per person in employment in 2005: Americans worked 1,800 annual hours; Italians, 1,780; Japanese, 1,700; Spanish, also 1,700; and French, 1,540 – or 10 per cent less than in neighbouring Spain.

It needs no explaining that less work failed to provide the French with a better standard of living, which has been further damaged by the fact that French social costs are exorbitant. The employer who pays a worker more than the minimum wage has also to pay half as much again to the state in social security contributions. The employee is not happy either, because he or she has to hand over 22 per cent of their pay in social security contributions, on top of income tax. To get back their money, the people exploit the social security system – which leads to deficits and creates a vicious cycle.

Another imbalance, according to experts, lies in the fact that only one out of two French men and women pay income taxes, being excused from taxation because of low earnings.[9] Theoretically, the rich are heavily taxed; practically, they have found ways to move their wealth abroad. This leaves the middle class, the other 50 per cent of the population, paying income tax for everybody else. *If* you guess they like it, *then* guess again. By contrast, everybody pays value added tax (VAT) which, with few exceptions, stands at 19.6 per cent.

But the greatest risk is social immobility. Three decades ago Alain Peyrefitte, author and former French diplomat, predicted that the *mal français* would stifle creativity and innovation and entrench resistance to change. Other critics, too, added their salt when they wrote about a more profound sickness in society than anybody imagined a couple of decades earlier. The common thread in these critiques is that they attributed France's downfall to:

- a heavy and inert state machinery that blocked the evolution of business and of society at large; and

---

9    This statement seems to contradict the one made on page 97, that minimum wages tend to be too high. However, another way of looking at this issue is that indulgences from taxation are set at a rather high level.

- politicians who consistently failed to explain to French citizens why the country could not afford the nanny state (Chapter 3) and at the same time move forward by managing change.

In a way not too dissimilar to Britain, French society also faces a multi-ethnic, but mainly Moslem, population in revolt. But unlike what goes on in Britain, in 2006 French students and labour unions revolted against change, not against inertia, holding country-wide strikes, university sit-ins and protest marches – a policy which is totally counterproductive in regard to their own future. This, too, has been a show of *déclinisme*.

## 3. Coming Up from Under: The Presidential Candidate's Promised Reforms

Up to the magic date of the final election of 6 May 2007 both leading candidates for the French presidency, Nicolas Sarkozy and Ségolène Royal, had painted a picture of a dazzling future paradise on earth with full employment, bigger pay packets, plentiful housing and general national well-being. This set the clock ticking. Public opinion was divided on a number of issues, ranging from the 35-hour working week to the goodies of the nanny state and law and order. Beyond verbal exchanges, however, there were clear indications that:

- voters wanted deliverables, and

- these would necessarily involve change; therefore they would not come easy.

To better appreciate what Sarkozy stood for in terms of change, one should step back to the end of the Chirac years of do-nothing policies (section 1) and look at the promises made by three presidential candidates – (then) centre-right Sarkozy, centre François Bayrou and centre-left Royal – as well as what public opinion had to say.

'I don't like her,' said a Frenchman about Ségolène Royal. 'She never talks about real life. She is like a good mother, too oriented towards social issues. She says she wants schools to listen more to parents, but you can't listen to everybody.' 'She is not convincing,' said another. 'But I may have to vote for her – or for Bayrou, why not?'[10]

---

10  *The Economist*, 24 March 2007.

As presidential candidate, Bayrou was third in the polls, and sometimes it looked as if he could overtake Royal. But many voters feared that his reign would resemble five more years of Chirac, and those who doubted Bayrou's ability to change things were by majority thinking to vote for Sarkozy.

Sarkozy was seen as being better prepared to focus on problem solving rather than point scoring. Many among French voters, however, were unhappy with all three leading candidates,[11] because they were proposing massive spending increases but not saying how they would finance them. None was eager to address the important question of how to reform the social security system. Two things were clear, however:

- Ségolène Royal, who had veered to the left, was hardly a testimony to the politics of national renovation. She was just keen to tax the rich.[12]

- Sarkozy wanted to reduce inheritance tax (in a country with one of the most favourable inheritance tax regimes in the world) and overhaul the 35-hour week through reforms.

Sarkozy had come forward with good ideas about labour market reform. The two most important measures he proposed were a single employment contract (that offered a gradual increase in employment protection) and more flexibility for workers who wish to work longer than the statutory 35-hour week.

Both were put in effect in the first one and a half years of his presidency. To the contrary, little headway was made in youth unemployment, a longstanding problem whose solutions would have made one of the most important contributions to reducing social tensions in French society. In terms of youth unemployment, not only France but the whole EU is facing real social and economic difficulties.

Unlike Sarkozy's presidential campaign, Royal's got off to a poor start. Her programme was intended to unite the Socialist Party behind a single platform, but it failed both in that goal and in bringing about the desired improvement in her poll ratings. Moreover, despite criticizing her country's unsustainable level

---

11   The National Front's Jean-Marie Le Pen was lying fourth in the polls.
12   By November 2008 in the French Socialist Party Congress Royal had swung to the centre right.

of public debt, she said almost nothing about how she would deliver all these promises without worsening the public finances. Royal:

- talked vaguely of streamlining the bureaucracy;

- hinted at the idea of 'taxing capital more than work';

- presented a catalogue of ideas about how to redistribute wealth, but few on how to create it; and

- damaged her own standing by engaging in monologues rather than in debates.[13]

No wonder that, as different polls indicated, the majority of the French electorate failed to find her speeches convincing. Some political analysts said that during the presidential campaign both Sarkozy and Royal had either played down European issues or used the EU as a scapegoat for France's problems.

If both presidential candidates had something to offer to everybody, they also touched some sensitive nerves. French citizens who had come to like the euro's monetary stability were dismayed by criticisms of the European Central Bank and of the euro, whose strong exchange rate was blamed for French industrial problems (Chapter 8). They were also dismayed by the portrayal of EU competition policies as bad for ordinary citizens.

In connection with national policies Royal made some *faux pas*. To appeal to the Greens she spoke against nuclear energy production, saying that it represented 18 per cent of France's electricity needs (not a minor error; the actual figure is nearly 80 per cent). During an electoral meeting on 2 March 2007 at Anglet, Pyrénnées-Atlantiques, she said to the local Basque population: 'I wish France to sign the European Charter of Regional Languages.' Critics answered that the socialist candidate to the presidency of the Republic either:

- did not know better, or

- faked a memory lapse.

---

13  '*Vous me connaissez. Même quand je discute, je monologue*' [You know me. Even when I discuss, I monologue], quoted in an article in *Le Canard Enchaîné* on 13 June 2007.

France had already signed that European Charter on 7 May 1999 in Budapest. At the time the prime minister was her socialist colleague Lionel Jospin and Royal was member of the government. But the Conseil Constitutionel, the country's highest political authority, judged that the Charter of Regional Languages was in violation of articles 1 and 2 of the French Constitution which state that 'France is indivisible' and 'the language of the Republic is French'.

Royal also returned to her old and unappealing, to the electorate, campaign techniques of surprising her base with unorthodox ideas. In mid-March 2007 she stunned her anti-capitalist wing by insisting that 'we must throw out the ideology of punishing profits'. Days earlier, she had tried to reclaim the value of patriotism by arguing that:

- socialists should sing the 'Marseillaise', the national anthem, at party meetings; and

- the French people should keep the tricolor in their homes to emphasize their national identity.[14]

While Royal's economic policies were vaguely socialist, Sarkozy's defied classification. On industrial policy, he was an unapologetic interventionist, proud of having rescued Alstom, an engineering firm, from bankruptcy with taxpayers' money when finance minister in 2004. But he wanted to lower the overall personal tax rate and believed in minimizing taxation.[15]

Taking everything into consideration, Sarkozy's approach came closer to themes matching many people's priorities, like unemployment, labour market, tax system and higher education. Also, his opinions were more concrete than Royal's; the centre-right candidate clearly said that the above issues were targeted for significant reform. Sarkozy's policies were 'a hijacking of the left and the centre', said some political commentators, while others characterized them as shrewd political manoeuvring.

After Sarkozy's election, and judging from the composition of his first government, which included several people from among the socialist and

---

14 'She had nine months for campaigning,' said one of Royal's closest political advisors, 'and if this is enough to make a baby, it is not enough to make a (social) revolution', *Le Canard Enchainé*, 9 May 2007.

15 Critics point out, however, that within a year after he became President he increased taxes eight times.

centre parties' leaderships, they proved to be shrewd indeed. Sarkozy appeared to have saved his political pace-making appointments for posts where either he or prime minister François Fillon had specific goals to achieve.

With one major exception, European public opinion has been favourable to Sarkozy's propositions. The exception has been his political attacks on the European Central Bank (ECB), which were unwonted but serious – causing cynicism about the euro in France and tension with Germany for whom a robust central bank is an existential precept. They also raised doubts about ECB independence and the euro's stability.

## 4. What Sarkozy's Reforms Have Achieved So Far

Sarkozy called for the 'liquidation' of the values of the 1958 generation. The motto of the May 1968 student revolution might have been 'bring imagination to power' but, as we saw in section 1, when the revolutionary-minded 1968 generation came to power it did absolutely nothing about renovation or the ideas it had posted through graffiti on the walls. Its nearly 40-year reign has been characterized by:

- indecision,

- inertia,

- defensiveness,

- aversion to change, and

- total lack of imagination.

Contrary to expectations, May 1968 increased the weight on the economy of so-called 'social entitlements' and people were unwilling to be deprived of them without a fight. Among other labour leaders, François Chérèque, boss of the moderate CFDT union, promised to 'fight tooth and nail' for union rights won in 1968, whose legacy the newly elected French president wanted to abolish.

The irony was that the majority of the French people wanted change and a reversal of *déclinisme*. But everybody assumed that this had to be done at somebody else's expense, not their own – in application of the age-old economic principle that it is a recession when somebody else loses their job and a depression when I lose my own. Political analysts predicted that, as a pragmatic individual, Sarkozy was not going to spend the next five years on the grandeur of the past centuries because he:

- viewed the presidency as an executive office not a ceremonial function;

- seemed intent on changing the political values; and

- aimed to end the 'stop-go' policies of his predecessors.

This mattered a great deal for the EU because France is Euroland's second-biggest economy and home to ten of Europe's 50 larger companies. But above its entrenched unemployment and the weakness of its economy, the country also had to face the very negative mood of the *banlieues* (suburbs), home to many jobless youths from ethnic minorities, which frequently blaze into riots (Chapter 3). The as-yet-unanswered question is whether Nicolas Sarkozy will:

- prove as good a strategist in turning around the country; and

- win the war against rigid labour protection, high taxes and what seemed to be an unmovable economy.

The way an article in *Paris-Match*, the French weekly, had it, the difficult reforms of the French labour market and social system – those which would swamp the endowments and impose individual responsibilities for all French people – are always left for some time in the future.[16] Will this continue? If not, it is not enough to talk in general terms. Precise measures are needed – for instance:

- revamping the franchise for health care;

- going ahead with restructuring of unemployment insurance;

- finding dependable economic sources to pay for endowments which are retained, without increasing the public debt.

---

16   *Paris-Match*, 14 July, 2007.

Another major challenge for the new government has been cutting down the expenses of the state by decreasing the bloated number of bureaucrats. This is easier said than done, because French bureaucrats are legion and they stick together. Moreover, even if half of them were weeded out there would still be too many.

The risk assumed by the new President of the Republic was that his popularity was bound to fade in direct proportion to his novelty. And by promoting himself as the country's chief executive and concentrating so much power in the presidency, he also opened himself up to the impact of the success or failure of his government.

Like Margaret Thatcher, the new French President needed to change the thinking of a generation, stressing wealth creation above its distribution, as well as introducing incentives for business to invest in France, and for talented people to stay in the country rather than migrate for their careers to Britain, Canada or the US. A tall order.

One statement that turned off many believers in free market principles was Sarkozy's demonization of free competition. He even pressed to have the free competition principle erased from the new European Union mini-Treaty (Chapter 6). 'What has free competition given to Europe?' he asked after the Brussels meeting which led to that mini-Treaty.[17] British, Dutch and Germans interpreted this as the icing on the cake of a belief that France is hurt by the free market.

This has been a most curious twist, because the French companies that show the best results are those which globalized – they are the firms that have been conquering international markets. Conversely, the most defensive French companies were languishing. The government promoted the French companies' acquisitions in foreign markets. As a trade expert was to suggest, it looks *as if* in Paris there exist double standards about globalization.

In London, the largest electric utility is the state-controlled Electricité de France (EDF), through acquisitions largely made with taxpayers' money. 'Anticapitalists in their work and in the street' wrote this same *Paris-Match* article, '[the French] become archicapitalists during the weekend when they do their shopping' – and like everybody else they like globalized vacations too, except that not everybody else is an economic nationalist.

---

17  *Paris-Match*, 14 July 2007.

Critics warned that at times Sarkozy's language on Europe and globalization had fiercely protectionist overtones, which pointed to the fact that his first domestic attempt was to see disgruntled Airbus workers who were demanding that a restructuring plan proposing thousands of job cuts at the struggling plane maker be scrapped. On that occasion, Sarkozy gave them a vague response, saying that his government was prepared to inject new money into EADS, the Airbus parent company (Chapter 11).

Following Sarkozy's first year in office, a feature article in *The Economist* had this to say about the results: 'Judged by his own standards, Mr Sarkozy's first year has been disappointing. After winning a strong mandate for change and a big majority in parliament ... [and] a few symbolic battles, it all went flat. His reform agenda lost its focus ... and his popularity slumped.'[18] This commentary is unfair because:

- a great deal still remains to be done to turn the country around;

- but Sarkozy's first year in office brought interesting (albeit not spectacular) deliverables.

One would be well advised to remember that in the more than quarter-century under Mitterrand and Chirac, France's economic growth was mostly slower than Europe's average, unemployment among the young was consistently higher, the scourge of a dynamic economy (inordinate public spending) grew to well over half of French GDP and the national debt rose faster than in any other major European economy. This happened in spite of Euroland's Stability and Growth Pact.

In addition, as should have been expected, attempts at reform were consistently and vigorously stymied by labour unions and other vested interests, most often by following the anti-democratic tradition of taking to the streets. On most of these issues Sarkozy's first year brought a measure of change, even if the hallowed street demonstrations continued.

On the other hand, as of late 2008 and early 2009, the economic recession, public deficits and rising unemployment have put the brakes on reforms. Some changes which passed through parliament, like the restructuring of the state's audiovisual authority, were far from achieving unanimity even among deputies of Sarkozy's party, or of being a priority – while the government soft-pedalled on other more important changes.

---

18  *The Economist*, May 2008

For instance, the government left for better times the all-important educational reform which was one of the fundamental electoral promises. In part this was motivated by the mobilization against it by labour unions of French teachers, who fought the reform tooth and nail, and in part by the December 2008 student revolt in Greece. Ironically,

- the Greek socialists called on the Greek students to imitate the French in street demonstrations and car burning;

- while the French government retrenched and abandoned (or at least delayed) the promised educational reform from fear the French students emulate the Greek.

Regarding external relations, in an interview which he gave on 10 December 2008 to *Le Parisien*[19] Bernard Kouchner, the French foreign minister, said that 'one cannot decide the foreign policy of a country only as a function of human rights. The responsibilities of leading a country obviously obliges to take some distance from certain *angelisms*.'[20] The contradiction between human rights and foreign policy can be productive, Kouchner added, noting that he had asked himself whether it was necessary to create a secretary of state for human rights.

On other issues critics say that little has been achieved in stopping Turkey's entry into the European Union and that relations with Germany have deteriorated. The pros answer that plenty has been delivered on the need for strengthening the alliance with America, the role of France in Europe and the French President's contribution in organizing the G20 meeting on the global economy on 15 November 2008 in Washington.

Sarkozy has been opposed to Turkish membership in the EU on the ground that most of the country is geographically in Asia, a position which polls show is shared by an overwhelming majority of French voters.[21] 'I don't think Turkey has its place in the EU – it's a question on which I have not changed my mind', Sarkozy said in a joint news conference with José Manuel Barroso, President of the European Commission, on his first visit to Brussels as French president.[22]

---

19  On the occasion of the sixtieth anniversary of the Universal Declaration of Human Rights.
20  Playing as if one were an angel. *Angelism* can best be translated as a cross between being nice and utopianism.
21  This position could lead to a dispute with Britain, a staunch defender of Ankara's ambitions.
22  *Herald Tribune*, 24 May 2007.

## 5. 'Liberté' and 'Egalité' Need Impartial Not Imperial Justice

To the reader, this section title may sound preposterous; but it is not so. To document it, it has been a deliberate choice to focus on a real-life case study rather than making general statements. Though names are withheld (but remain available), this case involves events that have taken place at end of the twentieth and early twenty-first centuries and document that:

- equality before the law has taken a holiday;

- while liberty of expression may not be far from taking the same road (the theme of section 6).

Here are the facts. French law prescribes severe penalties for those who fake and/or use faked documents. Article 441-2 of the Penal Code[23] stipulates that a fake committed on a document delivered by public administration as evidence of a right, identity, quality, or authorization is punishable by five years' in prison and a penalty of €75,000. French law also states that penalties may rise to seven years in prison and €100,000:

- if the use of fakes is committed in an habitual manner;

- or in a way leading to, or aimed at, assuring impunity of its author.

Within this legal framework, which briefly describes the law of the republic and associate penalty procedures, comes the case of a lady whom we shall call Mrs W. This lady has committed not one but a series of four fakes and uses of fakes; hence she acted in a habitual manner as the law stipulates. At the same time, however, the lady in reference was protected by occult interests – a protection which saw to it that she was above the law.

The first fake Mrs W created was done in an ingenious way of substituting one page for another, in connection with the 7 December 1992 decision of the Tribunal des Grandes Instances (TGI) of Nice. The text of the new page inserted through this substitution not only changed the nature of the court's decision, but also turned it around by 180 degrees. (An Huissier de Justice, who in France is a legal person, has certified the original and fake texts, subsequent to an order to investigate the case by the president of the court.)

---

23　And Ordonnance no. 2000-916 of 19 September 2000, Art. 3; published in the *Journal Officiel* of 22 September of the same year and applicable as of 1 January 2002.

The objective of the fake in question was to obtain from city authorities a construction permit that normalized what Mrs W had already built without any authorization. In this way, she escaped prosecution procedures initiated by the city itself, the Ministry of Equipment and Ministry of Agriculture. These authorities had made *procès verbaux* (PVs) because she had built a staircase in the bed of a creek and on somebody else's property, without the owner's accord or any legal permit.

Mrs W's second fake was equally audacious. Apart from that stairway, she had constructed a whole two-storey house in violation of a limited authorization she had obtained. Her building permit specified 57m² of covered area, the maximum her lot of land would allow. Instead she had constructed nearly 240 per cent of the building permit's limit plus a big bungalow – and never got, or even asked for, a certificate of conformity. Since she was protected by occult interests,[24] which in the French Riviera have created a state within the state, she felt free to do as she pleased.

Occult interests that distort the law of the land are one of the contributors to *déclinisme*, because they bias justice and increase the fragility of the state whose laws are violated. Mrs W knew very well that she had done something illegal, and that she needed a certificate of conformity, but she could not obtain it. So, in a police investigation she lied in her deposition and signed up a document that she acted according to:

- her building permit and

- her certificate of conformity, which she never had.

Because sometimes enough is enough, the different illegal acts mentioned in the preceding paragraphs were challenged in court. For her protection Mrs W manufactured a fake '*Certificat de Conformité*' which her lawyer incorporated into his conclusions, and submitted to the court to win the case. Dated 11 April 2003, a report of the French gendarmerie confirmed that this document was a fake – in fact, a fake which was made on another fake. Translating from the report of the Gendarmerie:

---

24  *Intérêts occultes* has nothing to do with metaphysics. It is a French term identifying actions by secret societies promoting their interests and those of their members, in violation of public liberties, equality before the law and fraternity. The result is a state within a state.

*... we ascertain that the piece [of paper] which has no title does not exactly correspond to the piece with a title.*

*... the two copies are not identical though [Mrs W] has declared that they were both originals.*

Still another fake was a declaration to the French tax authorities, written and signed by Mrs W. In this, she stated that the covered area of her house was 100m². By so doing, she explicitly admitted that she had built more than the 57m² she was authorized, but at the same time she lied because the covered area she really built on two floors was 135m², plus the 50m² illegal bungalow.

Then came the fourth fake. This was committed by her lawyers who submitted the aforementioned fake documents salted over with still another false declaration to the Court of Appeals in Aix. While in their deliberations lawyers often cross the line between truth and lies, when this is done orally it is not considered to be an offence. But submitting *false documents to a court* and basing one's thesis on them is an offence, and very serious one for that matter.

Taken together, this tandem of drawing up and using false documents in a court of law has proved beyond any doubt that the fabrication of fakes and their employment in legal cases was a habitual practice of Mrs W and of her counsels. But as the reader is already informed, all of them were protected by occult interests and therefore there was no way of challenging her in a civil court.

The hypothesis that it would be different in a penal court also proved wrong. When confronted with the evidence, the *juge d'instruction* (a one-man grand jury in France) looked the other way in spite of the long list of fakes and use of fakes, as well as the fact these were done by the same person in a habitual manner. When he was first appointed in Nice as attorney general, Eric de Montgolfier made a major critique of local justice, denouncing:

- 'the disappearance of files

- lack of rigorous management of certain legal cases and

- presumed influence of certain occult networks'[25] (more on this in section 6).

The decision by the *juge d'instruction* to forego four cases of fakes provided evidence that the Attorney General might be right. Of course, what the Juge d'Instruction decides is subject to appeal, and the lawyer diligently did so. Then came another surprise.

The law prescribes a delay of ten days for appeal, *after* the parties have been informed of the judge's decision by registered letter with receipt. The lawyer's document to the Appeals Court was submitted in seven days. But the court in Aix found that 'it was submitted too late'. Within the legally prescribed deadline, this decision, too, was appealed to the highest instance: the *Cour de Cassation* in Paris. There the judge said that Day 1 is when a judge 'writes' his decision – not when it is posted and received by the person to whom it is addressed.

That's not what French law stipulates. Nor is this true in any other European country which follows Napoleonic law. Apart from the fact that the letter of the law is absolutely clear, *if* it were the case that the deadline starts on the day of writing a decision, *then* there would simply be no way to appeal, since the judge could mail his decision after the legal delay is over. All told, this was a sad day for French justice and one that turned the two-century-old Napoleonic law on its head.

Experts said that the aforementioned Court of Appeals decision has created a loophole in French jurisprudence, which lawyers will be sure to exploit. One might even accept that occult interests administer justice in the provinces, but when their reach extends all the way to the summit, in Paris, the Republic and its institutions risk falling apart.

By all evidence, all this is a machination by agents of a state within a state which are not only perverting the law, they *are* the law in Alpes-Maritimes. One needs only to remember what Thucydides, the ancient Greek historian and author, has pointed out in this regard: 'Only enemies of democracy need secret organizations.'[26]

---

25  *Nice Matin*, 28 October 1998.

26  The complete file concerning this case was sent by registered mail to the Minister of Justice of the first Sarkozy government, right after it was formed. Since then the minister has not replied; she did not even acknowledge receipt.

## 6. Courts and State Must be Guardians of Civil Freedoms: Two Case Studies

*Law* is a structural form of human relations reflecting rights, limits and meaningful continuity. Biasing the administration of law has costly effects on society. Moreover, the impact of occult interests in rendering justice can go beyond favouritism for parties protected by occult interests, to include Stalinist-type kangaroo courts and prosecutions. Another perverse result is the suppression of basic freedoms which are sacrosanct because:

- they constitute the basis of our civilization;

- they characterize the way a democracy and its institutions work; and

- they represent gains attained by society from the Age of Enlightenment and Century of Reason to the American and French Revolutions.

A significant incident concerning lack of freedom of expression in the French Republic came to the public eye in late 2006 when Marc Baldino, editor of *Les Nouvelles Niçoises*, was condemned in the first instance by the court for writing that the mayor of Nice was a *'très haute insuffisance'* (highly placed insufficiency).

Surprised by this decision, many people expressed the opinion that whether one is mayor of a town, government minister or president of the republic, he or she is far from being a reincarnation of Louis XIV. Critics looked at this case of condemnation of a journalist for *lèse majesté* as:

- an attempt against freedom of opinion and of expression; and

- a sign that in our society the trend may be turning backwards, with suppression of basic human freedoms being the new guideline.

It needs no explaining that freedom of thought and expression is a basic constituent of individual values and rights. The fact that a court decided against free speech in the country of Voltaire, one of the main actors of the Century of Reason, has been interpreted by many as indication that somebody is turning off Voltaire's lights. The question is *who*. Is it the President,[27] the mayor, or general *déclinisme*?

This happening, cognizant people commented, sets a very bad precedent because in a democracy the people who have words as their only weapon *must be protected*, not prosecuted by the state and the courts. By contrast, in an autocracy whether royal and imperial justice prevails – or in a jurisdiction under the spell of dictators, oligarchs and occult interests – it is the other way around.

This decision of first instance against freedom of expression has been appealed, while for their part, throughout France, the media were mobilized against such an unwarranted but formidable attack on personal liberties and democratic principles. Experts suggested that what happened in Nice in late 2006 is the latest incident in a campaign to turn back the clock to the Middle Ages, by obliging people to differentiate between what is:

- *politically correct*, therefore in conformity to the regime, and

- *politically incorrect*, such as the liberty of expressing a critique or dissent.

By banning anything other than the 'official opinions', and by penalizing those who dare to criticize, our society moves straight into a new era of Stalinism, Nazism and other *isms* of the bloodstained twentieth century. False heroes of the governing oligarchy are trying to maintain themselves in power through suppression of adverse opinion.

It is indeed ironic, but unfortunately true, that principles which guided the Age of Enlightenment and Century of Reason should start fading away. Current trends to control free opinion contrast sharply with the nineteenth and early twentieth centuries when many newspapers and weeklies, and their journalists, had the freedom to express themselves as they saw fit. They were able to criticize what they felt were repressive attitudes, government insufficiencies, or plain scandals.

- Critics could exercise the liberty of speaking and publishing against the regime of the hour; and

---

27  Who at the time was Jacques Chirac.

- the different regimes did not dare to toy with the democratic culture which prevailed *then* but, if we are not careful in preserving it, it may go under.

Only a few years have gone by since, on 27 October 1999, the parliament in Paris voted a motion made by deputies who solicited the intervention of the Juridical High Council (Conseil Supérieur de la Magistrature (CSM)) and of the Inspectorate General of juridical services, to clear up certain events taking place at the Court of Nice. This motion was sent to the President of the Republic and to the Minister of Justice, for further action.[28]

For its part, the Court of Nice found itself in an unprecedented situation of doubt and suspicion; an after-effect of declarations made by Éric de Montgolfier, the (then) newly appointed Attorney General, and published in the press on 7 October 1999. The central theme of these statements was the malfunctioning of the Nice jurisdiction. A short time thereafter Judge Jean-Pierre Murciano and the Attorney General of Grasse, Bernard Farret, were put under examination.[29]

One of the parties who also found himself in rough seas was Joseph-Marcel Giordadegno, an intermediary known as 'Monsieur bons offices' and 'Marcel la Salade'. He was considered to be one of the most powerful people of the French Riviera, with strong links to politicians, judges and ministers who participated in private weekend parties he organized at his property. Accused of 'traffic of influence and swindle', Giordadengo was arrested.

Nobody seems to have bothered about the fortunes of 'Monsieur bons offices', but there have been doubts as to the reasons why Judge Murciano was prosecuted. According to some opinions, he was punished for having denounced the role played by occult interests.[30] To the contrary, the dean of *juges d'instruction* of the Nice jurisdiction, Jean-Paul Renard, accused of having used his right to access sensitive personal files to serve occult interests, was simply moved to another jurisdiction.

In an interview he gave to the *Journal du Dimanche* in 2001, Judge Renard said that he had indeed consulted the penal files of different persons (for reasons other than those connected to his juridical mission), and that he did

---

28  *Nice Matin*, 28 October 1999.
29  *Nice Matin*, 4 December 1999.
30  *Le Nouvel Observateur*, 29 June/5 July 2000.

so because there had been a strong increase in offenders in Nice and he did not want to see them becoming members of masonic lodges. He justified himself by saying that it was the (then) newly appointed Attorney General who inspired the penal policy; when he came to the Nice jurisdiction he said: 'Nice, it's Palermo.'[31]

Publicly, Judge Renard also insisted that the Attorney General who had put him under examination wanted to damage his reputation. Years down the line, on 13 January 2006, came the decision of the penal court of Paris where Renard's file had been sent. He was condemned for violation of professional secrets, a sanction equivalent to a reprimand and therefore a light sentence. It might have been worse.

This decision by the higher judicial authorities should be seen in the context of an environment where accusations and counter-accusations have continued for many years. In mid-2003, in an article published by *Nice Matin*, the Attorney General was quoted having said: 'This palace [of Justice] has exploded at all floors. The phenomena of clans and confrontations are all over. One has to be distrustful of everything, and when starting an investigation ask who will be charged'[32] (in the penal sense).

The general trend described by the preceding paragraphs gave ground to accusations that the court in Nice was subject to all sorts of obscure issues and associated problems. Those reported in the press included: voluntary delays of legal procedures; curious decisions whereby the accused party was found to have done nothing wrong (*'non lieu'*, the case of Mrs W); compromised juridical opinions; and persistent rumours of a dark affair of *paedophiles*.[33] It therefore came as no surprise that the conclusions of the Inspectorate General of the Ministry of Justice, released on 20 June 2003, suggested that conditions necessary to normal functioning of justice did not exist in the Nice jurisdiction.

The daily press asked, 'Who is responsible?' The president of the court whose 'authority has been weakened'? Attorney General Montgolfier and Judge Dorcet,[34] who the report of the Inspectorate General reproached as having distilled the poison of rumours? Judges Renard and Rousseau, as well as a substitute judge Thévenot, who the inspectors from the Ministry of Justice

---

31  *Journal du Dimanche*, 17 June 2001.
32  *Nice Matin*, 28 June 2003.
33  *Nice Matin*, September 2001.
34  Who had rendered the '*non lieu*' decision for the four cases of false official documents produced and used by Mrs W (see section 5).

described as imprudent, not-so-rigorous, and incompetent?[35] Or is it, rather, that all these cases have been the after-effect of general *déclinisme*?

---

35   *Nice Matin*, 2 July 2003.

# PART 2
*The EU'S Conflicting Aims and Inadequate Business Practices*

# 5

# Politicians, Managers and Parliamentarians of the EU

## 1. The European Union's Institutions

The pillars of any organization – whether it is a company, state, federation or union of states – are its *institutions*, its *objectives*, its *leadership* and the *direction* it takes in attaining its objectives. The best managers and hardest-working labour force will be frustrated and ineffectual without a plan and a direction, which presupposes the clear definition of:

- aims to be achieved;

- timetables to be met; and

- resources put into the job to be done.

To this there is a corollary. Politicians in charge of an organization of independent states should strive for effectiveness in attaining results while respecting individual freedoms and they should be keen on acquiring knowledge: legal, administrative, of a business nature and scientific.

While trying to motivate each member state's citizens and reach an exemplary professional standard, the people in charge of the EU and of its institutions should also be alert to the need to bring greater efficiency to the execution of processes and projects connected to these institutions. As envisaged by Jean Monnet, the European Union's basic institutions are:

- the European Commission;

- the European Council;

- the Council of Ministers;

- the European Parliament; and

- the European Court of Justice.

Based in Brussels,[1] the *European Commission* is the EU's executive arm. Originally, each member-state government appointed one or two commissioners depending on the state's size (section 2). Now the membership has grown to 27, each national government appoints one commissioner for a five-year term, which will probably change if the mini-Treaty is ratified (Chapter 6).[2]

Bringing the membership of what is supposed to be a governing council to 27 is the right prescription for galloping ineffectiveness. It is a big negative as well because, among other duties, the Commission also has the sole right of initiating legislation, administering the budget and executing other powers, including deciding competition cases, representing the EU in trade negotiations and engaging in negotiations about further (God forbid) enlargement. (More on the EU Commission in section 2; and on its lobbyists in section 3.)

Basically, the Commission is an executive arm addressing tactical, not strategic, issues. Its political orientation is given to it from the *European Council*, made up of the 27 heads of government, which meets four times a year and also nominates the Commission's president. For any practical purpose, the European Council is the highest EU authority, followed in terms of decision-making power by the *Council of Ministers* – which is the main law- and budget-making body.

Theoretically, the European Council is all-important as an instrument of strategic guidance. Practically, it has become a major media event which (together with infighting) detracts from efficiency. It is a platform for big egos and small results, but also helps in letting off steam as many of its quarrels become public, and this feeds the media.

---

1   And therefore often referred to simply as 'Brussels', a label which includes the associated bureaucracy.
2   Theoretically, only the bigger states will have a permanent commissioner; the others will rotate. This, however, is not certain because the Irish have been offered one commissioner per country if they vote 'yes' in a new referendum (which second referendum, if it happens, will violate their country's constitution).

As its name implies, the *Council of Ministers* brings together the ministers of each member state under the chairman of the minister whose government holds the six-month rotating EU presidency (under the current statutes). This may be foreign affairs, finance, transportation, agriculture or any other.

- In most cases, decisions are made by a qualifying majority, essentially a weighted system.

- On crucial issues, however, such as taxation, decisions have to be unanimous.

Also part of the Council of Ministers are the so-called 'high representatives'. So far there is only one; his remit is foreign policy and he reports to national governments. This job is ill-defined because the EU Executive, too, has a commissioner for external affairs (a policy of two people stepping on each other's toes, which will continue with the mini-Treaty; Chapter 6).

Theoretically, the *European Parliament* is outside the Brussels bureaucracy. It has (at present) a swarm of 736 members and it is directly elected in rough proportion to each country's population. Like the Commission, members of the Parliament serve for five years and it holds its plenary meetings in Strasbourg *and* in Brussels, with parliamentary committee meetings in Brussels (more on this in sections 5 and 7).

The relation between the European Commission and the European Parliament is murky at best, its best description being that of the Byzantine eagle: one body, two heads. EU Commission members are appointed by member governments, whereas parliamentarians are elected by the people of member states, but:

- parliamentarians have no authority over the Executive; and

- sometimes there are two texts circulating on the same issue, one from each institution.

Another two-headed inefficiency characterizes most EU laws, which are subject to a curious sort of 'co-decision' by the Council of Ministers and Parliament. However, in the most important areas like foreign affairs, defence, justice and home affairs, the Parliament has no say. It only has the right to approve the choice of the Commission President and could dismiss the entire

Commission – though not individual commissioners. (One attempt has been made so far in that direction.)

A very important and fairly independent institution is the *European Court of Justice* (ECJ), based in Luxembourg. It is made up of one representative from each member state, appointed by common accord of the governments of EU members for a six-year term. The ECJ consists of 13 judges and six advocates-general and is assisted by a Court of First Instance. Cases are decided by simple majority. The justices choose a president from amongst their number, who serves a three-year term but may be re-elected. The ECJ's official function is to assure that:

- law is applied uniformly in each member state; and

- if a decision or situation is open to debate, requiring a court of appeal, to decide such a dispute.

Theoretically, this reinforces the EU Executive's work of monitoring and policing the application of directives and regulations, as well as the treaties themselves. Practically, there is little to sustain such argument, because the EU Executive is not renowned for its policing functions. Moreover, there exist statutory constraints.

For instance, the ECJ acts as the EU's supreme court in some areas; but in others, such as criminal law, it has no authority. Even so, in line with EU provisions for referral, the ECJ's judgements on matters relating to the interpretation and application of EU law are important because they create jurisprudence.

This is particularly true of judgements on specific cases brought before the ECJ which had wider implications and referred to the EU's supranational character. For instance, in its 1963 judgement on the *Van Gend en Loos* case, the ECJ established the principle of direct effect: EU law confers both rights and duties on individuals that national courts must enforce. As an after-effect, it became possible for companies and private individuals to use the national courts to oblige governments to implement EU provisions. Another important legal principle has been the primacy of EU law over national law, enunciated in *Costa* v. *ENEL*. Still other EU institutions are:

- the *Court of Auditors* (based in Luxembourg) which audits the EU accounts every year;

- the *European Investment Bank* (EIB, in Luxembourg), which has become the world's largest multilateral borrower;

- the *Economic and Social Committee* (based in Brussels) which brings together the 'social partners';

- the *Committee of the Regions* (also in Brussels). This one has rather unclear objectives.

The committees in the last two bullets lack proper authority and are characterized by an absence of clear definitions of their duties and responsibilities. This has made both of them ineffectual, no matter what their title might be. It has been part of an old tradition to give corrupted spine-chilling titles to medicine – in the same way modern tradition mandates giving social-sounding titles to committees.[3]

As the careful reader will observe, there is something missing institution-wise. In a loose 'union' of independent states it would have been normal to have a *Constitutional Committee* with fairly broad powers. This does not exist. Instead, the process of debating on the EU Constitution and institutions is relegated to an Inter-Governmental Conference (IGC).

This is a sort of 'summit' event which has invariably left different member governments dissatisfied, leading to perpetual calls for another IGC. The merry-go-round began with the Single European Act in 1986, which extended qualified-majority voting to a range of policy areas needed to see through legislation for the 1992 Single Market programme.

The 1986 Single European Act, whose major provision has been majority voting, came into force a year later and it was followed by the Maastricht Treaty of 1992 which targeted monetary union, common foreign policy, justice and home affairs. The next IGC took place in 1997 and led to the Treaty of Amsterdam which focused on:

- social policy;

- more majority voting; and

---

3   Sixteenth-century pharmacy manuals defined that the title of medicine should be registered in clear Latin. But this did not work until the eighteenth century because encoded figurative titles, like dragon's blood (*sanquis draconi*) were often used.

- the Schengen Agreement.

The Schengen Agreement was named after a small town in Luxembourg where it was first discussed. Its goal was to remove all border controls between signatory EU nations, harmonize visa requirements for third parties and institute cross-border police procedures. This is putting the cart before the horse, because both external cross-border controls and cross-border cooperation leave much to be desired. The contemplated and only partly executed provisions include:

- common criteria for political asylum seekers;

- right of hot-pursuit on each other country's territory; and

- exchange of information on criminals, undesirables and missing persons (which is more or less accomplished).

Only some of the EU countries participate in Schengen. Italy, which wanted to join, was excluded because of its exceptionally long coastline; Denmark did not qualify because of its passport-free arrangements with other Nordic countries; and Britain simply did not wish to join. To the contrary, against all logic as far as the security of Swiss citizen is concerned, Switzerland joined in November 2008.

The next IGC event was the Treaty of Nice in 2001, on a new voting system, the need for a smaller commission and provisions for enlargement to 27, with an Irish declaration added later.[4] This was followed in 2004 by the Constitutional Treaty which was voted down by the French and Dutch referendums of mid-2005 (Chapter 6). It projected more majority voting and new institutional settlement as well as establishing a constitution for Europe. The simplified treaty of 2007 (voted down by the Irish in June 2008) has not been ratified (as of the time of writing).

## 2. The EU Commission: Bureaucrats cannot be Leaders

Europe's misfortune, said one of the cognizant people who contributed to this research, has been that those who followed the founding fathers of the EU as

---

4    A 2001 summit at Laeken, near Brussels, considered Nice leftovers, such as greater transparency (it never happened), and larger role for national parliaments.

heads of state had neither the value nor the broad view which characterized their predecessors. As for the EU commissioners who are supposed to lead the 'union', they are mainly bureaucrats appointed by autocrats to whom they owe their allegiance and respect. The people warming the EU's armchairs in Brussels:

- are not leaders elected by the people of the old continent; and

- are not directly responsible to the European public.

Additionally, they suffer from the fact that the different state autocrats dislike a strong EU Executive, because it may act in favour of the European people against the wishes of the oligarchy or oppose itself to industrial, political and linguistic nationalism (Chapters 3, 9 and 10). When, a few years ago, the capable and highly experienced Chris Patten was proposed to head the EU Commission, his candidacy was blocked by Chirac because he does not speak French.

The story of the nationalistic ping-pong played by heads of EU member states directly affects the EU Commission and its deliverables. The commissioners are appointed by national governments and, though they are expected to detach themselves from national loyalties, they can hardly afford to do so because their terms will or will not be renewed by the autocrats. The result is a policy of nepotism which:

- is followed all the way past the commissioners themselves; and

- includes the group of advisors and assistants who constitute their cabinets.[5]

Favouritism comes at the expense of the single most valuable component of management: the objective evaluation of performance. With incentives showered on political friends, promotions and demotions are zealously monitored by all bureaucrats in the organizational tree, which serves their personal purposes but not those of the EU.

Organization-wise, the EU Executive is divided into Directorates General (DGs), whose number keeps on increasing to match the number of the

---

5    There have also been several scandals associated to these advisors, their functions and their pay.

commissioners. With 27, this executive branch of the EU has become a small crowd, rather than an efficiently functioning body, and new duties had to be invented to give the recently appointed commissioners from Romania and Bulgaria something to do.

Prior to the European Union's major enlargements, the five larger member states – Britain, France, Germany, Italy and Spain – had two commissioners each; the smaller states had one. Now the rule is one commissioner from each state and, as we saw in section 1, this may change if and when the mini-Treaty is confirmed (Chapter 6).

Theoretically, but only theoretically, the EU Commission is one of the three *supranational* institutions which are *independent* of national governments. Practically this is not true. The Commission is under the thumb not only of the European Council of heads of member states, but also of each one of them individually, as the Chris Patten example documents. Of the other two independent EU institutions:

- the European Parliament is toothless to the point that the word 'parliament' is a misnomer (sections 4 to 5); and,

- while respected, the European Court of Justice is snowed under with many trivial cases, while it cannot bring heads of member states to justice for misbehaviour.

The pros say that the Commission is no paper tiger, even if its strength has varied over the years and it has considerably less prestige than it had achieved at the end of the 1980s. Critics answer that the EU Commission's influence is particularly threatened by national interests which are in the ascendant, and by the strong will of some chiefs of state who use the EU to acheive their own ends.

- National interests always loom large in political, social, economic and technical EU discussions; and

- faced with divergent financial goals or implications, governmental authorities of member states usually have their way, even if this is against the common good.

European politicians who are worth their salt should bring to public attention and public decision critical issues like liberalizing the labour market, cutting payroll and corporate taxes, and balancing the budget of each member state. They must also put their names in writing on concrete proposals like Sarkozy's selective immigration (filtering who is given EU citizenship and sending back to their country of origin those unwilling or unable to integrate).

Arguably, writing something down in clear terms is not what politicians like to do, their preferred approach being to switch around. Macmillan's fast switch regarding Suez has become a legend. At the beginning of the Suez campaign, Harold Macmillan was a keen advocate of invading Egypt, but then became the main protagonist of withdrawal. This led another Harold (Wilson) to refer to him as 'First in, first out of Suez'.

In the late 1940s Greece had a Prime Minister, Konstantin Tsaldaris, who always signed with a pencil. When a major political client complained to him that a certain government decision hurt his interests, Tsaldaris used the eraser – and his signature was gone. By contrast, politicians who want to leave a legacy behind them would be well advised to remember what was said to the visiting Solon by an old Egyptian priest, the law-setter of ancient Athens:

> *Nothing great or elegant has been done that has not long since been put in writing.*

Among social philosophers, Georg Wilhelm Friedrich Hegel (1770–1831) understood well that the objective of the ancient Egyptian scribes was not socializing, but rather the preservation of an esoteric greatness and of a ritual. This does not seem to be characteristic of EU Commission presidents and members, in their majority.

Among the few exceptions of EU Commission bosses with personal authority is Jacques Delors, who had the guts to suggest that political union was a prerequisite. As a rule, however, the EU Commission does not have any heavyweights.[6] One of the reasons is Commission-bashing by heads of EU states; another that it has become a favourite refuge of minor or inept politicians.

---

6  *'Comme ministres j'aurais préféré des épiciers, parce que au moins un épicier sait compter'* [As ministers I would prefer grocers, because at least a grocer knows how to count], said François Mitterrand, while President of the Fifth Republic. The ministers (and, by extension, EU commissioners) supposedly don't.

## 3. The European Union's Lobbyists

Lack of authority is far from being the only flaw of the EU Commission. Another serious one is that the current regime is characterized by lack of transparency. On 21 October 2005 the *Financial Times* reported that a drive to make decision-making in Brussels more *transparent* and *accountable* had run into practical difficulties and opposition from José Manuel Barroso, the European Commission's President. His reaction was particularly negative regarding plans to:

- allow public inspection of submissions made by third parties to the EU; and

- maintain a register of the estimated 15,000(!!) lobbyists trying to influence the EU Executive's decisions.

As a term, *lobbyist* stands for any person or group attempting to influence political decisions, or contribute to changing the letter of the law.[7] Such action can take different forms and it may have different sponsors: industries, labour unions, professional bodies and the churches can act as a lobbyist either directly or through intermediaries – the legions of 15,000 lobbyists of the EU. Their action usually targets economic interests (about 70 per cent of lobbyist money in the EU is paid by industry). But there are also:

- structural lobbies, trying to avert change;

- public function lobbies, defending the bureaucracy's 'entitlements';

- spiritual lobbies, promoted by different religious groups, and so on.

Critics say that real power in Brussels rests with the EU's numerous lobby groups, some 500 of them, who employ many of the aforementioned 15,000 busybodies. These lobby groups chiefly focus their activities on the EU Commission, which seems to be open to such pressures – and therefore lobbying has become an important part of the EU's decision-making pattern:

---

7    In English, the word *lobby* identifies an area on the ground floor of a hotel. Around 1830, in the British parliament, the term was used in connection with a large antechamber where pressure groups tried to influence the MPs' decisions.

- this emulates Washington, and

- it goes even further, since some of the lobby groups belong to the EU's member states.

In May 2008, the European Parliament voted in a new law on registration and control of lobbyists. That's good, except that a short time earlier the EU Commission had also done its investigation and reached its decision, evidently without consulting the Parliament. In the aftermath, the rules featured by these two 'decisions' are not the same. This and similar cases have led several critics to suggest that instead of spending taxpayers' money on fruitless investigations, the European Parliament's committees would be well advised first to assure that they have the authority to act and, second, where the limits lie between their authority and that of the Commission.

In addition, because lobbying in the European Union has become big business, it is a very serious issue that the EU Commission, Directorates and subsidiary authorities are averse to public inspection of their finances and of their wheeling and dealing with thousands of lobbyists. Any authority using tricks to avoid or wrong-foot inspections gives the signal that it has something to hide – indeed, something that is most disturbing.

The way it has been reported in the press, Barroso and his team have argued that further technical discussions are needed to 'improve' the transparency proposals – an excuse often used to avoid control. But, Jim Murray, the director of an association of European consumers, said: 'We want to know who is telling the Commission what to do … On the whole, it is ludicrous that somebody could make a submission to a public body on an issue of pubic importance, and have a guarantee of total confidentiality.'[8] Ludicrous and unethical, too.

## 4. The Violation of Management Principles

As section 1 has hinted, *political nationalism* has seen to it that decision-making power in the EU always rests with the different heads of state in their frequent and empty-of-content 'summits'. Regarding second-level matters, this decision-making power has been delegated to the EU Council of Ministers which

---

8    *Financial Times*, 21 October 2005.

deliberates on issues affecting member states as a whole – usually by horse-trading in tit-for-tat deals.

Made up of heads of state, the so-called *European Council* (briefly discussed in section 1) stands above the Council of Ministers. Established in 1974, it post-dates the Treaty of Rome but did not follow its spirit. Its decisions are political, nationalistic and a sort of grand design, with further details and transposition into EU law left to the Council of Ministers.

When coercion does not work, the stage is taken by compromises. A basic reason why political leadership tends to become schizophrenic is that over the years politicians observe that the public has three wishes: finding jobs, being well paid while reducing working hours and making these jobs permanent. These three goals are incompatible and therefore cannot be reconciled in any meaningful sense. Politicians, however, don't have:

- the guts to say so publicly; or

- the knowledge to explain that labour markets which are rigid and inflexible are the worst enemies of the public's other wishes.

The end result is that those who currently work have taken as hostage those who don't have a job – including the young who enter the labour market but stay unemployed over long stretches of time. Instead of liberalizing and opening up the labour market across the EU, each member state tries to find ephemeral solutions which mainly consist of patches applied with a great deal of opportunism. The labour market aside, there are other problems awaiting an effective pan-European solution which have been mismanaged. Here are two examples.

1. University education is at its lowest, partly because the output of secondary education is low.

Among the top 50 universities of the world,[9] a list largely dominated by American institutes of higher education, there are only five European: two British (Cambridge, Oxford), two Swiss (ETH Zürich, EPFL Lausanne) and, at 50th position, French: Sorbonne/Porte Dauphine. Yet, until World War II European university education topped the list.

---

9   A rating established and re-evaluated every year by the University of Shanghai.

2.      Cross-fertilization between postgraduate research, new product development develop and rapid marketing.

University research is an ivory tower in Europe. In some countries (I'd better not mention them) getting R&D money from industry is considered to be dirty business. Quite to the contrary, in America brilliant ideas are brought at lightning speed from university labs to start-ups and from there to the market.[10]

Quality of education, R&D and global marketing should be a pan-European policy with the EU Commission directly managing imaginative pan-European projects. In short, 'Brussels' must take the lead, but this runs contrary to the political nationalisms which keep education, R&D and productization inside every country's narrow borders – while Brussels limits its work to:

- trivia, which are hardly worth the effort; and

- administrative work, which is simply an overhead.

Instead of working for the future, the Brussels oligarchy and (at state level) successive governments of the left and the right have rewarded dysfunction, showered bureaucrats and welfare claimants with cash – but required nobody to deliver and even less checked on what people, departments and projects have been doing through regular reviews. In short, there has been no Rudy Giuliani around the house.[11]

Sound governance has taken leave, basic management principles are violated daily and lessons which should have been learned from the past are conveniently forgotten. Many lessons relating to sound management practice have been taught by Alfred Sloan, who provided an illuminating example of what is required for governance. Very rarely do CEOs achieve an industrial triumph from a vast bankrupt junkyard, as Sloan did. Typically, at state or corporate level, chief executives fail because:

---

10  Some years ago Siemens put up a budget to invest in start-ups, and 80 per cent of it was invested in America where promising start-ups can be found.

11  Prior to Rudy Giuliani's mayorship, in the Big Apple crime raged unchecked, aggressive beggars ruled the streets and the city was atrociously governed for decades. Giuliani's rule was tough on crime. He slashed New York's crime rate, was unflappable as the World Trade Center came down and instilled a sense of sound governance.

- they do not listen to the public (their customers) and they are unable to create vast wealth.

- Instead, they struggle, they stumble, they underperform but are overcompensated.

Not all national leaders make good managers. Mao, for one, was a great political leader but second-rate as an administrator. 'Under Mao, China didn't drift,' said an article in *The Economist*, 'it careened. The propellant came from the top. Policies were poor, execution dreadful and leadership misdirected, but each initiative seemed to create a centripetal force, as everyone looked toward Beijing to see how to march forward (or avoid being trampled).'[12]

Two books recently published in France are most revealing.[13] Valéry Giscard d'Estaing, a former president of France, treats Jacques Chirac, his first prime minister (and 20 years later president of the Republic), as being almost a felon. For his part, based on a testimony of the Gaullist party's bosses, Jean Mauriac says that Chirac was an opportunist, without any convictions, and full of contradictions. Leadership, in other terms, was an alien word over the 12 years of his presidency.

It is always interesting to look back in time and use recently published evidence to reinterpret past events. In Volume 3 of his book, Giscard d'Estaing publishes the 1978 Cochin affair, in which Chirac opposed the idea of a United Europe. That's hardly a politician who would have laboured to make the European Union a vibrant democratic institution.

But even François Mitterrand, the former French president, who was both a better politician and more European than his successor, did not contribute a great deal towards political union. His efforts were largely oriented towards the EU's economic solutions. What Mitterrand did with Helmut Kohl, the then German chancellor, in the 1991–1992 timeframe, did not add up to a United States of Europe – even if some people say that it was a step along that path. Several experts suggest that:

- neither the phrase 'an ever closer union' laid down in the Treaty of Rome,

---

12   *The Economist*, 22 December 2007.
13   Giscard d'Estaing, *Le pouvoir et la Vie-Choisir*, Editions CE 12, Paris, 2006; and Jean Mauriac, *L'après-de Gaulle*, Fayard, Paris, 2006.

- nor the goal of 'European Union' employed in the Mitterrand–Kohl summits have ever been properly defined.

This left plenty of room for contrarians to reverse the process of political union which, up to a point, was set in motion. It also led to conflicting interpretations, including the nightmare of a socialist, collectivist European superstate run from the ivory towers of Brussels. At the Conservative Party Conference in Brighton in October 1988, Margaret Thatcher declared that she and her government did not work over the years to free Britain from the paralysis of socialism only to see it creep in through the back door of bureaucracy from the EU Executive.

This *rule from Brussels* has been practically everybody's *bête noir*. Bureaucracy and its lobbyists aside, a general issue used by critics of the way the EU is run has been the politicians' aversion to the involvement of *foreigners* (meaning anybody other than their nationals) in their domestic affairs. Even the pro-Europeans are not quite convinced about full federalism, and they lived with the false hope that elimination of trade barriers would be political unity's alter ego.

Worse yet, though they are European Council members, the different heads of state accuse the EU Commission of not exercising its non-existing powers, like Chirac did when Hewlett-Packard decided to downsize its French factories (Part 3). Or, they hijack the whole EU and its institutions to serve *their* national aims.

An example of hijacking is Poland's veto of an EU energy deal with Russia, because Russia had put a ban on Polish beef and beef transiting through Poland. The surprise was that no smart fellow called the Polish bluff. As Plato, the ancient Greek philosopher, had it, 'Those who are too smart to engage in politics are being punished by being governed by those who are dumber.'

## 5. What's the Role of the European Parliament?

There is a story heard in the Soviet Union in the time of Mikhail Gorbachev (1980s) which constitutes the best allegory of the EU's current affairs, because it points to unprecedented mismanagement. Asked why the train of Communism had come to a halt, a highly placed official replied: 'Because all of the engines' steam was spent on the whistle.' Then, as now in the EU of 27, whistling is the favoured play – particularly on the side of parliamentarians.

Going back to the fundamentals, since the democracy of ancient Athens, one of the leading characteristics of a good parliamentarian has been to relish combat in defence of his or her convictions. This has not changed over time. 'You will be measured in this town by the enemies you destroy,' Treasury Secretary John Connally advised the young Henry Kissinger, 'The bigger they are, the bigger you will be.'

In a democracy, a good parliamentarian is both a destroyer and a builder. There is no escape from the fact that a legally *elected* parliament is a source of ideas, an authorizer and a censor at the same time. To perform their legislative and control duties in an able manner, parliamentarians must:

- have statutory rights;

- assume explicit responsibilities, like independence of opinion;

- exhibit extraordinary self-confidence in their decisions; and

- follow up on the application of laws censoring the executive branch's deviations or inaction.

Given these well-established prerogatives of national parliaments, it would be foolish for the EU parliamentarians, known as MEPs (Members of European Parliament (EP)) to admit that their work amounts to nothing. Critics, however, say so openly – and they add that the real problem of *defending democracy* emerges from the response to the question of how much control MEPs exercise on the EU Executive. The answer is *none*.

Some of the reasons are historical. Until 1979, MEPs were appointed by national parliaments from among their own members. This does not sound democratic, but critics of the current parliamentary solution argue that when it was controlled by national parliamentarians, the European Assembly (as it was often called in the earlier years) provided:

- better,

- truer, and

- more effective counterbalance to the Council of Ministers and EU Executive.

By contrast, with the current system MEPs for Brussels are not selected but elected directly with five-year mandates. While the introduction of direct elections might have been a victory for those who wanted greater European integration, it did not improve the European Parliament's effectiveness in the least. The pros answer that direct election is a better system, and it is no fault of this approach that the EU has abdicated its democratic duties.

Theoretically, the European Parliament calls to account the EU Commission; also theoretically, it has a sort of (undefined) authority over the Council of Ministers. Practically, although it has the power to dismiss the Commission, it has never done so. Only on one occasion, in 1999, did Parliament express lack of confidence in a weak and chaotic EU Commission and it engineered the Commission's resignation.

Again theoretically, according to its status the European Parliament affects EU policies through the legislative process. Practically, its influence is rather feeble, non-binding and dependent on the policy area which determines the extent of the EP's procedural rights. Under the consultation procedure the EP merely gives its opinion, but it has no effective sanction over the real decision-making agency,

- the Council of Ministers and

- heads of state in the European Council.

Seen from this perspective of real-life EU events, it would be difficult to find European parliamentarians who follow Connally's dictum. In the long years of the EP's existence nobody coming in or out of its ranks has been given the opportunity to exercise leadership. Nor is anybody in the European Parliament known to have truly fought for his or her convictions. Critics say that the MEPs have repeatedly defaulted on their duties, because there has been no censoring even if there were plenty of reasons to censor the EU Executive branch for:

- slow motion,

- high costs,

- low efficiency,

- different scandals, and

- very poor deliverables.

To its critics, the European Parliament has a reputation as an expensive talking shop, with a ridiculous monthly transfer of people and files between Brussels and Strasbourg that adds an annual €250 million to its costs. And though by some accounts the average quality of its members has risen over the years, its authority has not.

Indeed, the EP's influence over the European Commission is so low that it has no way of acting as a natural conduit connecting citizens to the European Union's institutions. This is having fatal consequences on its standing. Few European voters know (or even care to know) who their MEP is, and fewer still know what he or she does when in Strasbourg or Brussels. No surprise therefore that:

- turnout at European elections is low and falling;

- campaign issues are mainly national, not European; and

- voters see little connection between how they cast their ballot and what happens in EU decisions.

This is direct result of two facts: to avoid ruffling the feathers of nation states, in statutory terms the European Parliament has been deprived of any real authority; and, partly as a consequence of this first factor, there have been no great leaders in its ranks. Parliamentary leaders worth their salt would have found a thousand reasons to raise hell over the years. Instead, the issues to which the MEPs address themselves are:

- rather cosmetic and

- largely subaltern.

For instance, in mid-February 2007 the European Parliament endorsed a report criticizing several European governments for complicity in secret CIA flights used for extraordinary renditions. These included the transport of suspected

Islamist terrorists to third countries to face justice.[14] This is one of the issues about which the large majority of the European public cares exceptionally little, prizing security over the well-being of terrorists. It is also an example of:

- how priorities have been turned on their head,

- while many important subjects are left untackled, rather than being brought to parliamentary debate.

It is proper to bring to the reader's attention that this lack of focus and of emphasis on salient problems is not just one party's fault, but that of all European parliamentarians. This reference includes MEPs forming a broad spectrum of political groups:

- the European People's Party (centre-right),

- the socialists,

- the liberals, and more.

Had it been endowed with full powers as due in a democracy, a truly transnational representation in the European Parliament would have attracted public attention and appreciation; and it would have raised little or no resentment to its decisions if these were against 'this' or 'that' national sovereignty. But the member-state autocrats running the show in the EU look at the impotent Parliament with disdain, and feel no obligation to account for the will of the European public.

- They believe fanatically in their own importance; and

- they use ways and means to advance *their* personal cause, which is synonymous with personal advancement.

This is one of the main reasons why, deprived of decision-making power, debates in the European Parliament have never been exciting. Yet, in a democratic society, parliamentary debate is the device and platform through

---

14  A European Parliament committee concluded that EU countries, including Britain and Germany, were aware of the abduction of terror suspects by the CIA. The 'committee' also criticized EU officials for not cooperating in its 'investigation'.

which political, economic and social conflicts can be animated, torn apart, recombined and settled by reason, argument, or persuasion.

- The parliament's sovereignty over the executive branch is a guarantee against arbitrary force or coercion; and

- parliamentarians must assure the rule of law is enacted by means of popular consent through the ballot box.

To do so, like any other organization, the European Parliament needs inspired leadership, including a full acknowledgement of the voters' wishes and, most particularly, those of practical importance to the EU. Voters want not only economic success and greater prosperity, but also security and decision-making power over vital issues like EU enlargement (Chapter 7), which has so far been handled by heads of state in the most cynical and inept way.

As for the parliamentarians themselves, they have done nothing to gain the sympathy and appreciation of the European public – their voters. The way an article in *The Economist* had it, the claims to democracy by the women and men in the 736-strong European Parliament are being questioned, and not only because of the low turnout in the mid-2009 elections.[15]

For instance, the judges of Germany's Constitutional Court (see Chapter 6) found that MEPs enjoyed only a second-class form of democratic legitimacy when compared with national parliaments, and they identified structural flaws. EU voters are not equal under the Lisbon Treaty, as the vote of some of them carries 1,300 per cent more weight than that of others.

- A Maltese MEP will represent only 67,000 voters;

- s Swedish MEP 455,000; and

- a German MEP 867,000 voters.

The European Parliament 'is not a responsive democracy', says Frank Schorkopf, a German constitutional law professor.[16] Not only are EU citizens

---

15  The European elections saw a record low turnout of 43 per cent. The centre-left did badly in most countries, which means little because centre-right and centre-left are adjunct and indistinguishable.

16  *The Economist*, 18 July 2009.

unequal in voting terms, but also the different political parties club together in big coalitions that haggle with national governments and the European Commission. Therefore, the common people do not know how to vote if they want to influence EU laws.

## 6. European Parliamentarians and Duties which go Unattended

One of the European Parliament's duties which goes utterly unattended is planning for the old continent's future generations. This is not a subject limited to birth rates, family planning, sex education and abortions, but one which goes all the way to health care and who will pay in 10, 20 and 30 years from now for retirement benefits and other social goodies.

In the decades after World War II, European countries experienced a significant drop in birth rates. At the same time, in a way broadly similar to a trend which had shown up in America, the bonds of traditional family life began to slacken. People sought enjoyment and satisfaction more and more through individual pursuits, rather than in families. More women got jobs and this unavoidably had an impact on raising a family.

In 1957, the year of the European Union's founding, every one of the 27 countries that are now EU members had fertility rates above 2.1.[17] Fifty-two years later none does; EU member states find themselves well below replacement level, the point at which the population stabilizes. In the twenty-first century fertility fell below 1.3 in Italy and Greece and, with the exception of Ireland, where it stands at just under 2.1, the demographics in other EU countries are not much better.[18] Here is a sample:

- France, 2.0[19]

- Sweden, 1.9

- The Netherlands, 1.8

- Britain, 1.8

---

17  The fertility rate is the number of children a woman can expect during her lifetime.

18  A reviewer said: 'Birth rate is not a percentage but a reproduction rate.' That's a funny statement. A reproduction rate is a percentage. Another one wrote, '2 being replacement population.' That's near-sighted because it forgets longevity – therefore leading to a wholesome mistake.

19  Beefed up by high reproduction rates among those of Arab descent.

- Spain, 1.4.

France was the largest country in Europe in Louis XIV's years and during the Napoleonic Wars, accounting for about a fifth of the old continent's population. Today, demographers say that second- and third-generation Moslems, those born in France, account for a disproportionate share of the country's high fertility: 2.5 compared with about 1.6 for French-origin women.

The demographics characterizing tomorrow's EU are a top issue for the European Parliament to debate and come up with factual and documented recommendations – even laws designed to implement parliamentary policy decisions. The same is true of the policy that the EU (not just each member country on its own) should follow on abortions, which is also a worldwide problem.

Some years ago, a useful formula was coined by Bill Clinton – that abortion should be 'safe, legal and rare', but the world is still far from that point.[20] Of a total of an estimated 46 million abortions thought to be carried out each year (with over 25 per cent of pregnancies terminated),[21] nearly half are illegal, resulting in the deaths of around 70,000 women a year, according to the World Health Organization.

- What's the European Union's response to family planning, sex education and use of condoms?

- What's the policy regarding abortions as a last resort when other measures fail?

- What might be a better place than the European Parliament, supposed to represent all of the EU people, to discuss and decide on family, education and health-related issues, and make such decisions EU laws?

European industry, too, has urgent and important requirements which should be openly and thoroughly discussed by the MEPs. This is written in full appreciation of the fact that the mosaic of rules and regulations prevailing today in the EU is not even decent for a free trade area. Every member state

---

20  *The Economist*, 19 May 2007.
21  That's an average figure. In Romania, for example, reportedly 75 per cent of pregnancies end in abortion.

does as it pleases with its interpretation of obligations under the Treaty of Rome, and inefficiency all over the EU has produced some glaring *diseconomies* of scale. Here are a couple of hilarious examples.

- Dutch potatoes are trucked to Spain to be cleaned and peeled, then trucked back to The Netherlands for sale there.

- Shrimps are trucked from Denmark to Morocco, via Spain, to be cleaned, then hauled back to Denmark.[22]

All that shipping back and forth is done by road, simply forgetting that Europe produces no oil and has to pay for it dearly; and it takes place in the middle of a campaign (itself awfully ill-studied) to drastically reduce $CO_2$ emissions. At the EP, nobody seems to be taking account of environmental pollution, in spite of all those Green MEPs. The rail system might have been an alternative for such insane to-ing and fro-ing, but it is decaying and infested with wildcat strikes.

Additionally, the infrastructure itself is not maintained. France, for example, has spent profusely on building high-speed passenger trains, but relatively little on freight. There is no evidence that either the EU Executive or the MEPs have looked seriously into the rail versus road options, including opportunities and costs associated to them and the implied reduction in $CO_2$ – which suggests that the latter is a red herring.

Experts are right when they say that it would have been only reasonable to expect the European Parliament to take a close look at transport efficiency and spoilage and at constraints connected to energy supplies. They are also right when they say that protectionism is sanctioned because it is counterproductive. A case in point is German and French efforts to protect their carmakers, which have only succeeded in widening productivity gaps.[23]

In short, there are plenty of key issues on which the European Parliament's authority and inquiry should focus. Another example is high minimum wages EU-wide and associated ultra-high social costs accused of keeping low-skill workers out of a job. Individually, EU governments find it difficult to redress the lower wage/lower social costs challenge. By contrast, the European Parliament

---

22  *International Herald Tribune,* 11 July 2005.
23  Import restrictions on Japanese autos, experts say, have held Toyota to a 5 per cent share of the French market and to 16 per cent of Germany's.

is ideally situated to study it and propose ways and means to right the balances – which it does not do.

Another EU-wide issue which should be the subject of investigation by European parliamentarians is government subsidies. The support provided by governments worldwide to different pressure groups is often covert. For instance, while the US government does not give cane sugar and sugar beet farmers direct cash subsidies:

- it supports them with low-cost loans from the US Treasury;

- guarantees a price much higher than the world market's; and

- restricts imports, therefore increasing the cost to the consumer.

Similar cases of covert government subsidies abound in Europe, from the Airbus to 'you name it', and the result is largely an ineffective industrial system with government subsidies feeding the producers' weaknesses rather than their strengths. The EU commissioners, too, should have been preoccupied by this important question of unexpected consequences of parochial solutions to problems which are EU-wide.

In conclusion, there is plenty of conflict between duties that should be fulfilled, lack of authority of EU parliamentarians and deliverables which are hard to come by. Up to a point, that sort of conflict between duties and their execution is always present in a parliamentary democracy, but it is made much more acute in the EU setting, where, to preserve their influence and connections, a horde of pressure groups fights *against* parliamentary democracy.

## 7. The Many Origins of Outrageous Expenses

Historically, the European Parliament's function was consultative, which leads many people to suggest that the term 'parliament' is incorrectly used. Only since 1970 have MEPs started taking a look at the EU budget. This, however, amounted to very little because the EU budget is finally settled by EU heads of state even if the Treaties of Maastricht and Amsterdam extended a power of the so-called co-decision (first invented by the Single European Act of 1987).

*Co-decision* is a curious word which theoretically, but only theoretically, made the Parliament an important part of the European Union's legislative process. Often, nice words are used to express hope, but they are contradicted by experience. As we saw in sections 5 and 6, for all practical purposes today the European Parliament is:

- a talking shop,

- a paper tiger at best, and

- an out-of-date institution.

Beyond the issues outlined in the preceding sections that should be treated with authority at European Parliament level are the fixed costs of *being a country*. These vary widely among EU member states, mainly because of historical residues, but also due to irrational reasons. For starters:

- The fixed costs of being a country are not only for infrastructure, schools, and health care.

- There are many cost centres which run out of control, such as the excessive cost of embassies, armed forces and cabinet ministers who are too expensive for what they produce.

Parliamentarians who have done their homework should know that quite often budgeted costs turn into inordinate expenses because of mismanagement. This makes not only individual countries ineffective, but also the whole EU. By contrast, *if* countries were to be run along the lines of well-run commercial enterprises rather than also-ran states, efficiency would be held in high regard. On these premises, the European Parliament should:

- look into country cost issues from an holistic EU perspective; and

- take decisions on issues national parliaments are afraid to tackle because of conflicts of interest and other near-sighted reasons.

One of the excellent examples where the responsibility of MEPs should be engaged is the effect of each and every entitlement – which varies with EU member country – on labour costs and social costs, which makes European industry uncompetitive in the global market. Another is the twisted way in which practically every EU country finances its welfare state through a payroll tax which hits on the head the chances of European manufacturers exporting their wares.

In the aftermath of this loss of competitiveness, in country after country in the old continent full-time jobs and their attendant social security contributions disappear. This is creating a vicious cycle. In Germany, for example, matching contributions by workers and employees now add up to over 40 per cent of gross income, compared with 27.5 per cent in 1970. The result is to cut down take-home pay, which has been further hit by a massive increase of value added tax (VAT) from 16 per cent to 19 per cent. A European Union policy on VAT – a means of indirect taxation totally at the discretion of EU member states – is still another issue which the MEPs should be keen to study and analyze. The European Parliament is also ideally placed to:

- deliberate on the divergent fiscal policies of the 27; and

- debate changes necessary to social and economic practices to improve the continent's overall performance.

Moreover, the cost of the European Parliament itself is an important issue to be brought under control, one which from time to time makes the parliamentarians burst into anger. Such was the case in late April 2006, when MEPs were said to be outraged by claims that the city of Strasbourg was overcharging them for rent for two of their buildings. On that occasion, many MEPs said they would rather relocate entirely to Brussels, where they already had lavish quarters.

Not only do the European Union's dysfunctional institutions not come cheap, but also particularly objectionable to the critics of the current EU parliamentary system is the fact that the number of MEPs has significantly increased with each enlargement – and so have the costs.

In 1997, with the entry of Sweden, Finland and Austria, 626 members sat in the European Parliament. In December 2000, during the EU's head of state Nice meetings, the decision was taken to limit the number of members to 732, no matter how large the Union grows; they did become 785 and this extravagant number fell to 736 (as previously discussed). This growth for growth's sake has been highly anti-economic because:

- MEPs reward themselves lavishly with expenses and other goodies; and

- that's money going down the drain, having scant correspondence with the MEPs' deliverables.

Ironically, the EU's member states don't agree on what a parliamentarian's fair pay is. MEPs of Italian origin have the highest salary among their colleagues, to the tune of €11,000 *per month*.[24] Yet, Italy is one of the economically weaker EU members and is in constant breach of Euroland's Stability and Growth Pact. Multiplied at least by a factor of three for overheads, lavish travel allowances, hotels, secretarial help, other assistance, office space, utilities and so on,

- this adds up to €400,000 per head, in terms of MEP charges paid by Italian taxpayers; and

- no matter which metric one wishes to apply in terms of end results, *it is not worth it.*

MEPs, however, have friends who protect their turf. In mid-March 2005 the Luxembourg EU presidency said that it was necessary to harmonize pay rates for MEPs at about €7,000(!) per month, taking up to a decade to phase the change in. Even when they receive the same as national parliamentarians in their home state, it is in the MEPs' favour that they are also paid full expenses, with expense accounts often being abused.

Pat Cox, the Irish former president of the European Parliament, warned that unless the pay situation was resolved it would be only a matter of time before a scandal broke. One would be justified in adding that the huge, unwarranted expenses paid to the MEPs are already a grand scandal. For instance, in Germany there is a tax rebate for driving to work.

- If a common citizen lives in Köln and works in Frankfurt, a distance of 190 km, he or she will get a tax rebate of €57.

- But if one is an EU parliamentarian, the tax rebate becomes Euro 131 – up by 230 per cent, in favour of those who do nothing.

---

24  While Italian MEPs earn €11,000 a month, their counterparts from Baltic States get about €800 per month, or less than 7 per cent of what the Italians take home. New accession countries have tried to close the gap. With taxpayers' money Hungary decided to raise its MEPs' net salary to about €2,300 per month, putting them on a par with government ministers – which is absurd.

It may not be at all irrelevant that many parliamentarians are lawyers. As an old joke has it, a lawyer dies and arrives, very angry, at the Pearly Gates: 'Why me, I am only 57 years old?' he asks. Saint Peter consults his Big Book and replies: 'Well, according to your billing hours you are 89.'[25]

As far as the European Parliament and its MEPs are concerned, June 2009 was renowned for two reasons. One was the increasing rate of abstentions at the EU elections, which varied widely by country but continues to be fed by the citizens' disgust with the MEPs do-nothing practices and spending excesses. For instance, flat-rate travel charges are often worth five times the actual cost of an air ticket.

The second interesting event of June 2009 was how quickly new rules aimed at bending the curve of MEPs' excesses were put to rest. Under what was supposed to be a 'clean-up' directive, an era of personal accountability should have started – but the more shameless MEPs may still take home €200,000 a year.

On paper, the new system offers each MEP a €92,000 annual salary (which is outrageous), plus a generous non-contributory pension funded wholly by taxpayers. In practice, the members of the European Parliament also get:

- an annual allowance of more than €50,424 to run a constituency office, even if some don't have one;

- attendance allowances of €293 per day, which amounts to double pay; and

- top-up travel expenses worth hundreds of euros a week, with no receipts needed for any of these 'expenses'.

In addition, the new EU rules for parliamentarians have failed to waive a clause voted for in March 2009 by nearly 70 per cent of MEPs, which permits them to keep future expenses secret. No wonder, therefore, that across Europe the majority of voters did not bother going to the polls on 4–7 June to elect a new European Parliament. Taxpayers were sure to be looted no matter which party won.

---

25  Quoted in *The Economist* by Paul Berkeley.

There is good reason why scientists don't care to spend their time, and their lives, in dysfunctional parliaments – or even high up the state organization's ladder. In 1952 Albert Einstein was offered Israel's presidency. He declined, saying he thought he was too naïve in politics, but he is also quoted having said: 'Equations are more important to me, because politics is for the present but an equation is something for eternity.'[26]

---

26  Cited in Stephen Hawking, *A Brief History of Time*, Bantam Books, New York, 1988.

# 6

# The EU's Constitution and Constitutional Referendums

## 1. Snapshot of the EU Constitution's Troubles

A well-known art of politicians is to say one thing, mean something different and do something else entirely. But at least Gisela Stuart, a British MP, spoke her mind. Stuart was the Labour Party's parliamentary representative on the convention drawing up the ill-fated EU Constitution. In late 2003 she went public with her misgivings about the whole business surrounding the constitutional draft by arguing that:

- the British government should be wary of a constitution drawn up by 'a self-selected … European political elite'; and

- these self-selected elitists (read: autocrats) were engaged on a politically motivated attempt to transfer power to Brussels irrevocably.[1]

The way Gisela Stuart put it, not once in the 16 months she spent on the constitutional convention did representatives question whether deeper integration was what the people of Europe really wanted; whether it served the European citizens' best interests; or whether it provided the best basis for a sustainable structure of an expanding union. In a nutshell, Stuart's statement practically captures much of what has been wrong with the ill-fated EU Constitution:

- the people of the European Union were not allowed to say anything about the draft, yet it cast a big shadow over their lives; and

---

1    *The Economist*, 13 December 2003.

- headed by a former president of France, the self-selected oligarchs tried to hijack all EU authority, depositing it in the hands of the bigger nations – in the most arbitrary way.

Stuart's criticism was right, whether or not one agrees with her thesis that less EU integration is the better solution. I, for one, would have thought precisely the opposite: that political integration is not only the better solution, but also the only one that can work in the longer term. But Stuart has put her finger on precisely what democratic rule is all about:

- Let the sovereign people decide by majority on the most basic condition – and solution.

By contrast, the high-handed management of the EU's Constitution, and of its fortunes, by oligarchic and inept politicians has created an organization that is impenetrable to ordinary voters; one that makes a mockery of the citizen's will and undermines democratic accountability – and it therefore lacks popular support. Instead of a constitutional settlement that enhances democracy and accountability, those who prepared the draft EU Constitution headed for further constitutional instability (sections 2, 3 and 4).

Yet, given their past and present political careers, the oligarchs had enough experience to know that nowadays steamroller policies don't succeed even in the heart of Asia, which has a tradition of one-man rule. Pol Pot's Cambodia provides an example. After taking power, Pol Pot ordered the total evacuation of all towns and cities. This concerned not just the middle class, but also labourers, mechanics, street-cleaners, war refugees, everybody. Dictated from above:

- All Cambodians were to become workers on the land. There were to be no wages.

- Meals were to be provided by collective kitchens for 'unity of feeding'.

Each Cambodian had to refer to him- or herself as 'we' – they were forbidden to use the first-person singular. When one region found it did not have enough food, supplies were not sent from better-off places; rather, the hungry were marched off to look for them.[2] The rest is history, but it has a message that it is wise to retain.

- Pol Pot's steamrollering of Cambodians led to his own downfall; and

- those in charge or secretly drafting the EU Constitution should have had the brains to know that nothing would come out of it, because of lack of popular support.

This, indeed, was the case. Railroading the European people ended in a backlash. The curious logic that in a democracy of equals the larger EU countries make all the decisions, turns the smaller EU member states into Soviet-type satellites. 'We are never deceived, we deceive ourselves,' Johann Wolfgang von Goethe (1749–1832) once wrote.

- The EU's lop-sided Constitution was signed by the heads of state of member countries in October 2004, without consulting the people.

- Then, it had to be ratified by all (of the then) 25 states in order to become legally valid. That's where troubles came in.

The critics were vocal. Having read the EU Constitution, they rejected it outright. Others said that it should not be confirmed by governments, but put to a *public referendum* in every country of the European Union. A third school of thought was of the opinion that, at the very least, the European Parliament should have a free and secret vote on the Constitution before ratification by member states. In retrospect:

- a European Parliament vote was not a bad idea, but it was not enough;

- a country-by-country referendum should have followed it, so that the people, not the oligarchs, could make the final decision.

The autocrats rejected these proposals. In plain conflict of interest with their democratic duties, some prime ministers decided to ratify the EU Constitution high-handedly, on their own. Stalin would have been proud of that action. This was the case, for example, for Gerhard Schröder in Germany, where the parliamentary ratification process was completed with approval by

---

2    Philip Short, *Pol Pot: Anatomy of a Nightmare*, John MacRae Books, London, 2004.

the Bundestag on 12 May 2005 and by the Bundesrat on 27 May 2005. It could not have been otherwise, since Schröder's Social Democrats and their Green allies had a parliamentary majority.

Misjudging the French people's willingness, or lack of it, for further expansion of the European Union, which allegedly involved a Stalinist approach to Turkey's entry – as well as the French people's response to the undemocratic approach in drafting the EU Constitution – Jacques Chirac called for a referendum on its ratification. His advisors probably told him that, because of his 'popularity', the referendum's positive result was as safe as an atomic bunker.[3] Disguised on the agenda were both:

- the question of the EU's borders and

- the thrust and speed of further economic integration.

The first issue roused against the Constitution all those who did not want Turkish entry into the EU. The second roused those who were against different economic provisions they considered unfair. Joining two different currents into a 'No!' vote was an act of political suicide. And suicide it was.

On 8 June 2005, a fortnight after the results of the French referendum (see section 2), *Le Canard Enchainé*, France's top weekly magazine,[4] devoted a feature article to the political damage inflicted on Chirac's by the 'No!' vote. 'He is crushed', the article said, 'with three quarters of the French electorate no longer believing in his ability to lead.' The article reached two conclusions:

- 'He [Jacques] has reached an abysmal level of popularity': and

- 'Public respect for his authority has been severely damaged.'

The foreign press was no kinder. In London, the *Daily Telegraph* wrote that the French President had paid a high price for having adopted an oligarch's approach, which belatedly he put to a referendum. Personally humiliated, the British paper said, he is looked down on by the French. And the *Libre Belgique*

---

3   One evening, according to a Soviet joke, Stalin decided to see if he was as beloved as his cronies insisted, and went to a cinema in disguise. As the newsreels began, the dictator was moved to tears when the audience stood and wildly applauded his image on the screen. His pride, however, was cut short when his neighbour leaned down and hissed: 'Comrade, we all hate him. But it is safest to stand and clap.'

4   And the only really free press. See footnote 10, p. 296 for a further explanation of this.

wrote: 'Since the summit of Nice, the European strategy of Chirac is bluff and high-handed action.'

Hard-headed politicians, however, never learn. In spite of the very negative popular rejection of the EU Constitution in France and The Netherlands, and because it was totally out of touch with European popular sentiment, in June 2005 the European Council decided to continue with the ratification process. Tiny Luxembourg voted for it,[5] but several member states subsequently announced that they would postpone their referendums or parliamentary decisions. Or, they would even suspend the ratification process indefinitely; Britain provided an example.

In mid-2005 it was not foreseeable *whether* and, if so, *when* and under *what* conditions, a restructured EU Constitution, originally envisaged as entering into force on 1 November 2006, would come to life. Many people, however, had no doubt that politicians and autocrats who had lost touch with the European public's wishes would once more go against popular will and risk another popular rejection.

## 2. In the Shadow of French and Dutch Referendums

The French referendum, which rejected the EU's Constitution with a nearly 53 per cent majority, took place on 29 May 2005. A few days later, on 1 June, in the Dutch referendum on the same theme, almost over 60 per cent of Dutch people said 'No!' In the aftermath of the two votes, political analysts suggested that:

- the intrigue by the political oligarchy which had tried to squeeze in Turkish membership to the EU by reinterpreting the positive results it expected to get, loaded the 'No!' side; and

- the French and the Dutch voters' flat rejection of the EU Constitution left no room for double talk, or for doubt about where the people of Europe stood, as opposed to the ideas of many of their oligarchs and other pseudo-representatives.

---

5   Luxembourg and Spain have been the only countries whose people were asked for their opinion and voted 'Yes'.

Critics added that Chirac's blunder was the best present he could make to his friend Tony Blair, by letting him off the hook on his promise to have a British referendum on the EU Constitution. Indeed, one week after Chirac's debacle Blair decided to postpone referendum plans, because from public polls it appeared that in Britain the EU Constitution was heading for a two-thirds 'No!' vote.

It does not take a genius to appreciate that, for all practical purposes, the French and Dutch referendums meant that the process of forming a European superstate has been stopped dead. The 'No!' votes were also a strong signal of profound grassroots dissatisfaction over how Europe's political elites had steered the European Union. In France, fresh from the personal rebuff he had received, Jacques Chirac responded by picking a new prime minister. According to political analysts, that showed:

- complete misunderstanding of the meaning of the French popular vote; and

- lack of sensitivity, on the part of worn-out European politicians, to the message they should take from the public's anti-oligarchic sentiment.

In fact, according to critics of the way the European Union is managed – or, more precisely mismanaged – following in the footsteps of the French voters, the Dutch had not only killed the EU Constitution stone-dead; they had also left little room for resurrecting it because there was simply nobody around with the status to pick up the pieces. However, the events that followed proved that public opinion had underrated the oligarchs' resolve, even if their contract totally lacked:

- a clear statement of common identity;

- a coherent pan-European foreign policy and defence policy;

- a new voting system, which made national governments transparent by reaching the people;

- focused goals and timetables; and

- more democratic means for law-making, with referendums on all crucial issues, such as constitutional changes and enlargement.

It is probably too much to ask for these things from autocrats and bureaucrats. As General George S. Patton, of WWII fame, once said, 'A civil servant is sometimes like a broken cannon – it won't work and you can't fire it.' The sad thing is that the EU is stuck with its oligarchs, bureaucrats and lobbyists (Chapter 5), whose motto is that 'democracy is the regime where one can say what one thinks, provided one does not think'.

The public is disillusioned by the fact that the EU is *dead* as an entity willing or able to share foreign policy and defence goals. Today's European Union is first and foremost a limping economic project – and that's why economic nationalisms matter so much (Part 3). Theoretically, the EU's political oligarchy remains mired in the idea of a 'union', persistently talking of the Constitution's resurrection (section 3). Practically:

- it is contemptuous of European voters and their wishes; and

- it is inviting a still more explosive anti-autocratic backlash.

The fact the political autocrats and their bureaucracy in Brussels have repeatedly attempted to ignore the clear message sent by voters, by saying that 'the show must go on', has indeed been deceitful. This lack of political acumen by second-raters shows up at several levels. For example, among members of the EU Commission are numerous senior officials who have stated publicly that the French, Dutch and (more recently) the Irish 'No!' votes are:

- only a little bump in the road; and

- somehow the integrationist process will continue in spite of them.

It needs no explaining that these are utterly biased opinions, expressed by people out of touch with the electorate; and they are not only very wrong, but also self-deceiving. Instead of indulging in more wrong-headed risk, the European Union's political oligarchy should draw two broader lessons from the French, Dutch and Irish votes.

1.    Political union in the EU should have been attained right after the Treaty of Rome, or at least after de Gaulle's retirement.

Now with 27 members and (quite likely) more to come into the EU, this is no longer feasible. The rejection of the Constitution signals that deeper political integration is a pipe dream, and the euro is sure to feel plenty of aftershocks. Today's Germany is not that of the late 1980s which accepted, maybe reluctantly, its role as 'locomotive of the EU and of the world'.

2.       The political oligarchy's days of dictatorial powers are past. To survive, its members must pass more powers back to the voters, as is due in a democracy.

Decision-making on crucial issues, such as EU constitutional powers, agricultural policy, health and retirement benefits (as well as who pays for them), or Turkey's entry, must be made at the lowest sensible level of government – the voters themselves. In a democracy, the oligarchs should not be able to impose their policies on the people – if for no other reason than because this increases public disenchantment with the entire EU project and its mismanagers.

What *The Economist* wrote on the first anniversary of the French and Dutch 'No!' fits aptly into this discussion because it foretold things to come: 'Over the next few years, everyone and his dog will be offering advice about the EU constitution. Next week, the European Commission will present its proposals; Angela Merkel, Chancellor of Germany and thus leader of the traditional guardians of EU integration, will deliver hers. Two weeks later, EU foreign ministers will debate the matter.'[6] Indeed, a short time thereafter came the mini-Treaty (Section 3).

Here in a nutshell is how another article in *The Economist* looked at the Lisbon Treaty five months before the 'No!' of the Irish people: 'For British critics, the treaty is a bid to bamboozle voters, and smuggle into law most of the failed EU constitution … As the British debate began, critics demanded to know why Lisbon did not merit the referendum promised on the constitution … One Tory asked it the government thought the British public "too thick to understand its benefits".'[7] In the end Gordon Brown saw to it that the British people were denied the right to express their opinion hence it was left to the Irish voters to answer for them by proxy.

## 3. The June 2007 Summit on a New EU Constitution

Part 1 has already informed the reader that 'summits' are a visible part of politicians' tendency to indulge in wishful thinking. In the EU, they are also a

6    *The Economist*, 6 May 2006.
7    *The Economist*, 26 January 2008.

way of hiding the fact that the question of sovereignty has not been observed; the public's worries have not been answered, and the likelihood that the real priorities will be confronted in a decisive way is practically nil.

- By all evidence, the major contribution of the 'summits' is the photo opportunity.

- They offer little, if anything, of substance, nor do they help those who take part, let alone the EU, boost their reputation.

Summits are about power, particularly political power, which cannot be divorced from personality. That holds true for heads of states as well as for corporate CEOs in negotiations, agreements, secret deals, mergers and acquisitions. Whether discussions in the course of so-called summits are nice or nasty matters less than how strongly the politicians feel about personal power.

In line with these summit principles, on 21 and 22 June 2007 European Union leaders gathered for a summit in Brussels. Angela Merkel, the German Chancellor, who at the time held the rotating EU presidency, hoped to reach a deal on a new simplified treaty to replace the draft EU Constitution originally signed in October 2004 and rejected by French and Dutch voters in 2005.

Since the French and Dutch 'No!' in the 2005 constitutional referendums, the EU had drifted from 15 to 27 members, which is a negative in obtaining a positive public response. Still, Merkel made agreement on a new constitution top priority for her EU presidency. She was pushing for a new text which, she hoped, would preserve as much as 90 per cent of the substance of the rejected constitution. Nicolas Sarkozy, the French President, came up with a proposal for a mini-Treaty (a simplified Treaty) by merely dropping some labels and symbols such as:

- the EU flag and anthem,

- the word 'Constitution', and

- the appointment of an EU foreign minister.[8]

---

8    Rechristened as 'high commissioner'.

Merkel's hidden goal was to avoid putting any new text to the vote anywhere, save Ireland, where a referendum is constitutionally required for all EU treaties. Yet, she should have known that it is wrong for EU leaders to avoid the risk of more negative votes by simply going back on their pledges to consult the public on all major decisions. Back in 2005, no fewer than tencountries had promised a referendum on the original constitutional treaty.

- Two voted 'No!'

- two voted 'Yes' and

- the other six suspended ratification.[9]

Secretive treaty-making behind closed doors is hardly an idea destined to endear oligarchs to disenchanted voters. The most widespread opinion among the European public was that the mini-Treaty which was then being discussed and in the end was tentatively confirmed during that Brussels meeting was nothing more or less than the old rejected EU Constitution under new clothing – 'a constitution in drag', as one of the political leaders commented.

Not only was the voted-down EU Constitution – rechristened 'Treaty' – no clear answer to what the European people wanted, but also, to become more acceptable, its better and more fundamental parts in a Union sense, like the flag and hymn of the EU, were dropped. But bureaucratic jobs were preserved, like that of the President of the EU to replace the rotating presidency and warm an armchair for two and a half years.

The way public opinion had it, it was simply not enough for EU leaders to chop off some branches of the rejected EU Constitution, or use different terminology like 'high commissioner' rather than 'foreign minister'. In this connection, it is good to remember that the process leading to the European Constitution which was launched in 2001 hoped to bring Europe 'closer to its citizens' – but the result was precisely the opposite, which was repeated with the simplified Treaty.

Critics said that the attempt to smuggle the rejected constitution past the public by denying them a vote was a pitiful end to the project and to the concept of a democratic European Union as well. To the large majority of the European

---

9    Britain and Poland set out negotiating 'red lines'.

public, 'institutional reform' was a non-issue. By contrast, the subjects close to its heart were:

- the EU's irrational but steady enlargement (Chapter 7);

- stopping Turkish accession, because Turkey is not part of Europe;

- thorough examination of the Union's lopsided budget, 40 per cent of which goes to farm subsidies; and

- a greater respect for European citizens, so that people are not taken for a ride in the name of the EU.

'The people don't like the government so we must replace the people.' This satirical comment, made by Bertolt Brecht, the German playwright, on the crushing of workers uprising in East Berlin in June 1953, gloriously describes the resuscitation of a rejected EU Constitution. (It is also ironic that Angela Merkel, a former citizen of East Germany, should have entered this controversy 54 years after the events in East Berlin.)

One of the reasons why voting by referendum rather than by rubber-stamp governments and parliaments was, and is, the better solution can be found in the fact that the 27 EU countries are deeply split over which parts of the constitution are useful (to each of them) and which are not. One group is the 18 countries that have ratified the Constitution (albeit 16 through parliamentary steamrolling). These 18 have been sulky at having to revisit a deal they thought was settled.

A second group is the French and the Dutch – joined by the Irish[10] – who almost certainly would have voted 'No!' again had they been given the chance. In fact, Frans Timmermans, Dutch Minister for Europe, told the *Financial Times*: 'The No vote was deafening. To re-establish the confidence of the Dutch public in the European project we need to show clearly that we understood that message and acted upon it. We are hard-headed on these issues.'[11] But in the end, on 22 June 2007, Timmermans ate his words and his hat.

In a group of their own were the Poles, asking for leverage. The rules established at the Nice 'summit' gave Poland almost as many votes (27) as

---

10   Who voted 'No!' to the reworked Treaty in June 2008.
11   *Financial Times*, 20 June 2007.

Germany (29), although Germany's population is more than twice as big. Instead, the voted-down EU Constitution provided that a majority must mean 55 per cent of EU members representing at least 65 per cent of the EU's population. The Poles asked that rather than a country's absolute population numbers, the square root of the population should be taken as proxy to voting weight – a curious self-serving algorithm.

The other hold-out, also a country alone in its group, has been the UK. Tony Blair promised a referendum on the EU Constitution. It never took place because in mid-2005 the French and Dutch let him off the hook with their 'No!' vote. By June 2007, Blair was gone and, afraid that the British public's vote would be a resounding 'No!', Gordon Brown chose the anti-democratic approach of passing the Treaty through parliament – where he was assured of his party's majority.

Indeed, both Merkel and the Brussels bureaucracy made no secret of their view that the two trickiest countries were Britain and Poland (missing out the fact that the Irish, too, would not take the railroading lightly). Britain asked for, insisted on and got an opt-out on criminal justice policy and police and judicial cooperation, as well as on the universality of EU labour laws. The Poles also obtained exceptions – with the result that:

- the mini-Treaty ended up with incompatible versions; and

- it's a Treaty which resembles Emmenthal cheese rather than a constitutional document.

At the expense of incompatibility among Treaty versions, compromise was reached, seeing to it that the charter cannot overturn national labour laws – more evidence that the EU is nothing other than a free trade area. (The British position did face resistance to its other request to strip all legal force from the charter of fundamental rights. This involved a sweeping list of social rights that was part of the defunct EU Constitution.)

The Dutch, too, got some goodies to take home. Their request was to insert a clause protecting so-called 'services of general interest' from competition. They argued that some private services, notably social housing agencies, perform public duties and should be safeguarded from EU competition policy.

The most beautiful of all the twists and turns suffered by the mini-Treaty was the far-reaching request by Nicolas Sarkozy, the French President, for a clause against free trade.[12] Adding its weight to the public's disillusionment, this one-sided request was accepted in no time in an atmosphere of *bon enfant*, becoming a pillar of the EU Treaty and raising some pointed questions:

- Do European politicians trust the free market?

- Is the new EU Treaty grounded on economic nationalism?

The clause against free trade is particularly curious due to the fact that, for all the critiques in parts of the continent against capitalism, Europe is good at business. But free trade seems to be bad. With all these twists and exceptions to the Treaty's clauses, one wonders what is left of it; also, even more importantly, if it makes any sense and how it may eventually function.

## 4. Is the Lisbon Treaty Dictatorial?

The mini-Treaty was rebaptized the 'Lisbon Treaty' because of the town in which the heads of state of the 27 EU members met to confirm it.[13] After the Irish voters rejected it, however, many people said that its death should be acknowledged by Brussels and in the different EU capitals that favoured it. Trying to achieve a resurrection by telling the Irish people to 'keep on voting till you get it right' would be in one shot:

- contemptible and

- counterproductive.

Some critics were particularly concerned by the fact that, in their judgement, the Lisbon Treaty was basically dictatorial. As evidence, they pointed to the code of Roman emperor Diocletian, who crafted the political system from which the Byzantine Empire emerged and saw to it that the rich and powerful lusted and revelled while the mass of the degraded population knelt – setting the pattern for serfdom.[14]

---

12  Which in one stroke cancelled out the most basic premise underpinning a free trade area.

13  On 19 October 2007 the EU heads of state reached agreement on the simplified Treaty, which they signed in Lisbon on 13 December 2007.

14  Some people look at the Diocletian model as a variant of Lycurgus' Sparta, better known as the 'oligarchical model'. This was defeated by Alexander the Great but it was to be established under the hegemony of the murdered Alexander's Ptolemaic successors.

Looked at as a system, the EU's new Treaty made several changes to the 'Union's' general institutional framework. An example is the establishment of a permanent president for the European Council, elected for a term of two and a half years, renewable once. This president represents the EU externally and chairs meetings of the European Council which, as the careful reader will recall, bring together the heads of state and president of the European Commission, which became a Union institution.

In regard to the European Council, the definition of a 'qualified majority' was amended by introducing the so-called double majority approach which will become mandatory from 2017 (provided the mini-Treaty is voted in). Its essence is that a measure will (usually) be approved by the Council if it is supported by:

- 55 per cent of member states and

- these represent at least 65 per cent of the EU population.

Many but not all areas of the council's voting will be decided by such qualified majority; the veto right, however, does not disappear altogether since there exist exceptions to the rule.

Theoretically, but only theoretically, the EU Commission became smaller. The original plan (approved in Lisbon) was that from 2014 the number of commissioners would be reduced from 27 to two-thirds of the number of member states, including the Commission president and the high commissioner, chosen on the basis of an equal rotation system. But after the Irish 'No!' of June 2008, and in order to induce the Irish into a second referendum (in violation of their constitution), the oligarchs offered to keep the number of commissioners at 27. That in itself explains how serious this whole business is.

Also theoretically, the EU's foreign affairs apparatus was strengthened through the aforementioned institution of a high commissioner for foreign and security policy responsible to the European Council.[15] He or she became vice president in charge of external relations, and chairman of the EU Foreign Affairs Council. But, to please the different politicians, the current rotating presidency system has been maintained for chairing the Council's remaining formations – leaving the EU with two presidents, as typically happens in a banana republic.

---

15  On a five-year term.

Contrary to that nonsense, two positive aspects of the new treaty are that: (i) the European Central Bank (ECB) was given the legal status of a union institution, with the ECB and European System of Central Banks (ESCB) guaranteed their independent status;[16] and (ii) the European Parliament became involved in more legislative areas and the number of its members was reduced to 751 (still way too large). Co-decision by the Council and the European Parliament is supposed to become the ordinary legislative procedure (Chapter 5). Other innovations include:

- a role for national parliaments in monitoring the application of the subsidiary principles; and

- introduction of an 'exit clause' allowing a member state to leave the EU in an orderly fashion.

But a very important reference concerning respect for the will of the European people is definitely missing, and this sees to it that European citizens feel betrayed by their own governments. Many also feel uneasy because of the second-class position reserved to the EU's smaller countries. Two counts – failure to institutionalize referendums and treating smaller countries lightly – create a 'second-class citizen' spirit which adds to the severe criticism that:

- the Lisbon Treaty is dictatorial and

- it somewhat adds up to the Sovietization of Europe.

The argument goes like this: with the fall of the Berlin Wall, dictatorial fervour spread westward by stealth, to infect the European Union whose complex treaties (hated and feared by the overtaxed, overregulated peoples of Europe) parallel the Soviet Constitution more closely than they do any constitution of liberty or democracy. According to Jens-Peter Bonde, this is so much the case that, if the European Union were to apply for membership of a democratic nations club, its application would be thrown out on the ground that it is not democratic.[17]

---

16  Most importantly, price stability, which was already the primary objective of the ECB and ESCB, is now included in the EU objectives, one of which is the sustainable development of Europe based on balanced economic growth and price stability.

17  *EIR*, 4 April 2008.

According to this school of thought, like the Soviet Politburo, the European Commission has the sole power to propose and hence to reject European legislation. Also like the Politburo, the Commission is unelected and self-perpetuating. Moreover, any commissioner (or Kommissar) has the power to issue an edict which has the immediate force of supreme law throughout the subject territories.

This is admittedly too bleak a picture, but it is by no means deprived of any truth. In Britain, respected members of the Labour Party such as Frank Field and Gisela Stuart describe their government's position on the Treaty as neither honest nor coherent.[18] As for the Tories, who were once divided on the EU, they are now uniformly Eurosceptic and are voicing the public's wish for a say.

Opponents of the Treaty have grounds for concern, and in Britain the European Scrutiny Committee (ESC) of the House of Commons seems to agree. Polls show that voters want a referendum on the Treaty and would vote against it, despite Gordon Brown's dictatorial ratification. A 20 October 2007 article in *The Economist* pointed out that David Miliband, the Foreign Secretary, was attacked by the ESC chairman for accepting incursions across Britain's vaunted 'red lines'. The ESC chairman compared Brown's support for the Treaty to Neville Chamberlain's enthusiasm for the Munich Agreement of 1938.

It needs no reminder that politicians always find a way to bypass the public's will, and the ratification of Lisbon's Constitutional Treaty (or mini-Treaty) has been no exception. In violation of Ireland's constitution, which does not allow a second referendum on something already decided by a referendum, that second event took place.

This happened after the severe global economic crisis of 2007-2009 (which, as yet, has not ended) decimated the Irish economy as the government rushed to guarantee deposits to, and debts of, the bigger Irish banks. These banks had already fatally wounded themselves through superleveraging, subprimes and derivatives; along with some British banks in Ireland.[19] With the country ont the edge of bankruptcy, this time:

---

18  *The Economist*, 20 October 2007.
19  It is, however, to the credit of the Irish government that it took measures to redress the economic situation, while Greece, Spain and Portugal (like Iceland and Latvia) are not sure if they choose to float or sink.

- The Irish did not have much of an option, and

- Public opinion saw to it that, the 'yes' vote carried the day.

What has happened with Poland and the Czech Republic to get their signature on the EU constitution is a different case, and unethical. Both countries received indulgencies for any claims by German citizens regarding their property, which was confiscated in formerly German territories (now part of Poland) and in Sudetenland. The Germans were made to pay their dues, but Poles and Czechs have been given a papal abolition of sins.

## 5. The EU's Failure in Economic Discipline

The No. 1 preoccupation of Angela Merkel when, in 2007, as Germany's chancellor, she chaired the European Union for six months, was how to revive the draft EU Constitution. When Nicolas Sarkozy occupied the Union's six-month rotating presidency in the second half of 2008, he made this same issue his overriding priority. Surprisingly, neither paid due attention to the crucial issue of economic discipline in the EU, which is missing both from the Constitution and from the Treaty. We will see where this led.

Not only did Merkel and Sarkozy, respectively in 2007 and 2008, not pay attention to the need for economic discipline by EU member states, new and old, but this is also an alien issue to the EU's rules, laws and bylaws in all of their incarnations – from the Treaty with Rome (1957) to the mini-Treaty (2007). In connection to economics and finance in the EU, this lack of attention has been:

- the Achilles heel and

- a source of future troubles and sorrows.

True enough, Euroland has its Stability and Growth Pact, which is steadily attacked by the French and poorly observed by the other 15 Euroland members; but the 16 are just a subset of the EU's 27. Some of the other 11, like Britain and Sweden, are in charge of their economies, but the Baltic States and several

---

Here is an example of what I mean. A couple of years ago I took a taxi at 6am from a hotel in central Athens to the airport. The streets were full of vehicles. I said to the driver, 'I'm happy to see that people go to work so early.' He asked, 'How long have you been away from Greece?' I answered, 'For over 50 years.' 'Gentleman,' said the taxi driver, 'these people don't go to work. They return home to sleep after a long night in the nightclubs.'

others are not. Indeed, as we will see in Chapter 7, Eastern Europe is on the brink of bankruptcy – and not only Eastern Europe is affected.

To put it mildly, in spite of all the signatures which it features from the heads of state of Euroland's member countries, the Stability and Growth Pact has become a joke. As of March 2010, the budget deficit of Greece is over 12 per cent, Spain nearly 12 per cent, Ireland a little less than that, France 9 per cent and even Germany features a hefty budget deficit of 6 per cent. There is no better way to describe what the French call *lettre morte*.

EU-wide discipline in economics and finance is not part of the different treaties because, in the mind of second-raters, it did not attract the attention that it deserves. Instead, the fact that weighted their judgement, influencing their reasoning, is that the union which they have unwisely over expanded can no longer function without structured bylaws of a political nature.

In the background of this attention to structural issues, like voting rights by member states, lies the fact that the European Union's original institutions were designed for six members, not for today's 27. But though a constitution could improve on the current chaotic situation, different structural mismatches and the absence of financial discipline rules would prove its undoing. Nor is there an agreement about how to get from 'here' to 'there' in terms of organization and structure:

- some member countries want a bigger treaty with social provisions;

- others want a smaller one with no new powers for Brussels;

- still others want to reopen all the institutional compromises; and

- a few also say that the EU works without a constitution. Hence, why bother?

Behind the challenges posed by the last bullet point lies the fact that the EU has plenty of disillusioned citizens who are not interested in complex and opaque institutional arguments. In so far as they care about Brussels, they want concrete results (which are difficult to find) and a say in decision-making.

The more sophisticated EU citizens suggest scrapping such pointless bodies as the Economic and Social Committee and the Committee of Regions; they also ask for the replacement of the European Parliament, which cannot win legitimacy, with a European senate made up of presidents of national parliaments. But what European citizens want most of all from the EU is a timetable of real deliverables, especially economic ones, rather than theoretical constitutional arguments. This is true both of the old EU members and of the newer ones.

That's also the message given by public opinion polls. A poll conducted in January 2007 among the ten accession countries of 2004 (Poland, the Baltic States, and so on) has shown that the public takes a very dim view of the EU as it presently stands. With the exception of tiny Slovenia, this public feeling has been widespread, with the worst responses to the current status obtained in:

- Hungary, where only 39 per cent voted for the EU and

- Latvia, where the score was even lower, at 33 per cent.

This is indeed very interesting because Latvia (and the other Baltic countries) is much more an embarrassment for the EU than the EU is for Latvia.[20] Indeed, in December 2008 a little-publicized dramatic and controversial financial rescue took shape in the Baltic countries, led by the International Monetary Fund and backed by neighbouring countries, the European Union and other institutions.

The problem came to public knowledge when Latvia's central bank burned through €1 billion ($1.40 billion), about 20 per cent of its reserves, in a month and a half between mid-October and 1 December 2008 to defend the lat, its national currency.[21] Like Argentina's currency of old, the lat is pegged to the euro in an arrangement emulating a currency board – but high inflation ate up the value of local money and foreign currency reserves.

---

20  Latvia's economy is expected to shrink by 4 per cent in 2009, only a notch better than the -4.6 per cent of hugely mismanaged Zimbabwe.

21  As a stop-gap measure, the Swedish and Danish central banks offered a combined €500 million in short-term swap facilities.

The IMF-led bail out stood at the level of €7 billion (about $10 billion) and there were also major contributions from Nordic countries.[22] Nor have the other currencies in the Baltics been in much better shape. Yet, a couple of years earlier the Lithuanians got angry because the EU and European Central Bank rejected their application to join the euro on grounds that:

• their current account balance was highly negative;

• their inflation was not under control; and

• their currency was far from stable.

As if this was not enough, in the intervening years the Baltic countries' current account balance significantly deteriorated over the years (Table 6.1). For Lithuania, doubling its current account deficit in three short years is an act of high irresponsibility. In its way, the case of Lithuania and of the other Baltic States dramatizes what is wrong with the EU in its current status, whether or not the mini-Treaty is confirmed.

**Table 6.1     Current account deficit of the Baltic countries as percentage of GDP***

|  | 2005 | 2008** |
| --- | --- | --- |
| Latvia | 12.4% | 14.2% |
| Estonia | 10.0% | 11.9% |
| Lithuania | 7.0% | 14.4% |

\*      Statistics from *The Economist*, 20 December 2008.
\*\*     At the same time, year-on-year in 2008 Latvia's GDP plunged by 5 per cent and Estonia's by 4 per cent.

• These are independent countries which joined the EU for a free lunch.

• Since their independence from the Soviet Union they have been under very poor leadership; and

---

22  At least for the time being, that deal does not require Latvia to devalue its currency, which is controversial because the IMF knows very well that the memories of the debacle over Argentina's abandonment of its currency board and declaring bankruptcy are still vivid.

- the 'old boys' attitude of the EU, which will not change with the new Treaty, made matters worse because nobody really is in charge.

In parallel with this lack of leadership, financial discipline and accountability, in Brussels and at member countries' national level, Western financial institutions which are exposed in these states use their lobbyists to protect their investments. Swedish and Finnish banks, which own the bulk of Latvia's banking system, could easily find their own creditworthiness suffering if Latvia abandons the peg, let alone declares bankruptcy.[23]

The 2008 global financial earthquakes make a mockery of events like the 26 January 2007 economic meeting when 20 European Union countries[24] gathered in Madrid to pay homage to the Union's 'magnificent' constitutional treaty (the full version of it), and the top brass gave warnings that those blocking the revival of the stalled text could be relegated to the slow lane of a two-speed Europe. Big words but small deeds, as the 2008 events in the Baltics, Hungary and elsewhere documented.

## 6. Creating New Jobs Through the Organization Chart

On 25 June 2008 the European Central Bank published its Structural Issues Report for the year, entitled *Labor Supply and Employment in the Euro Area Countries: Developments and Challenges*. Its contents described and analyzed the main developments in labour supply and its determinants in Euroland since the early 1980s; they also reviewed the links between labour supply and labour market institutions:

- assessing how well the supply of labour reflects demand for it; and

- identifying future challenges to which policy makers in Euroland must bring their attention.

---

23  In late October 2008 the Swedish government launched a loan guarantee plan of $190 billion to calm fears about Swedish banks' stability.
24  Seven of the EU's 27 members did not take part in that controversial Madrid meeting of foreign ministers and senior officials – the UK, the Czech Republic, Denmark, France, the Netherlands, Poland and Sweden – because none of them had yet ratified the constitution and most argued that the only way forward was to adopt a modest mini-Treaty, focusing on rule changes and institutional reforms deemed absolutely necessary.

This is a tall order because, as is well known, 2008 was a year of Western banking crises and the credit crunch, which led to a global economic crisis,[25] with after-effects expected to spread over the next years. Employment will be particularly affected, adding to the fact that the EU already has some chronic unemployment problems. Jobs have been hard to find at the middle and bottom of the labour pyramid – but not at the top.

Jobs at the top can be created a dime a dozen, particularly for political friends. An example is the job created by the Lisbon Treaty of the first permanent president of the European Council, the body that brings together all 27 heads of EU member states. That President, it has been suggested, may well turn into the EU's public face in dealing with his or her American counterpart. Call him or her EU President No. 1.[26]

- Is this not a great innovation for the EU, and an enviable position?

- The answer is not self-evident, as much depends on the job's statutory rights and on who fills it.

In terms of personalities, the die is not cast in advance. Here is what Bob Woodward has to say in *State of Denial* about a presidency of great statutory authority whose filling, however, left much to be desired: 'The President put down the phone and started to cry, a deep convoluted cry (p. 352)... The President liked old comfortable shoes. His staff had become comfortable shoes' (p. 354).[27]

As is typically the case, the inner circle of the staff consisted of a small group of people. Woodward states: 'Even the President's father had confirmed he was unhappy with Rice. "Condi is a disappointment, isn't she? ... General Myers, the outgoing chairman of the JCS was a broken man ... General Pace was worse ... To [Brent] Scowcroft, Rumsfeld was a wholly negative force ... Cheney was the worst, Snowcroft felt." What's happened to Dick Cheney? ... It's a chorus. "We don't know this Dick Cheney"' (all references from p. 420 of *State of Denial*).

25  D.N. Chorafas, *Financial Boom and Gloom. The Credit and Banking Crisis of 2007–2009 and Beyond*, Palgrave Macmillan, London, 2009.
26  To this day, not only is speculation over candidates to the European Council presidency rife, but the functions of the job remain fuzzy, as does its relationship to governments that hold the rotating EU presidency.
27  Bob Woodward, *State of Denial. Bush at War, Part III*, Simon & Schuster, New York, 2006.

In a way quite similar to the EU Commission's, people who had independence of opinion were not welcome in that tight club. A meeting between the highly respected Senator Chuck Hagel and George W. Bush provides an example. Quoting Woodward: 'Mr President,' Hagel said, 'let me ask you a question. I believe that you are getting really bubbled in here in the White House on Iraq. Do you ever reach outside your national security council?' (p. 399). The text implies he had not done so, nor did he appreciate Hagel's question, asking the Senator to talk instead to his national security executive.

One has also to account for the fact that George W. Bush was an elected president. Think about the degrees of freedom of action and of independence of opinion the *selected* president of the European Union will have. The evident answer is zero point zero. They will be cocooned by the 27 chiefs of the EU member states who selected them and might or might not authorize their reappointment.

In addition, there is absolutely no assurance that the EU's top job will be filled by a person able to think about the aftermath of his actions, or able to challenge his own assumptions. There is, however, no chance he or she could be successful unless he does so not only once, but steadily. One of Henry Kissinger's private criticisms of Bush, according to Woodward, 'was that he had no mechanism in place, or even an inclination, to consider the downsides of impeding decisions. Alternative courses of action were rarely considered' (p. 455).

The management principle of unity of command is also sacrificed at the altar of creating new jobs at the top of the EU's hierarchical pyramid. The Treaty stipulates that, apart from the EU President No. 1 selected to a two and a half year term, there will also be a rotating president – call them EU President No. 2 – who, as head of government, will warm another CEO armchair. And one should not forget EU President No. 3, who heads, and will continue heading, the Brussels-based European Commission.

An article in *The Economist* was on the right track in making fun of this plethora of presidents. Referring to the Biblical King Solomon who, when faced with two women claiming the same baby, threatened to cut it in half, which swiftly revealed the real mother, the article pressed the point that the European Union is different: 'Faced with two rival plans, its approach is to say yes to both, delay a reckoning for years and then throw money at the compromise.

If EU leaders were running Solomon's court they would award both women custody, build parallel nurseries with public funds and review progress in 2014.'[28] It might be added that:

- none of these three presidents, who will be inevitably stepping on each other's toes, has any statutory authority to oblige the governments of EU member countries to put their financial houses in order (section 5);

- by contrast, there will be dreadful rows over the top job, of which the EU has a history – like the 'summit' to launch the euro (in May 1998), which degenerated into a 12-hour squabble over who should run the European Central Bank.[29]

In a lecture they gave to the students of Paris-Dauphine University (the former Sorbonne) on 9 December 2008, Valéry Giscard d'Estaing, a former President of the French Republic, and Daniel Cohn-Bendit, one of the leaders of the May 1968 student revolution and currently European Parliament deputy, found a way to agree on what is wrong with the present-day EU.

Talking about the EU's political construction, Giscard d'Estaing said that it is 'a trampling, as a minimum'. Cohn-Bendit commented that it is 'too many words, but no thinking'. To this Giscard d'Estaing added that what there exists is 'a *brouhaha* of ideas and formulas'.[30] He might also have stated 'and not even of clear ideas, while the necessary leadership and discipline are on permanent leave'.

## 7. In the Shadow of the Irish 'No!' Vote

A short while before the now famous mid-June 2008 Irish referendum, an Irish friend was saying that if he were a playwright he would have written a comedy about the new Treaty of the EU and its pork-barrel strategy. As an example, he took the current General Affairs and External Relations Council (GAERC),[31] which prepares summits as well as policies on such matters as Iran. With the

---

28  *The Economist*, 15 March 2008.
29  It was settled by a dubious deal to split the eight-year term between a Dutchman, Wim Duisenberg, and a Frenchmen, Jean-Claude Trichet.
30  *Le Canard Enchainé*, 17 December 2008.
31  Headed on a rotating basis by the foreign minister of the country whose turn has come to chair the EU.

multiplication of EU presidents and other 'top' officials projected by the Treaty, the GAERC will be split:

- creating a foreign affairs council (FAC), chaired by the high commissioner, who will lead on foreign policy and defence; and

- leaving the foreign minister of the rotating presidency with a general affairs council (GAC), whose intended job is vague and uncertain.

'It's plain nonsense,' said the friend, 'and we Irish should use our vote to stop that nonsense.' That's precisely what the public of the Republic of Ireland did. The voters rejected the Lisbon Treaty in the referendum held on 12 June 2008, and this means that the Treaty cannot come into effect, as this requires its unanimous ratification by all EU member states.

Immediately after the Irish vote, the Germans, French and others who pushed the EU Treaty condemned the Irish as well as the fact that 4 million people are 'permitted' to thwart the will of 490 million other Europeans.[32] That argument is bogus and dangerous: bogus because (as an exception in EU business) the rules for ratification were clear and unambiguous.

- To change the rules when one is losing is a violation of fair play and lacks honesty.

- Respect for the rule of law is even more important than the fate of the Lisbon Treaty, or of any other document.

The arguments presented against the Irish 'No!' vote are dangerous too, because they not only constitute a negation of democratic procedures, but also show that the Brussels bureaucrats and heads of state don't understand the Treaty's weaknesses. In addition, trying to isolate and intimidate a small country is not the proper foundation for the formation of a vibrant EU.

Aside from all that, the Treaty itself was written *as if* its authors wanted it to fail. One of the reasons is that by being so voluminous it became unreadable by, and incomprehensible to, the common citizen. Its consolidated version, plus protocols, annexes and declarations, runs into 392 pages. Trying to read its legislative jargon is an almost hopeless task. No wonder that both

---

32  They also called Brian Cowen, the (newly appointed) Irish Prime Minister to go explain himself to Brussels. Cowen should have told Brussels and its brass to go to hell.

Brian Cowen, the Irish Prime Minister, and Charlie McCreevy, the Irish EU Commissioner, said that they have not read this 392-page document cover-to-cover.

No mention was made of the fact that this lack of reading and understanding of the fine print of the Lisbon Treaty no doubt also characterized other EU commissioners and other heads of state – which makes some of the comments that followed the 'No!' vote very funny; for example, Ireland will be offered additional guarantees of its sovereignty in areas such as:

- taxation,

- family law, and

- military policy.

As for insulting the Irish voters, this has not only been anti-democratic but also in bad taste and grossly unfair. The French and Dutch referendums of 2005 (section 2) had already shown that public opinion in the EU was very unhappy with the politicians cooking up things. What was special in 2008 about the Irish is that they were constitutionally compelled to hold a referendum on the Lisbon Treaty, while the other 26 EU countries could push it through by an oligarchic (even if theoretically parliamentary) trick. At the end of the day, the fact is that:

- the Irish 'No!' to the Lisbon Treaty was backed by a 53-per cent majority;

- this followed the French and Dutch referendums which rejected the EU Constitution (the Lisbon Treaty's predecessor) in 2005.

The reader should also notice that neither of these 'No!s' was the first negative popular vote on EU issues. The first 'No!' in a popular referendum was given by the Danes in 1992 and it concerned the Maastricht Treaty. Then in 2001 the Irish turned down the Nice Treaty, though they later approved a modified form of it. These precedents led the different EU governments to bypass popular opinion and adopt the approval of EU-binding decisions through simple parliamentary voting. But in the end the arms of the Irish people have been twisted, and they said 'Yes!'

Precisely because writing off the citizens' opinion has become everyday practice, the results of the Irish 'No!' to the EU Treaty were like a slow-motion car wreck, but the Irish are by no means the only EU people to dislike the Treaty. Václav Klaus, President of the Czech Republic, who from 1 January to 30 June 2008 chaired the EU, has declared Lisbon dead.[33] Diplomats also expect difficulties in Poland, where parliament has approved the treaty, but President Lech Kaczynski has held back from signing it. 'It is not a very popular treaty in Poland,' said a European government official in close touch with the Polish.

Other opponents, too, look towards the 2009 European Parliament elections and are preparing arguments as well as platforms that include rejection of the Lisbon Treaty – though their No. 1 objective is to allow the European public to express their views on important issues by direct vote. Another objective is to make the oligarchs more accountable to the people. It is not possible to continue with the policy that every time one of the EU member states ventures into holding a referendum and gets a negative popular vote, the autocrats' reaction is that of:

- declaring that the EU is in deep trouble and unable to function;

- accusing the country that has said 'No!' of sabotaging the EU;

- hinting that the voters in question should change their minds;

- asking the political leadership of that country to explain itself for the 'No!' vote and then to find a solution; and

- as an alternative, threatening that country that it may be forced to leave the EU.

Quite to the contrary to this policy, *if* in a democratic society the people don't approve of the government and its treaties, *then* the political leadership has to undertake an autocritique and change course.

It is indeed surprising that those who are supposed to lead the EU find it difficult to appreciate that a whole range of EU commitments, from

---

33 According to polls, in the Czech Republic 55 per cent of the population opposes the Treaty. Nevertheless, as we saw in section 4, after he got the indulgences he asked for (to avoid paying indemnities for confiscated properties of German citizens), Klaus signed the Lisbon Constitutional Treaty.

enlargement to treaties, are too monolithic, too little exposed to critical review and too complex to be the object of a simple 'yes/no' vote. They are also too manipulated by the different governments and their bosses, to the point that they are not working as they are supposed to be.

## Note to the Reader

Events that have taken place in September and October 2009 brought up the need to update this text. These updates appear in this chapter as well as Chapter 7 and Chapter 12.

While the workings of the EU remain mysterious, even to the insiders, a couple of happenings are worth recording.

One of these critical events to EU's future is the reappointment of José-Manuel Barroso as head of the European Commission. The European public did not quite appreciate it, as evidenced by an opinion poll conducted by Euronews: 32 per cent approved it; 55 per cent *disapproved* it; and 13 per cent expressed no opinion.[34]

Then there has been the (unconstitutional) repetition of the EU Treaty referendum in Ireland. The best comment came from *The Economist* who wrote: '... the Euro-establishment's delight ... is just as nonsensical and self-serving as most of the Yes and No arguments.'[35]

The third milestone to the EU's uncertain path has been the signing up on November 3, 2009 by Vaclav Klaus of the Lisbon Treaty – after the latter was dented to accommodate his requirement that not all citizen who suffered by World War II's aftermath are equal in front of the law. This also revealed that the Poles, too, had been given indulgencies.

And then there was the fading star of 'President Blair'. Britain is divided on the idea of his candidacy to one of the three EU 'presidential armchairs'. Since the start, insiders suggested that there are many reasons to expect the former prime minister to fail in his bid. He did.

---

34  *Euronews*, 17 September, 2009.
35  *The Economist*, 10 October, 2009.

# 7

# Perils of the EU's Enlargement

## 1. EU Enlargement. A Policy Followed by Default

Linguistic nationalism (Chapter 3), economic nationalism (Chapters 10 and 11) and a plethora of other wrong-way 'patriotisms' prevailing in the European Union would have been enough to dissuade accepting more member states. This is what a rational mind would have suggested. Till the many 'isms' are ironed out, taking on board more members is:

- counterproductive and

- an exercise in futility.

But the EU does not work in a rational way. Decisions are not taken after a thorough study of 'pros' and 'cons'. Most frequently they are reached by default – a policy which dates back to the nineteenth century. As a Parisian joke had it, in 1870 after Marechal Mac-Mahon capitulated in Sedan and Marechal Bazaine in Metz – thereby opening wide the gates for Prussian conquest of France – 'Bazaine had finally joined forces with Mac-Mahon'.[1] That's exactly how Bulgaria and Romania joined forces with the EU in 2007 and still at the gates is Turkey.

The capitulation of two major French armies was a curse and not a joke, but it can also be seen as a precedent to other misfortunes like the steady drifting of the EU towards a larger and worse group of states characterized by varying degrees of linguistic and economic nationalism. The aftermath of this policy of letting others decide one's fate is that in 2009 European citizens have no more confidence in, or respect for, the different political chiefs. As a 2007 poll conducted among the original 12 countries of the EU has shown, the most negative public reaction centred on two issues:

---

1    F. Sarcey, *Le Siège de Paris*, Collection Nelson, Paris, 1871.

1.     unstoppable influx of migrant workers and

2.     accession of Romania and Bulgaria to the EU.

On average, such a negative reaction stood at 42 per cent, outpacing positive opinion by two-to-one.[2] In Germany, positive opinion about Romania's and Bulgaria's accession was only 17 per cent, while negative opinion stood at nearly 60 per cent. For every 'yes' there have been 3.5 'no's, yet the EU Commission and the swarm of heads of state continue their negotiations with Turkey.

It is indeed surprising that highly paid individuals who play heads of state are incapable of judging what they should and should not do. To some of them 'enlargement' is like morphine. They go dopey, feel better and are worse off. Europe may be a rich continent, but like anybody else it has both

- priorities and

- finite resources.

Rather than absorbing at high speed and high price poor countries who expect huge amounts of financial assistance after joining the EU, one of its priorities should be to redress the depressed regions of its current members – without the waste of money observed in the past. Here is what an article in the highly respected *Monthly Report* by the Deutsche Bundesbank had to say about the aftermath of unstoppable enlargement for the support former East Germany still requires:

> ... *EU assistance for eastern Germany will be reduced as, post-enlargement, its economy will no longer be as weak compared with the new EU average.*

> *Far more significant is the agreement contained in Solidarity Pact II (which has been in effect since 2005) to gradually reduce the special supplementary Federal grants which the east German states receive ... to ease the burdens resulting from the former partitioning of Germany.*[3]

2   *Financial Times*, 29 January 2007.
3   Deutsche Bundesbank, *Monthly Report*, July 2006.

Because of 'enlargement' German funds had to be diverted to Bulgaria and Romania rather than helping Germany again become the economic dynamo it once was. Worse yet is the plight of decaying industrial suburbs in Britain and elsewhere – the 'forgotten underclass' as an article in *The Economist* had it, adding that 'Moslems and blacks get more attention. But poor whites are in a worse state.' This combines the after-effects of uncontrollable immigration and enlargement into one odious act. As this article aptly points out:

> *When politicians say that some communities are failing to integrate with mainstream society, they mean Moslems from the Indian subcontinent.*

> *When campaigners complain that schools are failing some children, they often cite black boys.*

> *Yet the nation's most troubled group, in both absolute and relative terms, is poor, white and British-born.*[4]

The common theme behind these British and German real-life references is that something wrong happens because of the EU's misguided policies and wrongly perceived priorities. In Britain's case, the victims are poor, white children between the ages of 14 and 16, who are left behind in education, which damages their professional life. As *The Economist* has pointed out, the parents and grandparents of these kids have come to the same conclusion.

In spite of its plethora of heads of member states, commissioners and other Brussels bureaucrats – or, more likely, because of it – the EU has never really had a policy towards its own people; 'enlargement' has been its banner. When new members from central Europe joined the club in 2004, Europeans faced an even greater problem than the previous enlargements had brought:

- these new member states were a relatively incoherent group; and

- their labour laws, social policies and wages were totally incompatible with those of Western Europe, which led to labour restrictions in violation of the Treaty of Rome[5] and other acts.

---

4  *The Economist*, 28 October 2006.
5  For instance, the 'Polish plumber' in France, and British restrictions on labour seekers from Romania and Belgium.

The British attitude after Bulgaria and Romania joined the EU contrasted with the one adopted in May 2004 when the European Union expanded to the east. At that time, together with Ireland and Sweden, Britain was one of the few countries to open its labour market to workers from the new member states (particularly Poland), giving up the right to impose restrictions lasting up to seven years – as France and other EU countries did.

But openness also has its limits, and on 24 October 2006 that open-door policy was slammed shut for Bulgaria and Romania. John Reid, the then Home Secretary, announced a list of controls which were designed to keep out all but a trickle of migrant workers from the EU's two new members, starting on 1 January 2007.

There is little doubt that Britain had good reasons to reach that decision. The point, however, is that the facts which have motivated it were known to Tony Blair, Jacques Chirac, Angela Merkel and the rest of the decision-makers well before Romania and Bulgaria were admitted to the EU. Also known to them was the high level of corruption and crime in these two countries, particularly in Bulgaria. This being the case, it would have been much more rational – and more honest – not to admit them rather than to bend, post-mortem, the EU rules.

## 2. Britain's Entry into the European Union

The first enlargement ever contemplated concerned Britain. In 1963, however, de Gaulle unilaterally vetoed Britain's entry into what was then the EEC (Chapter 1) and only in May 1971 were the last obstacles overcome.[6] Willy Brandt, the then German Chancellor, supported Britain's membership in the Common Market, at least in part to give balance to his *Ostpolitik*. And Georges Pompidou, the then French President, a former banker and university professor, abandoned de Gaulle's reservations if for no other reason than because he feared that France would be left alone with a potentially nationalistic Germany.

- De Gaulle did not want competition from Britain for leadership of the EEC, and he also resented certain events from World War II.

---

6   The Conservative government of Harold Macmillan had already applied for EEC membership in 1961. The 1963 rejection was in conjunction with British, Irish, Danish and Norwegian applications.

- However, procedurally and substantively his actions irritated the other five governments, particularly in 1967 when he vetoed the second British application.[7]

This affront against the wishes of other EU members did not end with the unilateral rejection of Britain's application. For de Gaulle, Hallstein, the Common Market's first CEO, was moving too much towards budgetary autonomy for the EEC, and he regarded this as a major threat to national sovereignty because it would mean that French interests could be overridden in the European Council. In June 1965 France withdrew from the workings of the Council of Ministers, a solution was not found until January 1966 in the so-called Luxembourg Compromise – which essentially confirmed the EEC's future impotence.

British membership of the EU had to wait till Edward Heath, the then British Prime Minister, and Pompidou met in late May 1971 to resolve the remaining issues, which were mostly technical.[8] With this done, Pompidou made his famous statement: 'It would be unreasonable to think that we will not reach an agreement', thereby welcoming British membership in spite of the reservations of many of his assistants.

By 1973, with Britain's accession to the EEC, it looked as if hard-core Gaullists had had to swallow their pride. But those opposed to British entry into what was then the Common Market did not disarm. Voices were raised, particularly in France, that Britain was historically and emotionally committed to the United States. Contrarians to its EEC membership claimed that:

- Britain was closer to America than to Europe; and

- whatever the facts of geography may be, they were only an illusion.

In Britain, too, not everybody welcomed the country's entry into the EU. The public was divided into a three-way split: *pro-European* more or less the minority, *anti-European*, and *Eurosceptic* – the fence-sitters. These were the commonly used terms and they were deliberately misleading because 'pro', 'anti', and 'sceptic' are geographically, politically and socially inaccurate.

---

7   This time made by the Labour government of Harold Wilson.
8   Pompidou was de Gaulle's Prime Minister, but the latter never pardoned the former for running for president of the French Republic. *'C'est sur mon lit de mort qu'il me reverra,'* the general had said. When Pompidou went to Colombey for the funeral, de Gaulle's coffin had already been closed by his family (*Le Canard Enchaîné*, 4 October 2006).

Indeed, since EEC accession, one of the most prominent themes of British politics has been the nature of the relationship between Britain and the mainland continent. Across the Channel similar feelings prevail. It is nobody's secret that the French still regret (and many even reject) Britain's EU accession,[9] pointing out:

- Britain's link to America and

- the history of Britain's relationship with continental Europe.

Included in the second bullet are: late application for membership, rejection of some of the EEC's early principles (like supranational institutions), squabbles, renegotiation, budget rebate (in Thatcher's time), objections to the single currency and opposition to extra powers for the European Parliament – *as if* other member states welcomed such extra powers!

Irrespective of the merits of the *for* or *against* stands in regard to British entry, the political elite seems to have taken the strategic decision that Britain's future security in Europe was more important than other considerations – and that 'togetherness' could improve such security. In Britain, too, some political analysts and businesspeople think that part of that decision was an appreciation of the fact that the nation states of Europe could no longer be independent of each other the way they were before World War II.

Not everybody, however, was in accord with this school of thought. Several opinions I heard in London converged with the notion that implicit in the Eurosceptics' rejection of Europe is an instinctive defence of parliamentary authority against its weakening from continental influences. Other conditions advanced by Eurosceptics for agreeing to entry are:

- freedom to plan the British economy and

- freedom to pursue an independent foreign policy.

In the background of these conditions and objections can be found the notion that democratic rule, economic freedom and policy independence are questions to be decided by the British Parliament and nobody else. (By all the evidence, Ted Heath was committed to joining Europe, convinced of Britain's need to enter the Community from its early years, and he pursued his vision

---

9    'It was a deadly mistake to let Britain in,' said a friend in Monte Carlo, 'almost a catastrophe.'

with unyielding determination. In contrast, Harold Wilson, who had a record of U-turns on European issues, set a policy of fence-sitting – which transcended his departure from political life.)

Across the Channel, apart from the French, who were generally hostile to Britain's entry, in the rest of continental Europe sentiments reflecting Britain's place in the EU were milder but divided. Proponents of political union worried that this inevitably meant:

- a shallower European Union and

- a solution which would be nothing more than free trade areas marred by endless wrangling.

People who had thought that the 1957 Treaty of Rome meant, *One Europe*, worried about progress towards closer integration being stalled by the difficulty of finding agreement on anything but the most general level – which actually happens. Gaullists, who were against political integration anyway, were particularly concerned that with Britain in, France was losing its predominant position in the EU.

Not every adversity, however, was political. Some problems were technical, such as finding a generally acceptable solution on institutional matters, a task that presented particular difficulties. At the core was the question of the balance of power between states. Britain's entry rekindled arguments that were never really resolved, like:

- how much acknowledgement should be given to national independence and sovereignty;

- how much weight should be given to the size of EU members' population in the making of decisions; and

- in what way differences between Napoleonic law prevailing in continental Europe and Anglo-Saxon law[10] could be resolved.

It is appropriate to notice that from 1971, when these three points were raised, to 2009 nothing has been done to resolve them. People who brought up legal issues

---

10  It would have been more precise to write English common law, but Anglo-Saxon law is the term currently used in continental Europe, and also covers American law.

connected to 'more Europe' also noted that crime increasingly crossed borders. Indeed it did; and so did terrorism. The EU set up Eurojust to help prosecutors cooperate in dealing with the worst cross-border crimes only in 2001.

The issue of how convergent legal decisions could be reached has also been obscure, as every member state has a veto at the bargaining table and a high court to account for. Critics of the prevailing big differences in legal systems among jurisdictions say that involvement in criminal justice may hit the rocks. This has indeed happened when in 2006 the European Court of Justice (ECJ, Chapter 5)[11] struck down an EU deal on sharing airline-passenger data on the ground that law enforcement cannot be decided using Single Market rules.

## 3. The EU's Unstoppable Enlargement: A Case Study in Mismanagement[12]

Back in 1953 one of my professors at UCLA taught his students that the most important principle of *mismanagement* is that if you cannot do anything right, do a lot.[13] The more you have going on, the longer it will take for its disastrous consequences to become clear. In the long run, of course, the facts will find you out. But who cares? We will all be dead in the long run.

That is a principle to which the European Union has subscribed wholeheartedly, and it has also espoused mismanagement's second most important principle: marking its acts as myths, invented and/or based on exaggerated tales by Brussels bureaucrats as well as heads of state.

Euromyths are the order of the day irrespective of whether they are made up at the EU's headquarters or in this or that member country or whether they have to do with the unstoppable enlargement, obscure policies, or incoherent proposals for far-reaching institutional reforms 'to keep the EU functioning'. For example:

- scrapping the practice of one European commissioner per country;

---

11  Not to be confused with the European Court of Human Rights (ECHR).
12  Beyond the current 27, three countries have been granted candidate status: Turkey in 1999, Croatia in 2004 and pseudo-Macedonia in 2005. All the other Balkan countries are potential candidate countries and have the prospect of eventual EU membership.
13  Correspondingly, according to Dr Neil Jacoby (the same UCLA professor and dean of the School of BusAd), one of the basic principles of management is that the best way to get rid of a bad executive is to give him enough rope to hang himself.

- weighing national governments' votes by some magic formula;

- continuing to enlarge the EU because 'it has been so far very successful'.

Against all good sense, the latter myth has been coined by a former Finnish Prime Minister who, after having messed up negotiations on Kosovo, was awarded the Nobel Prize for Peace.[14] (The former Prime Minister in question would have been wiser to apply Abraham Lincoln's dictum: 'Better to remain silent and be thought a fool, than to speak out and remove all doubt.')

Looking back in a snapshot, after Britain and Denmark stepped over the line in 1973 to become members of the EEC came a torrent of new applications. The second enlargement in 1981 was Greece's; in 1986 Spain and Portugal joined; in 1995 membership was extended to Austria, Sweden and Finland; in 2004 the new members were Poland, the three Baltic States, Czechoslovakia,[15] Slovenia, Hungary, Cyprus and Malta. The sixth enlargement in 2007 let in Romania and Bulgaria. *Basta*.

This growth for growth's sake in EU membership has proved to be a huge miscalculation by the oligarchs who run the destiny of the European Union and that of its member states. They distracted themselves, strained available resources, confused growth with quality and missed the chance to turn to good advantage the once-in-a-lifetime opportunity for integration and Franco-German collaboration presented by the Treaty of Rome.

Anyone who has not yet become senile or is permanently confronted by deep conflicts of interest would appreciate that it is not logical for EU enlargement to continue without an end in sight. Following the Brussels train of thought adopted by bureaucrats, lobbyists and second-rate heads of state, the EU may as well include the whole world under one God-sized administrative structure which envelopes mountains, valleys, oceans and kitchen sinks.

The urge to do something which enlarges one's ego or serves one's interests is so great that no attention is being paid to the legacy new EU members bring along. Examples are provided by Estonia, Latvia and Lithuania, which have

---

14  Or was it for a piece of Serbia?
15  Now the Czech Republic and Slovakia.

nudged the European Union into a tougher stance towards Russia,[16] but also became living examples of:

- lack of economic discipline (Chapter 6) and

- paving the way to financial bankruptcy (section 6, in this chapter).

With the fifth and sixth enlargements of 2004 and 2007 the EU's political ranks were enriched with plenty of ex-communists relabelling themselves as social democrats and hanging on to power across the East European landscape. Brussels is full of talk about *backsliding*, to describe the way politicians in the new member countries:

- forgot or

- actively undermined

reforms that the EU demanded and they had agreed to implement. Promises made and agreements signed during accession negotiations were written on the wind. By contrast, corruption and organized crime prospered, while parliaments and ministerial suites sheltered too many unwanted persons – with the worst record shown after Romania's and Bulgaria's accession.

Another part of the legacy, or more precisely the dowry, new members brought to the EU has been the large numbers of illegal immigrants. Millions of people with no fixed domicile, loosely labelled as Roma or gypsies,[17] started to move west in huge numbers, exploiting EU laws.

(There are no reliable statistics available but a 2005 UNICEF report stated that 84 per cent of Roma in Bulgaria, 88 per cent in Romania and 91 per cent in Hungary lived below the poverty line.) Italy has got the bulk of this massive new migration promoted by the EU's open frontiers. Having won a landslide election in early 2008, the fourth Berlusconi government said it would make illegal entry into Italy (from outside the EU) an offence, as it already is in Britain, France and Germany. It would also confiscate property rented to illegal immigrants, restrict the granting of asylum and make it harder for legal immigrants to bring in family members. But these measures are not the whole story.

---

16  Unlike Estonia and Latvia, Lithuania no longer shares a common border with Russia.
17  Estimates range widely between 4 and 12 million altogether.

After the murder of a couple of young Italian women, allegedly by Romas, Italian police carried out checks and raided Roma settlements. In Naples, an alleged attempted abduction of a child by a young gypsy woman prompted vigilante attacks on camps, one of which was torched after its inhabitants were removed by the authorities for their own safety.[18] To stop social unrest from taking the upper hand, the Italian criminalization of illegal entry will allow the authorities to:

- lock up migrants arriving in rickety fishing boats and

- escort to the border those already in the country found not to have the right papers.

The European Union simply cannot be the world's collector of people who abandon their domicile, as certain 'socialists' and other eggheads want it to become. Italy's measures have been sovereign acts, but they did not please those politicians who are ready to sell the European way of life. Spain's socialist Deputy Prime Minister, Maria Teresa Fernandez de la Vega, loudly condemned the Italian government's policies – which was not her business. Not unexpectedly, this sparked trans-Mediterranean reproaches that strained relations.

Not to be left behind, another Spanish socialist, Celestino Corbacho, Minister of Work and Immigration (notice how the two have been combined), affirmed that the Italian policy is accentuating discrimination against diversity rather than managing the phenomenon and it is intended to criminalize diversity – adding to his statement various accusations of racism. The minister would have done better to condemn:

- his own country's policy, which has become a gateway via the Canary Islands; and

- the absence of any effort by the alien communities to put their own house in order and convince the citizens of the countries they inhabit that they can be orderly and productive members of society.

---

18  All this is a double mystery to me. Firstly, why don't European parliaments take the initiative to finally settle the Romas in agricultural areas which have been decommissioned – recommissioning them again for the production of biofuels. Secondly, the Romas themselves have responded negatively to some European efforts aimed at providing them with permanent settlements. Allegedly, centuries ago the Romas migrated from India and they were from the cast of the untouchables. But European culture does not have a cast of untouchables.

If the No. 1 problem of Romas is failure to settle down and give high priority to education, No. 2 is political leadership. Instead of trying to instil some civil respect and discipline in her own people,[19] Viktoria Mohácsi (an MEP of Roma origin) toured gypsy camps in Italy and made inflammatory statements that conditions were the worst she had seen in Europe.[20] On 20 May 2008 the European Parliament added its voice by censuring Italy for its treatment of gypsies. De la Vega, Corbacho, Mohácsi and the parliamentarians are old enough to know that:

- the best way to improve one's lot is through education and personal initiative;

- people no longer take responsibility for themselves when the government does everything to please them; and

- the Ponzi game of taking money away from those who work to throw it to economic migrants falsely claiming refugee status, or refuse an honest day's work, must come to an end.

The same day that Mohácsi spoke, and with the memory of the Spanish verbal assault still fresh, Franco Frattini, Italy's Foreign Minister, said his government wanted to ensure the effective expulsion of all those who break the law or act antisocially no matter what may be their origin, and that it would do so in full compliance with European rules.

Therein lies the catch. The grounds on which one EU country can expel citizens of another are severely limited by a 2004 EU directive on freedom of movement. Many of Italy's gypsies came from Romania and Bulgaria after they were admitted as members of the EU. That's part of the dowry they brought along when they joined – or, if you prefer, of the 'success story of EU-enlargement', the myth intended to cover the facts about the EU's *déclinisme*.

## 4. A Two- or Three-Speed EU is the Worst Possible Scenario

We can't compare the EU with an integrated polity like the US, José Manuel Barroso, speaking as chief of the European Union Executive, said on 15 February

---

19  Italy's estimated more than 150,000 Roma gypsies.
20  That is a superficial contribution to social peace. An MEP is, at least theoretically, a political leader – and it is the job of a political leader to instill respect and discipline to the people he or she represents.

2006. He then added that: 'We are 25,[21] not one. They [probably meaning the meetings and discussions] take a lot of time. We are not China or the US It is the essence of Europe. We want to be 25 free democracies.'[22] Who are 'we'?[23]

Leaving aside the fact that references made to both the US and China are out of context because the EU can be compared to neither, Barroso might have been right if he was talking as Prime Minister of Portugal, which he previously was. But he is wrong in making this sort of statement as EU's chief executive – though he did manage to explain, in a nutshell, what the salient problem with today's European Union is.

- *If* the EU was composed of the original six members – or even the 15 – *then* decision-making would have been much more effective.

- *If,* alternatively, each member state wants to have its own monetary and fiscal policies as well as its own culture – from schooling to laws and jurisprudence – *then* we don't talk about a 'union' but about a travelling provincial theatre cast.

Barroso's reference, moreover, is in full *contradiction* to the position taken by one of his (much more famous) predecessors. 'We're not here just to make a single market, that doesn't interest me,' Jacques Delors, the European Commission President repeated in the 1980s and 1990s, 'but to make a political union.' In all likelihood, the EU's founding fathers thought the same, but instead of political union, we had unstoppable enlargements which:

- diluted the pseudo-union and

- proved that indeed growth for growth's sake is the philosophy of the cancer cell.

It is quite curious that highly paid (and pampered with taxpayers' money) presidents, prime ministers, EU CEOs, commissioners and other managers do not realize that more means less. Precisely because of less and less cohesion we

---

21  Prior to the entry of Romania and Bulgaria.
22  *The Economist*, 10 September 2005.
23  The way the *Financial Times* saw it, in the 1980s the fear of Europe was that the British would be in charge of foodstuffs and the Germans of the police. But in the intervening decades new perils have taken the spotlight. In mid-2009 the nightmare of Europe is that Tony Blair becomes President of the European Council and José Manuel Barroso is reconfirmed as President of the European Commission (*Le Canard Enchaîné*, 5 August 2009).

have trivial deliverables. And we also see that the EU's powers of persuasion rest only on the lure of full membership to countries that are not necessary parties of choice.

Critics are right in saying that this is tunnel vision. Its aftermath is an unstable, one-dimensional approach further undermined by *enlargement fatigue*. In 2006, one of the EU commissioners, who had more brains than his colleagues, said that the EU should let in Romania and Bulgaria but then close its doors. Bulgaria, however, did not (and does not) satisfy even the EU admission requirements and Romania is not a much better fit.[24] This, plus the spectre of Turkish admission (section 7):

- has turned the majority of EU citizens against further enlargement; and

- makes it harder and harder to dole out interim benefits that (most irrationally) go with membership talks.

Closing the EU doors, even at this late stage, would leave out not only Turkey (which, anyway, is a culture most alien to the European[25]) but also Croatia, Bosnia, pseudo-Macedonia, Montenegro, Albania and Serbia. It would also cut the link between admission criteria and political manoeuvring.

Serbia's arm is being twisted by the EU to make it give up its citizens in exchange for EU membership at some unspecified date. A growing number of people now say that the fact the EU gave the Serbian government a deadline to deliver General Vladic to the Hague Tribunal is a disgrace, because the EU is a political body, not a police state or a tribunal.

- It is enough that Islamists integrate politics and religion.

- *If* we are going to confuse politics and judicial action, *then* we are opening the door to a new dictatorship.

---

24 Both countries are characterized by a high level of corruption, all the way up to the government, although this is worse in Bulgaria. In both countries, monetary policy is in shambles and tax collection is no better. Moreover, in the years after their admission to the EU, there has been no significant improvement.

25 Turkish culture is perverse by Western standards, like a father ordering his son to kill his sister – in a case involving Turkish immigrants that recently went to court in Germany. (The father got life imprisonment, the son 8 years in prison because he acted under his father's command). This has to do with religion, but not only with religion.

Critics of EU irrationalities also point out that even with the 27-nation membership, language barriers have become significant, setting the various countries and their people apart. Political union would have been instrumental in overcoming some of the differences, because it would have made all EU citizens active players, rather than keeping them as passive watchers. And it might have been instrumental in avoiding a *two-* or *three-speed* EU – because at the 15-member mark, all member countries were at about the same level of industrial development.

According to its proponents, the defeated EU Constitution would have seen to it that the ever bigger number of member states would move as a convoy at *slow speed*, even if without much to say about the direction of things. Some of its proponents, however, add that the selected few of the EU (read the bigger states) should be free to move at *high speed*.

The French invented this two-speed scenario. It needs no explaining that this is an unacceptable idea to the smaller EU members. It is practically reinventing colonies in the European continent: the smaller countries will be expected to pay the huge budget deficits of the 'high-speed' nuts, whose leaders do not seem to have read the advice of Dr Ludwig von Mises, the Austrian economist and mathematician of the early twentieth century.

Von Mises put his thoughts in the clearest possible manner when he stated that: 'It may sometimes be expedient for a man to heat the stove with his furniture, but he should not delude himself by believing that he has discovered a wonderful method of heating his premises.' That's what the EU is currently doing. Some countries, the high speeders-to-be – as well as the high spenders – try to propel themselves through big budget deficits to be paid by the others.

Worse yet, in the EU of 27, for the '27 plus' the two-speed dichotomy will become a multi-speed and soon thereafter multi-tier Europe, with those in the lower tiers frozen out. Proposals to create a 'hard core' or even 'a group of pioneers' fall into this category. Nor would a multi-speed arrangement work if those who pursue a project can capriciously stop others joining if they want to, thereby:

- creating categories of first- and second-class memberships; and

- fragmenting the 'union' by accommodating diverse views on how far and how fast to go.

On the practical side, high speed in economic development is, of course, a pipe dream, as Mao discovered with his Great Leap Forward. Take as an example France and its slow path to economic reform. Studies which identified the chief brakes on growth provide plenty of food for thought. The brakes include:

- high taxation, particularly for the social net;

- a rigid labour market, and

- the public sector's inordinate weight on the economy.

Critics suggest that the difficulty most EU governments, including those of recent accessions, face is not that of deciding what to do but of doing it. For instance, in the Group of Ten (G10) countries, France is today the one with more bureaucrats than any other: 5,100,000 people, amounting to 25 per cent of the working population, are in the government payroll. Men and women in these jobs are riding desks rather than horses, and their number exceeds by more than 10 per cent employment in the private sector.

An article in *Le Figaro* stated that the more than 5 million bureaucrats of the French government could be reduced by 15 per cent to 20 per cent without impairing any service (Sarkozy is correctly trying to do that, starting with the teachers). Government employment of 25 per cent of the workforce compares badly with 15 per cent or less in Britain, Germany, the Netherlands and the United States. It also consumes an inordinate 40 per cent of the total government budget. Another interesting statistic is that since the mid-1960s,

- the number of bureaucrats in France has multiplied by three,

- while more and more people, including graduating students, seek some sort of *rent*.

This may not be so surprising because all over the European Union today – and most particularly in the former Soviet satellites – there is a growing trend towards *rent-seeking*. Living on state subsidies and taking out of the common purse rather than contributing to it has become a widespread policy assuring that, if nothing else moves, at least the EU's rent-seeking industry is growing by leaps and bounds.

This is surely leading to economic ruin, but good examples that might induce people to change course are missing. 'The Queen is being kept by the taxpayer so why shouldn't we be?' said jobless Brian Deighan in Britain, on £26,000 a year in benefits paid to himself, his pregnant wife and ten children. Those who pay the 12 Deighans' rent are the British people who are hard-working, but also heavily taxed. Is that a fair social policy?

## 5. The Transfer of Jobs to Accession Countries

The majority of EU citizens think that enlargement speeds the transfer of jobs to countries with cheaper labour. This is only partly true. According to a European Restructuring Monitor survey, about 8 per cent of EU jobs lost to restructuring between 2003 and 2006 involved offshoring. In addition, the transfer of jobs to lower-cost countries is part of globalization without limits,[26] which started long before enlargement, though EU enlargement, too, has contributed to it.

- Renault transferred jobs to Logan, a low-cost carmaker it bought in Romania; and

- Nokia was heavily criticized when, in early 2008, it announced the closure of a mobile-telephone factory in the German city of Bochum[27] and transfer of work to Cluj, also in Romania.

Soon after the Berlin Wall came down, EU firms began investing heavily in Central and Eastern Europe. And this accelerated with ascension. Even subsidized factories, like Nokia's in Bochum, shifted to lower-cost countries. (The latter case led a German government minister to demand assurances that EU funds would not be used to subsidize such moves.)

While labour costs are the overriding reason, excuses can always be found for these job transfers. Renault's plan, reportedly, was to produce a new low-cost car with few gadgets and sell it in emerging markets like Eastern Europe, Turkey and North Africa. The Logan, however, was designed to meet Western European norms because it was also marketed there and some of the other target markets were candidates to join the EU.[28]

---

26  D.N. Chorafas, *Globalization's Limits. Conflicting National Interests in Trade and Finance*, Gower, Farnham, 2009.
27  For which it had received considerable subsidies.
28  Production began in 2004 in Romania, where Renault had bought a local carmaker, Dacia, but contrary to the drummed-up original idea, Logan sold all over the EU. Indeed, Renault rushed

One of the ironies with these job transfers is that Western European manufacturers who took that road miscalculated how fast new accession countries would learn to put wages and social costs up. Salaries paid by Renault in Romania have been rising and in 2007 they jumped by 20 per cent, to an average of about €450 a month. A three-week strike at the Dacia plant which ended in April 2008 achieved a pay award of a 28 per cent increase.

Still, in spite of the French government's open aversion to the dislocation of jobs and of wage raises in the 'near abroad', the movement of factories, big and small, continues. Almost every week there is a story of Western European workers left high and dry because their jobs have relocated. On Christmas Eve 2008 workers in a French province occupied the factory in which they used to work to block the transfer of its equipment and raw materials to Slovakia.

Even the factories of big companies in which the government has a major stake are on the move. In October 2008 the President of EADS, the maker of Airbus (Chapter 11) announced that part of the production currently in Toulouse would be moving to Tunisia (not an EU country, for the time being). There is plenty of evidence that:

- globalization is fragmenting;

- supply chains are breaking into ever smaller parts; and

- the rush to lower wages is sending jobs in all directions.

While, however, much lower wages abroad have been a key reason behind the dislocation of jobs, little to no attention is paid to the quality of the product which in many cases is dismal – particularly from offshoring in Turkey, North Africa and Southeast Asia, where quality control leaves much to be desired. By contrast, the quality of produce from the former Soviet satellites is better, but wages are rising fast partly because of inflation.[29] Year-on-year, first quarter 2007 to first quarter 2008:

- inflation and wages in Latvia rose by 30 per cent and inflation by about 20 per cent;

---

to organize distribution in Western Europe, beginning with France and in 2007 nearly 80,000 Logans were sold in Western Europe.

29 Furthermore, countries with strong trade unions, mostly former state outfits, have already seen strikes over pay and social advantages.

- in Estonia wages rose by 22 per cent and inflation by 12 per cent;

- in Romania wages rose also by 22 per cent and inflation by 8 per cent;

- in Lithuiania wages rose by 21 per cent and inflation by 12 per cent;

- in Bulgaria wages rose by 18 per cent and inflation by 14 per cent and so on.

A different way of looking at these statistics is that all of the above countries are in the process of pricing themselves out of the low labour-cost market. By contrast, Slovenia, the Czech Republic, Slovakia and Hungary (in that order) are more in control of their labour costs, followed by Poland. Even so and though new Western European investments and jobs are arriving in countries whose proximity still counts, their attraction for offshoring is diminishing.

The risks that the poorly governed East Europeans are taking come from the fact that the globalization of jobs has got legs, and relocation plans increasingly involve complex moves. As an example, a German company shed 400 jobs in Slovenia and sent the manufacturing end to China while bringing engineering and research back to Germany.

To make matters worse, while costs are rising in Eastern European EU members, productivity is not growing, even from its present low base. The Eastern EU countries are relying too heavily on Western European investors to bring technology and jobs, rather than creating indigenous centres of research and development and taking their future into their own hands.

In addition, some of the companies which have moved their manufacturing operations to Eastern Europe comment that there is no substance to the myth that the newer EU members are crammed with highly-educated people and a great number of intellectuals. This has also been confirmed by a 2008 OECD survey of educational standards in science, reading and mathematics, which stated that:

- only young Estonians and Slovenians performed above the OECD average in all three counts;

- by contrast, young Bulgarians and Romanians were not just way below average, but they also performed dismally in reading and maths particularly.

The issue of Bulgaria and Romania is particularly touchy because underperformance and low educational standards are joined (as already discussed) by corruption and mistaken spending of EU money. In mid-July 2008, complaining of a striking absence of convincing results in Bulgaria's anti-corruption fight and of a grave problem over the 'lack of accountability' when spending EU funds, the European Commission announced severe sanctions, suspending aid worth €486 million ($690 million).

In spite of promises made by Bulgarian governments to fight corruption before joining the EU, no case of high-level official corruption has led to a successful conviction, just as not one of more than 120 gangland shootings since 2001 has been cleared up. In fact, EU officials believe that organized crime reaches the highest levels of government. Additionally, in both countries:

- gangland killings are frequent and

- they typically go unpunished, according to accounts published in the press.

Klaus Jansen, a senior German law-enforcement official, complained recently of a 'kiss my ass' attitude among his Bulgarian counterparts.[30] Romanians have a joke about driving through Bulgaria, for instance to Greece: fill your tank before you get to the Bulgarian border, lock the doors and windows, put your foot down and don't stop until you reach the other frontier. Bulgarians say the same about driving through Romania to Hungary.

OLAF, the EU's anti-fraud agency, accused highly-placed officials in Bulgaria of being a political umbrella for gangs who have stolen millions of euros meant for the country's backward and dirt-poor countryside. 'Influential forces' in politics and the bureaucracy, suggested one of OLAF's leaked letters, are 'not interested' in punishing those linked to notorious bosses.[31]

Even in Slovenia, once seen as an example of good government, a member of Euroland and a country which chaired the EU in the first half of 2008, law-makers

---

30   *The Economist*, 20 May 2006.
31   *The Economist*, 26 July 2008.

are trying to close down the commission for the prevention of corruption. Their argument is that it is expensive and unnecessary, but the real reasons are:

- disdain for all public watchdogs and

- fear of the commission's repeated attacks on the government's credentials.

If this is the case with Slovenia, think what will be the tsunami of corruption in the EU if and when Turkey and Croatia join – two countries which, when it comes to graft,[32] have no equals. And behind them in the list of EU 'candidates' roster come Albania, Bosnia, pseudo-Macedonia, Montenegro and Serbia, all of which are close to the tail of Transparency International's Corruption Perceptions Index. Indeed, as the former Finnish Prime Minister and Nobel Prize winner for Peace said 'EU's enlargement has been a great success' – a success in the spread of corruption.

## 6. Eastern Europe on the Brink of Bankruptcy

The spread of corruption is not the only success story the EU encountered with the former Soviet satellites. Throwing good money after bad to avert their bankruptcy is another, as Chapter 6 has already brought to the reader's attention through the discussion on total lack of economic discipline.

The mid-December 2008 subsidy of $7.5 billion (theoretically an IMF loan) to Latvia corresponds to a gift of about $2,000 to each of its citizens – and it constitutes a huge reward for mismanagement. To place this subject under perspective, Table 7.1 presents some very interesting statistics on the late 2008 cost of insuring government debt against default for the EU's Eastern European member countries, plus the Ukraine, which is being promoted by Poles and America's for membership in the EU and NATO.

As 2008 came to a close, ungovernable Ukraine was nearer to bankruptcy than any other country in Eastern Europe, as the figures in Table 7.1 document. The hryvnia, its currency, lost 50 per cent of its value against the dollar that same year and its further stability is questionable. Inflation stands at 25 per cent. Moreover:

- Prominvest, the country's sixth largest bank suffered a run;

- Ukraine's economic growth has taken a dive; and

---

32  Here the word 'graft' should not be interpreted in the sense of hard work.

Table 7.1    Third-quarter 2008 cost of insuring government debt against
             default (based on three-year CDS spread)* and negative
             current account balances for Eastern Europe**

| | CDS spread in basis points | Positive or negative current account as % of GDP |
|---|---|---|
| Ukraine | 1,944 | -7.2% |
| Latvia | 662 | -15.1% |
| Romania | 483 | -13.8% |
| Estonia | 433 | 10.8% |
| Lithuania[a] | 428 | -14.9% |
| Hungary | 418 | -5.5% |
| Bulgaria | 417 | -24.4% |
| Poland | 147 | -4.7% |
| Slovakia[b] | 108 | -5.1% |
| Czech Republic | 22[c] | -2.2% |

*    As of 21 October 2008; *The Economist*, 25 October 2008.
**   These statistics belong to years past. They have been purposely included to provide evidence that
     the economic and financial problems with the EU are not just a 2010 affair. They have deep roots.
a    Which missed entry into the euro by a small margin.
b    Which entered the euro on January 1, 2009.
c    That's the only acceptable statistic. CDS spreads for Belarus and Moldavia are unknown. Their
     current account deficits are respectively -5.9 per cent and -1.99 per cent, bad enough but much
     better than EU members Latvia, Romania, Lithuania and Bulgaria.

  •    credit-rating agencies issued downgrades.[33]

The Ukraine is not, however, the only sick man of Eastern Europe.
Practically every other former Soviet republic, Soviet satellite or some other
part of the defunct Soviet Union is in deep trouble. The only exception is the
Czech Republic whose three-year CDS spread is contained and whose current
account balance, though negative, is not outrageous.

Less well off but not under dramatic conditions are Poland and Slovakia.
Curiously enough, the latter has been welcome to join Euroland as of 1 January
2009. Only the Lord saved the euro from Lithuanian membership, its huge
current account deficit and high CDS spread (Lithuania's 428 basis points in

33  And in spite of a massive aid of $16.5 billion by the IMF it cannot even pay its gas bills to
    Gazprom.

three-year CDS spread roughly corresponds to a 6 per cent default likelihood, which means junk credit).

In terms of current account deficits as percentage of their gross domestic product, the worst off are Bulgaria, Latvia,[34] Lithuania, Romania and Estonia (in that order). Not only were none of their economies ready to join the European Union, but also during their years of EU membership they did not make any significant effort to improve on the Soviet-era disasters; they just waited for a *Deus ex machina* to save them.

Furthermore, each of EU's nine member states in Table 7.1 (one-third of its membership) has its own folklore. In Hungary, this has been homeowners' penchant for loans in Swiss francs (which for a while featured lower interest rates). This popular trend (also found in Latvia and in Iceland) has demonstrated:

- how little the general public knows about the risk of the carry trade; and

- how much the borrower has to pay when the market changes and exotic loans turn on their head.

To save the day, on 16 October 2008 the European Central Bank provided a short-term credit line of €5 billion ($6.8 billion) to Hungary, because it had an economy closely linked to Euroland (Austria is particularly exposed to Hungary and other countries of its former empire).[35] This did not ease the fears of the foreign exchange market nor appease worries about:

- debts,

- growth prospects, and

- public finances.

Hungary is among the most vulnerable EU member states. Public debt is more than 60 per cent of GDP, which is large by the region's standards, thanks to communist-era twisted principles of lending and borrowing, a huge

---

34 In addition, like Spain, Latvia has found itself in the middle of a real-estate crash.
35 The loans books of Austrian banks are loaded with Eastern European liabilities to an incredible 43 per cent of Austria's GDP, compared with 5 per cent for Italy and 1 per cent for Sweden.

and growing budget deficit and the fact that recent debt auctions have been cancelled because of a buyers' strike.

Though the rise and fall of a country's currency exchange value is affected by more factors than economic conditions, exchange rate changes are an indicator of the market's trust. Between 1 January and 21 October 2008, Hungary's currency fell by 19 per cent. That's not as bad as the 31 per cent of South Korea's won or 25 per cent of Brazil's real, but it is bad enough. (In Brazil's case the sharp fall in commodity prices hit the currency hard.)

It is a foregone conclusion that the Eastern European countries at the top of the list in Table 7.1 will go to both the EU and the International Monetary Fund cap-in-hand for loans.[36] That's not the best time for doing so because some other highly mismanaged countries are already queuing up – Iceland and Pakistan among them. The former has already gone bust; the latter is ready to do so.[37] On 26 October 2008, the Ukraine had already received $16.5 billion to support its economy and banking system.[38]

The IMF's list of would-be borrowers from Eastern Europe includes (in alphabetical order) Belarus, Bulgaria, Hungary, Latvia, Romania and Serbia – two-thirds of them EU members. As for the Baltic countries, Fitch Ratings, the rating agency, downgraded all three of them in October 2008 because the money they needed for foreign debt repayments and their current-account deficits in 2009 represented:

- 400 per cent of likely year-end forex reserves in Latvia;

- 350 per cent in Estonia; and

- 250 per cent in Lithuania.

---

36  Their situation has become so critical that the IMF has been considering whether to raise the borrowing limit for members and waive its standard demand for economic austerity measures.

37  Pakistan first sought an emergency loan of $2 to $4 billion from former ally China; Iceland got several hundred million dollars from Sweden, hoped to get $4 billion from Russia, and finally received a couple of billion dollars from the IMF.

38  In spite of the fact that a couple of days earlier S&P downgraded Ukraine's credit rating to B from B+, with a negative outlook.

These are the highest ratios in emerging Europe, and some of the banks which lavishly loaned money are going to get burned. Swedbank, for one, has 16 per cent of its loans in the Baltic States to the tune of $32 billion. No wonder that, at end of October 2008, the Swedish government launched a $200 billion bail-out plan to quieten the market's nervousness.

There is an irony associated with this turn of events. It is not that long ago that the Baltic countries were looked at as the jewels of the EU's expanding frontiers; now they seem to be a pain in the neck. Even more of a drag (and this should have been expected) are Bulgaria and Romania, with their huge current-account deficits, bursting property bubbles, corporate bankruptcies, poor quality of banks' loans books and total failure to fulfil commitments to clean up organized crime and corruption.

The silver lining in all that is that it might help in opening the eyes of the different European autocrats, bureaucrats and heads of state who disregarded rational criteria for membership to the EU, and used its membership as a cross between hubris and political weapon. One can only hope that a cash-strapped EU would think thrice about the money it is prepared to spend not only on infrastructure and public services to jump-start its economy and as a fire brigade to pull its eastern members away from the brink of bankruptcy, but also in what it regards 'new member states' in the East.

Western European banks which rushed to make a fast buck in Eastern Europe paid a heavy price for it. The trouble is that, because of the 2007–2009 deep economic crisis, Western governments rushed to recapitalize them with taxpayers' money, increasing the national debt.

During the 2 April 2009 G20 summit in London (see the Epilogue), Dominique Strauss-Kahn, IMF's managing director, told the *Financial Times*: 'The risk of spillovers or contagion in central and eastern Europe exists ... with possible impact on other countries whose banks have a big exposure to central and eastern Europe ... so the situation needs to be watched carefully.'[39]

- The cumulative exposure of Austria's banks stands at 76.7 per cent of Austrian GDP;

- Swiss banks come next with cumulative 13 per cent exposure relative to Swiss GDP; and

---

39 *Financial Times*, 13 May 2009.

- these statistics are followed, in terms of assumed risk, by Italy's (11 per cent), Germany's (7 per cent) and France's (6 per cent) respectively of each country's GDP.

British banks are next in line, while the exposure to Eastern Europe by American and Japanese banks is less than 1 per cent of their home country's gross domestic product. Still, given the level of US GDP the committed sums are important – particularly so as there is the challenge of rollovers in 2009 and 2010, with the IMF estimating that the region's financing gap (the money that cannot be found in the market) will be at the level of $120 to $125 billion in 2009 and still some $65 billion in 2010.

The risk is greater than these numbers suggest, because many of the important East European banks are largely run by West European financial institutions and they could face non-performing loans of up to 25 per cent. According to the IMF, West European banks, with a regional exposure totalling $1,600 billion, could see losses of $160 billion. In the aftermath they will need $100 billion new capital, which could rise to three times as much in the case of fully-fledged regional crisis.

## 7. Rolling Back the EU's Red Carpet for Turkey

In March 2006, Edmund Stoiber, then Bavarian Prime Minister and CSU chief, travelled to Brussels with his cabinet to emphasize that its 'accession automatism' has to end – even if this means breaking some agreements and promises. Several politicians even suggested decreeing a 30-year accession moratorium.[40] To appreciate the importance of Stoiber's initiative it should be noted that for decades Germany was a proponent of every new member state to the EU. Theoretically, the reasons for an enlargement moratorium have been:

- the failure of the EU Constitution;

- competition by cheap labour from some of the (then) ten new members; and

- the prospect of further cheap workers taking German jobs, which has changed the minds of many citizens.

---

40  *Der Spiegel*, 13/2006.

Practically, however, the reason was totally different and it had to do with the growing wish of the German public to stop the intriguingly obscure manipulations of new EU memberships. Unfortunately for the Europeans, the different oligarchs masquerading as politicians failed to take notice of the most significant changes in voter sentiment. In principle, who forgets the public mood prepares him- or herself for a lacklustre showing at the next polls – but this is the EU.

Angela Merkel, for one, who once backed only a 'privileged partnership' for Turkey that fell short of full membership, changed her tune and suggested that membership may be attainable after all. The switch led several people to question whether the reason was a sudden conflict of interest or a limited ability to think of the consequences.

For his part, when he campaigned for the French presidency Nicolas Sarkozy not only opposed Turkey's bid to join the EU, but also spoke openly against the nearly unanimous EU agreement to open membership talks.[41] Yet, during 2007 and 2008 he did nothing to stop these membership talks and the distraction through Club Med (the so-called Mediterranean union) has been only a passing issue.

True enough, there is the fact that Jacques Chirac, the former French President, has always favoured Turkish accession, even if he did not dare to promote it when it became an issue in the referendum campaign in 2005. But like his dear friend and foe Tony Blair, Chirac is now a non-entity and:

- history does not speak about him even in a remotely favourable way;

- the vast majority of Frenchpeople look at the 12 Chirac years as being a time of rapid decline for France.

It is not only the European public – and most particularly the citizens of France and Austria – who are dead-set against Turkish entry into the EU, but also those who say that Turkey is far from fulfilling the 'Copenhagen criteria' for membership and they have plenty of evidence to sustain their thesis.

---

41  Entry negotiations began with Croatia and Turkey in October 2005.

The spectre of Turkey and its 80 million impoverished citizens  as well as its government (characterized as 'mildly fundamentalist') joining the EU is a nightmare. It looks as if the different second-class politicians who parade as heads of state, EU CEOs, commissioners, bureaucrats and lobbyists cannot see that the prospect of Turkey joining the EU represents another step in the erosion of any distinction between Europe and the Islamic world. Even accession by tiny pseudo-Macedonia would be a disaster.  In pseudo-Macedonia:

- More than a third of its workforce is unemployed; hence cheap labour ready to migrate to the EU, like the Turkish; and

- The country features a most curious interpretation of democracy, as in the recent past its Albanians (who make up about one third of the population) who fought an on-and-off civil war against the Serbian majority.

Beyond all these considerations, the EU is no longer able to finance poor countries whose governments push for membership as only way to get out of trouble. In November 2006 the Swiss taxpayers were put to the task of financing, with Swiss francs 1 billion (€680 million; $900 million), the 2004 accession countries that the European Union had no more money to support. Why should the Swiss taxpayers pay for other people's pleasures?

At the root of the problem is the fact that the political oligarchy in the European Union is totally out of step with the European people's will. Heads of state are paid to worry, and they should be very worried about bringing doomsday closer with Turkey's contemplated accession to the EU. But what can one expect from irresponsible politicians?

- Only a few clear heads have stated so far that indeed the risks go well beyond rent-seeking by Turkey.

- Turkey is an Asian state, with nearly 95 percent of its real estate being in what has for centuries been known as Asia Minor; and

- An eventual Turkish accession is nothing less than a Trojan horse for the conquest of Europe by Islam.

Today's Turkey has reverted to the culture and morals of the old Ottoman Empire, which means nearly medieval standards.  Its misfortune has been that Mustafa Kemal Ataturk, its great leader and founder of the Turkish Republic, died relatively young (in his mid-50s). This did not leave him much time to modernize the country and manage the change necessary to bring it into modern times. Still,

- in the dozen years he was in power, Ataturk covered nearly half the distance to modernizing the Turkish nation;

- but his untimely death and the fact that corrupt politicians gained power[42] turned back the clock of Turkey's history.

As an example, among his most important feats is that he convinced the whole population to do away with the fez and the Anatolian dress. Even more impressive is that against all odds he changed the Turkish Arabic alphabet, replacing it with Latin, and he did so in just six months. (Under a lesser person it might have taken a generation or more.) Ataturk also dropped Turkish medieval symbols of the Ottoman Raj, and he was on his way to changing the Turkish culture, too – but after his death the old habits gained the upper ground.

But all that is history. Today's central theme is Europe's pending Islamization and odious acts such as the (allegedly Kissinger-blessed) Turkish invasion and occupation of northern Cyprus – Cyprus being an EU member state. EU law is suspended in the north, which is now under the heel of 30,000 Turkish troops who never left after invading the island in 1974 and driving a third of the Greek-speaking population from their homes.[43]

Just as repulsive is the tacit acceptance by Brussels that there is no problem if the Turkish government continues to turn a deaf ear to the EU's requests to improve its attitude towards the state of Cyprus. A case in point is its refusal to open Turkey's ports and airports to Cypriot ships and airliners, despite a promise to do so.

Against this background comes Sarkozy's plan to close the door to Turkey's EU membership providing, in exchange, an association through the Union for the Mediterranean, also known as the Barcelona Process[44] and nicknamed 'Club Med'. This was planned to include only France, Spain, Italy and Greece

---

42  This reference does not include Inonu, who was Ataturk's right hand and for some time succeeded him as Turkey's president.
43  Since 1983 the northern side has called itself the Turkish Republic of Northern Cyprus, an isolated non-state recognized only by Turkey.
44  Whose origins however predate Sarkozy's effort as they date back to 1995, when the EU intended to forge a Mediterranean Free Trade Area by 2010.

from the EU. as well as Libya, Tunisia, Algeria and Morocco from the southern Med shores.

Germany reacted negatively to the Club Med plan, not the least reason being that it was unilaterally cut out of it while it was sure that the Mediterranean union will be using EU money. To solve the Franco-German row, the whole EU got itself associated with Club Med but without showing any urgency for moving ahead – while Turkey itself is not sure that it wants to participate and Libya stayed out because the local chief wanted to be Club Med's co-president while the job went to Mubarak.

If it ever gets off its feet, in all likelihood the Club Med will closely emulate the EU. All sorts of politicians will get up to speak and say nothing. Nobody will listen to them, but everybody will disagree and nothing will be done.

## Note to the Reader

The most ugly political plot by Turkey's friends inside the EU has been a defamation campaign against the French President, Nicolas Sarkozy, the only European politician who had the guts to publicly state his opinion that Turkey does not qualify as EU member state.[45] As if to confirm Sarkozy is right, and (probably also) to punch Barack Obama's ambiguous Middle Eastern policy, Recep Tayyip Erdogan visited Teheran and aired his full support to Iran's nuclear projects. For its part, the Turkish state television featured televisual wares depicting Israeli soldiers as brutal killers[46] – which was greatly appreciated by some Arab audiences.

---

45  See 'Sarkozy and Morality. We are in it up to here', *The Economist*, 17 October, 2009.
46  *The Economist*, 31 October, 2009.

# PART 3
# *The EU'S Economic Nationalism*

# 8

# Business Opportunity? Take it or Leave it

## 1. Wealth Creation

Wealth is the stock of assets one has accumulated minus debts one has contracted. One of the basic characteristics of wealth is that, with some exceptions, its creation requires meticulous planning, hard work and attention to costs. In addition, it is shared much less equitably than income. Historically, more than half of the world's wealth is held by just 2 per cent of the population, and sometimes by just 1 per cent – an observation which in the late nineteenth century led Vilfredo Pareto, a Swiss-Italian economist and mathematician, to establish Pareto's Law.[1]

'The new empires are the empires of the mind,' Winston Churchill once said. Wealth, too, is a state of mind. People, companies and countries may have resources that they do not know how to exploit, they do not care to exploit, or they simply do not put in the effort. Lack of leadership makes matters worse than they might have been. The after-effect is that:

- plenty of people in poor countries have next to nothing;

- but also quite a lot of people in rich countries have even less than that, because their liabilities exceed their assets.

Wealth is not created; indeed it is destroyed by distributing a little to everybody from what exists. The fate of communism in the Soviet Union and of socialism – in France, pre-Thatcher Britain and Sweden – provides plenty

---

1   Briefly, Pareto's Law states that large part of a certain factor A corresponds to a small part of another factor B.

of evidence on that. For example, in the classification of personal wealth, the bottom half of Swedes have a collective net worth of less than zero.[2]

'Success is 95 per cent perspiration and 5 per cent inspiration', Ralph Waldo Emerson (1803–1882) once said. Hard work creates wealth when husbanded by business opportunity and a benign environment promoted by good governance. Usually a growing economy is characterized by:

- the rule of law,

- good education,

- avoidance of excesses,

- low taxes,

- high savings, and

- high investments.

Economy does not consist in saving coal but in using its heat while it burns. Excesses destroy wealth in the medium to longer run, and wealth destruction is also promoted by the policies of misery. In 1958, Mao Zedong declared war on songbirds, sparrows in particular, claiming they consumed scarce grain.

In 2007–2009 the housing bust in America transited across the Atlantic, hitting Britain, Spain and other EU countries. In 2008, gross domestic product (GDP) in all European countries fell from already low annual growth rates. That Europe slipped is no surprise; even in brighter times for the world economy it has struggled to maintain its growth. America's GDP, too, was badly hurt as it endured a painful shock from:

- its burst housing bubble and

- the crash of its banking industry.

---

2    *The Economist*, 9 December 2006. The French and Swedish social models were characterized by a web of labour and welfare laws offering a 'high degree of social protection'. They largely emerged during the post-World War II boom, when living standards soared across Western Europe, raising the level of unaffordable entitlements.

How much difference six decades can make. When World War II ended, both Europe and Asia were devastated, and, although Latin America had a relative prosperity, the only truly wealthy country in the world was the United States. For the other states, including Britain, the mid- to late 1940s were miserable even if the Marshall Plan ingeniously and generously helped to lift up Europe's economy – but the 1950s were prosperous as the rebuilding effort got into gear.

In the 1960s, with America caught in Vietnam, European industry enjoyed an amazingly low degree of competition. In 1960 a West German car worker had little to fear from Eastern Europe and Asia. Skodas and Nissans were pretty horrid; Chinese workers were lost to the madness of Mao. But when China, India and the ex-Soviet bloc joined the capitalist world three decades later, the global labour pool grew from 1.5 billion to 3 billion. This has literally been an explosion[3] and its aftershocks have been felt over several decades.

- The explosion saw to it that American and European businesspeople and workers would never again live in a world with trivial competition.

- With globalization, new economies grew out of what was widely considered to be a backwater and they prospered while formerly wealthy economies went into decline.

With this came the surprise. Mid-way through the first decade of this century Goldman Sachs coined the label BRICs to include in one envelope four major emerging economies: Brazil, Russia, India and China. To this should be added a second small group: Mexico, South Korea and South Africa, bringing the number of challengers to the US and Europe to seven.


## 2. BRICs and PIIGS

The BRICs are major countries with rapid economic development which benefited from foreign direct investments (FDIs), put themselves in high gear and started to weigh heavily on the twenty-first century's economy. It is projected that, for some of them, by 2040 their gross national product will approach or exceed that of current frontrunners (USA, Japan, Germany), and

---

3    Called 'the great doubling' by Richard Freeman, a Harvard economist.

China will probably overtake the United States ten years or so later – unless something happens that reverses gears, such as:

- a major Asian war or

- a protracted global depression.

Several things have come together to produce such an extraordinary boom and put the economy of BRICs on an expansion course. The first is that prosperity in the West has been fuelled by *debt* and the West's appetite for low cost imports gave the better-positioned developing countries a head-start. The second factor is that BRICs governments have been more effective than their predecessors in:

- cleaning up public finances;

- pushing through unpopular reforms;

- actively courting foreign investors; and

- negotiating favourable trade agreements.

Not all these countries, of course, have been equally successful. In some, 40 per cent of the population is still living in poverty and unemployment is rather high. Moreover, the weakness of using one envelope for four, and even more so for seven, different countries is that, economic growth aside, they don't share common characteristics. Russia, for instance, has a demographic deficit and a good deal of its growth is based on the energy economy which dramatically changed in 2008 when the cost of a barrel of oil briefly went from $147 to $35 per barrel, then fluctuated between $60 and $80.

For its part, India has a large section of its population under the poverty line and this could have an important social aftermath during the coming years, while China's rapid track to industrialization has been accompanied by a vast amount of environmental pollution. China also faces the prospect of rapidly growing unemployment as its dynamic export engine slows down.

In spite of all this, however, it is no less true that the impact of the aforementioned countries on the global economy finds a negative counterpart in the shrinking weight of the current developed world – and most particularly of some of the countries in the European Union. In May 2008 a new label was coined, identifying the four laggards among the (then) 15 countries of Euroland: PIGS.

PIGS stands for Portugal, Italy, Greece, Spain. That's the negative version of the fast growing BRICs. The PIGS economies and labour laws contrast to those of other EU countries like Austria, Finland, the Netherlands and to a lesser extent Germany, which found the power to implement reforms to make their economies:

- more competitive and

- more flexible than they have been.

There is, however, a mistake in the Goldman Sachs classification, because it has failed to account for Ireland; not one 'I' but two 'I's are present in this group of Euroland countries, making their common label PIIGS. Ireland profited handsomely from EU membership and from the euro, but in so doing both the country and its banks overleveraged themselves and they are now facing very strong headwinds all the way to the ongoing speculation that Ireland may become the new Iceland.[4]

When, in the third quarter of 2008, economic conditions turned ugly, the Irish government rushed to guarantee all deposits in Irish banks, the British and others cried foul. When in January 2009 the Anglo Irish Bank was about to go under and was also hit by a scandal involving its CEO, the Irish government took it over. With all that, however, the government itself came to the frontline within clear view of the economic precipice.

Nor were Greece, Portugal and Spain unscathed. All three Euroland members lost their rating, downgraded by Standard & Poor's, but with a difference. Spain's credit rating dropped from AAA to AA+, while that of Greece went from A to A-, just a notch above BBB+, which is not a good sign. Other countries, too, were flirting with a credit downgrade as January 2009 brought bad news to nearly all economies around the globe.[5]

---

4  Which went nearly broke in mid-2008 and was saved at the eleventh hour through financial support by Scandinavian countries and an IMF loan; but its banks went under.
5  Other countries in Europe, within and outside the EU, have done even worse. As of January 2009, among the ten economies in the world most likely to default the large majority comes from Central and Eastern Europe while one is in Asia (Pakistan). Ecuador has defaulted.

The other side of the coin was that Ireland, Portugal, Greece and Spain had all enjoyed a cyclical boost that led to overheating. Portugal's economy was the first to break down, with its boom in the second half of the 1990s fed by a decline in borrowing costs on the prospect of euro membership and by EU financial aid. In this century Portugal struggled but failed to:

• regain a cost advantage and

• get its economy moving again.[6]

Spain and Greece benefited from similar booms fuelled by big spending and financial aid. For a while it was thought that they would avoid a sharp downturn, but then they got Portugal's hangover and suffered from a rapid loss of international competitiveness. For all three countries the stable euro has turned from friend to foe, but abandoning the euro has its own major dangers (section 6).

Italy has shared some of the same ills: a high and unabating real exchange rate (because of the loss of its classical devaluation policy), a current account deficit and a weak economy frequently shaken up by labour strikes. Over and above that, however, Italy missed out on the boom after the euro came into effect.

All this, plus the French pressure to devalue the euro, confronts the European Central Bank (ECB) with the difficult job of running a multispeed currency. Analysts say that in the second decade of its history the ECB will face the fact that the PIIGS quartet, and to a lesser extent France, are still abiding by the old inflexible model of a highly structured labour market. This holds them back from reaping benefits associated with a globalized economy – while the rewards of a globalized economy will become more and more questionable.

The irony is that so far the effects of inaction have been highly variable. Portugal and Italy have undergone longer-term stagnation as Italy's economy was propelled by tourism. Until the 2008 severe downturn, Greece and Spain were booming, but France grew only modestly. What these five countries have in common is that the measures their governments have taken were very short-term.

---

6    Its current-account deficit is still large, at about 8 per cent of GDP.

- They treated the adoption of the euro as the end of their reforms, rather than the beginning, as should have been the case; and

- they were left way behind by Austria, Finland and the Netherlands, which looked at the common currency as the milestone for a new start for reforms.

Not unexpectedly, the differences are spectacular. Unit labour costs in all four PIIGS have risen significantly, resulting in a sharp deterioration in economic conditions and in competitiveness. Within the EU this is in stark contrast to the fact that unit labour costs in the three restructured economies and in Germany have fallen.

Critics say that the PIIGS countries should change their attitude before falling further behind, which would make things worse than they currently are and probably cross the point of no return, but that to do so they would have to undergo the necessary pain. Critics also add that with the 2007–2009 financial crisis the structural change necessary to usher in greater competitiveness is far more necessary than in the past because the global economy is darker than it has been in many years, and there is simply no excuse for waiting for a *Deus ex machina*.

## 3. Is the EU a Model of Financial Integration?

Available evidence suggests that the first globalization in the (then known) world saw the light in the second millennium BC. This attenuated over time, took off again, lost steam and was then followed by centuries of economic integration of Western Europe, the Middle East and North Africa under Roman reign. In 154 AD Aelius Aristides spoke of Rome as 'the universe which became one city'.[7]

Rome, of course, was not the only empire of its time, but with the exception of Persia it had no challengers (under the Sassanides). Other mighty nations which extended a nearly global jurisdiction (in their region) had no common border with Rome. Examples are the Chinese, Indian, Indo-Scythian empires and, after Rome fell, that of the Mongols. History books say that in the second, third and fourth centuries of our era:

---

7    Cited in Michel Rouché, *Les Empires Universels; IIe-IVe Siècles*, Larousse, Paris, 1968.

- globalization was sustained through commercial relations between these empires; and

- then it subsided again but was reinvented by the great global explorers of the thirteenth to sixteenth centuries.

The mid- to late nineteenth century saw a new wave of globalization, but two world wars in the early and middle twentieth century turned off globalization's lights. By the 1980s, however, it took off again and it intensified in the 1990s as well as in the first seven years of this century.

Nobody is able to say how long this will last. Maybe we are at the end of that particular cycle. The worsening macro-data resulting from economic and financial crisis affect globalization the big way. The global economy has hit a wall recently, and no country is an exception. Early indicators suggest that in a rapidly deteriorating economy the growth of global trade is headed for single-digit, or even negative figures.

- Because of the problems in the global financial system and failing demand, growth in global trade is set to plummet.

- Many economists expect that both export and import growth could head downwards, bending globalization's surge as home-centred bias increases.

This message is valid not only for the larger globalization perspective, but also for regional ones – from free trade areas to regions supposed to undergo a serious economic integration, like the European Union and NAFTA in the Americas. Other factors than economics also play a role.

Because of lack of political integration the EU does not quite meet the basic criteria for financial integration, or even a well-tuned regional globalization – no matter what its proponents say – and this is also true of Euroland. For instance, economists consider the market for financial instruments to be fully integrated when investors and other market participants:

- are subject to a single set of rules when they decide to deal with them;

- have equal access to this set of financial instruments or services; and

- are treated equally when they operate in the market.[8]

Among the classical indicators of an integrated process are legislative and regulatory frameworks for the financial system, infrastructural solutions (such as the payments and settlements system) facilitating collective action and central bank services that foster financial integration. Of these three, in Euroland, the last two are in good shape but the legislative and regulatory frameworks are in tatters.

In addition, Euroland's securities infrastructure which underpins both bond and equity markets is not yet sufficiently integrated and, while interbank activities show signs of increasing integration, retail banking markets continue to be standalone. As for capital market-related activities in Euroland, the price structure of government bonds behaves according to the jurisdiction issuing them and its creditworthiness rather than in a uniform way.

A basic reason is found in the fact that no two Euroland countries have the same budgetary and fiscal policies or exposure to public debt and to current account deficits. The public debt of Italy and Greece, both early Euroland members, is among the world's four largest, equivalent to over 100 per cent of GDP.

- The fear has long been that this poorly controlled public debt would escape and wreak havoc; and

- the results would be felt not only in Italy and Greece, but also across Euroland.[9]

In Italy, in early December 2008, this fear crystallized in the form of an answer by its Welfare Minister Maurizio Sacconi, to market rumours that he was at odds with the Finance Minister, Giulio Tremonti, over how much to spend on stimulus measures. Sacconi said 'I too am worried by the risk of default,' adding: 'There is something worse than recession, and that's state bankruptcy: an improbable, but nevertheless possible, hypothesis.'[10]

---

8    European Central Bank, *Financial Integration in Europe*, March 2007.
9    Italy's debt currently stands at €1.6 trillion.
10   *The Economist*, 13 December 2008.

No wonder, therefore, that to find buyers for Italian sovereign bonds the government must pay up to 150 basis points (1.5 per cent) above similar German bonds, which are the safest in Euroland (followed by the Dutch). Italian taxpayers have been taken to the cleaners by their own actions and reactions in the post-World War II years:

- as the yield on Italy's bonds goes up, the government pays more in interest; and

- this further erodes investors' confidence, prompting them to demand still higher yields.

Among other things, Italian productivity is low and absenteeism among public employees is four times higher in the public sector than in private companies. The inefficiency of Italy's 3.5 million-strong public employees has become a big drag on the economy. (In 2005 state workers took an average of 18 days' sick leave. In the health service, the figure was almost 30 days, while over the past six years wages have risen by 15 per cent more in the public sector than in private firms.)

Germany's government bonds are at a premium within Euroland because its economy is better managed and the Bundesbank cares a great deal about financial stability. While Italy, France and other Euroland countries have huge current-account deficits, at end of 2007 Germany had net external assets of €645 billion, representing 26.5 per cent of GDP. This was essentially an accumulation of current account surpluses since 2001.[11]

In the years 2004 to 2007, Germany's industrial output increased by 18 per cent, that of France by 3 per cent and Italy's by 2 per cent. Over the same period, Germany real exports grew by 33 per cent, while those of France increased by barely 10 per cent. By contrast, the growth in German and French imports was not that different, leaving Germany with a sizeable current account surplus.

- Germany has succeeded in conquering foreign markets without state intervention in the way the industrial engine ticks.

- France has been much less successful in spite of massive state intervention – or, more likely, because of it.

---

11  Deutsche Bundesbank, *Monthly Report*, October 2008.

The irony of government intervention for patriotism, protectionism (Chapters 9 and 10), nepotism and other fancy reasons is that the more it meddles with the markets the worse are its results. These range from the fall of barricades against Mittal Steel's hostile bid for Arcelor, a big employer in France, to plenty of other cases where the government's heavy hand risks wrecking even flourishing industries.

In conclusion, while differences are expected to exist among different EU countries, statistics speak louder than words. Within Euroland, during the period being considered, Germany has significantly improved its performance while that of other countries has remained stagnant or has even deteriorated. There is more than one reason behind these differences, providing evidence that globalization does not work the same way for everybody and that economic integration in the EU is still an abstract notion.

## 4. The EU's Common Industrial Policy is in Tatters

While the member states of the European Union are at a loss about how to deal with themselves, their challenges and their partners in an entity supposed to be the 'union' of its members, a much bigger issue, requiring strategic planning, looms on the horizon: should the EU welcome or object to the purchase of its industries by third parties?[12]

The industrial policy question, and associated acquisitions challenge, can best be brought into focus by taking a quick look into corporate Europe, starting with type of industries and corporate global size in terms of revenues and profits. As 2007 came to a close, of the largest dozen companies revenue-wise, six were American (Wal-Mart, ExxonMobil, Chevron, Conoco Philips, General Electric), one Japanese (Toyota), one British (BP), two Dutch (Royal Dutch Shell, ING), one German (Daimler) and one French (Total).

Therefore, nearly half of this top dozen were European firms and they were all very profitable, unlike General Motors which, in 2007, had managed to lose $38.7 billion. The largest profit in 2007 was made by Exxon to the tune of $40.6 billion, 5 per cent higher than GM's losses. None of the big European companies wrote its end-of-year (2007) accounts in red ink.

---

12  This is not written in the strict sense of economic nationalism, which is the subject of Chapter 9, but rather as the establishment of a policy for mergers and acquisitions.

In terms of shareholder relations, US corporate boards were confronted by many activists, including big institutional investors, contesting corporate elections and trying to bring about change through the equity owners' pressure, as well as litigation. This is a literally unknown practice in Europe, with one interesting exception.

On 3 October 2007 the European Commission abandoned its long-running attempt to introduce the principle of 'one share, one vote' into European law. The change would have strengthened legal protection for minority shareholders, which is notoriously weak in several jurisdictions of the European Union.

- The prime opponents were lobbyists for big shareholders.

- Their trick has been to use special shares to retain control of the dynasty's businesses.

In Japan, too, an August 2007 decision by the Supreme Court dealt a blow to the nascent shareholder activism there. Foreign investors, mainly from the United States, had put companies under pressure to return some of their large cash piles to equity owners. The decision, which basically concerned the free use by managements of poison pills,[13] made the activists nearly powerless.

Another factor where the Japanese and European corporate scene correlate and, up to a point, contrast with the American scene is by government intervention in who can buy which business assets. As we will see in Chapters 9 and 10, there are lots of interesting questions about state interference, because in a mergers and acquisitions (M&A) transaction shareholders are not necessarily permitted to decide what is to be done.

Anyone thinking of selling what might supposedly be a strategic asset, or agreeing to be taken over, has to let the government know who its potential purchasers are – which does nothing to encourage price competition. In this regard, Britain and the US are much more liberal than continental Europe, though the US Congress did react very negatively when it came to the purchase of an oil company by a Chinese firm or of port authorities by Middle East interests.

---

13  The practice of (and term) poison pills was invented in the 1960s in the US during the wave of mergers and acquisitions. Companies which did not want to be acquired loaded themselves with debt and/or took other measures with very negative results to their net worth. Still, this did not always repel the acquiring company, as the case of Time Warner documents.

One of the side effects of government interference multiplied 27 times over is that it makes it impossible for the EU to establish a common strategy in the globalized economy. Theoretically, nobody denies the urgency for the European Union to elaborate factual common policies. But, practically, when this touches cross-border mergers and favoured partnerships, there is only discord. Because of this, according to experts, the 'unions'' strategies at large – and most particularly its policy on mergers, acquisitions and takeovers – are totally:

- irrational and

- asymmetric.

As if to prove the critics right, in late 2005 François Loos, France's Industry Minister, published a list of the country's strategic industrial sectors that would be *protected* from foreign takeovers. This came in the same week that a French building materials firm made a €5.4 billion (then $6.7 billion) hostile bid for a British rival.[14] Ironically, in that list of protected species was steel and that led to the Arcelor merger opposition and debacle shared by three EU governments (Chapter 10).

Shortly thereafter, in February 2006, the then Prime Minister Dominique de Villepin posed for the cameras flanked by the CEOs of two French energy companies, Suez and Gaz de France, who had 'agreed' to merge their firms. The French Prime Minister felt that the shotgun marriage he had pulled off was a spectacular trick, but many experts said this was a big mistake in terms of industrial policy.

Lost in the cloud of enjoyment and self-congratulation on the grounds that economic patriotism would reign and block takeovers of national industrial jewels was the fact that GDF-Suez provided further evidence that the EU's common industrial policy is in tatters. Political analysts pointed out that when the elated French Prime Minister announced his defensive position:

- he was still enjoying a honeymoon with members of parliament and the electorate;

- but a short while thereafter his credibility was battered by mass street protests and university sit-ins, as well as the *Clearstream* affair (Chapter 11).

---

14  *The Economist*, 3 September 2005.

Villepin was also under pressure over the mess at the European Aeronautic Defence and Space Company (EADS, Chapter 11), in which the government held a big stake, while France's financial regulator was investigating the share options exercised by Noël Forgeard, the company's ex co-CEO, who was alleged to be a protégé of Jacques Chirac, then President of the Republic.

Some people say that this stonewalling within the EU is a residue of socialist governments' policies, which did not change in spite of the fall of communism. Others maintain that in its background is not really economic nationalism but 'conservatism'. The latter argument is wrong. Andrew Sullivan says there are two types of conservatism:[15]

- the divinely inspired fundamentalism, Iran-type, also known as *theo conservatism*; and

- conservatism, British version, which is sceptical, but also tolerant and open-minded with regard to change.[16]

Contrary to the model described by the second bullet, economic patriotism or nationalism (as you please) works by creating national champions, and by manipulating takeover laws. The European Union is dead and we should act accordingly, said Giulio Tremonti, Italy's former Finance Minister, in the aftermath of the bid by Enel for Suez, which was blocked by the French government. Not so, answered José Manuel Barroso, President of the European Commission.

According to Barroso, these are just growing pains. Deplorable as it may be, the reaction from national capitals is just a backlash against inevitable change, Barroso suggests – but he finds it difficult to prove it as, in the couple of years which have elapsed since that statement, economic patriotism continues to be alive and well. While those EU nations and companies refused equal rights don't share Barroso's opinion, today the trend is towards more Colbertism, not less (see Chapter 9).

## 5. Tax Harmonization in the EU is not for Tomorrow

Back in 1962, five years after the Common Market was born, European politicians began to realize that a major step towards financial integration among the six

---

15  Andrew Sullivan, *The Conservative Soul: How We Lost it, How to Get it Bank*, HarperCollins, London, 2006.
16  Which is capitalism's characteristic as well.

countries which had signed the Treaty of Rome would be tax harmonization. It took a quarter of a century until, on 2 May 2007, the European Commission gave a rather positive report on its progress towards legislation on a common consolidated corporate law, which is nothing more than a first step towards corporate tax harmonization.

Under the Commission's still rough plans, companies would adopt a tax base for their EU-wide activities, rather than face a tangle of 27 different regimes. The EU says that this will lighten compliance costs and boost the single market. But:

- many of the details, such as the delicate issue of how to split revenues between countries, are still to be worked out; and

- disagreements are the order of the day with not only tax receipts, but also economic nationalism playing its part.

The only issue on which there seems to be agreement is that each EU country's Ministry of Finance will continue to set its own rates. This is precisely the opposite of what is required for tax harmonization. As is to be expected, the whole scheme has become a matter of playing politics, in an EU where one country's veto means full stop. The way the chips fall was revealed more than three years ago at an April 2006 informal meeting of finance ministers:

- 12 EU countries supported a common tax base;

- eight cautiously played for time; and

- seven were die-hard opponents.

Interestingly enough, the opponents included Britain, Ireland and Estonia; the latter has a flat tax, while the former two have theological objections to ceding tax powers to Brussels. Both opponents and fence-sitters should, however, appreciate that even in a free trade area, let alone a 'union', tax harmonization has significant influence on price formation.

A similar statement covering fiscal policies by the 27 EU members is valid – from value added tax (VAT) to direct and other forms of taxation. Two decades of rulings from the European Court of Justice have theoretically constrained member states' fiscal independence, but in practice they had no result in rate-settings because its opponents are in the majority.[17]

The lack of tax harmonization in the European Union is another example of the failure to proceed with political union. There are two reasons why a bunch of independent states have great difficulty in coming up with a common plan for taxation. The first is more evident and the second is every state's secret hope.

- From direct personal taxes to VAT corporate taxes and import duties, taxation is the government's prerogative and income; and

- every government tries to outwit its neighbours in bringing more water to its mill (protectionism), forgetting that the rising of import duties in the late 1920s and early 1930s fed the fires of the First Great Depression.

In retrospect, a major failure of the Maastricht Treaty has been that it did not provide a strong link between monetary policy, which came under the European Central Bank, and fiscal policy, which was left totally at the discretion of every one of Euroland's member states. This left fiscal policy, including taxation and budget deficits, as the exclusive domain of independent governments. An example of where it led is provided by the five larger member states of the EU. In two consecutive years, 2007 and 2008:

- Britain, France and Italy had budget deficits ranging from 2.5 per cent to nearly 3 per cent of GDP.

- By contrast, Germany and Spain had budget surpluses ranging from 0.2 per cent to 1.8 per cent GDP (both numbers come from Spain, with Germany's surplus standing at about 0.5 per cent in both years).

In connection to Italy's 2008 budget, Romano Prodi, the then prime minister, mused that it could be hard 'to distinguish the real issue – about which nobody ever talks – from the fictitious one which is fought over ferociously.'[18] His centre-left government had decided that the low-paid citizen would get

---

17  For instance, Ireland fears a harmonized base would be a slippery slope to common rates, eventually forcing it to raise its highly competitive corporate tax rate of 12.5 per cent.

18  *The Economist*, 6 October 2007.

reduced property taxes and either an income-tax break or a cash handout (Prodi also cut the corporate tax rate from 33 per cent to 27.5 per cent and trimmed a regional business tax). These measures were aimed at relaunching the Italian economy, but the shortfall created by them was not compensated by trimming the government's expenses.

Trimming the government's expenses always upsets the bureaucrats, trade unions and their allies in parliament. Yet, practically all public sector spending is characterized by waste, corruption, overstaffing and underperformance, which puts a huge burden on the economy. Spending cuts are followed in southern Europe in the most democratic manner through:

- street demonstrations and

- general public unrest.

America, too, is falling into the same trap. Under George W. Bush it experienced hyperleverage of national debt because of disastrous budgetary deficits. National indebtedness under the Bush administration has been greater than under all preceding 42 American Presidents, with little appreciation of the fact that the way to economic ruin rests on two pillars:

- consumers spending more than they earn and

- the government spending much more than it collects in taxes.

A common trait of all big spenders is their inability to understand that no government has money of its own. The money the government obtains comes from its citizens and from the companies in its jurisdiction. This is done in two ways:

- through taxation and

- by means of inflation, which is the worst taxation of them all.

While the government can borrow large amounts of money, like any other debt this has to be served by paying interest and eventually it has to be repaid out of money collected through taxation. (That's a reason why economists distinguish between internal debt served through higher taxation and external debt for whose servicing the government must have foreign hard currency reserves.)

'What's creating inflation?' Arthur Burns, a former chairman of the Federal Reserve, asked his students at Columbia University, answering his own question by saying 'Government deficits create inflation.' All governments are doing so but at widely varying degrees, therefore making very difficult, if not outright impossible, the establishment of a common taxation policy in the EU.

## 6. The Euro: Advantages and Constraints of a Common Currency

Take Britain as an example of an EU member state with its own currency. The kingmaker in the fortunes of the pound is the Bank of England's (BoE's) Monetary Policy Committee (MPC). But the government, too, has a say. For instance, in late April 2007 it allowed the Bank of England to issue a large amount of gilts to fund the purchase of mortgage securities from banks. (Banks in Britain, as in the US, curtailed their mortgage lending, as they have been unable to sell on the mortgages they had previously funded.)

Euroland's government encouraged banks to get their businesses in order, but (excluding covert pressure and big words) they could in no way emulate the interplay of the British government and the BoE because the European Central Bank was not part of their remit. The silver lining of the lack of political union has been precisely the fact that:

- the umbilical cord between government and central bank has been cut; and

- this constitutes a major advantage in monetary stability, because it does away with the government's heavy hand on monetary policy.

In different terms, the lack of full-scale political union imposes a welcome constraint on each one of Euroland's governments. There is no mixing with monetary policy affairs. When he was German chancellor, Helmut Kohl saw that political union was not on the cards and, in a speech only ten days before Maastricht, he spelled out his conditions: 'Political union and economic and monetary union are inseparably linked. The one is the unconditioned complement of the other. We can and will not give up sovereignty over monetary policies if political union remains a "castle in the air".'[19]

This followed almost to the letter a roadmap set down in 1963, almost three decades earlier, by Karl Blessing, the first Bundesbank president: 'The final goal of the Commission is a European monetary union ... A common currency and a federal central banking system are only feasible if, apart from a common trade policy, there is also a common finance and budget policy, a common economic policy, a common social and wage policy – a common policy all round.'[20]

From monetary convergence criteria for Euroland's member countries to the Stability and Growth Pact, the steps that have been followed at least partially correspond to Blessing's criteria. In addition, at least so far, monetary policy strategy and instruments have proved their worth, but the future is more uncertain. Given the huge divergence in tax and fiscal policies (section 5) it is not sure that Euroland is well equipped to meet the coming challenges. Among the benefits of the single currency are:

- elimination of exchange rate uncertainty within the monetary union;

- a credible monetary policy framework for maintaining price stability;

- significantly lower long-term interest rates based on creditworthiness;

- greater resilience against economic and financial shocks; and

- substantially reduced transaction and information costs.

One of the problems with common discipline has to do with the fact that the different heads of state want to gain their 'independence', benefiting from the common currency but accepting no constraints to guarantee its stability. The corresponding obligations are those of:

- adopting and following prudent fiscal policies;

---

19  Jouy-en Josas, 3 December 1991, speech by Kohl on Franco-German relations.
20  Cited in David Marsh, *The Bundesbank*, William Heinemann, London, 1992.

- implementing further structural reforms;

- allowing adjustment mechanisms to operate efficiently within the enlarged currency area; and

- promoting open, competitive and flexible markets.

The latter is a factor as important as fiscal discipline to the smooth conduct of the single monetary policy. Steep as this price may be, it is no less true that no advantages can be gained from a monetary union without paying one's dues. Cheating one's neighbour is no medium- to longer-term solution. Another problem with the common currency is the lack of precise definitions in the EU Stability and Growth Pact on both:

- the fine mechanism of monetary stability and

- its contribution to sustained growth and employment.

Article 105 of the still to be ratified EC constitution (Chapter 6) states that the primary objective of the Eurosystem is to maintain price stability. The Treaty, however, does not provide a quantitative definition of price stability, which is a pity because a good definition has been provided by the Governing Council of the ECB back in October 1998 and should have been quoted:

> Price stability is 'a year-on-year increase in the Harmonized Index of Consumer Prices for the euro-area of below, but close to 2 per cent'.

At 2.1 per cent on average, Euroland's annual inflation rate was consistently above this stability target during the first seven years of monetary union. This, however, was no big deviation like the one which came in 2007 with a series of upward price shocks originating in the international energy, commodities and agricultural markets as well as changes in taxes. Euroland's inflation reached 3.4 per cent in early 2008.[21]

Commodity prices aside, an inordinate growth of the euro's M3 money supply metric,[22] largely propelled by a sprint in private sector loans, was a main contributor to the fact that the hydra of inflation raised its heads. This provides further documentation of the detrimental effects of lack of political union.

---

21  Spain even hit an annualized 7 per cent inflation.
22  D.N. Chorafas, *Capitalism Without Capital*, Palgrave/Macmillan, London, 2009.

- The ECB has responsibility for monetary policy but it does not control the banking sector's leveraging and lending policies; and

- there are divergences in overall supervision in terms of assumed risk, capital adequacy and liquidity because this rests with the national central banks (NCBs) and regulatory authorities.

Theoretically, close cooperation among national central banks in Euroland and the ECB assures that all contribute equally to the preparation and implementation of the single monetary policy. But while this broad-based decision-making and opinion-forming process has advantages, in practical terms the fact that it involves 16 NCBs[23] sees to it that it is less than perfect.[24]

This is precisely an argument against enlarging Euroland's membership, even concerning countries such a Britain, Sweden and Denmark. *If* 16 find it difficult to find a common wavelength and coordinate action aimed at meeting the aforementioned obligations, *then* more countries means more sources of trouble.

If Britain and the Scandinavians pose coordination and policy problems, think of the poorer EU member states where prices tend to climb faster because wages are moving rapidly upwards (Chapters 6 and 7), productivity is growing slowly and capital-intensive export industries are non-existent. There is a long list of well-documented reasons why the ECB may prefer to keep transition economies out until convergence is fully satisfied over several years.[25]

Also of material importance to this discussion is the fact that even under current membership a majority of citizens in Euroland countries believe that the euro has damaged their income and even their national economies. Led by populist politicians, many people confuse the euro with the EU's free movement of labour. On the other hand, it is no less true that in Italy, Greece and Portugal a combination of strong wage increases and weak productivity growth has undermined both:

- standards of living and

---

23  With Slovakia which joined the euro on 1 January 2009. When the ECB was created in 1998 it set monetary policy for 11 prospective euro members.
24  Since the currency's launch in January 1999, five countries have joined – Greece in 2001, Slovenia in 2007, Cyprus and Malta in 2008 and Slovakia in 2009.
25  It is the European Commission in Brussels which gave its blessing for Slovakia's entry into the euro. The ECB was afraid that inflation might then pick up as it did in Slovakia.

- cost-competitiveness.

The same challenge of higher wages and sluggish productivity clouds the outlook for one of the fastest-growing European economies: Spain (see section 2, BRICs and PIIGS). In the last decade, its economy has expanded by an average of 3.7 per cent a year, nearly twice the average rate for the whole of Euroland, but by 2009 high labour costs proved to be Spain's undoing. Olivier Blanchard, of the Massachusetts Institute of Technology, sees Spain as a plausible next victim of what he calls 'the rotating slumps under the euro'.[26]

The story is different in Germany where the majority of citizens think that mismanagement of EU's economies and stiff labour laws in many member countries make the euro unattractive. Two German citizens in three prefer the country's former national currency, the Deutsche Mark, whose stability was managed by the Bundesbank in the most able fashion.

In late January 2007, a short six months before the economic and banking crisis, an FT-Harris survey provided interesting results. To the query: 'What impact the introduction of the euro made on your country's economy?', the answer has been negative for 78 per cent of Italians, 77 per cent of French and 68 per cent of Spaniards – with a Euroland average of nearly 60 per cent.

## 7. 'Stimulus' at Any Cost is Disrespect for the Value of Money

On 26 November 2008 the EU Commission unveiled a plan for a so-called coordinated fiscal stimulus across the European Union worth €200 billion ($280 billion). Behind that 'plan' was a cocktail of temporary cuts in employment and sales taxes, more generous state support for the low-paid and jobless, and other goodies – mainly socialist-type measures which:

- largely involve throwing away money and

- are unlikely to give the EU's economy even a short-term lift.

Critics said that this was another of the EU Executive's ill-documented proposals brought up a few weeks before an EU summit in December 2008 and unlikely to be accepted by Angela Merkel, the German Chancellor. Merkel had reportedly decided not to bend her policies to the wishes and whims of

---

26  *The Economist*, 27 January 2007.

the big spenders.[27] To boost support, Sarkozy and Barroso went to London to meet with Brown – another socialist throwing other people's money down the drain.

What is indeed most surprising is that right after the London meeting of 6/7 December 2008 with Brown and Sarkozy, Barroso went public with an open critique of Merkel, characterizing her resistance to big spending plans as being incomprehensible. The President of the EU Commission should not only have been more polite towards the German Chancellor,[28] but also the first person in line to express respect for Euroland's Stability and Growth Pact and its restrictions on budget deficits.

The choice of Gordon Brown as a partner is by no means accidental. As of late 2008, Britain was contracting new debt of $222 billion because the crisis had reduced the Treasury's revenues. Adding to this were the various spending plans of the Labour government, which was trying to reacquire its socialist credentials. Economists foresee that Britain's debt as percentage of GDP will surge.

Part of the torrent of red ink is the government's own fault. After having allowed the British banks to run wild in terms of assuming mountains of risks, the Prime Minister engaged in an extravaganza of spending £500 billion ($750 billion) in salvage operations which cost the British taxpayer £8,000 ($12,000) per person, including newborns. And this is a conservative estimate. George W. Bush could not have done better (or rather worse) in his mismanagement of public money.

A short time before these visits and consultations of the big spenders' league, and after calling for the suspension of the Stability and Growth Pact, Sarkozy, during a visit he made to a Renault factory, had already announced a similar plan for the French economy to be financed through deficits. The Germans did not appreciate this unilateral action; they are weary of Euroland governments adding deficits to already high deficits because:

- time and again such moves proved to be counterproductive;

---

27 She finally did go along with reservations and conditions, in the mid-December 2008 'summit' in Brussels.

28 It was also a very bad policy for an appointed bureaucrat publicly to criticize an elected official and head of state because she disagreed with his spending plan. Besides, Barroso should have remembered that these plans met with a stony hostility not only from the Germans, but also from the Dutch.

- they lead to a vicious cycle of price increases; and

- they damage the stability and credibility of the euro as common currency.

For other governments, however, a policy which would dampen the euro fitted well with their spending plans. For instance, since 2007, as President of France, Sarkozy had adopted the socialists' beloved motto that the euro is overvalued. According to this opinion, the euro's value against the dollar – and not the ultra-structured labour market – is at the origin of the difficulties French manufacturers have with their exports. Many economists contest this argument, because:

- *if* it were true,

- *then* Germany would also face the same problems with its exports.

Instead, German manufacturers say: 'We love the strong euro.' The way an article in *The Economist* had it, Sarkozy has repeatedly questioned the tenets of Europe's single currency, especially its strictures on budget deficits and on the independence of the European Central Bank. Germans are getting increasingly fed up with the French style, says Daniela Schwarzer of the Stiftung Wissenschaft and Politik, a think-tank. And not only Germans – other Euroland citizens, too.

Moreover, apart from some exceptions like the Franco-German Airbus, which competes against Boeing with dollar-denominated prices for airframes (Chapter 11), the euro's value against the dollar is a weak argument. Half the French exports go to the other countries of Euroland where French-made goods are losing market share. This is particularly true in Germany, which has classically absorbed a large amount of French-made wares.

It is also in Germany that the 1922 hyperinflation of the Weimar Republic has left the deepest wounds.[29] To better understand the German Chancellor's position, the reader should keep two things in mind. First, Germany's renewed vigour in 2005 to mid-2008 reflected stringent control of real wages, which secured a fall in unit labour costs when they were rising elsewhere in the EU. This has not characterized other Euroland countries like France, Spain, Portugal, Italy and Greece. In addition:

---

29  The French francs, too, has suffered in 1922, having lost half of its value as it became the play of currency speculators.

- giving *carte blanche* to inflation is precisely the opposite of what the EU's founding fathers wanted to achieve; and

- the concept of bringing France and Germany closely together was damaged by the 2008 big-spender policies.

Still another reason for Merkel's reluctance to become a big spender is the negative example on monetary policy provided by the Bush administration, the *bête noir* of Jacques Chirac, the former French President. Under its watch, the Fed and Treasury took on more commitments than they could credibly keep. With budget deficits that could top $1 trillion a year, plus trillions of dollars more in guarantees to mortgages and bank debt, both investors and economists have questioned the US's ability to shoulder all this leverage.

## 8. Is the EU a New Edition of Orwell's *Animal Farm*?

Dr Paul Volcker, the respected former chairman of the Federal Reserve, once likened global capital markets to a vast sea that cannot escape the occasional big storm. That storm swept across global financial markets and their underlying economies in 2007–2009, shaking confidence in the stability of the system.

As a way of getting the markets moving again and pushing the banking industry into returning to its role of intermediation, central banks (particularly the Federal Reserve and Bank of England) aggressively cut interest rates. For their part, governments pumped trillions into the treasuries of banks and other institutions, nationalizing some of them. But:

- the gloomy economy has hurt the public's trust;

- overleveraged consumers retrenched, trying to repair their balance sheets; and

- as should have been expected, neither nearly zero interest rates nor the hastily assembled stimulus plans had any short- to medium-term effect.

Furthermore, huge interest rate cuts, like those of early December 2008 by the European Central Bank, had their critics. A week before, Lorenzo Bini Smaghi, a member of the ECB's rate-setting council, argued that slashing interest rates to insure against a deep downturn can harm confidence, as well as limit policy-makers' future options. This is precisely what has happened with the Fed since late 2007 and more recently with the Bank of England.

Worst of all was the lack of prior consultation and agreement on common policy among heads of state. Wouter Bos, the Dutch Finance Minister, pointedly told Sarkozy that Europe should not be like *Animal Farm*, in which 'some are more equal than others'.[30] This remark concerned efforts to reopen old debates about how sovereign states should or should not care about the common currency's stability.

For his part, when Sarkozy addressed the European Parliament in mid-December 2008, Graham Watson, a British MEP and leader of the liberal group of deputies, first praised him for his work as president of the EU over the (then) ending six-month period, then added 'You don't need to do everything. Leave the finance responsibility to Jean-Claude Juncker and that of the euro to Jean-Claude Trichet.'[31]

Brussels, too, was upset by the 'go get it' policy. EU officials don't like to hear Sarkozy talking about a strong euro choking exports. Statistics compiled by the EU Commission document that France's trade surplus with America has grown despite the weak dollar, whereas French exports to Germany have fallen even though they share a currency.

Many economists point out that not only are efforts to bend the euro's value misdirected, but also big spending policies, supposed to relaunch the economy in the middle of a global financial crisis, are typically poorly planned and ineffective. Nor is it wise to target several goals at the same time. An example is the case of the French 'strategic investment fund' of €20 billion ($28 billion) announced on 20 November 2008, and vowing to hit two birds with one well-placed stone, to:

- protect French industry from foreign predators and

- lift the French economy from a worsening economic slump.

Even more of an anathema to the Germans, Dutch and other Euroland members who prize monetary stability were suggestions to cast aside the

30   *The Economist*, 14 July 2007.
31   President of the Eurogroup's finance council and of the European Central Bank respectively.

Stability and Growth Pact because of the ongoing economic crisis. Initiatives like Ireland's guarantee of all deposits made to its banks no matter what the amount also weaken the euro's exchange rate because of assumed liabilities.

There are also other incidents justifying the reference Wouter Bos made to Orwell's *Animal Farm*. Competition experts fault the EU Commission for failing to stand against the move to downgrade the status of competition in the Lisbon Treaty (Chapter 6). Because of a demand by Nicolas Sarkozy, competition will no longer be one of the EU's main objectives if the Treaty comes into force. No attention has been given to an important precedent:

- competition law was suspended in the US during the Depression, resulting in widespread price fixing;

- many economists today say that price collusion during the 1930s prolonged the American economy's slump.

Collective bending to one party's present, as well as unilateral moves, are not welcome because they cast aside the necessary unity which should have characterized the European Union (and most particularly Euroland) – all the way from guaranteeing its future to facing up to the challenges of the ongoing banking and credit earthquake. Mindful of the effects that big spending of government money has on the stability of the currency, plus the fact that such massive credit allocations are often misdirected, the Netherlands and a couple of other Euroland members are asking for proof of:

- financial discipline and

- free-market principles.

For years the Germans bankrolled initiatives approved at EU summits, but in late 2008 they feared having to pick up the cheque for spending plans in the EU economy. Germans, Italians and Poles also asked for an easing of the burden of overambitious $CO_2$ reduction measures.[32] Merkel's leadership has been challenged within the EU because of her caution, but she seems happy to

---

32   Angela Merkel made it clear that she will seek to shield Germany's heavy industry, and about 90 per cent of EU industrial producers, from proposal – to combat climate change – unless other countries outside the EU agree to similar moves. Poland and Italy also objected to unilateral environmental rules which put their industry at a huge disadvantage, and they finally got their way mid-December 2008.

stick to her guns even if her opponents present her as 'Madame Non', as she has been dubbed by the French media.

Acute political observers now think that Franco-German tensions will outlast whatever negative chemistry affects Sarkozy and Merkel. The greater risk is missed opportunities rather than one of sudden rupture. Germany's allergy to economic tinkering contrasts with the inflation/devaluation cycle France and Italy adopted after World War II. This makes it very difficult to implement a one-size-fits-all monetary policy without political union – but political union is not on the cards.

# 9

# The European Union's Economic Nationalism

## 1. Colbertism and Economic Nationalism

After the Treaty of Westphalia (Chapter 1) the nation state got organized, became conscious of its authority and made economic nationalism current currency. This manifested itself in a variety of ways, from the protection of national industries to the competitive devaluations that contributed to the Great Depression of 1929.[1]

One of the original demonstrations of economic nationalism has been the building up of selected industries in vital sectors of the economy with the explicit objectives first to curtail imports and then to gain global market share. 'Strategic industries' reduce dependence on other countries, a practice known as *Colbertism*, after Jean-Baptiste Colbert (1619–1683) who, under Louis XIV, subsidized and built up from scratch several French industry sectors. An example is the founding in 1665 of Saint Gobin, aimed at replacing imports of Venetian glass with homemade wares.

There is no record of whether Colbert ever explained to Louis XIV and his court Colbertism's downside: the double cost to the consumers and taxpayers as well as the fact that the collapse and resurrection of state-supported strategic industries becomes embarrassingly public. Here is an example. In the 1980s and 1990s nationalized Crédit Lyonnais set out to be the banking champion of Europe and of the world. In 1991 it even took over MGM studios. Eventually, Crédit Lyonnais collapsed and had to be rescued with public money, but in

---

1    As we will see in Chapter 10, even the clauses of the downsized EU Stability and Growth Pact give free rein to a new sort of competitive devaluation within Euroland, by huge budgetary deficits at the expense of one's partners.

the meantime people close to the Mitterrand regime profited. In addition, as a government inquiry found:

- the state's role as shareholder and regulator in the bank was 'close to nil';

- but there were scandals galore and, after years of wheeling and dealing, Crédit Lyonnais went under.

Misused public money is not the only cost of state ownership. One of the harder ones to spot is that, for political reasons, former deputies and civil servants with no experience of business are parachuted into the top of large companies, and that usually ends in disaster. In addition, strategic industries age and decline, with the result that protecting old champions hinders the emergence of new and more dynamic ones.

Still another aspect of economic nationalism is that of playing the weeping boy to get as much as one can from other people's assets, under the excuse that one clearly needs them for subsistence. This has been explicit in the case of the Doha Round[2] and of covert aspects in trade negotiations that preceded it. Confronted with elements of globalization which are not favourable to them, different nations provide growing evidence of economic nationalism.

Often, the barriers of economic nationalism are raised through red tape. A former EU commissioner for enterprise and industry estimated that European firms spend €600 billion (then $800 billion) a year on compliance with regulations. A poll of 1,000 British CEOs found that, in the opinion of 540 of them, red tape outweighs the benefits of the single market.[3]

Ironically, the opposite to Colbertism is also Colbertism. It consists of protecting local industries from foreign takeovers by using the heavy hand and purse of the government as *Deus ex machina*. For instance, in 2005 the US Congress saw danger in China's CNOOC bid for Unocal. Most of Unocal's oil and gas reserves happened to be outside America, but oil and gas reserves are now considered by everybody to be a national treasure, even if located in another sovereign state.

---

2    D.N. Chorafas, *Globalization's Limits. Conflicting National Interests in Trade and Finance*, Gower, Farnham, 2009.
3    *The Economist*, 9 December 2006.

What has happened between the US and China is not what should be happening between member states of European Union (Chapter 10). Still, economic nationalism is precisely what many European Union countries demonstrate in negotiating with other EU members, or in opposing takeovers of what they consider to be their economic and industrial jewels.

## 2. The Treaty of Rome is Put on the Backburner

Any unilateral action by an EU member state puts the other 26 at a disadvantage. This needs no explaining but few chiefs of state pay attention to it, as attested by facts recorded during the last ten years. When initially established in 1957, the Treaty of Rome characteristically described four freedoms of movements for the eventual European Union:

- goods,

- capital,

- labour, and

- services.

But in a growing number of cases, the free movement of capital, labour and services in the EU is undermined by self-styled *economic patriots*. This happens not in one but in several European countries, but most particularly in France, Spain and to a lesser extent Poland, though other EU members, too, are beginning to have second thoughts.

Conversely, the more liberal EU countries present no obstacles when foreign companies buy their firms. Examples are the takeover of Abbey National in Britain by Spain's Santander and EDF's purchase of Edison in Italy, as well as the acquisition by BNP Paribas, a French bank, of Italy's Banca Nazionale del Lavoro (BNL). In contrast, France did not permit Italy's Enel to purchase Suez, an energy and water company.[4] In the aftermath, Italy, too, became an economic nationalist.

---

4   Originally, this was the Compagnie du Canal de Suez, owner of the waterway of the same name. After Suez's nationalization by Nasser, it converted itself into a holding, specializing in energy and water.

Thanks to the new wave of Colbertism, the takeover of firms by foreign capital has excited a curious sort of patriotism, whose intensity, however, varies from one EU country to another. France and Spain fear a 'foreign conquest' of their economies. They also object to what they call 'impersonal capitalistic management', where the owner only looks for profits and cares for neither the company nor its employees – *as if* socialist governments do care.

EU countries practising economic nationalism justify their action partly by their fear of losing jobs for their nationals, partly for security purposes and partly because of the 'need' to preserve their industry's secrets. This reminds one of Harry Houdini (1874–1926), the great illusionist, who was constantly worried that thieves might steal his techniques, so he never revealed his secrets. But one day he admitted:

> One of my secrets is overcoming fear, keeping a completely clear mind
> in order to work with great subtlety and lightning speed. Free of every
> mental block, I may apply all of my powers to the job in hand.[5]

This is precisely what heads of state and prime ministers would be well advised to do – *overcome fear*, the fear that other EU nations and their companies will buy their assets to steal precious secrets. In an age where education, research and innovation are the motors of the economy, hanging on to old connections is not just unwise, it is also the worst possible strategy.

In the EU, this policy of *hanging on to the past* is being practised widely. While several cases of economic nationalism preceded 2004, it is in that year that economic patriotism acquired its current importance. In 2004 the French government was frightened by a bid by Novartis, the Swiss drug company, and engineered the marriage of two French drug firms[6] by threatening to deploy regulatory levers.

A short time thereafter, the heavy hand of the government fell on the alleged takeover of Danone, the French dairy products company, by Pepsi Cola. Of course, in the case of these examples one could argue that neither the Swiss nor the Americans are EU members. But then why was the bid by Italy's Enel opposed by the French government and the German E.ON's bid for Endesa blocked by the Spanish?

---

5    'Ulisse 2000', Alitalia, Rome, Italy.
6    The smaller, Sanofi, acquired the bigger one, Aventis.

The answer is that a new illness is spreading in the EU: economic nationalism drums up the theme of conspiracy against the 'nation and its citizen, as José Luis Rodriguez Zapatero, the socialist Spanish minister, imprudently[5] stated in a televised interview in the aftermath of E.ON's bid for Endesa (for more detail on E.ON/Endesa, see Chapter 10). At the time, within less than a month,

- Jacques Chirac, supposedly the man of the French right, and

- Zapatero, the man of the Spanish left, were united through the strategy of the red herring.

Apart from adding insult and injury to the spirit of the Treaty of Rome and (why not?) of the European Union, which theoretically seeks to create strong cross-national industrial units able to compete globally, the French refusal of Enel's takeover of Suez had unexpected consequences on the French government's internal front.

The first was that, to accomplish its plans, the French government had to privatize Gaz de France (GDF). The move was opposed not only by labour unions, but also by many deputies of the ruling party; as a result in June 2006 the government could not put together the majority it needed to pass the privatization bill through parliament and had to wait for several months to do so. Finally it got its way, and GDF merged with Suez.

This was not without other after-affects, ranging from the Belgian government's request that Suez sold some of its creation of another energy monopoly over and above EDF. As Eric Emptaz wrote in his feature article in *Le Canard Enchaîné*, in reference to the Suez/Gaz de France affair, '… it is the economic conjuncture which, like the birds, got the flu'.[7] Indirectly, Emptaz pressed the point that *'Allons z'enfants de la patrie économique'* is no answer to economic difficulties, as it is not a medicine for bird flu.

The second unexpected consequence was that the originators of the Suez nationalistic stonewalling were hard hit by the Clearstream affair (Chapter 11) of illicit financial investigations against members of their own government. Allegedly initiated by Dominique de Villepin, the Prime Minister,[8] the smear campaign of Clearstream created a tsunami in French politics because it

---

7    *Le Canard Enchaîné*, 1 March 2006.
8    Who, in December 2006, was put under examination by the juge d'instruction in charge of the
     Clearstream affair.

targeted Nicolas Sarkozy, the then Interior Minister, and other senior officials of the French government. A house divided within itself cannot stand, Abraham Lincoln once suggested

## 3. Overcoming Structural Problems and the Summits' Irrelevance

Angela Merkel, the German Chancellor, planned to start her 1 January to 30 June 2007 presidency of the EU with an effort to relaunch the moribund European Union institutions. But as 2006 came to an end, Spain and Portugal pulled the rug out from under her feet by inviting themselves to a conference with the other 14 member countries which, like themselves, had ratified the EU Constitution – mainly through parliamentary vote, by short-circuiting public will.

This conference among 'the friends of Yes', led by the socialist Spanish government, was scheduled for 26 January, while the same socialists planned a conference for the 'friends of No' for February. In the background of the Spanish move was the intention to undermine Merkel's target: the principle of so-called double majority in EU decisions, which would account for a member state's population.

With 82 million people, Germany would have a weight in EU voting of 18 per cent versus 9 per cent today. France would obtain 13 per cent versus 9 per cent today. Other countries, including Spain, would lose out proportionally speaking, and this was expected to reignite confrontations inside the EU, including different latent animosities.

Interestingly enough, all the rush was about votes and gravy, and it did not take account of the EU's salient problem which, since the Treaty of Rome, has been one of crumbling old structures – including the unreformable labour market and the question of a growing deficit of the right skills for a post-industrial economy. Yet, it is nobody's secret that the most urgent need was for:

- labour reform (see also section 5) and

- a thorough restructuring of the educational system.[9]

---

9   The old education structure is unfit for the twenty-first century's economy, the proof being that in the EU there are millions of vacancies which people who are currently unemployed are unable to fill.

The two bullets correlate among themselves, with the opening up of career opportunities. Take Germany as an example of positive after-effects of ongoing changes. This is a country that has found a way to move ahead of the curve, after a period of stress and suffering which lasted for a decade after post-reunification euphoria gave way to a hangover. In 2006 and 2007 GDP grew by almost 3 per cent year-on-year, small by Chinese standards but large by those of the EU.

Prior to this necessary change – for instance, in 2002 and 2003 when the economy was at its lowest – many economists said that the drag was the prevailing stiff labour laws. The labour changes Gerhard Schröder brought forward saw to it that employment rose significantly in 2006, with domestic demand adding its weight to already strong manufacturing exports. Something structural has shifted in Germany's economy, and not only in labour. Corporate Germany's balance sheets changed, too.

Another example of changing social and commercial winds in Germany, that affected consumer spending was the rapid rise of discounting in food retailing. Cut-price operators now have some 30 per cent of the market, while shopping at Aldi and Lidl is the norm for rich and poor alike. This 30 per cent is also the case in Norway, while in France food discounting stands at 7 per cent, in Italy at 6 per cent and in Britain at 3 per cent. 'It's the best business model for retail in the world,' says Philippe Suchet of Exane BNP Paribas.[10] Discounters stock a fraction of the goods that a normal supermarket offers, resulting in:

- fewer suppliers;

- higher volume of purchases and sales; and

- massive economies of scale.

Many economists say that the shifts in the market for labour and capital, as well as in retailing,[11] have been just as important as the government's persistence in moving ahead with reforms – a Thatcherite model. Taken together, they brought forth jobs as they:

- stiffened the terms for unemployment benefit and

---

10  *The Economist*, 16 August 2008. Aldi and Lidl dominate the world in discounting, with annual sales estimated respectively at €43 billion ($60 billion) and €35 billion – while, with over 35 years of history, Carrefour has sales of €102 billion ($142 billion).

11  Which make the now classical supermarket obsolete.

- made life easier for enterprises which struggle to survive, as do many of the *Mittelstände*.[12]

*Zeitarbeit*, as temporary work is known, has also helped in reducing unemployment even if in Germany it accounts for 1 per cent of all jobs. (It has proved to be an excellent buffer in job seeking.) Having reduced permanent staffing levels and carrying no reserves, many companies and other entities like hospitals turn to temporary employment agencies as their requirements fluctuate. By contrast, temporary employment is anathema to labour unions and to the majority of employees and workers, yet it is unavoidable in a globalized economy with its accompanying job mobility. Therefore these two themes, which are:

- putting the brakes on economic nationalism and

- actively promoting temporary employment

should have been at the top of the EU's priorities in terms of establishing a uniform policy on industry and jobs, which is far from being the case. The evidence is provided both from the most recent EU summits and from the global ones.

Here is an example. On 7 October 2008 an ECOFIN[13] meeting addressed the following themes: interventions to salvage wounded banks, protecting legitimate interests of competitors and negative spillover effects. Nowhere is there a reference to economic nationalism associated to the salvage of big banks (the first of that meeting's themes) or temporary employment perspectives for the tens of thousands who have lost their job as banks undergo restructuring.

A week later, on 12 October 2008, there was a summit of Euroland countries with the following subjects: assuring appropriate liquidity conditions for financial institutions; facilitating the funding of banks and allowing for an efficient recapitalization; bending the implementation of accounting rules (presented as a matter of 'flexibility'); and enhancing the cooperation procedures among EU members with regard to distressed banks. Again, labour issues and industrial patriotism were absent from the agenda.

---

12  Small and medium-sized enterprises.
13  Euroland's Council of Finance Ministers.

These two themes were absent as well from the agendas of the G7 Summit held on 10 October 2008, the G8 Summit which took place five days later on 15 October and the G20 Summit on financial markets and the world economy. The latter was held on 15 November 2008 in Washington and its agenda was:

- unsound risk management practices, opaque financial products and macroeconomic imbalances as root causes of the ongoing economic crisis;

- stabilization of financial markets and economic growth through national measures as well as IMF and World Bank emergency loans (therefore more debt);

- enhanced transparency and accountability and expansion of international bodies, including the Financial Stability Forum (FSF);

- commitment to an open global economy with a regulatory framework (to which labour problems were not attached); and

- the request that finance ministers initiate processes to implement the action plan and formulate additional recommendations by 31 March 2009.

That 'action plan' was non-existent, but reference to it must have been judged as something positive for the communiqué. By contrast, attention to the economic nationalism that has crept into the salvage of big banks – and made the finding of effective solutions, like the establishment of a global regulator of the financial industry, so much more difficult – fell by the wayside. Instead, other themes were included in the communiqué of the 15 November 2008 G20 'summit', which were totally irrelevant to its primary focus. Examples are:

- environmental issues and

- the resurrection of the long-dead Doha Round.

Environmental goals may be commendable, but their aims clash with the objective of putting the global economy back on its feet, as well as providing employment opportunities for those who have lost their jobs. As for the Doha Round, its resurrection is sure to cause disarray virtually everywhere else. The people who participated in the mid-November 2008 Washington summit should have been mature enough to know that attacking every issue across the board is the best prescription for making headway on none of them.

## 4. Case Study on the City of London

To better appreciate why a case study on employment in the City of London is within this chapter's objectives, we should step back a moment and look at the impact of sectors of the economy on British gross domestic product. In the decade from 1997 to 2007 British GDP grew by about 35 per cent or, on average, somewhat better than 3 per cent annually, but not all sectors have contributed at that level.

- The manufacturing industry's growth has been practically nil.[14]

- By contrast, the banking industry, including securities and derivatives, grew by about 17.5 per cent per year.

In the mid-years of this decade, the City of London-led expansion of finance in Britain saw to it that a sector worth about a tenth of the economy was responsible for 30 per cent of overall sprint in GDP. Moreover, this happened despite the fact that the City was hit by the downturn in international finance after the dotcom crash.[15]

Even at the end of 2007, six months after the great banking crisis and service slump had started, and though bank shares have fallen by nearly 20 per cent since that year's summer, the City had kept up its spirits. Bonuses were untouchable and, although banking jobs were being axed, many people took it as a necessary cutting of excess personnel or of dead wood.

As 2007 came to a close, the biggest casualty was in Newcastle, the north-eastern base of Northern Rock. The mortgage lender's woes had an aftermath as they undermined confidence in the ability of one of the country's industrial regions to bring itself into the post-industrial society.

---

14  Employment in manufacturing has been in decline, and while Britain's manufacturing grew somewhat, its share of GDP has fallen.
15  In the 1997 to 2007 period Britain's financial sector also contributed about 30 per cent of all corporate tax revenues.

Time and again analysts in the City of London commented that even if a prolonged banking crisis like the one that crippled the Japanese economy in the 1990s and first decade of this century could be ruled out, current difficulties may not be just a temporary reverse. This assessment was mixed with the hope that banking and securities, insurance and specialist services like shipbroking would continue making a healthy share of British national output,[16] but analysts also warned that:

- there was really no place for economic nationalism and

- fair play under the free-market principle would not have allowed it in the first place.

The rather favourable assessment was based on the fact that what makes a big difference is the City's role as a global financial hub, where big banks and leading moneymen congregate (even the taxation of foreign businesspeople by the Labour government did not send them away). London remained a centre for international finance:

- dominating off-exchange dealing in derivatives;

- hosting most news share issues, by value; and

- positioning its foreign-exchange markets at over twice New York's share of trading.

At the same time, however, like New York before it, globalization and financial liberalization saw to it that London faced a lot more competition than it used to – particularly from the Middle East and Asian financial centres like Hong Kong and Singapore – while, as New York slipped, many American politicians did not take lightly this loss in global financial centre leadership. In a covert show of economic nationalism:

- some accused the British government of deliberately lowering bank supervision standards while the US kept them high (later these proved to be nil under George W. Bush's watch);

---

16  About 6 per cent.

- while others blamed the Sarbanes-Oxley Act of 2002[17] for New York's second position in financial services.

Experts said that as far as New York's financial market was concerned, the bigger loss has been in the sector for initial public offerings (IPOs), which is an important barometer of financial well-being. Measured by proceeds, America's share has shrunk since the late 1990s. In 2000 the New York Stock Exchange dwarfed London and Hong Kong, but by 2007 it was beaten by both.

The US message of economic nationalism was grim for Britain, but according to cognizant people it will be virtually impossible for New York to recapture the banking business that has moved away to other major financial centres. Indeed, some financial experts suggest that the best New York can hope for is to slow or stabilize this flight, as the banking and economic crisis of 2007–2009 made a bad situation worse.

(In mid-January 2007 a report by McKinsey commissioned by Michael Bloomberg, New York mayor, and Chuck Schumer, a senator, warned that, if the then ongoing trends continued, New York could lose up to seven percentage points of its share, equivalent to 60,000 jobs, over the next five years. In December 2008 this was raised to between 200,000 and 250,000 jobs lost as a result of the severe US banking and economic crisis.)

As bad news never comes singly, a recently heard opinion in the City of London is that more dark clouds are on the horizon because of ratification of the EU Constitution (Chapter 6) by Gordon Brown's government (through a parliamentary vote), and of ongoing talk that Britain may join the euro. The point some experts make is that the Treaty redistributes powers in the EU in a way that will make it easier for Brussels-based EU institutions to influence the regulation of financial services.

What specifically bothers these experts is that, by all available evidence, new financial regulation will be considerably more intrusive and politically driven than the City is accustomed to – a fact that could damage its interests. Qualified majority voting, they argue, will make it harder for the British government to fight the City's corner at the EU negotiating table:

---

17  D.N. Chorafas, *IT Auditing and Sarbanes-Oxley Compliance*, Auerbach/CRC, New York, 2009. Restrictions placed after the 11 September 2001 terrorist events and virtual privatization of US visa services were much more of a problem than Sarbanes-Oxley.

- opening up a big area of uncertainty and

- making it harder for British bankers and lobbyists to form alliances of blocking minorities, which they have done to stop the Financial Services Authority from extending its powers.

Critics of this thesis answer that this is plain economic nationalism in reverse and a negation of fair play. They also add that it essentially confirms the American position that the City of London overtook New York's financial market by significantly lowering regulatory powers.

But those worried about London's recovery of its previous global financial position, and the EU Constitution's negative effects, aren't laying down their arms. They point out that the Constitution's reform of European Parliament procedures will give a stronger voice to the EU's more populist elements who view the City with suspicion and are averse to the fact that it is:

- the EU's largest financial centre by a long way and

- closely identified with a single member country.

It is also true that the City of London has few champions in Brussels and Strasbourg, while Britain's power to influence events is curtailed by the EU Constitution. The same executives and financial experts are also worried that the EU is planning to centralize financial regulation and liquidity management measures, which become easier to push through under the Treaty's new structures. *If* the new EU regulations go that way, *then*, critics say, passive resistance to them may become a necessity – but this will be a new form of Colbertism.

## 5. The Myth that Economic Nationalism is the Solution

Responding to questions from the *Financial Times* a few days before the 6 May 2007 election, Nicolas Sarkozy described his role in the rescue of Alstom as a success story and said he wanted a new ethic of capitalism. For her part, Ségolène Royal wanted to make the state a dynamic shareholder (as if bureaucrats can be dynamic) which she said would allow companies 'not to reason by financial or even very short-term speculative targets, but to establish their role as leaders'.[18]

---

18  Leaders of what?

Among the French public, businesses which valued the free market's contribution to the economy stated that they were not convinced by the arguments of either presidential candidate and that the striking thing about these two very different personalities was the similarity of their views and approaches. Both were signalling:

- state intervention,

- economic nationalism and

- other issues linked to dirigisme.

Some political analysts commented that the message conveyed by all three bullets went against the European Union's attempts to promote competition. In surprisingly similar statements, Royal and Sarkozy – who contended the presidential election from the left and the right respectively – said prices would have to take account of consumer purchasing power and the competitiveness of French companies. But:

- *if* both issues were indeed political goals,

- *then* they clearly contradicted one another.

They were also impossible to realize, as subsequent events demonstrated. As an example, energy prices are not decided in Paris, London, Berlin or Washington and not even in Moscow or Riyadh, though the latter two cities have something more to say about energy than Paris, Berlin or any other European capital – no matter how much economic nationalism one might like to preach.

Royal said that Europe's energy policy should have the objective of 'maintaining the public service missions that are specific to each company and so allow a regulation of energy prices'. Leaving aside the fact that even were she elected president, Royal could have talked only for France, not for Europe, that stance:

- looks like a nineteenth-century socialist manifesto, rather than 'a dynamic' way to manage the twenty-first century economy; and

- is not the only anachronism which found its way into one of this century's 100 per cent populist and utopian political programmes.

It is indeed surprising how little attention politicians pay to the real cost of economic nationalism and wrong-way 'labour protection' programmes which contribute in a big way to the dilapidation of the manufacturing base. France's overprotected job market provides a vivid example of what has just been said. In 2000–2002, under the socialists, the government reduced the country's standard working week from 39 to 35 hours without loss of pay.

- Employers secured some flexibility in return;[19]

- but the new rules have caused headaches, particularly in the service sector.

To spread the shorter hours over a year, many office workers were given about three weeks' extra holiday, in addition to their normal five weeks of paid vacation. Some companies said that this encouraged absenteeism, and, taken together, absenteeism and the shorter working week were instrumental in their decision to relocate.

To counterbalance this jobs drain, the government instituted various other protections while national collective-bargaining agreements, which apply to all employees in an industry, entrenched union power. The collective agreement for the bakery industry goes on for an epic 480 pages while the general labour code is a heavy pile of paper featuring 2,730 pages. These thousands of pages:

- all favour the job market's insiders,

- but do little to nothing for the outsiders: the young, the poorly skilled, the long-term jobless.

Years after the 35-hour week was implemented, there is plenty of proof that the winners have not been the workers but the big global forms. Whether we talk of France or of any other country of origin, such firms make between 50 per cent and 80 per cent of their profits outside the country where they started, and provide daily proof of their ability to benefit from globalization.

- To them, economic nationalism is a joke, because a large chunk of their shares is held by foreign investors from pension funds to hedge funds; and

---

19  Some efforts have also been made to lighten the burden on employers to encourage them to hire.

- shareholder pressure helped to prompt change within the firms, including the act of altering the corporate culture.

An example is Air France. After the company was floated, a capable CEO, Jean-Cyril Spinetta, took some bold strategic gambles, such as the merger with KLM and an ambitious expansion of routes in the late 1990s. The change is even more impressive if one accounts for the fact that Spinetta inherited a confrontational workplace with widespread distrust between management and rank and file. But he introduced novel approaches, such as being frank, communicating with employees and explaining things.

Economic nationalism has nothing to offer to well-run companies, and salvage plans which try to be everything to everybody, doing miracles with a little bit of money, are of no use either. Even if money thrown at the problem is labelled 'strategic investment fund' it has nothing strategic in the first place. Strategy is a master plan against an opponent, but the opponents of industrial patriotism are several and elusive. In addition, strategy not only involves a series of actions to achieve a goal, but also entails answering questions like:

- What is going to be done?

- By whom, when and how?

- What's the expected aftermath? The costs? The risks? The targeted benefits?

Nationalistic aspirations are no strategy, and the simple wish to win, though admirable, is no strategy either, which paints a very bleak picture of economic patriotism and its deliverables. To outsiders, at least, it looks like a process made for the evening news, with no great impact and with even less in terms of longer-range effects. But people feel more comfortable if they think their interests and those of their families are protected, and politicians are ready to oblige.

Other issues, too, have the potential to hit the public eye via the media, like the 'Marseillaise' of Ségolène Royale. 'I had to respond to Sarkozy who stopped his fall in the opinion polls with his Ministry of Immigration and Nationality,' the presidential candidate said to her socialist followers in April 2007 to justify her new-found love for the 'Marseillaise' and the French flag, adding: 'I cannot only defend the illegal immigrants.'[20]

## 6. The Maginot Line Mentality of Economic Nationalism[21]

The wider becomes the phenomenon of populist action against the very idea of the European Union, the less the EU has a reason for being. In Greek popular theatre there is a smart comic character called Karagiozis, whose credo in negotiations is: 'What is mine is mine, and what is yours is mine.' As a way of doing business, this Karagiozis strategy accurately describes the mindset of economic nationalists.

Critics of the way in which the European Union's business is being conducted, and of the rising resistance to political integration, say that the basic reason is lack of real leadership. They see economic nationalism as another manifestation of *déclinisme*, with nobody being in charge. Others suggest that part of the reason the future looks so bleak lies in the facts that:

- the industrial policy prevailing in today's EU dates back to late nineteenth and early twentieth centuries; and

- even these antiquated principles are very much guided by a Maginot Line mentality of static economic defences, which damages the EU as a whole and benefits nobody in particular.

At least in some of the EU member states, this way of thinking backwards is not alien to the public. The way an article in the *International Herald Tribune* had it, a sweeping survey of people in 22 countries, which took place in January 2006, found that France was alone in disagreeing with the premise that the best economic model is 'the free enterprise system and free market economy'.[22]

---

20  A short time earlier in the presidential campaign, during her appearance in the 'Grand Jury RTL', she had promoted the policy of regularizing everybody. Immediately her public opinion poll moved south. So the next day she denied having said so and promoted the idea of a case-by-case examination of the illegals (*Le Canard Enchaîné*, 28 March 2007).

21  Bearing the name of a World War I veteran who served as war minister, the Maginot Line, designed to protect France, and most particularly its border industrial areas, from a new German invasion, was started in 1929. In World War II the Maginot Line became an irrelevance, since the Germans invaded France through Belgium. Ironically, it was used by the Germans in their resistance to the advance of Patton's Third Army.

22  *International Herald Tribune*, 28 March 2006.

Three years later this is no longer true. Several EU countries have joined the economic patriotism bandwagon.

The poll referred to in the preceding paragraph was conducted by the University of Maryland's Program on International Policy Attitudes. Based on their findings, the pollsters concluded that to the question on whether they like the market economy and its deliverables, only 36 per cent of French respondents replied 'Yes'. This compared poorly with:

- 59 per cent in Italy;

- 65 per cent in Germany;

- 66 per cent in Britain;

- 71 per cent in the United States; and

- 74 per cent in China, where three out of four people subscribed to the global market economy.

The fact that nearly two out of three Frenchmen and -women voted *against* the free market and free enterprise system explains the French government's love of an economic and industrial Maginot Line mentality. Immediately after listing 11 strategic industries, and promoting the shotgun merger of Suez and Gaz de France (section 2), the government used state-owned Caisse des Dépôts et Consignations (CDC), which is a trustee and should be free of government interference, to build up core shareholdings in French companies[23] – and it is doing so in full knowledge of the fact that:

- the trustee's money is engaged in an operation involving considerable market risk; and

- practically everywhere in the world, risky investments violate a trustee's statutory requirements.

To appreciate the stratagem, the reader should know that the French CDC is a huge financial organization managing savings of €220 billion ($295 billion), plus pension and other funds. This is an impressive endowment, but – even if risky investments were legal – that money would not have been enough to

---

23  See also the reference in section 4.

build up blocking stakes across the French stock market, which prior to the 2008 slam had a capitalization of €1.5 trillion.

Moreover, CDC had already invested more than half of its own surplus in French equities[24] and, with such a concentration of risk, it could not commit more depositors' funds without jeopardizing its position as a responsible custodian of savings and pensions, or without going way outside its mission while trying to make up for the fact that:

- France lacks domestic private institutional investors and

- some 45 per cent of French shares are foreign-owned.

Beyond the use of CDC funds as a way of reinforcing this Maginot Line mentality of economic nationalism, the French parliament has approved a Villepin-proposed amendment of the European Union takeover directive. This amendment makes it easier to introduce 'poison pill' defences to ward off hostile bids from foreign entities and investors that acquire French equity.

Critics say that these tricks could turn the country seven decades back in its history. State intervention in the economy flourished at the time of the original Maginot Line, between the two great wars. In 1936, a few years after the 1929 stock market crash, Léon Blum's Popular Front nationalized the defence industry, the railways and the Banque de France. Then, in the aftermath of World War II, the communists and socialists in de Gaulle's government:

- nationalized more big chunks of industry and finance; and

- presented these takeovers as part of an ingenious state-run effort to get France back on her feet.

Three and a half decades later, following the socialists' victory in the 1982 elections, François Mitterrand's government engaged in a new frenzy of nationalizations of banks and industrial companies – paid for through inflation, higher taxation and successive depreciations of the franc. Many of these firms were reprivatized in the 1990s, but this did not eliminate the state's shadow over French industry, which still looms very large. Experts suggest that the French government's intervention is one-sided because the government did not object to:

---

24  Which means that it has lost plenty of funds in the banking and economic crisis.

- Suez's takeover of the 49.9 per cent of Electrabel, the Belgian electricity company that it did not already own (which the Belgian government wanted back in case Suez merged with GDF);

- Electricité de France's (EDF's) takeover of Edison, the second-biggest Italian energy firm (together with AEM, the power supplier for the city of Milan), among other acquisitions, particularly in Britain; and

- the French banks, continuing expansion in Euroland through acquisitions, like the aforementioned BNP Paribas purchase of BNL, different Italian credit institutions by Crédit Agricole and BNP Paribas's acquisition of the remains of Fortis.

Those who say that it is wrong to have double standards also point out that Chirac did not object when, in April 2006, Alcatel, the French telecommunications company, bought Lucent Technologies, the American firm. The two telecom manufacturers were on the block together in 2001 and for good reason. Right after the bursting of the stock market's bubble, telecoms vendors had huge overcapacity to strip out and they definitely needed to squeeze their expensive R&D, which stood to the tune of:

- €2 billion (2.7 billion) a year on Alcatel's side and

- $1.2 billion on Lucent's, or about 12.7 per cent of sales.

In the opinion of financial analysts there were some synergies in the Alcatel/Lucent merger, but most of the economies were planned by cutting staff in overlapping areas rather than creating value to be added. Cutting staff? This should have rung alarm bells on Chirac's side. But since it was a French company taking over a big American name, it did not.

The US government made no move to block that deal. On Wall Street, analysts were fairly sure that, left to its own devices, neither company could survive in a tough competitive global market for telecommunications equipment. The financial analysts' comments made sense:

- Aa hugely downsized Lucent was too small to rank in the Big 5 and had no choice but to find a new owner.

- Alcatel had a huge cost structure and was apparently hoping to disguise it through the Lucent acquisition.

This merger was welcomed by Jacques Chirac for prestige reasons, since Alcatel paid for Lucent. But was it economically viable or were French shareholders going to pay for it in a way similar to that of Eurotunnel? After the M&A announcement the fall in the combined value of the two companies was equivalent to 11 per cent of Lucent's market capitalization.[25] The celebrations some months earlier in Paris about a French company taking over a big American name proved to be premature.

## 7. Industrial Patriotism is Competition under a New Guise

It would be wrong to think that the French are the only economic nationalists in Europe, much less in the world. Within the EU this is becoming a policy; Hungary, Spain (Chapter 10) and, to a lesser extent, Italy are other examples. When, in mid-2007, in an apparent move towards a takeover, the Austrian oil and Gas firm OMV raised its stake in its Hungarian rival, MOL, the Hungarian government intervened. It advanced money to MOL to purchase its own shares and the firm assumed control of 40 per cent of its own equity – a sort of government-approved poison pill:

- in violation of a Hungarian law that prohibits a firm from holding more than 10 per cent of its own stakes; and

- in spite of the fact that Hungary was on the edge of bankruptcy and a year later, in 2008, it required both a huge IMF loan and EU money to save the day.

Like economic nationalists everywhere else, in spite of the country's financial mismanagement and lack of funds, Hungarian politicians believe that more should be done to prevent foreigners from meddling. In fact, the Hungarian government is threatening to pass a law preventing foreign firms, including those of European Union origins, from buying 'strategic' Hungarian assets.[26]

---

25  Afterwards the stock recovered, but it remains volatile.
26  *The Economist*, 11 August 2008.

The reader should know that government interference may come from many sources, not only from the ministerial council or from parliament. On 23 May 2008 Antonio Fazio, a former Bank of Italy governor, was ordered to stand trial over alleged wrong-doing in the country's banking scandal of 2005. As governor of the central bank he has allegedly behaved improperly while a group of Italian bankers and financiers waged a battle with ABN Amro of the Netherlands for control of Banca Antonveneta.

Fazio faces a maximum penalty of six years in jail plus a fine, according to Roberto Borgogno, one of his lawyers, who added, however, that his client had done nothing wrong in his relationship with Gianpiero Fiorani, then head of Banca Popolare Italiana. During the investigation into the scandal, prosecutors looked into the opaque methods Fiorani and others were alleged to have used to build up a stake in the bank and defeat ABN's chances of an acquisition. According to published accounts:

- Fiorani had Fazio's blessing when allowed to turn a small mutual bank, from near Milano, into a bigger player through more than a dozen acquisitions; and

- the governor's supposed impartiality was a sham after leaked telephone transcripts exposed friendly late-night conversations with Fiorani about the battle for Antonvenata.

Milan prosecutors accused Fazio and others of market-rigging – a broad accusation implying that the participants' actions improperly influenced the movement of shares traded in Milan. Though ABN Amro eventually prevailed through the heavy intervention of prosecutors in Milan and Rome, its coveted Italian expansion turned out to be short-lived, as in 2007 the Dutch bank was acquired by a consortium of other banks and broken up, with Antonveneta being first taken over by Santander (a Spanish bank) and then bought by Tuscany-based Monte dei Paschi di Siena.

This has been an interesting case of economic nationalism's dead-end. After allegedly illegal acts were committed by the governor of the central bank to stop Antonveneta from being acquired by another EU bank, ABN AMRO fell to a consortium of Royal Bank of Scotland (RBS), Fortis and Santander – with the result that Antonveneta returned to Italian ownership.

It is also important to notice that two out of the three members of that acquisitive consortium hit the wall. While Santander made a discreet profit by selling Antonvenata to Monte dei Paschi, RBS went bankrupt because of its excesses and was salvaged, then nationalized, by the British government, using taxpayers' money. Fortis also went bankrupt:

- one part was salvaged with Dutch[27] and Belgian taxpayers money; and

- the remainder was sold to BNP Paribas, with the sale subsequently suspended because of a court decision[28] – which had its own after-effects, bringing the Belgian government down in flames.

Compare all this to the liberal attitude taken by the British and Dutch governments in connection with the battle between Tata, an Indian conglomerate, and CSN, a Brazilian steelmaker, for Corus, the Anglo-Dutch company that absorbed what was once British Steel and Hoogovens. (Tata and Corus had already agreed a takeover deal when CSN barged in on 17 November 2006.)

Both Tata, which finally took the prize, and CSN were the number two steelmakers in their home markets and (at the time) were highly profitable; but they were small in comparison with their main suppliers and customers. Acquiring Corus, one of the few independent large producers of flat steel, was part of their strategy to gain a way into the European market. The same strategy was followed by Mittal in its acquisition of Arcelor (Chapter 10).

If France, Spain, Hungary and other EU countries are not sorts of economic patriot, the US is not alien to this concept. In February that same year, 2006, American congressmen of every stripe were up in arms when the government's Committee on Foreign Investment in the US (CFIUS) approved the acquisition by Dubai Ports World[29] of P&O, a British firm that operated several ports in America. The storm abated only after Dubai Ports World agreed to spin off the American operations to an American-owned firm.

This incident was preceded by Congressional concerns over the sale to overseas buyers of Global Crossing, a telecoms firm with optical fibres in the Pacific seabed and (as already discussed), of the would-be purchase of Unocal,

---

27  The Dutch government bought the local operations of dismembered ABN Amro.
28  Related to a suit brought by minor shareholders who complained of having been abused.
29  Controlled by the government of Dubai.

an oil company, by the China National Offshore Oil Company (CNOOC). Many foreign firms interpreted these moves as proof of American hostility to foreigners buying some types of US company.

Other tools than plain cash are used as means for stonewalling in a globalized world. One of the 2007 and 2008 themes, for example, was how the delayed effects of the dollar depreciation over the previous five years influenced US export competitiveness, leading to what was characterized as manufacturing renaissance. The people at EADS (Chapter 11) hold firm on that opinion, pointing to the weak dollar as the reason why they lost many contracts to Boeing's Dreamliner.

New rules, too, may become the tools of industrial patriotism. A case in point is $CO_2$ emissions and other factors which might be used for reasons of trade discrimination. Indeed, there exists a whole toolkit of overt and covert limits to a liberal acquisitions and trade policy, allowing somebody:

- to be openly in favour of free capital movements, investments and trade,

- but at the same time promoting different sorts of self-serving controls.

As 2008 came to a close, for example, transport-related $CO_2$ emissions in the European Union constituted nearly 29 per cent of the EU total – with cars and vans responsible for about half. While there has been some reduction since carmakers were threatened with legislation a decade ago, progress has been painfully slow and uneven.

- In 2008 the best year-on-year results were achieved by Toyota (-0.5 per cent).

- Honda, BMW, PSA Peugeot Citroen and Nissan came next (between -3.8 per cent and -1.6 per cent).

Volkswagen, Renault, Fiat, Ford and GM (in that order) have produced some fractional improvements in $CO_2$ emissions but Daimler Benz contributed nothing to this process and the same is true of Chinese- and Indian-made cars.

While as the above reference suggests, with some exceptions motor vehicle manufacturers have at least been making an effort to improve their environmental credentials, these improvements are small fry to the ambitious plans for $CO_2$ reduction the French and Italians[30] are championing in the EU – and the Germans resist for obvious reasons. They also say that these ambitious plans:

- are selfish, a Trojan horse to cut the market for German cars; and

- are a charade of economic nationalism under a different form, but just as discriminating and lethal.[31]

Behind these $CO_2$ arguments and counterarguments lies the fact that in major auto manufacturing countries between 7 and 10 per cent of the working population is linked to the motor vehicle industry (including suppliers, service networks and so on). It is simply unthinkable that, $CO_2$ or no $CO_2$, a government would allow leadership in the auto industry to slip away.

It is no less true, however, that $CO_2$ rules are far from being the only factor that can destroy a motor vehicle industry. As Roger Bishop aptly wrote, MG Rover, a formerly British-based car-making enterprise, was 'destroyed over a very long period by corporate and shareholder greed. Successive buyers downsized and rationalized slashed R&D budgets and generally did everything they could to cut costs before selling on the carcass to the next new "investor". That's no way to run a car company (or any other business for that matter) that need to keep its products fresh for future generations of customers.'[32] This is a profound observation that governments and companies should keep in mind. Economic nationalism is no silver bullet.

---

30  The Italians, however, were against tough $CO_2$ limits for industrial emissions and so were the Poles, who feature over 90 per cent of power production from coal.

31  A new car takes five to seven years to develop, and new technologies cannot be incorporated straightaway. Moreover, both the EU and the US currently lack sufficient engineering resources to pursue many hares simultaneously.

32  *European Automotive Design*, June 2007.

# 10

# Case Studies on Economic Nationalism

## 1. 'The Government Will Put Up the Money'

A socialistic state, which nationalizes the country's industries and financial institutions, and a nationalistic state, which blocks foreign companies from acquiring control of private companies in sectors such as energy, system engineering, aerospace, pharmaceuticals, food processing and others, have at least one thing in common. They exercise their populism by using and misusing assets that don't belong to them.

To find out whether everybody appreciates that fact, I asked a number of people where this silly business of economic nationalism's Maginot Line comes from. The most frequent answer was: 'The government is going to put it up.' Then I reminded the respondents that the government does not have any money of its own. The only money any government has is what it takes from you, me and the businesses and industries we work for. As has been already brought to the reader's attention, this happens in two ways:

- in the form of taxes or

- through huge budgetary deficits, feeding inflation.

Both, and most particularly the latter, are used by the government, any government and any central bank, 'to put up the money'. Inflation is the worst tax of the two. 'We must tax the poor, they are the more numerous,' said André Tardieu, a socialist French prime minister of the early 1930s. Value added tax (VAT) and inflation are the best ways to do so, because:

- they can be turned on and off without apparent limits.

- Inflation, however, is more dangerous than VAT because it escapes control and it burns up not only savings but also parts of the economy.

People I interviewed were surprised to hear that the money going down the drain was not 'the government's' but their own. They were also interested to learn that to tax, tax and tax, socialism, and economic nationalism require that the country has a sound and prosperous industrial economy to loot. *If* that is not the case, as happens in big chunks of the EU, *then* the only alternative for financing socialistic and nationalistic programs is huge budget deficits.

Politically speaking, populism is at the core of both socialistic and nationalistic economic, social and financial measures. But what is really meant by *populism*, and does is it really worth paying for? The way an article in *The Economist* had it, José Manuel Barroso, the CEO of the European Commission, identified two kinds of populism, both of them negative:

- one is against the market and

- the other is against the very idea of Europe.[1]

Spain's José Rodriguez Zapatero is an example of the first and Jacques Chirac, the former French President, of the second. This book has made many references to Chirac, but not enough to Zapatero. It is therefore time to balance the scales. The Spanish economic nationalism of recent years came to public attention with the now famous case of two utility companies:

- Germany's E.ON and

- Spain's own Endesa.

E.ON's interest in gaining control of Endesa started in 2006. This was a long-lasting battle, and the position taken by the Spanish government against the acquisition of Endesa by E.ON is a good example of populism, which negates the very idea of a European Union, as well as the need for pan-European utilities and other infrastructural services firms.[2] All this started in late February 2006, as Spain took a very frosty approach towards Germany's E.ON, an energy

---

1   *The Economist*, 15 October 2005.
2   In spite of the large amounts of money it received, and continues to receive, from the EU, much of it coming from the German taxpayers' pockets.

company, launching a €29.1 billion ($37.8 billion) bid for Endesa, a Spanish power provider. This would have been the largest-ever transborder deal in the EU utilities sector.

Right after the Irish 'No!' to the June 2008 referendum on the EU Treaty (Chapter 6) a horde of politicians said that the Irish were out of their minds to go against the Brussels Commission's and plenty of heads' of state wishes concerning ratification. After all, this argument said, the Irish had received so much money from the EU. Curiously enough, nobody spoke against the Spaniards when they blocked the takeover of Endesa by E.ON. After all, in this case, too, the Spaniards had received (and continue to get) plenty of money from the EU.

## 2. E.ON's Failed Takeover of Endesa

Without first doing his homework and examining the most likely after-effects, as well as being careless about the need for previous consultation with Brussels, on 22 February 2006, José Luis Rodriguez Zapatero put the brakes on E.ON's offer. The socialist Spanish Prime Minister did just the opposite of what the EU spirit demanded in terms of cross-border mergers. He announced that his blocking of the bid for Endesa was necessary because of:

- 'the interests of our citizens' and

- 'the interests of our country'.

In other terms, Spain is *über alles in der Welt* (or at least in the EU) and the interests of the European Union should be damned. What sort of 'union' is this when every country is out for itself, cares only for its own nationalistic interests and stonewalls – no matter what is written in the agreements which it signed when it joined the EU.

Zapatero did not bother to explain why blocking E.ON protected the interests of Spanish citizen. But it could be read between the lines that he was much more concerned about satisfying national voters than keeping his obligations towards his European partners. As for the 'interests of Spain' being protected from the Germans, the Spanish government seemed forget that for more than two decades:

- Spain benefited from lavish agricultural and other subsidies, largely paid by Germany,

- while the Federal Republic and its taxpayers had been, for long, too long, Spain's and the EU's cash cow.[3]

Timidly, the usually weak EU Commission asked Spain not to intervene in the E.ON bid, but this seems to have fallen on deaf ears. The Spanish government had decided to stop the German energy company's bid, which it saw as unwelcome. For this reason, it backed another Spanish utility's, Gas Natural's, offer for Endesa despite its rejection by Spanish antitrust authorities because their merger would create a monopoly. In one move, the Spanish socialists violated both:

- European Union rules and

- Spanish antitrust laws.

Critics say that this was not the result of a sort of one-off bad humour. Under 'socialist leadership' Spain's EU spirit has taken leave of absence, and shame has gone along with it. Following that first silly reaction and under mild EU pressure and for fear of ridicule José Luis Rodriguez Zapatero agreed to a half-way takeover by E.ON, but the EU commissioner for competition was not satisfied. Insisting that Spain must abide by EU rules, the commissioner contemplated bringing the country to the European Court of Justice.

Those who cared about how well the European Union functions were hoping that, at the end of the day, Spain and the other economic nationalist EU states would stop treating the 'union' as a non-entity – but they were deceived in their hopes. Critics of the 'I do as I like' Spanish attitude pointed out that Zapatero does not only excel in economic nationalism, Spain wants to be both in- and out-of the EU as it suits it best.

- Its government fails to recognize in how deep a hole it is in terms of EU esteem and what it would take to get out; and

---

3   Spain exploits its EU membership in many ways, because it is a rich country and still benefits from subsidies provided to poor EU countries. Also because its illegal immigration policies are anti-EU, as they aggravate the EU's problems with illegal immigrants.

- the country's policy of continuing to play the fool, however, violates the First Law of Holes: 'When you are in one, stop digging.'

As for the Spanish economy, it simply cannot afford to play '*über alles*'. On 14 January 2009, the day Standard & Poor's, the independent rating agency, downgraded Greece's credit rating from A to A-, it also placed Spain and Portugal on negative credit watch. The global financial and economic crisis exacerbated an underlying loss of competitiveness in all three economies.

The gag about building Spanish castles on foundations of sand does not end there. The same socialist/nationalist José Luis Rodriguez Zapatero had no objection when Ferrovial, a Spanish construction company, made a bid to buy the British Airports Authority (BAA), owner of Heathrow, Europe's busiest airport, when Telefónica made a bid for O2, a British mobile-phone operator; or when Santander, a big Spanish bank, bought Britain's Abbey National bank and parts of other credit institutions that had failed in England.[4] This is the 'European Union' of:

- double standards;

- narrow views; and

- very bad management.

Like the flu, nationalistic policies are contagious. The British did not object to Spanish companies cherry-picking their firms, but the Italians did so. Until recently, Italy was liberal on takeovers, but it changed policies. Under government pressure, the purchase of Autostrade by Spain's Abertis, a €25 billion ($33 billion) deal, was scrapped in mid-December 2006.

A couple of months later Italy and Spain found a way to get together with cross-holdings. Telefónica, Spain's big phone company bought a large share in Telecom Italia, which suited the Romano Prodi government well because in that way it blocked a takeover of Telecom Italia through a combined bid by AT&T and a Mexican telephone company.

As a reminder, in April 2007 AT&T and Mexico's América Móvil, a mobile-phone operator, had tried to secure a stake in Telecom Italia. Their endeavour

---

4  Also when Scottish Power was bought by by Iberdrola, a Spanish utility. Indeed, Spanish businesses have spent nearly $60 billion (£40 billion) snapping up British firms.

met stiff resistance from the Prodi government and other Italian politicians, who argued that the country's highly indebted telephony 'jewel' was a strategic asset that should not fall into foreign hands.

Instead, the equally 'foreign hands' of Spain's Telefónica (together with a couple of large Italian financial institutions) bought the €4.1 billion ($5.6 billion) controlling stake in Telecom Italia held by Pirelli. This decision of the Italian government to interfere with the markets cost the Telecom Italia shareholders dearly, as they were deprived of the added value of a takeover, which was substituted by private placement – but it did open the way for a Spanish–Italian rapprochement as in the Franco-Mussolini years, with Zapatero and Prodi in the leading roles.

With this new-found friendship, at the end of February 2007 the Spanish government gave the green light for Enel, Italy's big state-controlled electricity firm, to plunge into the fractious battle for Endesa. Enel started with a bid for a 10 per cent stake in the Spanish utility, because it needed the approval of Spain's energy commission to buy more than 10 per cent share. But the important thing was that:

- its move had the blessing of Spain's socialist government, which came just three weeks before a critical meeting of Endesa shareholders; and

- that revealed the other side of state intervention – favouritism following the heads of state whims for Enel but against E.ON.

With this evidence, who can ever say that the European Union is a free market? That thought is awfully mistaken. 'There will probably be a kind of pact,' said Juan Clos, Industry Minister in the Zapatero government. 'I would say a Spanish solution had greater chances of success [than the German bid].'[5] That 'Spanish solution' was understood to have been discussed by Spanish Prime Minister Jose Luis Rodriguez Zapatero and Romano Prodi, the Italian prime minister, at a meeting in Ibiza at end of February 2007 just before Prodi's government fell.

In spite of the widely aired government-manipulated 'Spanish/Italian solution', E.ON said it would pursue its bid for Endesa. But the chances of success for the biggest and longest-running takeover in utilities history suddenly

---

5    *Financial Times*, 28 February 2007.

looked very small. The Germans were faced not only with staunch opposition from the Spanish government, but also with a cash-rich and expansion-hungry Italian rival. Looking at the odds, in the end E.ON opted out of that deal.

## 3. Lessons from the 'Spanish/Italian Solution'

People favourable to the Spanish government's position against E.ON suggest that it opposed the German bid from the outset because, like most European governments, it is keen to create a home-grown energy champion in anticipation of full deregulation of the energy market. This could have been retained as a hypothesis as long as it had backed a lower offer for Endesa by Gas Natural, the other Spanish energy firm, despite its rejection by the antitrust authorities in Madrid.

By all evidence Gas Natural was used as a red herring. In November 2006 the Spanish government found an ally in Acciona, a Spanish construction firm, which built a stake of more than 21 per cent in Endesa and said it wanted full control. Then came Enel, the 'Spanish/Italian solution' and the Italian energy firm's plan to increase its stake in Endesa to 24.9 per cent (above that level it would have had to launch a full bid for the company).

To appreciate the Zapatero government's Germanic xenophobia better, the reader should know that under previous prime ministers non-residents in Spain had come to control 57 per cent of the turnover in the Madrid's stock exchange. These were largely American and British funds. Spanish investment holding companies represented about 19 per cent, different financial groups another 19 per cent and a mere 5 per cent (just peanuts) was left to individual investors.

- The Spanish stock market was, and is, in the hands of a small group of big players[6] (more on the Madrid stock exchange later).

- Zapatero's socialist government changed nothing in all that. As section 2 has shown, it has simply been anti-German.

According to a cognizant opinion, besides his own reservations about E.ON, Zapatero fell under Prodi's spell. One reason why the Italian government was happy to see Enel buy into Endesa was that Endesa's Italian subsidiary, which

---

6    Though not to the same extent as the Russian stock market.

first entered the Italian market in 2001, had become the second largest private electricity producer in Italy. If E.ON were to acquire Endesa, it would give the giant German energy group a foothold in the Italian market, a prospect many ministers in the centre-left Italian government did not welcome.

- It's alright for the Germans to support the Italian lira from the 1970s to 2000;

- but it is wrong for the Germans and the Dutch to acquire equity in Italy.

Opposition to German expansion in the energy industry in southern Europe was common territory for the Spanish and Italian governments. The 'Spanish/Italian solution' was put in motion even if Enel's entry into Endesa was condemned in Madrid by the opposition Popular Party, which said that the Zapatero government had acted unlawfully – and also criticized the fact that the socialist government was not *protecting* the minority shareholders.[7]

Both the small shareholders and business ethics were trapped by the Spanish socialist government's whims. A lesson taught by these dubious standards prevailing among EU member states is that the open economy is a myth.

Britain's liberal policy has made it a favoured landscape for takeovers, because the Spanish encounter less opposition there than they do in France and Italy. But the Spanish themselves are stonewalling in their own country, and the French mounted defences over a bid by Sacyr Vallehermoso, a Spanish construction company, for the Eiffage construction group which, in the nineteenth century, had built the Eiffel Tower.

In M&As companies choose the path of least resistance. After the Italians' refusal to let their Autostrade company go, the Spanish Ferrovial teamed up with Australia's Macquarie Group to buy two motorways in America: the Chicago Skyway and the Indiana Toll Road, through its quoted subsidiary Cintra.[8] Ferrovial, moreover, bought Amey, a British services and project-management firm that maintained three London Underground lines.

---

7    At €38.75 per share, E.ON was offering more than double Endesa's undisturbed price from September 2005.
8    It also managed a motorway in Texas (with the state government).

This hyperactive strategy of Spanish firms in acquiring other countries' assets, wherever they can, in a big way, has after-effects in terms of leveraging. Spain's current-account deficit is second only to that of the United States. At more than 9 per cent of GDP, it mirrors the thirst for borrowing of Spanish companies. Just prior to the July/August 2007 financial crisis:

- lending to Spanish industrial firms had risen by 30 per cent in 2006; and

- Spain's deficit revealed how tilted towards gearing up the country's economy had become.

Privately, several Spanish bankers and executives were worried about the leverage going on, as the ambitions of Spain's big companies were riding on too much borrowed money and their loans were sometimes backed by their stakes in other quoted companies whose equity was crashing in the stock market. This meant that, triggered by a property downturn which came in a big way in 2008, the fall in the Spanish stock market had damaging effects on:

- the leveraged companies and

- the Spanish economy as a whole, which was further hit by the crash of the building industry.

The fragility of the Spanish economy was further documented by the fact that Madrid's stock market reflected a rapidly rising level of corporate debt with net debt/equity ratios nearly 2.0 in 2006 and early 2007, versus 0.6 in France and less than 0.1 in Switzerland. *Leverage* has been the name of the Spanish game.

When it joined the European Union in 1986, Spain was a backwater with a per capita GDP about 25 per cent below the EU average. German money, as well as the fiscal and monetary discipline that came with EU membership, has underpinned dramatic economic growth in Spain. But all that changed with the recent government.

Regarding the Spanish companies' overseas adventures, these were boosted by the transformation of their home economy from an also-ran into one of the better performers of the European Union. At the same time, however, a 15-year domestic expansion, buoyed by low interest rates and a construction and property boom, reached its limits. Therefore:

- it would be wrong to think the Spanish had found the elixir of perpetual life;

- nearly a year before its collapse, the construction boom suddenly started receding, signs of which the socialist government failed to take notice.

As the American economy also found out the hard way, both business expansion and the real estate boom need lots of leveraged financing, and currently Spain is seeing the other side of life in the euro zone: the economic crisis environment. Critics add that while the country has achieved one of the most rapid increases in wealth in Euroland, largely with EU money, it remained stuck with an unbalanced economy and low domestic productivity. Hence the rush to develop global champions to:

- draw on markets outside Spain and

- prove that Spanish business is not limited in its scope.

The 2008/2009 economic crisis, however, brought with it the need for rebalancing the economy. Devaluing the currency, the trick usually played by Italians and French prior to the euro, is ruled out. Hence Spain must find a different method of pulling itself up. This is problematic because the country's higher-than-average inflation rate brought with it high wages. Productivity growth has been trivial. Taken together, these factors led to a nearly 15 per cent increase in unit labour costs, relative to the Euroland average, since 2000, a mark of uncompetitiveness shared by Italy – which brings into perspective one of the broader aspects of the 'Spanish/Italian solution'.

## 4. Committing Corporate Suicide. Case Study on Alitalia

Examined in its fundamentals, the 'Spanish/Italian solution' has much deeper roots than economic nationalism against E.ON might suggest. At its roots are government and corporate mismanagement, made worse by the meddling of labour unions, which both pushed the envelope for greater labour benefits and lost control of their base. Companies, too, are badly mismanaged and Alitalia, Italy's flag airline, provides the perfect example.[9]

---

9   Spain's Iberia is another basket case. Years after having absorbed Argentina's bankrupt Aerolineas Argentina, it ran into rough weather and is now for sale. It was a deliberate choice

Poor service, old aircraft, overstaffing and wildcat strikes have brought Alitalia to its knees; for more than a couple of decades it has survived only through massive injections of public money. A relic of the immediate post-World War II years, the Italian national airline practically collapsed in September 2008 but was brought back to life at the eleventh hour – and a couple of months later became the object of a French-German rush for an alliance, even as a government rescue of the airline ran into new obstacles.

Air France was no newcomer as a suitor for Alitalia. It was one of the few remaining bidders to take control of Italy's national airline after the government put it up for sale, following the end of March 2007 announcement that it had made a pre-tax loss of €405 million ($600 million) in 2006, almost three times as much as the previous year. (The last time Alitalia reported an annual profit was 1998.)

Air France had continued negotiating in spite of the fact that other potential buyers of a controlling stake in the beleaguered national airline had pulled out, not only because of the torrent of red ink but also because of:

- government conditions, like maintaining the hubs in Rome and Milan; and

- stiff labour unions' positions that what Alitalia's employees and workers had gained in the past decades in negotiating with weak Italian governments was untouchable.

Air France persisted but at the same time, because it was well-managed, chipped away several of the government's and labour union's 'musts'. Other critical issues, however, remained, and a new one came up: economic nationalism in the tourist industry.

The way friends in Rome and Milan explained it in January 2008, both France and Italy were competitors in the global market for tourism – a big income earner. Therefore, it was unthinkable to leave Italy's air routes in the hands of France's flag airline. This would have damaged Italy's tourist business in the longer run. Eventually, Air France left the negotiating table, but economic patriotism has a price and by the third trimester of 2008:

---

to keep Iberia out of this discussion.

- the tag attached to Italy's crippled flag carrier read: €5 billion (then $7.3 billion); and

- that was the cost of preserving the airline's inefficiency and *Italianita*.

The Berlusconi government, which inherited from the Prodi government the crippled airline's mess, was slow to come up with a solution. By late August 2008 this crystallized into the so-called Operation Phoenix,[10] a rescue based on funnelling Alitalia's €1.2 billion debts and its least profitable bits into a 'bad company' dumped on the Italian Treasury. More realistic estimates put the cost to the state at €2 billion (then $2.8 billion), with the government offering to guarantee seven years of alternative employment or welfare protection to the 5,000 or so workers who stood to lose their jobs.

The *Deus ex machina* in Operation Phoenix was Air One, Alitalia's main domestic rival. The two were supposed to merge into a new company, stifling competition particularly on the lucrative Rome–Milan route, with the government exempting the new company for three years from restrictions imposed by antitrust laws. One of Operation Phoenix's interesting hindsights is that it confirmed the loss of Milan Malpensa's hub status, which Air France had requested in earlier negotiations. As a result:

- a good deal of the intercontinental traffic from Italy's industrial heartland will be routed through other hubs; and

- with Air France-KLM and Lufthansa being the two parties remaining in the new round of negotiations, the names of the hubs were (respectively) Paris and Frankfurt.

Critics said that the rationale of Operation Phoenix was not really economic, but rather the desire to honour Silvio Berlusconi's claim, made ahead of the April 2008 election, that he had a better solution for Alitalia than the Air France-KLM offer, which he had termed offensive. But there were not many options on how to come out of Alitalia's long red-ink tunnel.

---

10  Phoenix was the code name of a consortium of Italian entrepreneurs, precisely 16 investors ready to put up €1 billion. They were led by Roberto Colaninno of Olivetti/Telecom Italia fame and CEO of the Piaggio scooter firm.

Under the rescue plan, CAI – the renamed investors' consortium – would take over from the government, buy Alitalia's newer planes and airport slots and merge them with those of Air One to start up the combined airline as a smaller carrier. The Italian government would take over Alitalia's other assets, which are practically worthless but loaded with liabilities. However, this plan relied on the reaction of labour unions who:

- thought they had found private investors to finance their featherbedding; and

- engaged in protracted negotiations, disagreements among themselves and more strikes – precisely the stuff of corporate suicide.

In the hope that all that would come to an end and survival logic would prevail, by late October 2008 Air France-KLM (whose bid was rejected in early 2008) Lufthansa and British Airways (which until then had denied any interest in Alitalia) wanted to negotiate a commercial alliance. The rush could be explained by the fact that the prospects for Alitalia improved by the aforementioned government-backed bail-out that would result in a debt-free and privately owned airline. On the other hand, the negatives were:

- two failed auctions and

- a looming bankruptcy filing.

These had seen to it that the airline's passenger traffic fell by 28 per cent in September 2008 alone. This did not particularly bother Lufthansa and Air France-KLM, each of which – as my friends in Rome and Milan had said in January 2008 – wanted a piece of Alitalia to strengthen their position in the booming Italian travel market and prevent Alitalia from falling into the hands of a rival.

Some financial analysts suggested that the enthusiasm over linking up with Alitalia was premature as its bail-out ran into new hurdles in connection with labour unions, and some other problems also came up. For instance, the 'new Alitalia' was initially scheduled for early November 2008, but that was delayed because CAI had yet to present a formal offer for Alitalia's assets. Augusto Fantozzi, the airline bankruptcy commissioner, said he hoped that:

- the deal could be concluded two weeks before cash reserves of the airline ran dry; and

- any further delays would require Alitalia to seek a new loan to keep flying.

CAI had been waiting for regulatory approvals before presenting its formal offer – which is a sort of deadly embrace. Moreover, the new investor was seeking a flying licence for the new airline while being at the same time worried that, after reluctantly agreeing to back its plan to avert a liquidation of Alitalia, its unions would again begin voicing complaints, turning the rescue into one with increasingly uncertainties – in a typical fashion.

There was also the European Commission, which had to approve CAI's takeover plan, but was unlikely to do so because of the Italian government loan of €300 million ($390 million) to Alitalia. The Commission found itself in a state of self-contradiction because at the same time competition officials in Brussels had long been pursuing, without results, two loss-making airlines, Alitalia and Olympic, milking their governments over illegal subsidies.

On 13 January 2008 the wires carried the news that the winner in the competition to get a piece of the new Alitalia was Air France-KLM. It paid about €450 million ($600 million) for a 25 per cent stake, valuing the whole company at roughly €1.8 billion ($2.25 billion), including its planes, human resources, slots, potential clients and other goodies.

That was a small fraction of what the Italian taxpayer had paid out over the previous few years to keep the rotten company afloat. It was also tantamount to abandoning the Malpensa airport (near Milan) as a hub – bending the economic nationalism resistance. In fact, right after this announcement Malpensa's personnel and Alitalia's employees went on strike (the old habit) because much of the big Italian airport's traffic was going to move to Paris.

In conclusion, from a macroscopic viewpoint, Alitalia is a good proxy of the way the European Union works. It has run up huge losses, it is viewed as badly managed, overstaffed, too heavily unionized and subject to political interference. As an entity, Alitalia has been characterized by chronic unprofitability, strikes, cancellations and turbulent labour relations. As a carrier, it is sustained for political, rather than business, reasons and beyond all logic it had classically insisted in operating two hubs – one at Rome's Fiumincino airport and one at

Milan's Malpensa – just like the EU is bent on expansion without any logic to sustain that policy.

## 5. Galileo versus GPS and other Mickey Mouse Investments

If Alitalia was an attempt to resurrect Lazarus from his well-deserved tomb, other 'investments' proved to be stillborn. Galileo is a EU project of radio navigation and economic nationalism supposed to be a competitor to the American GPS[11] but heralded as being one of superior technical qualities – except that it cannot manage to get off the ground.

The project began in June 2005 when the European Commission chose a consortium of eight big industry names to realize Galileo's objectives: 30 satellites to be put at an altitude of 20,000km. Wow! Members of this Galileo consortium were the Franco-German EADS (Chapter 11) of A380 fame, Thales and Alcatel of France, Inmarsat of Britain, Hispasat of Spain, Finmeccanica of Italy and TeleOp, a smaller German firm.

- This selection was made in 2005 but practically nothing was done until 2008; and

- according to reliable sources, it will take at least another couple of years to sign the contracts which are supposed to last for 20 years – another 'first' in industrial history.[12]

A milestone in the course between the life and death of the European satellite navigation system supposed to rival GPS came in mid-March 2007 when its development ground to a halt amid doubts among the project's consortium companies over its likely profitability. '[The companies] are just not working', said a European Commission spokesman.

The partners in this 'superior technology' global positioning solution were indeed sceptical that there would be enough customers to make Galileo profitable. 'There is a doubt over the revenues,' said one executive. 'Why buy Pepsi-Cola when you can get Coca-Cola for free?' asked another. The latter

---

11  The US global positioning system.

12  In the 1960s I was consultant to the board of AEG/Telefunken, and the executive vice president who introduced me to the newly elected CEO Dr Gamer told me: 'He will lead our firm for the next 20 years.' Dr Gamer lasted not quite two years.

executive also suggested that European governments would have to guarantee that their emergency fire and ambulance services would subscribe to the new global positioning system to bring in funds.

'It is looking increasingly like an Airbus in space,'[13] said Gerard Batten, an MEP from the British Independence Party (UKIP). Another MEP recalled that Galileo was originally conceived in the 1990s by the EU Commission to guarantee a European-controlled satellite guidance system free of the constraints of the US military, and:

- it was due to be operational by 2010,

- but nobody talked of that date as being a target any longer.

EU governments had good reasons to be concerned that long delays in development work, as well as the stop-and-go policies designed to milk more EU funds, could see to it that China launched a competitor satellite navigation system before Galileo was flying. Beijing said that its own system, called Beidou, would cover China and its neighbours by 2008 and would ultimately span the globe (it has not happened yet).

People who bothered to examine how and why Galileo was approved in the first place have come to the conclusion that economic nationalism was at the top of the list of reasons – and at the same time behind the difficulty to reach an agreement on:

- what had to be done;

- who was going to do it;

- what the acceptable cost level was; and

- how infighting between the members of Galileo's consortium could be avoided.

Infighting was more likely than cooperation, because each one of the national champions wanted to gain the major share of commercial advantages, while at the same time none was sure that the project would meet its aims. Next in the line of adversities came financing. The EU put on the table €1.5 billion

---

13   Rather than Airbus, the white elephant that preceded it: Concorde.

($2.1 billion), but the different companies were far from being sure that this was enough. They wanted €5.0 billion ($7.0 billion) from the EU, rather than contributing the difference themselves.

On 2 May 2007, amid signs that the private sector could not agree on how to get Galileo off the ground, the EU budget commissioner, Dalia Grybauskaite, proposed a 51 per cent increase in funding for the Galileo satellite project. Within a fortnight, by mid-May 2007, the EU agreed to pay *all* the money for Galileo's infrastructure.

It needs no explaining that throwing money at the problem is no way of guaranteeing its success. Quite to the contrary, projects put up for prestige reasons and assigned to quarrelling parties, some of whom have doubts about their partners as well as the project itself, do not produce deliverables.

- They are booby-trapped to start with; and

- the best that can be expected from them is to bring to life a Mickey Mouse.

As a policy, this is, of course, troubling, and Galileo has by no means been the only example. Another hilarious project brought to the public eye was a plan to develop a Franco-German Internet search engine to rival Google. Named Quaero, probably to indicate that hot air (aero) was its key feature, it was included in a list of initiatives designed to challenge America's dominance of the Internet by France's Jacques Chirac. Cooler heads in Germany:

- grumbled about the cost,

- but also indicated they would produce 'their own', scaled-down search engine.

Nothing was learned from past projects which were ill-studied in regard to their potential, repeatedly burned their schedules, loaded themselves with unnecessary costs and never really came out of the red. A glaring example is Eurotunnel, a public company which was used as comfortable seat for politicians with scant business experience. With over €9 billion ($12.5 billion) of debt,[14] the tunnel under the Channel became the greatest disaster to small French investors since the end of World War II.

---

14  Eventually converted into equity to avoid bringing Eurotunnel to bankruptcy.

Brought to its knees by chronic lack of sound governance, as CEO followed CEO over several decades, in mid-2006 Eurotunnel sought legal protection from its creditors and got it through safeguard procedures roughly equivalent to the American Chapter 11 bankruptcy provisions. At the same time, the company insisted that protection from creditors did not preclude its continuing talks with the two main creditor groups, while small equity investors – who stood to lose the most – were given no voice.[15] With it, the idea of responsibility for small shareholders who put their savings in the firm.

- flew out of the window, and

- that's economic nationalism's other face.

An alternative to keeping Eurotunnel going, also at the expense of minor investors, was an offer by Goldman Sachs and Austrialia's Macquarie which had proposed buying the French bank's loans at 60 per cent of face value, but the claims of bondholders at only 5 per cent – in a distressed debt operation. In that case bondholders would have paid a large part of the bill, but shareholders would not have been much better off.

Small shareholders have also been swindled by ill-conceived mergers and acquisitions, with economic nationalism the overriding reason. The merger of French telephony equipment manufacturer Alcatel and US Lucent Technologies, with the former officially acquiring the latter, was completed at the end of 2006 in a deal valued at $11.6 billion.[16] At the time, Alcatel promised annual cost cuts of €1.4 billion. But a year later, lacklustre results left investors in the cold.

- Alcatel-Lucent tried to soothe ruffled feathers at its results announcement, by saying it is likely to achieve its pre-tax savings target based on synergies from the merger.[17]

- The market, however, was not convinced, and its equities value hit rock-bottom as investors realized the company would fail to deliver on its restructuring programme.

---

15  More than 80 per cent of equity was held by small French investors. They conserved only 13 per cent of their equity, while the market value has crushed and it currently sells as penny stock.

16  The two firms tried to merge in 2001, but the deal fell apart at the last minute when the then Lucent's CEO Henry Schacht refused to agree to the terms pressed by Alcatel's boss, Serge Tchuruk.

17  That has been precisely the same argument advanced by Air France-KLM when it bought a 25 per cent share in the new Alitalia (section 4).

A second-tier management at Alcatel-Lucent tried to convince the financial analysts that a 'strategic rethink may not be far away'; rumour also had it that the labour unions backpedalled on agreed-upon job cuts. But investment banks downgraded the stock, and some repeated their advice to sell, citing disappointing gross margins and scant evidence that the business was moving forward.

All that was a far cry from the talk that the merger would create a network-equipment manufacturer rivalling Cisco Systems in size. Instead, Alcatel-Lucent continued to bleed heavily from its bloated cost of operations and burdensome restructuring requirements, while price pressure offset any cost synergies from the merger. As the company's share price caved in and stayed at a low one-digit number, the shareholders lost their savings.

## 6. Mittal's Conquest of Arcelor

The 2006 acquisition of Arcelor – a major French–Spanish–Luxembourg steel entity – by Mittal, an Indian steel company, was (at least so far) the biggest battle lost by economic nationalists. 'Mittal won because of a fragmented shareholder base interested only in making a quick buck,' fumed Jean-Pierre Chevènement, a former French socialist interior minister and leader of a splinter left party.[18] Chevènement blamed Europe's single market for what he called the 'triumph of globalized capital' which, in his opinion:

- leads to a dictatorship of cash and

- pits the global market at large against France's interests.

There was more populism than anything else in this statement, yet it deserves the reader's attention. Chevènement has failed to explain which of 'France's interests' are being hurt (isolation maybe?) or why French interests in the EU should differ from German or Italian interests. At the same time, however, Chevènement's thoughts demonstrate an attitude which is anachronistic but widespread, fed by the obsession of 'national' control of industry. Critics said that while Chevènement (a former student leader) might be a nice fellow, he has spent all of his life as a politician.

- He never built an industry; and

---

18  *The Economist*, 1 July 2006.

- he never created a single new job.

By contrast, a man who started as an office boy in his early teens, worked six days a week for less than $1 per day, studied on the seventh day at the local library and built the largest steel empire in the world was the Scottish-American Andrew Carnegie. Here is what Andrew Carnegie had to say on this same issue: 'The price which society pays for the law of competition ... is great; but the advantages of this law are also greater still than its cost – for it is to this law that we owe our wonderful material development.'

Lakshmi Mittal, too, started (nearly) from scratch as an Indian-born entrepreneur who went abroad and little by little put together the second of history's great steel empires, based on Carnegie's vision. Part of this process was Mittal's €18.6 billion ($28 billion) hostile bid for Arcelor, Europe's champion steelmaker, which politicians wanted to keep out of Mittal's reach but lacked a strategy on how to do so.

Not unexpectedly, Mittal's bid aroused a chorus of 'patriotic' outrage. Jean-Claude Juncker, Luxembourg's Prime Minister, scorned the offer as incomprehensible and vowed to use all necessary means to fight it. Thierry Breton, France's Finance Minister and a former businessman, voiced profound concerns, as did his counterparts in Belgium and Spain.[19]

In a call to arms, Dominique de Villepin, the then French Prime Minister, exceeded all other anti-Mittal warriors. In a televised address on 31 January 2006, he stated: 'Economic patriotism is the mobilization of all the participants, of all those concerned, the shareholders but also the company bosses', urging French and other European chief executives to be better organized to resist attacks by foreign companies.[20]

The EU Commission, however, took a different stand. Charlie McCreevy, the internal market commissioner, sent Breton a letter demanding justification for provisions in new legislation that gave the government the right to veto or impose conditions on takeovers in 11 'strategic industries'. Some Brussels watchers said that that reprimand might explain the initially subdued reaction to Mittal's bid by French politicians.

---

19  Together with the Franco-German pharmaceutical Sanofi-Aventis and the European Aeronautic Defence and Space Company (EADS, Chapter 13), Arcelor was one of the few pan-European corporate success stories.

20  *The Economist*, 4 February 2006.

There has nevertheless been no question that the French, Spanish and Luxembourg governments considered Arcelor one of their country's corporate jewels. Created in 2002 after the merger of Spain's Aceralia, Luxembourg's Arbed and France's Usinor, and incorporated in Luxembourg, the steelmaker had employees in France, Spain, Germany, Luxembourg and the Americas.

All three EU governments vowed to fight to the finish, yet Mittal Steel's hostile bid reached its objective. Here is a brief reminder of the epic battle for Arcelor's control. When the prospect of Mittal takeover materialized, all three governments raised hell, joining Guy Dollé, Arcelor's CEO, in a flat statement about the takeover's unacceptability for a variety of reasons which included:

- loss of jobs in the three countries and

- an even bigger loss of national prestige.

Months passed, but bureaucrats and politicians in France, Spain and Luxembourg failed to come up with a plan to keep Arcelor independent. The company's board and CEO were equally unsuccessful in the search for a white knight. Arcelor found only a murky 'solution', selling itself for peanuts to Severstal (credit rated B+ by independent rating agencies) and to Alexey Mordashov, the Russian oligarch and steelmaker's boss. In a clear show of mismanagement, this was done without any study of the possible consequences.

One of the issues Villepin and his Spanish and Luxembourg colleagues failed to explain was why a Russian oligarch was a better option than a hard-working Indian entrepreneur. Besides, Mittal Steel was registered in the Netherlands and run out of London, but in an unknown and mysterious way three EU governments, and Arcelor's board, decided that Mittal did not share Arcelor's European 'cultural values', while presumably B+ Severstal did.

There is irony and extreme bad judgement in this affair. What is known about Severstal is that it is an unquoted, opaque metals firm controlled by a tycoon who, without launching a bid, was to become the dominant shareholder of the combined steel group and titan of 'European cultural values':

- Under the terms of the proposed transaction, Arcelor would have acquired a 90 per cent stake in B+ Severstal; and

- in exchange, Mordashov would have owned a 38 per cent share in Arcelor, giving him the power to make decisions about Arcelor's future.

That speaks volumes about the brains of the three countries' top politicians – presidents and prime ministers included – as well as of the quality of Arcelor's top management. The politicians finally got cold feet and this rotten deal fell through. But the boss of Severstal made a killing at the expense of Arcelor's shareholders, as the Arcelor management had committed itself to a ridiculous €140 million ($175 million) 'break-up fee'.

This is one of the best examples to be found regarding the level of absurdity of economic nationalism. Therefore, it comes as no surprise that Arcelor's shareholders went into revolt. A lesson to be learned from this case is that, in the last analysis, shareholders' rights count and governments who try everything they can to muffle the will of equity owners lose face.

This was the conclusion analysts reached when, after almost six months of vigorous resistance, Arcelor's board finally succumbed to Mittal Steel's takeover offer. 'This is a marriage of reason,' said Joseph Kinsch, chairman of Arcelor, when he presented the proposed merger of the Luxembourg-based steelmaker and Mittal Steel to the press on 26 June 2006.[21]

- 'Reason of June', when the weather and the CEO's seat are hot,

- but 'unreason of January', because, in the winter months, brains hibernate.

Between 'unreason' and 'reason', Chirac and Zapatero, Kinsch and Guy Dollé, Arcelor tried every way it could find to rebuff Mittal's hostile bid. At shareholders' expense, its management mobilized politicians, bankers and public relations advisors. It also invited a curious sort of a white knight, B+ Severstal, and finally found out that the light at the end of the tunnel was that of an oncoming train.

Another important lesson from Mittal–Arcelor is that the heavy hand of governments distorts sound judgement and makes CEOs and board members decide as if they were living in Lalaland. Let's keep this lesson in mind. Companies the government backs are the ones that are falling to pieces and

---

21  *The Economist*, 1 July 2006.

need rescuing: France's Alstom, an engineering group, Bull, a computer firm and Crédit Lyonnais, a big but bankrupt bank – are other examples.[22]

## 7. The NYSE's Takeover of Euronext

The rise of national self-interest in the European Union has manifested itself in threats to the free movement of capital including, as we saw through several case studies, cross-border mergers and takeovers by companies residing in other member states. For many years EU mergers and acquisitions were seen by the European Commission as a vital tool for raising the continent's competitiveness, but the number of countries that think the opposite increased in a significant way.

- This change of heart is altogether bad news for the European Union.

- The good news is that the attention of the officers staffing the Maginot Line has limits and eventually their defences crumble.

One of the best examples is the merger of stock exchanges from both sides of the Atlantic, propelled by the globalization of capital markets. It looks as if the stonewallers were asleep when the New York Stock Exchange (NYSE) came shopping in the European Union. The economic nationalists' defences were down, yet stock exchanges are 'strategic industries' because:

- they are pivotal to the work the capital market, hence they can be seen as true 'national treasures'; and

- these 'treasures' are about to be taken away in the drive to merge into a global network.

In the last week of May 2006 the bidding intensity increased between the Frankfurt-based Deutsche Börse and the biggest stock market of all, the New York Stock Exchange (NYSE). Both wanted to expand and for both the target was Euronext, itself the product of M&As. This was a battle royal that the

---

22  It is interesting to note, as a postscript, that the governments of Britain and the Netherlands did not object when in October 2006 – a few months after Mittal's acquisition of Arcelor – Tata, also an Indian steel company, made a takeover bid for Corus (the result of a merger of former British Steel and Dutch Hoogovens), or when a Brazilian steelmaker made another bid for the same firm.

stonewallers lost because they could not make up their minds which way they wanted to act (more on this later).

Why was the New York Stock Exchange so eager to acquire Euronext? While the NYSE is currently by far the largest big board by value traded (followed by Nasdaq, the London Stock Exchange (LSE), the Tokyo Stock Exchange, Euronext and the Deutsche Börse, in that order), this merger would have made it twice as big, by value traded, as the next in line, NASDAQ. And it had a good chance of becoming even bigger if NASDAQ, the LSE and Deutsche Börse merged.

Euronext, the result of a merger between the Paris Bourse and stock exchanges of Brussels, Amsterdam and Lisbon, operated for several years undisturbed by acquisitions. Then it sought to acquire the London Stock Exchange (LSE), became subject to a bid by the Deutsche Börse and fell to the alternative bid by the New York Stock Exchange. By acquiring Euronext, both the NYSE and Deutsche Börse aimed at gaining clout through consolidation in the world's financial markets.

Approved by Euronext's shareholders in mid-December 2006, the merger between the NYSE and Euronext created the first transatlantic exchange at a price of €7.9 billion ($10.4 billion),[23] but its importance goes well beyond money. Experts point out that modern stock exchanges are sophisticated entities which have gone a long way from the conditions characterizing their early years. (They began their life in Georgian London's coffee houses through informal gatherings, but they were eventually structured and multiplied on global scale.)

Today, there are hundreds of exchanges worldwide, usually with spacious trading floors, though many of them are small. While old-style exchanges were traditionally organized as mutual trading clubs, modern entities are themselves quoted companies whose equity is bought and sold. In a number of cases the value of their equity continues to rise. For example, in June 2006 Deutsche Börse shares were worth about €100, up from €45 20 months earlier at the end of 2004.

The reasons for cross-border acquisition of exchanges may be geographic expansion, acquisition of new product lines, or both. To enter the clearing of debt instruments, the Deutsche Börse bought Luxembourg's Cedel (Clearstream, see Chapter 11). With its appetite intact, it then sought to acquire Euronext

---

23  Prior to it the NASDAQ had acquired a chunk of the LES, but had no majority control.

where the NYSE carried the day. However, judging from a late June 2006 announcement by the Economics Ministry of the German state of Hesse, the fact that the Deutsche Börse lost its bid might have been a blessing in disguise for the Frankfurt Stock Exchange.

In a show of economic nationalism *à la française*, the Hesse ministry let it be known that *in extremis* it might withdraw the Deutsche Börse's licence to operate the Frankfurt Stock Exchange, which it supervises. The ministry was afraid that, in its bid for Euronext, the Deutsche Börse had made concessions that would damage Frankfurt as a global financial centre.

Critics said that was a medieval mentality. What the Deutsche Börse's proposal for Euronext offered in essence was to delegate more power outside Frankfurt, with a holding company based in Amsterdam, risk control functions centred in Paris and dual locations being institutional in managing information technology and derivatives trading. But the CEO and chief financial officer were scheduled to stay in Frankfurt.

In a management sense, the geographic dislocation of key functions is not consistent with sound governance. But it is the price companies pay to satisfy economic patriots: making silly concessions so that business becomes unmanageable is the start of self-destruction. What particularly irked German politicians and labour representatives was that the Deutsche Börse/Euronext merger would have meant:

- the loss of local jobs; and

- the loss of ill-conceived prestige, because of choosing Euronext's software for trading rather than that of the Deutsche Börse.

Euronext, of course, is by no means the first stock exchange in the EU to be subject to takeover. The London Stock Exchange, too, has been the object of a takeover bid by OM, Stockholm's Stock Exchange (which did not succeed), as well as the target of a major investment by NASDAQ (at 29.9 per cent). The difference with Euronext was that it was partly French, which poses the question:

- *if* stock exchanges and capital markets which use them are so crucial to the economy (indeed, they are),

- *then* how does it happen that the officers manning the French economic Maginot Line did not raise the defences? Were they caught sleeping?

Some experts think that they were. Preoccupied with other problems, including Clearstream (Chapter 11), Chirac and Villepin, two people usually vigilant over national jewels, remained off the news as the New York Stock Exchange edged out the Deutsche Börse and emerged as a serious suitor of Euronext. All Chirac did was make a mellow comment that he would prefer Euronext to merge with the Deutsche Börse, but he did not stonewall the deal in a way reminiscent of Danone or Suez.

Experts also suggested that there were significant differences in the minds of the French government's top brass. Chirac favoured the takeover of Euronext by the Frankfurt Stock Exchange. But Thierry Breton, his finance minister, was inclined towards the NYSE. The stated reason for the choice of NYSE as suitor was that it had no clearing and settlement facilities; hence, there was less risk for cross-subsidies, which distort market competition.

But an article in *The Economist* was of a different opinion, seeing in this preference for the NYSE a covert nationalistic approach. Breton, the article stated, insisted that any merger should preserve a strong share-trading operation in Paris, which must be regulated by the Autorité des Marchés Financiers (AMF), the French regulator.[24] If so, why had Chirac declared himself for the Deutsche Börse?

- Did he suddenly abandon economic nationalism?

- Or, did he miss the fine print of Euronext's takeover?

According to the same article, Breton prevailed with his plan to maintain Euronext's federal corporate governance, which was doable with the NYSE because the NYSE intended to adopt just such a federal structure. If this was the case, then the guardians of economic nationalism were not fully asleep. National pride and self-preservation ring as clearly in their plans as the closing bell at the NYSE. But this did not quite answer two other queries:

- What had happened to the pure and hard stonewalling by economic patriots?

---

24  *The Economist*, 27 May 2006.

- Why did the French Minister of Finance have a diametrically opposed position to that of the President of the Republic?

In my opinion, deprived of knowledge in economics and finance, the 'pure and hard' core of the Maginot Liners was at a loss. Maybe they also remembered that the 2001 merger of the Paris, Brussels, Amsterdam and Lisbon exchanges into Euronext was advertised by the then French socialist government as '*le fer de lance de l'Europe boursiere*' (the spearhead of Europe of stock exchanges), under a CEO who was French but based in Amsterdam.[25]

On these grounds, Jacques Chirac, Lionel Jospin, then Prime Minister and Dominique Strauss-Kahn, then Finance Minister,[26] had allowed the Bourse de Paris to delocalize provided its CEO was French. The press, however, wrote about another motive – French banks benefited handsomely from Euronext's equity. They made a cool 33 per cent profit on their investment by selling their part to British and American funds.[27]

In conclusion, the takeover of Euronext by the NYSE passed more or less in silence, while in 2005 Villepin as prime minister and Breton as finance minister, shouted loudly to keep Danone French, and they repeated that show with Suez as well as with Arcelor. As *Le Canard Enchaîné* concluded its article on the Euronext affair: 'It is known that the government is pedalling in yogurt; but to this point ...'[28]

---

25  François Mitterrand had fallen into the same trap when the British offered to base the European Bank for Reconstruction and Development (EBRD) in London, with a French CEO, or in Paris, with a British CEO. The London-based French CEO, Jacques Attali (an excellent author but no banker) lasted only a couple of years – but the EBRD is always in London.

26  Currently President of the International Monetary Fund (IMF).

27  *Le Canard Enchaîné*, 7 June 2006.

28  Idem.

# 11

# The European Aeronautics Defence and Space Industrial Giant

## 1. EADS and Airbus

As its name implies, the European Aeronautics Defence and Space (EADS) Company is a conglomerate with products spanning a wide range of markets and activities. Two governments – French and German – are dearly interested in it, and the former has a participation[1] – but it is largely owned by investors. Among these investors are other conglomerates like Daimler-Benz (the maker of Mercedes) and Groupe Lagardère[2].

EADS has been one of the more dynamic European cross-border enterprises, with its fortunes conditioned by the market performance of two of its product lines: Airbus Industrie,[3] which resulted from the merger of Toulouse-based Sud Aviation, Munich-based Entwicklungs Ring Süd (the former Messerschmidt) and Hamburg-based Entwicklungs Ring Nord (the former Dornier); and weapons systems (more on the origin of EADS in section 2).

The Airbus company, maker of the airframes under the same name, which will interest us the most in this chapter, has been a great engineering entity, abiding by the principle that a superior product is:

---

1   In the case of Germany, government participation is limited to two states which bought half of Daimler's interests.
2   A French conglomerate specializing in missiles and satellites (the former Matra defence entity which merged into EADS) as well as the media.
3   At the time of the events discussed in this section EADS owned 80 per cent of Airbus. The balance was in the hands of Bae Systems, descendent of the former British Aircraft Corp.

- the best strategy for growth and survival and

- the best protection against intensifying competition.

A pioneering product that came out of Sud Aviation was Caravelle, the right-sized passenger carrier at the right time for the booming mid-range air traffic of the 1960s. By contrast, the government's interference led to mismanagement. An example is the supersonic Anglo-French Concorde, which proved to be a white elephant – a flying machine so heavily loaded with unnecessary costs that (commercially speaking) it could not get off the ground.[4]

Though the choice of a product like Concorde was due to the heavy hand of the state, which was at the time Sud Aviation's owner, it also proved that general management at Airbus's predecessor was not at the quality level of its engineering team. Apart from incorrectly estimating the market for supersonic passenger planes, at the time when Boeing's SST project was killed, a major flaw of Concorde was that it had been projected as a one-off flying engine. As Dr David Rockefeller, then CEO of Chase Manhattan, pointed out in a discussion which we had at the time:

- a big and expensive high-tech project will be a sure loser if it is designed in one size;

- to recover its R&D, manufacturing and marketing investments and leave a profit, it has to be projected in a way that it becomes a smaller and bigger product – like Boeing had done with its successful 700 series.

Both bullets bring us squarely to the subject of Airbus's fortunes. This name encompasses both a project and a company financed by the taxpayers of France, Germany, Britain and Spain. It started as a common European R&D development effort more successful than other joint EU projects, until it encountered turbulence with the A380 superjumbo. The concept of the original A300 Airbus series began in the mid-1960s at the height of American aircraft manufacturing supremacy. At the time:

- over 90 per cent of all jetliners sold around the world were American-made; and

---

4   As its designers joked in a meeting I had in the mid-1960s at British Aircraft Corporation, near Bristol.

- while US airframe producers were selling a third of all their planes overseas, European airlines complained that scant attention was paid to *their* needs.

In late 1966, Air France, Lufthansa[5] and British Airways, Europe's three biggest carriers, met in London to talk about their concerns regarding the latest plans of American's planemakers. Boeing, McDonnell Douglas and Lockheed were all working on the 'next generation' of aircraft, characterized by wide-bodied aircraft powered by three or four engines and geared for long-haul flights.

- This was *not* what European carriers needed for the continent's shorter distances; and

- the three main European carriers also thought that the US aircraft designs were not as cost-effective for their requirements as they would have liked them to be.

What the aforementioned EU airlines wanted was a two-engine, short-range, low-cost, wide-bodied aircraft– something like an upgraded Caravelle, France's most successful civil airplane of the early 1960s. But what British Airways and Lufthansa were prepared to buy would not be produced by Sud Aviation (Caravelle's maker) alone. This restriction by big clients was instrumental in the birth of Airbus. With important clients lined up for its products, the new consortium reaped a record harvest of orders at the Paris Air Show and prepared for a big boost in production.

The headwinds which came in the 1990s and first years of this century were due to the *faux pas* of the company's own management rather than competition. When on 17 January 2002 Airbus held its annual briefing for journalists and analysts, the successor of the former Sud Aviation and its then chief executive office, Noël Forgeard, had to answer a lot of tough questions.

- The company said that orders in 2002 could fall 60 per cent below the 2001 level;[6] and

---

5   It was most significant for Airbus's future that in December 2006 Lufthansa decided to buy Boeing's Dreamliner rather than the still uncertain Airbus A350.
6   *BusinessWeek*, 21 January 2002.

- that meant revenues would remain anaemic through 2003 and 2004, since orders are usually booked well over a year before the expected delivery date, with at least 80 per cent of the purchase price paid on delivery.

That slowdown in orders and cash flow projection could not have come at a worse time. Over the following years Airbus was committed to spending at least $11 billion on developing the A380, the double-decker scheduled for launch in 2006. Preparing to tighten its belt, the company froze a planned expansion of capacity and announced 500 job cuts in Britain. No layoffs were, however, planned in continental Europe as this was a highly political issue.

- Not only did costs have to be trimmed but investors also needed reassuring, as EADS shares had slumped 40 per cent in 2001.

- Boeing stock, too, was down 30 per cent, but since September 2001 it had rebounded more strongly than EADS.

One of Airbus's problems was that its cost base was clearly sized for a lot more than A300 series deliveries, and other flying machines were not in its pipeline. While the company had won tentative approval for A400M, its first military transport plane, that project was not expected to generate revenues for several years and therefore it did not feature in the spreadsheets of financial analysts.

Cutting costs was essential, but neither the heart nor the skills of the company's management were in that task. Moreover, there existed plenty of confusion about who could take what sort of initiative given that Airbus was formed less than two years earlier from a loose consortium of French, German, British and 'as minor partner' Spanish aircraft companies.

As if this was not enough, EADS itself was the product of a delicate cross-border merger whose fine print was still difficult to read. What happened between 2006 and 2008, a few years down the line, was the logical follow-up of these ownership uncertainties and of the management shortfall – whose synergy created the perfect storm.

## 2. The Government's Heavy Hand

Shortcomings in senior management are the right prescription for trouble, and trouble did come, further promoted by the fact that the state was part-owner of EADS, opening the door for meddling by politicians. The usual occurence with partly or fully state-owned enterprises is that they are treated as subsidiaries of the government, where political friends can serve themselves with jobs.

Poor governance sees to it that even industries which were prosperous and aiming for global leadership are brought to their knees. The rise and fall of EADS/Airbus, which had given Boeing a run for its money, makes interesting reading precisely for that reason. Here is what Jean Claude Noel, of INSEAD, the French postgraduate university, had to say in a letter he wrote to *The Economist* in October 2006.

> ... *The specifics of the situation in which Airbus now finds itself is partly the responsibility of previous management. Noël Forgeard,[7] who was ousted in June (2006) as co-chief executive of EADS,[8] Airbus's parent company, personified the arrogance and sense of entitlement of the French 'elite'. Graduating from the grandes écoles ... is no substitute for practical leadership.[9]*

Jean Claude Noël's thesis was that the severity of EADS's and Airbus's plight in 2006 should be enough warning that the cosy French model characterizing business, industry and social issues had reached its limits. In fact, not only that model, but also the practice of revolving doors between political jobs and those of top brass in nationalized industry, as well as in companies in which the government has a share, is in a terminal state.

A bird's-eye view of the company's origin explains why governments were trying, most unsuccessfully, to run the show. EADS was born in 1999 under a French socialist government with Lionel Jospin as Prime Minister and Dominique Strauss-Kahn as Minister of Finance and the Economy. Private interests also participated – particularly Daimler and Lagardère, as section 1 brought to the reader's attention.

---

7   A political appointee and friend of Jacques Chirac, who was at the time French president.
8   Who, as we saw in section 1, was previously Airbus's CEO.
9   *The Economist*, 21 October 2006.

The way an article published in the French press had it, Lagardère contributed assets valued between 5 and 10 billion francs (€0.76–€1.52 billion; then $0.95–$1.90 billion) and got counterparty equity in EADS estimated at between 80 to 160 billion francs (€1.22–€2.44 billion; $1.52–$3.04 billion).[10] That seems to have been quite a present from the socialist government or, alternatively, politicians and bureaucrats who engineered the deal were weak in mathematics.

Between the lines section 1 also suggested that in its first years of operation, EADS was a successful enterprise, one that competed successfully in the global market with Boeing, the only remaining American commercial aircraft manufacturer. This happened in spite of EADS's lop-sided management structure, which emulated the Byzantine eagle with two heads. Commonly known as co-chief executives, for eight long years the French and German top men reflected:

- each country's equity share in EADS; and

- most evidently, also each country's goals.

That sort of parochial thinking was absent when in the late 1960s the governments of Britain, West Germany and France agreed to put in seed money with the aim of exploring the design and manufacturing of a new commercial aircraft able to fulfil short-range requirements better than Boeing's. Taking the project's name as its own, Sud Aviation was chosen to coordinate production. Unfortunately, the governments' hands-off policy did not characterize the following years.

Critics say that it was a mistake that in 2001, when the market's reaction was favourable, EADS did not shed its government ownership – and this for a variety of reasons. The first was quality of management. With very few exceptions, like Volkswagen,[11] industrial history teaches that government-owned or partly-owned enterprises are very badly run.

- They are fiefs of political friends;

---

10  *Le Monde*, 2 October 1998 and *Le Canard Enchaîné*, 25 October 2006. Many people think that *Le Canard Enchaîné* is a satirical newspaper. This is not even half true. *Le Canard Enchaîné* is a political newspaper which, by all the evidence, is subsidized by nobody; hence, it has the courage to write against anybody when it obtains the proper documentation.

11  Where the government of Lower Saxony had a major participation and still has a golden share.

- attract all sorts of incompetence;

- are prone to political meddling;[12]

- are unable to sharpen up their goals; and

- when bad times come they find themselves with all sorts of sacred cows they cannot kill.

An example was given in section 1. When in 2002 EADS needed to cut costs with a sharp knife, it could not do so because of its state ownership. Yet, it was loaded with unnecessary personnel, particularly in its different headquarters, since it had never had the benefit of economies of scale after its constitution because of opposition to layoffs by the governments owning (directly or indirectly) parts of its equity.

While it is by no certain that a private company will have good management – and a study done in London by Goldman Sachs proves that one out of three companies is poorly governed – in a state-owned or partly-owned firm this percentage rises very substantially. EADS has provided one more confirmation of the fact that eventually state-run enterprises tend to become underperformers.

There is also another important factor to be kept in mind: the challenge posed by the firm's eventual privatization. The banks and insurance companies nationalized by François Mitterand in the first couple of years of the 1980s after he was elected president of the French Republic were reprivatized in the 1990s in a process accompanied by various stories of favouritism and abuses.

In Britain this likelihood has been pointed out by critics of the nationalization of Northern Rock and Royal Bank of Scotland, as well as the partial nationalization of HBOS-Lloyds TSB by the Labour government. It is a foregone conclusion, these critics say, that their eventual reprivatization will:

- be accompanied by inefficiencies and scandals; and

- hurt the interests of taxpayers whose money was used in 2007 and 2008 for their salvage.

---

12  See section 6 on Clearstream.

Still another example of how difficult it is to be in fairly good shape while getting away from the heavy hand of the government is provided by Sweden's €70 billion ($100 billion) sell-off of state companies. In early 2007, the multi-billion-dollar privatization of the country's state-owned firms by the (then) new centre-right government was in danger of turning into an 'Airbus-like structure', according to privatization experts.

Dag Detter, former head of state-owned enterprise reform for the Swedish government (between 1998 and 2001) and advisor to the World Bank and International Financial Corporation, said at the time that Prime Minister Fredrik Reinfeldt must ensure that he did not create a structure where political and commercial interests could be confused. Detter also added that the decision to put two ministers, those of financial services and of industry, in charge of its reforms was uncomfortably close to Airbus's arrangement of:

- two chief executives and

- two chairmen of the board.[13]

Critics of the Byzantine eagle organization further added that they questioned the wisdom of the government's approach, which had created separate working groups for each of the privatization candidates. To them, this meant that the process was in danger of being pulled in different and uncertain directions.

That's precisely what happens with the heavy hand of the government everywhere. The state's agents are not there to help anybody else but their own career and other interests, as well as those of the nomenclatura and of the political party to which they belong. They do so both when they buy and when they sell the different enterprises (and their people).

It comes as no surprise, therefore, that in the case of EADS/Airbus the heavy hands of not one but of three governments had a lot to do with the giant enterprise's self-destruction. As always, this has been orchestrated by second-raters who know that theirs is a political appointment and therefore they cannot be choosers.

---

13  *Financial Times*, 21 March 2007. Sweden's privatization was scheduled to be a complex enterprise as there was a stable of 55 state-owned companies to sell, though the government stated that the process would start with only six of them.

## 3. Second-raters and the A380 Fiasco

One, but only one, of the reasons why inferior management is so widespread in the majority of state-run enterprises is that politicians have no firm opinion about goals and priorities, which they change all too often. The late George Papandreou, a Greek Prime Minister at the end of World War II, was not the only one described by the public as *anemodouras* (turning with the wind). Old hands in politics suggest that candidates for an election must have simultaneously different opinions, because voters are not characterized by a unique frame of mind.

- The more contradictory opinions a politician has,

- the greater are his chances that he or she will be elected.

Indeed, even after one is elected, contradictory opinions bring dividends, particularly when expressed as being deep-rooted. The same is true of unkept promises. When in 1925 the French socialist government of Edouard Herriot fell, a published article made this comment: 'Whatever may be one's opinion of Herriot's government, it is proper to recognize that he respected the essential issues of his programme. He respected them so much that he did not even touch them.'[14]

While there exist politicians who are true leaders and innovators, the safe bet is that many of the figures revolving around them as satellites are second-raters. Here is an example of the second-rater's virtues which I borrowed from Max Hastings. In World War II, General Harold Alexander was beloved by many as a delightful military gentleman gifted with good looks, athletics, charm and courtesy. 'These gifts', Hastings says, 'masked laziness and lack of intellect. [Sir Alan] Brooke (British military chief in World War II) dismissed Alexander as a very, very small man [who] cannot think big.'[15] That's what is meant by second-rater.

It is wrong, however, to assume that such people cannot reach the top of an organization. On a misty night in 1920, the guard of a rail crossing in Seine-et-Marne (near Paris) heard somebody knocking on his window. Outside was a man in pyjamas who said: 'I am the president of the Republic.' The pyjama man

---

14  Jean Egen, *Messieurs du Canard*, Stock, Paris, 1973. François Mauriac had said: '*Ce que le Canard est lu! Même à l'Académie on m'a dit: Vous avez lu dans* le Canard Enchaîné?' And Jean Guéhenno had added '*Notre seul journal sérieux:* Le Canard Enchaîné' [Our only serious journal: *Le Canard Enchaîné*].

15  Max Hastings, *Armageddon. The Battle for Germany 1944–45*, Pan Books, London, 2004.

was indeed Paul Deschanel who had fallen from the presidential train, having confused the door to the men's room with the exit door from the carriage.[16]

Critics say that by far the No. 1 reason for mismanagement at EADS/Airbus was political interference by the French government, including the appointment of senior executives unfit for the job with which they were entrusted. A senior vice president of EADS is under investigation for the Clearstream political scandal (see section 6), while the then co-CEO has been accused of (and is under investigation for) manipulating his options based on inside information (more on this in section 5).

Led by second-raters, EADS/Airbus first designed the world's larger aircraft, the A380, for more long-haul civilian passenger flights than ever existed, and then it confronted supposedly unexpected technical problems and delays in deliveries. These suggested that even though the superjumbo A380, a 555-seater aircraft, was not a supersonic craft, it might well become another prestige-only object like Concorde.

It is an irony that the deep troubles of the A380 hit the news 15 months after prime ministers and heads of state from France, Germany, Spain and Britain (which participated in the Airbus consortium but not in EADS management) claimed credit for a European technological 'triumph'. They did so in January 2005 when the big new passenger jet was unveiled in a grand ceremony in Toulouse, France. The bad news which followed on the heels of this champagne party involved not one, but several, issues:

- technical problems,

- manufacturing schedules,

- deliveries and cash flows,

- new equity partners.

Within a few months of aforementioned grandiose event and self-congratulations exchanged by prime ministers and heads of state, Airbus slipped out news of a six-month delay in A380 deliveries. Then in June 2006 it announced a further six-month delay and said it would deliver a mere nine planes in 2007, rather than the promised 25.

---

16  Jean Egen, *Messieurs du Canard*, Stock, Paris, 1973.

Moreover, even that deadline did not hold as new delays were subsequently announced along with a torrent of red ink. The latest rollbacks of production schedules knocked a further €4.8 billion (then $6 billion) off EADS profits and €6.3 billion off revenues between 2006 and 2010. Mismanagement and the government's heavy hand:

- turned a profitable company into financial backwater;

- allowed serious technical problems to develop and left them unattended; and

- ended by eliminating thousands of jobs, in spite of the French and Spanish governments' boasts that they kept equity in EADS as a safeguard for employment.

Officially, the origin of the A380 delays was attributed to the cabling system of the aircraft. As a matter of fact this was a major challenge, given the complexity of a huge airframe and was therefore, something that should have been taken care of as a priority, precisely because of the problems it could have presented some time down the line. Steady design reviews should have kept track of technical progress, with priority given to corrective action.

## 4. Design Incompatibilities can Kill a Project

Technical problems must be taken care of when they are nascent, not after major roadblocks. As it later emerged, the A380 had not one but two cabling systems – one for the fuselage made in French factories and another for the part of the airliner manufactured in Hamburg, Germany. Each used different computer-aided design (CAD) software and coordination was found wanting. As with the origin of the disaster at Three Mile Island, the nuclear plant accident in the US:

- these two halves were using incompatible software; and

- over the years of development the project manager of the A380, boss of Airbus and co-chief executives of EADS had done nothing about this incompatibility.

Simulation is a powerful tool in project management[17] but by all evidence, senior executives of Airbus and EADS got the message that something was wrong only *after* the assembly line put the airframe's parts together and tried to connect them.[18] This happened way down in the production schedule, after the EU prime ministers' celebrations and also after having sold planes that were not deliverable, with the result that airline carriers (the EADS/Airbus clients) asked for damages.

It is inevitable that when a major product and the company itself are in trouble, issues connected to employment pop up, and the number can be large in an enterprise employing 110,000 people. With the heavy hand of the government all over the firm, Jacques Chirac could not even use the *coup* with the Hewlett-Packard (HP) affair to put the blame on somebody else.

The way politicians tackled the latter problem is an instructive example. In late 2005, when Hewlett-Packard decided to reduce its engineering and software presence in France, the then French President blamed the EU bureaucrats for the resulting loss of jobs. The EU Commission was to blame, Chirac said, because it did not care that the American computer company planned to axe a quarter of its French employees – and moreover Brussels did nothing to stop HP, a private firm, from downsizing, which plainly is not its business.

(At the time the EU Executive in Brussels, as well as a number of other EU politicians, answered that the government in Paris found the EU Commission to be a body to kick and a soul to blame. The real reason, some experts suggested, was the French government's failure to make hard decisions about restructuring the French anachronistic labour laws, which led to the HP downsizing. Additionally, a statement from Brussels explained that the EU had no power to intervene in this case.)

Excuses like Brussels' insensitivity to the labour problems of EU's member states had no place in the case of the aeronautics, defence and space industries as the government itself was in the frontline. Following the dismal news of technical glitches which grew to become a headwind, heads rolled both at Airbus and at EADS, its parent company. At the top level, two Frenchmen and the German boss of Airbus lost their jobs. Chopping off heads may be good

---

17  D.N. Chorafas, *Systems and Simulation*, Academic Press, New York, 1965.
18  Rear fuselages made in Hamburg were supposed to arrive in Toulouse with all their wiring ready to plug into the forward parts coming in from factories in north and west France. But in the end the 500km (!) of wiring in the two halves did not match up.

for the gallery but by itself it does not solve technical problems, nor does it advance the new aircraft delivery schedule.

- Quite to the contrary, management was destabilized as the musical chairs continued, and

- the newly appointed boss of Airbus quit because his plan for redressing the company and its production management was rejected as too radical.

Nor was it of any help that the investigators from the French regulatory authority searched the Paris office of EADS, Airbus's parent, looking into the sale of shares by Noël Forgeard in March 2006, before a further delay in the A380 was divulged. The co-chief executive of EADS used an appearance before a French parliamentary committee to defend his position, but investors in EADS continued to call for his removal.

After having detailed his professional career, Forgeard explained to the members of the Finance Committee of the French Parliament that he knew 'all corners of the company'. Henri Emmanuelli, one of the Committee members asked him: 'How is it that, as manager, you did not protect your company and its shareholders?'[19] Noël Forgeard answered: 'Managers and shareholders don't talk to each other'[20] – which should be written in mismanagement books as a new principle.[21]

Emmanuelli had a good reason to ask that question. Not only were the French government's interests harmed, but also from March 2006 some of the major shareholders of EADS wanted to sell their stakes. Britain's BAE Systems, a defence contractor, was one of them, having put its 20 per cent stake in Airbus on the block. But at what price?

- Rothschild, the investment bank, valued BAE's 20 per cent share in Airbus at €2.75 billion (then $3.5 billion), much lower than EADS or BAE Systems itself had expected.

---

19  Probably meaning the government's participation in the firm.
20  *Le Canard Enchaîné*, 5 July 2006.
21  Though personally accountable for the disaster as co-chief executive of EADS responsible for Airbus, Noël Forgeard adamantly refused to go. When he was finally pushed out on 2 July 2006, he insisted in a statement that he had 'no responsibility in the A380 delays' (*Le Canard Enchaîné*, 5 July 2006), as if the CEO did not bear the full responsibility for all of his company's misfortunes.

- With the shock from this low valuation still fresh, BAE planned to conduct a full audit of Airbus, but several analysts suggested this was unwise because there might well be nasty surprises.

The stock market, too, had to digest unfavourable news regarding the aeronautics defence and space industrial giant. Given that Airbus accounts for 70 per cent of sales and 80 per cent of EADS's profits (the balance comes from missiles, helicopters and so on), an educated guestimate by analysts has been that Airbus represents 75 per cent or more of EADS's worth. Therefore, Rothschild's valuation of BAE Systems' 20 per cent share put Airbus's value at €13.75 billion and that of EADS at €18.33 billion ($23.28 billion) at best – which was rather dismal news for shareholders.

## 5. The EADS Shareholders

According to expert opinions, major management troubles at EADS/Airbus started in 2005 when its German and French equity owners clashed in a fierce battle over the company's top jobs. The French government had 15 per cent and Lagardère 7.5 per cent, giving French shareholders 22.5 per cent; Germany's Daimler-Chrysler had another 22.5 per cent, and 5 per cent was held by SEPI, the Spanish government's industrial holding company. The remaining 50 per cent was publicly traded, and it was essentially these shareholders who paid for the sharp dive in the company's stock price.[22]

Since the company's early days in 1999, as far as the different French political parties are concerned, the government share in EADS has been everyone's preoccupation. This was one of the reasons leading to state intervention which weighed heavily, in a negative way, on the company's fortunes. When he was elected president of France, Nicolas Sarkozy put as one of his priorities finding a solution to EADS's management by engineering an agreement between shareholders. The problem was that the government shareholders were not of the same mind.[23]

---

22  The drop in the value of EADS equity after the announcement of A380 delivery delays wiped €5.5 billion (then $7.7 billion) off the stock market valuation of the firm in a single day.

23  It is interesting to note that the policy Ségolène Royal planned to follow with EADS/Airbus was no different. Her plan was to 'stabilize the shareholding of the group, by combining a responsible public shareholder and a reliable private shareholder'. This was, of course, an oxymoron because 'reliable' private shareholders who do only what the government tells them to do are not known to exist.

Matters were made even more complex by the fact that the Franco-German aerospace group has been paralysed by national rivalry and investor discord. During the campaign to the 6 May 2007 French presidential election, both candidates made clear their discontent about the dual-nationality shareholder structure set up under the French socialist government of Lionel Jospin and the German social democratic government of Gerhard Schröder.

Industrial history, however, teaches that it is difficult to change facts *post mortem*. In 1999 EADS was presented as 'a merger of equals' to which both the Germans and the French contributed what was left of their aerospace industry. This was done in a dual effort to create a global entity and cut the subsidies each government paid to its own aerospace enterprise(s).

- If either France or Germany were to leave EADS, they would be relegated to an underdeveloped country as far as aeronautics and space are concerned.

- Living together, however, has proved to be impractical, particularly under Chirac – a time which led to the dual A380 and management fiascos.

Have things changed with Sarkozy? Right after his inauguration, political analysts said that the new French President might not be averse to a wider European solution to the problems posed by the current shareholder structure of EADS. (One change that has, in fact, taken place is significant improvement in the company's management, as we will see in section 8.)

Regarding shareholding, a change had already come under Chirac: the British were *out* (of Airbus) and the Russians were *in* the parent company. Equity-wise EADS was no more the 50–50 Franco-German jewel, with Spain having a minor share. In mid-September 2006 it emerged that a Russian state-owned bank had taken a 5 per cent stake in the Franco-German airframe, missile and aerospace firm, making it the biggest investor in Airbus's parent company outside its 'core' group of shareholders.

At that time, an aide to President Vladimir Putin fuelled speculation about how deep a partnership Russia was seeking with EADS, by implying that the state bank might raise its holding to acquire a blocking stake. In addition, some analysts commented that the EADS equity holding was bought on behalf of a Russian state company set up to coordinate strategy in the country's aerospace industry. Another opinion was that this participation might develop as a second axis in Russian–German relations, particularly if the French tried to push the Germans into being second-class equity owners of EADS.

The Chinese government, too, was interested in getting part of the cake. In late October 2006 Jacques Chirac, the then French President, went to China with a delegation of some 100 French businessmen. Part of the pitch was to sell Airbus planes – at least the smaller ones. This succeeded and the Chinese government signed a big order, but also stipulated that a good deal of manufacturing and the assembly of Airbus would be done in China.

- A new factory had to be built;

- technology transfer was part of the deal; and

- it's a fair bet that years down the line the Chinese aircraft factory will compete with EADS, at *Chinese price level.*

If the Russians and Chinese were newcomers, as equity owners and manufacturing partners respectively, BAE Systems of Britain was not the only shareholder who wanted out. Another party who wanted to lighten its share in EADS was Arnaud Lagardère. Still another vendor was Daimler-Benz, which (at the time) retained 22.5 per cent of EADS equity – equal to that of the French government.

Analysts said that Daimler-Benz wanted to sell at least half its share, which in a depressed market for EADS equity, following the A380 deliveries 'SNAFU', was going to be neither easy nor profitable. By contrast, a state-owned Spanish holding which already controlled little more than 5 per cent of EADS was a buyer.

Spanish ownership was anathema to the Germans not only because the wounds from the E.ON–Endesa affair (Chapter 10) were still fresh, but also because it was tantamount to being cut off from one of the most dynamic industrial sectors which holds the keys to future competitiveness. Instead, the German government and German industry offered to pick up any Daimler equity being sold, in order to maintain the 50–50 balance with the French.

At the same time, EADS/Airbus needed cash. Having spent plenty of capital on the A380, mother and daughter were short of money for the development of the A350, planned as an answer to Boeing's 787 Dreamliner (which was originally presented as the American airframer's response to the A380). Experts bet that:

- Jim McNerney, the EU competition commissioner, would not approve a reimbursable French government loan which is against WTO accords; and

- Lagardère and Daimler would not participate to a capital increase since they wanted to reduce their shareholding.

The choice of EADS's major equity holders was that Airbus should issue bonds guaranteed by the French government, which had a 15 per cent share in the firm, but the Ministry of Finance refused to do so. An option which came under examination was to have new owners in EADS, like the investment funds of Qatar and Dubai,[24] while the Russian government also signalled that it was ready to strengthen its equity in the European aeronautics firm.

In the end, the French government, already a major equity holder in EADS, put the Caisse des Dépôts et Consignations (CDC, Chapter 10) to buy a 2.5 per cent share in EADS, in violation of its statutory limits. CDC bought half of Lagardère share (altogether amounting to 7.5 per cent of EADS equity). The German government was rumoured to have something similar in mind for part of Daimler's equity, but with taxpayers' funds from state governments.

In the end, the German government organized a special consortium to take up the 7.5 per cent share in EADS being sold by Daimler. The consortium included two German states with Airbus factories and a state-owned bank, as well as several private parties, and it helped to ensure parity between French and German shareholdings in EADS. Presumably, some experts said, this was part of an effort to protect most of Airbus's 29,000 German workers and not only to safeguard the German share in the big aerospace firm.

Resolving the EADS/Airbus shareholding issues was crucial because, as Sarkozy had correctly stated in his election campaign, EADS needed to recover its 'operational serenity'. This was a sort of recognition that EADS had, in the past, suffered from too much political intervention, and a new management had to take over with clearly defined lines of:

- authority and

---

24  *Challenges*, No. 58, 30 November 2006, 12–17.

- responsibility.

For several years there was, in fact, a sort of management warfare between German and French shareholders and executives as if to show how 'harmoniously' cross-border EU companies can work. A long-term objective of the French government was to have one CEO for EADS rather than two – and appoint, of course, someone French to this position. Noël Forgeard was supposed to do that, but encountered headwinds because, correctly, the German co-owners wanted to keep control of their investment rather than abdicate their responsibilities.

It does not come as a surprise that in an environment where infighting and poor leadership were the rule, strategic decisions like future development projects, which are integral part of better governance, were given little or no attention. Several experts expressed the opinion that while EADS and its subsidiary, Airbus, did well when development work kept within pre-established confines of aircraft designs which competed head-on with Boeing,

- weak management did not allow advanced engineering projects to flourish and,

- as should have been expected way ahead of time, this led to most regrettable results.

Not only did R&D priorities and schedules fall behind but the financial analysis and P&L projections were also found wanting. Orders for the new airliner were stuck at around 160, and each delay pushed up the number needed for break-even from the original figure of 250. The company was under stress, and experts commented that if Airbus did nothing to get out of the tunnel, its profit margin would be squeezed to 4 per cent and it would be destroying capital. (It's a safe bet that an advanced technology outfit could be competitive only with a margin of 10 per cent, at least.)

## 6. Options, Shares and AMF's Investigation

High-handed mismanagement was not the only thing for which those who brought Airbus and EADS at the edge of the precipice were to blame. There has also been lust and greed. After he sold his options for good profit while EADS's equity was still high, Noël Forgeard, then co-chief executive of EADS, claimed that Airbus (where he was previously CEO), was not late in admitting its A380 production problems. Hence, he sold his options in good faith.

To the contrary, informed sources commented that it took Airbus two months to make the technical troubles public. Forgeard, a political appointment, was accused of having used inside information when he sold his options well before the delays became public knowledge and the company's equity crashed. There has been some other misinformation, too.

- Forgeard stated in different interviews that the relationship between Airbus and EADS was completely transparent.

- But people who knew how the company worked suggested that, by contrast, Airbus was run as a semi-autonomous fief.

For its part, the Autorité des Marchés Financiers (AMF), the French regulator of stock exchange operations, was busy investigating the equity sales. Plenty of attention fell on options sales by Noël Forgeard, from which he made €8.5 million ($11.4 million). By mid-May 2007, AMF's hearings also involved EADS deputy chief executive, Jean-Paul Gut, former EADS co-chairman and Manfred Bischoff, another company executive was to be questioned, as well as Arnaud Lagardère (who said he had no idea about the A380 production problems and encouraged the AMF to investigate the stock sales).[25]

This action by the French regulator as part of an investigation into alleged insider trading got favourable reviews in the French press. The investigation focused on the sale of millions of euros-worth of EADS options and shares by top executives in March and April 2006, as well as on their timing – weeks before the company announced major delays to the superjumbo A380 which sent the stock price tumbling 26 per cent in one day.

In a parallel action, Paris prosecutors opened a preliminary inquiry into whether Forgeard's severance package constituted misappropriation of public funds, based on a complaint by an EADS shareholder. On 3 October 2007, a report by the Autorité des Marchés Financiers revealed that not just Noel Forgeard, and the aforementioned small group of people, but a total of 21 top executives of the aerospace firm allegedly used insider trading information for profits – selling their stock a short well before the EADS equity crashed.

---

25  *International Herald Tribune*, 24 May 2007.

For once, the French government asked for transparency. 'I want to know, at the end of the inquiry, what the state's responsibility was in the affair,' said Nicolas Sarkozy in mid-October 2007, as investigators into possible insider-trading at EADS turned to the state's own role.[26] At issue were two questions:

- When executives at EADS exercised stock options in November 2005 and March 2006, did they know about delays in the A380 which emerged in public only in June 2006?

- Did the government know about these troubles when in April 2006 the Caisse des Dépôts et Consignations helped Lagardère to offload part of its 7.5 per cent stake in EADS, landing CDC with a big loss?

Part of the second question derives from the fact that in January 2006, under Chirac's presidency, the Agency for State Shareholdings had advised Thierry Breton, the then finance minister, to reduce the French state's stake in EADS as the company would soon enter a zone of turbulence.

With the investigators' attention focusing on what he did or did not know, Breton said he knew nothing about A380's delays, also denying influencing or even knowing about the CDC's plans. However, if Breton 'did not know', what about Chirac?[27]

These questions, and the answers they should be receiving, were crucial because the conflict of interest confronting EADS/Airbus might also pop up in other state-run enterprises. As 2007 had come to a close, just prior to putting taxpayers' money into the big banks' treasuries because of the deep economic crisis (but after Northern Rock), France was leading the pack in terms of the size of state-owned companies whose combined weight was nearly 4.5 per cent of French GDP.[28]

(Using the same criteria regarding state-owned enterprises in relation to the country's GDP, the French were followed by the Italians at 3.6 per cent (in spite of the Mussolini legacy with IRI); the Germans, 3.1 per cent; Dutch,

---

26  *The Economist*, 13 October 2007.
27  Augustin de Romanet, who is now the CDC's director-general, was at that time a civil servant at the Elysée (*The Economist*, 13 October 2007).
28  With a value of about $400 billion prior to the 2008 market crash.

2.8 per cent; and Spanish, 2.6 per cent. The British state-owned enterprise share to GDP was somewhat below 2 per cent, but the Labour government was catching up fast with its sprint into the big bank nationalizations arena.)

As far as the insider trading investigation into the EADS options and share scandal was concerned, results did not take too long to become public. In April 2008 the Autorité des Marchés Financiers confirmed in the conclusion of a preliminary report that it had found evidence of massive insider dealing by 17 senior EADS executives and two core shareholders of the airframer: Lagadère and Daimler.

The AMF alleged that executives and shareholders sold equity in late 2005/ early 2006 in the knowledge that the 380 superjumbo was in deep trouble. One interesting hindsight in connection to this case of insider trading has been that the list of top executives of EADS, which extended beyond Noël Forgeard and Jean-Paul Gut (a former chief operating officer of EADS), had made a total of €20 million (then $32 million) from their dealings – a trifle compared to similar illegal profits in the US.

## 7. The Clearstream²⁹ Affair³⁰

French entrepreneurs who are worth their salt can see very well the pitfalls embedded in the different forms of statism, Colbertism and economic nationalism. A clear-eyed entrepreneur is Henri de Castries, CEO of AXA, the French insurance company. After the Danone case, where Pepsi Cola was fenced off from Danone's acquisition, de Castries warned that, as economic history has demonstrated, protectionism is based on an *archaic view of the world*.³¹ But nobody seems to have been listening on the government's side.

Many other French businesspeople, too, criticized the government's industrial policy asymmetry. They also pointed out that while they fight to keep other European Union companies, as well as American and Asians, from acquiring French firms, the authorities try to hold on what French companies acquired abroad – even if this may no more make sense because conditions have

---

29  Originally known as Cedel, and currently owned by the Deutsche Börse, Clearstream is a clearer of debt instruments with about 45 per cent of global market, the balance controlled by J.P. Morgan's Euroclear. Clearstream also has banking activities.

30  At the end of a long process, which created a great deal of press coverage and public excitement, everything has been whitewashed with a detergent more powerful than Tide. With some minor reprimands, which were the exception, the defendants have been acquitted.

31  *The Economist*, 25 March 2006.

changed either in the country where the acquisition was made or in the global market. A case in point is Alcatel-Lucent. Political interference in business:

- has led to business misjudgement and

- not only to the options, shares and other internal trading scandals.

When the Clearstream scandal broke out in 2006, it shook the French political system. From the start, many people have been obsessed by the identity of *le corbeau* (the crow) who was at the origin of denunciations. Only slowly was it revealed that the anonymous informer was Jean-Louis Gergorin, a top executive of EADS who, it was rumoured, was returning political favours he had received under Villepin, the then prime minister.

Gergorin had allegedly tried to link important politicians, including Nicolas Sarkozy, then Interior Minister and leader of the centre-right UMP party, to secret bank accounts in Luxembourg's Clearstream. The French media made the connection in no time, because Gergorin was reported to be a close confidant of Dominique de Villepin, Sarkozy's arch-rival. This raised the political stakes in the Clearstream affair, apart from highlighting long-standing and unhealthy connections between:

- the French government and

- top levels of French business.

At the eye of the smear campaign's storm was a fake list of public figures (anonymously leaked to a French judge in 2004) who allegedly held accounts at Luxembourg-based Clearstream, linked to kickbacks on the sale of French frigates to Taiwan in 1991. Nicolas Sarkozy, a rival of Villepin for the succession to Chirac, was one of the names on the list that was ruled bogus:

- Two judges began investigating the false accusations and

- in 2006 Sarkozy became a civil plaintiff in the case.

To get to the bottom of a complex plot, the judges put many people under formal investigation. They included Jean-Louis Gergorin and Imad Lahoud (who also worked for EADS), with Villepin already heard, first as a witness and then under formal investigation. People who knew what they were talking about said that Gergorin's has been a suicidal mission, with the French Prime Minister badly wounded by Clearstream. Additionally, several political commentators suggested that behind Villepin's role in this affair was Chirac, then President of the Republic.

If so, it backfired. Accounts published in the press revealed that General Philippe Rondot, the former chief of French espionage who was asked by Villepin (while he was Foreign Minister) to lead the Clearstream investigation, deposited to the judges that Chirac had a secret account of Francs 300 million ($57 million) in Japan.[32] In addition, apart from the fallout of the scandal and the fact that it distracts the government's attention from other matters, French business leaders were also concerned by the fact that Jacques Chirac and Villepin's government, although nominally conservative:

- were increasingly embracing the rhetoric of the anti-globalization left; and

- were dragging their feet in needed reforms, given that whatever was carried out during the Chirac years had been largely cosmetic.

Critics said that Chirac and his Prime Minister were not renouncing the concept of the *welfare state*; they were only trying to strengthen it by adding that of the *welfare company* – an enterprise that is ruinously generous to its employees and even uses them as agents in political scandals against all economic and commercial logic.

The Clearstream affair also proved to have long legs. Though it has not yet reached its judicial end and therefore the culpability of Chirac, Villepin, Gergorin and their presumed accomplices has not been proven beyond doubt so far, the news coming to the public eye as the judicial examination proceeds make interesting reading.

Among other things, the documents in the hands of the *juges d'instruction* (investigating judges) include references to Chirac's account at the Tokyo Sowa bank which he allegedly opened in the mid-1990s as well as an investment of $1 billion to be made in France by Shoichi Osada, a Japanese banker and friend of Chirac.[33] Published reports also indicate that in September 2001 the French president called General Rondot and asked him to clean up the files, but all

---

32  *Le Canard Enchaîné*, 10 May 2006.
33  *Le Canard Enchaîné*, 23 May 2007.

that information was already registered in the archives of the secret service and stayed put.[34]

'Is the judicial trail closing in on France's former president, Jacques Chirac?' asked an article in *The Economist*, after the investigation into the Clearstream affair took a new turn when Dominique de Villepin, confirmed that he had been summoned on 27 July 2007 to meet two investigating judges who may put him under formal investigation.[35]

Chirac's position has become critical because his presidential immunity expired in June 2007 and the two Clearstream judges have requested a hearing with him as a witness. But his lawyer told Europe 1 radio that he had refused, arguing that the constitution states that '[t]he President of the Republic shall incur no liability by reason of acts carried out in this official capacity'.

In the meantime, the Clearstream affair is going through turns and twists as judicial control forbids Villepin talking to his former boss, Jacques Chirac, as the judges seem convinced that both men have played a role in this business.[36] Nor is the press ready to let go in conveying to its readers the latest developments.

In December 2008, for example, Villepin struck back, saying that he has been unfairly singled out because of the long-standing rivalry between himself and Sarkozy. The former Prime Minister insisted that his 'innocence in this affair is total' and complained of 'a media lynching'.[37] He has also complained to the Conseil d'Etat, France's highest administrative court.

This case too, added up (at least so far) to nothing. In early 2010, the lower court acquitted Villepin due to a lack of unshakeable evidence, although it condemned the two people who had manipulated the records. The affair is, however, far from being closed as the Attorney General has appealed the acquittal decision.

---

34  Evidence found in deleted files retrieved from a computer belonging to General Rondot includes, according to leaks in the French press, notes of the General's conversations with Lahoud, who told him that 'Jean-Louis Gergorin received instructions from Dominique de Villepin, themselves formulated by the President of the Republic, to denounce Nicolas Sarkozy'.

35  *The Economist*, 14 July 2007.

36  *Le Canard Enchaîné*, 1 August 2007.

37  *The Economist*, 6 December 2008.

## 8. A New Management Takes Over at EADS

In mid-July 2007 EADS announced that it was streamlining its management structure. It was time for a new departure after a couple of tough years during which the European aerospace and defence company was hampered by meddling politicians in France and Germany and the dual-management structure was criticized by many for being unwieldy.

- Louis Gallois, who was co-CEO for a short time, became EADS's sole chief executive.[38]

- Tom Enders, who was EADS's other co-chief executive, became head of Airbus.

While the streamlining of management structure was finally taking place, some slimming down had already been decided by the previous administration when, in March 2007, it unveiled a long-awaited restructuring plan (which had been held up by last-minute negotiations between France and Germany). Some 10,000 jobs were to go over four years, split between Airbus and its contractors.[39]

The announcement of job cuts led to labour union protests both in France and in Germany, somewhat mellowed by the fact that EADS had a dismal year in 2006 when it reported that its net income had plunged by 94 per cent, to €99 million ($125 million). The turmoil in aircraft production at Airbus and a weak dollar were blamed for Airbus's first-ever operating loss.

As a good manager, Louis Gallois was trying to force EADS and Airbus to face a painful reality, even before becoming the parent company's single CEO. Under the plans he announced back in March 2007, half of the workforce at Saint-Nazaire Villeolant in Brittany, which makes components for fuselages, would take early retirement. Airbus was also aiming to increase its manufacturing productivity by 16 per cent by 2010. According to Gallois:

- engineering productivity should improve by 15 per cent and

---

38  And until then, the boss of SNCF the French state-owned railroad company.
39  To win backing for the plan in France, where outraged unions called for industrial action, final assembly of the A350 XWB was to be exclusively based in Toulouse, but Germany won increased production of the bestselling A320 narrow-bodied aircraft.

- aircraft development cycles had to come down from seven-and-a-half to six years.

For the A350, Airbus would outsource 50 per cent of the airframe structure, up from 25 per cent on previous programmes, in order to spread risk and gain access to outside capital and engineering resources. Like Boeing with the 787 Dreamliner, Airbus was seeking to become more:

- the systems architect and integrator and

- the assembling entity rather than one pursuing vertically integrated manufacturing.

The Gallois plan also aimed to eventually reduce the number of its manufacturing sites across Europe from 17 to 10 or 11, as part of a longer-term transformation of its engineering and manufacturing operations, targeting an increase in the firm's competitiveness against US rival Boeing, as well as countering the impact of the decline in the value of the dollar.

The EADS CEO estimated that each 10 cent rise in the euro exchange value costs Airbus €1 billion, as Airbus makes 76 per cent of its purchases within Europe, but generates over 60 per cent of its sales elsewhere. Hence the plan to shift some production abroad, which was looked down on by the French as *delocalization*.

With China being a low-cost producer, Airbus planned to open an assembly line for the single-aisle A320 in China, followed by a second site for making composite components. The conversion of the A320 passenger aircraft into a cargo variant was scheduled to take place in Russia, which will also get 5 per cent of the work on the new A350.

The new management of Airbus also revealed that it was in talks with Japanese companies to take on about 5 per cent of the A350 programme. Another plan called for new aircraft, like the A320's successor, to be made almost entirely outside Euroland.

At least some of the Airbus new game plan was influenced by results obtained by Boeing which, in the course of the last few years, had learnt how to outsource much of the work and associated business risk on new aircraft to suppliers in Italy, China and Japan. Boeing had also become more efficient by streamlining its final-assembly plant in Seattle.

The scheduled changes were no child's play because the model of a revamped in-house manufacturing structure stood in contrast to the current Airbus factories scattered over France, Germany, Spain and Britain – with one of the reasons being political. Because it depends heavily on government loans to launch new designs, the politicians have a powerful weapon with which to defend jobs in their fief.

This conflict between sound governance and meddling by politicians came up repeatedly at meetings between French and German officials but, until 2007, there were scant results in terms of measures needed to increase EADS/Airbus competitiveness. Both the fear that Airbus may be losing its market touch and new political leadership in France and Germany gave the green light for change.

The results did not take long to start showing. At the Bourget airframe industry show of mid- to late June 2007 Airbus announced a bumper crop of new aircraft orders. Louis Gallois claimed that the European manufacturer was now 'back in business', but he also seemed much more circumspect during meetings with European government ministers, acknowledging that Airbus, 'is in the worst state it has ever been'.[40]

The reason for the latter statement is that, even with new leadership, most of the problems undermining Airbus did not lift over the short term. Apart from financial woes, national rivalries continued to hamper much-needed industrial restructuring to enable Airbus to manufacture aircraft more competitively, and there has also been the question of how much could or should be manufactured abroad.

On 9 September 2008 Louis Gallois announced that, to reduce expenses by €1.4 billion ($1.80 billion), Airbus would build a factory in Tunisia and shift work there – while closing a plant near Bristol and selling it to GKN. This raised questions about quality and reliability and also came at a time when the euro, a *bête noir* of EADS, was falling against the dollar while rising significantly against the pound.

---

40   *Financial Times*, 20 June 2007.

Airbus and EADS also announced that they would expand their activity in India because of the supply of good engineering talent there and that factories in Mexico were a possibility. As for the production of A320s in China, it was going ahead because of the need, costs aside, to be close to that huge market.

According to some experts, without radically downsizing its cost base, Airbus may find itself in the paradoxical situation in which the more aircraft it sells, the more money it loses. There exactly lies the dilemma. Relying on Europe for 76 per cent of production is a recipe for financial disaster, but offshoring to lower-cost countries implies that the governments involved in Airbus will be prepared to sacrifice 'national jobs' – which is tough under current depressing economic conditions.

On the side of good news for Airbus was the fact that, as a 14 January 2009 company announcement had it, the A350 long-haul airliner was on track for first delivery in mid-2013. In the words of Fabrice Brégier, the Airbus chief operating officer: 'We know it is a challenge. We will face additional problems, but we have changed the mindset of our people.'[41] Optimism about the A350 was in stark contrast to the company's experience with the A380. *If* indeed Airbus could face the challenge and defy the sceptics, *then* it would close the competitive gap with the 787 of rival Boeing.

Other initiatives, however, hit the skids. EADS efforts to recoup up to €1.4 billion ($2 billion) in extra costs for developing the Airbus A400M were rejected.[42] Franz Josef Jung, Germany's Defence Minister, turned down a written request for discussions about reducing the penalties that the company has to pay a seven-nation consortium for delayed delivery of the military transport aircraft.

The aforementioned reply from Berlin came on the heels of a decision in Washington to review, and probably revise, a previous procurement decision which had chosen the A400M as the next-generation big military transport

---

41  *Financial Times*, 15 January 2009
42  One of the comments made at galleyproofing level (February 2010) was that the A400M has now flown. The answer is *jein* (a composite of the German words 'ja' (yes) and 'nein' (no). It is not enough that a plane passes a test to really 'fly'.
    In the mid-1960s I was in a meeting with engineers of British Aircraft Corp, near Bath (which has by now disappeared into BAE Systems, unfortunately for Britain). I asked 'When is Concorde going to fly?' One of the British engineers answered 'It is never going to fly, because it is loaded with unnecessary costs.' The same is true with the Airbus A400M – which is another white elephant.

refuelling plane, against a bid by Boeing. This matter is under review, and political pressures are believed to have been behind this change of heart.

On the financial front, the good news for EADS shareholders and the company's new management was that at end of November 2008 it reported a net profit of €679 million ($1 billion) in the third quarter, compared with a loss of €776 million a year earlier. This was helped by the rise of the dollar, which led to a revaluation of unprofitable contracts.

There was also good news for Boeing, which reached a tentative agreement with its engineers' union, which was threatening to go on strike. Boeing's commercial aeroplane units had already endured a strike by union machinists that lasted 58 days and ended in early November 2008, having cost the company a great deal of money and also having led to delays in the delivery of planes to the airlines. All this happened in the midst of a severe global economic crisis. Sometimes labour unions seem to live on a tralala planet.

The bad news for EADS came in April 2009 when it was officially announced that the Airbus A400M military transport was not only three years late but also €2 billion over budget. Talks to decide its fate became a game of high political stakes played by OCCAR – the organization founded a dozen years earlier to manage collaborative military projects on behalf of EU member governments. EADS and the four countries who have collectively placed 161 of the 192 orders for the A400M are not on the same wavelength.

- *If* agreement cannot be reached on how to continue with the €20 billion project,

- *then* EADS will have to return €5.7 billion in advance payments, which represents more than half its available cash.

The failure of Airbus to meet a commitment to have flown the A400M by the end of March 2009 gave customers the right to cancel their orders. But since three of the four governments are also EADS shareholders, they worked out an agreement to a three-month moratorium, during which time an attempt will be made to salvage the project. Available evidence, however, goes the opposite way, and this also means that, in the middle of a global crisis, up to 40,000 jobs are at stake.

# PART 4

# *The Decline of the Atlantic Alliance*

# Useful as Feathers on a Fish

## 1. The *Déclinisme* of NATO

The North Atlantic Treaty Organization was created with the goal of providing an American-led defence against what was perceived as the Soviet menace to Western Europe. The immediate post-World War II years were characterized by great uncertainty about what follows the division of Europe. The Korean War, however, signalled the first shift in emphasis from Old Europe to New Asia.

As a brief reminder of events which took place at that time, in March 1947 Britain and France signed an agreement of mutual military cooperation soon joined by Belgium, the Netherlands and Luxembourg. With the Cold War scare, a dialogue with America and Canada was instrumental in establishing an Atlantic Alliance formalized on 4 April 1949,[1] with the North Atlantic Treaty Organization (NATO) being its military structure.[2]

History teaches, nevertheless, that no alliances last forever. Over the years, and most particularly during the last two decades of NATO's existence, many things have changed: it expanded in membership but cohesion and strength went the opposite way. Today there are 26 states and mini-states under NATO's umbrella, but at the same time:

- there exists no clear goal about what this assembly of states stands for; and

- the leading nations in its membership are at odds over the future role of the alliance.

---

1   Joined by West Germany, in 1955.
2   NATO's Article 5 requires mutual defence assistance in case of an attack on the territory of a member state.

In an article published for the European Council on foreign relations, Nick Witney of the British Foreign and Commonwealth Office, said flatly that 'NATO is dying'. It should have disappeared when the Soviet Union collapsed but, because of the situation in the Balkans in the 1990s, 11 September 2001 and the Afghanistan War, it has been kept in business. But the idea of NATO with a US leadership and a European followership is no longer accepted. The whole concept of having a partnership between NATO and the European Union is a waste of breath.[3]

The original *raison d'être* of the alliance, US protection against a possible though unlikely rolling of Soviet tanks to Frankfurt and Paris, is long gone. It will soon be two decades since the Soviet Union disappeared. Today's Russia accuses America of misusing NATO territory to advance its own missile defence and this is far from being blue sky.

Within NATO different opinions are now heard. The Americans were taken aback when Nicolas Sarkozy, the French President, declared that their planned anti-missile shield, to be deployed in the Czech Republic and Poland, would 'bring nothing to European security'. And he is also advancing an idea, backed by the Russians, to hold a summit with the aim to rethink Europe's economic and security architecture.[4]

Important in this connection is the fact that Sarkozy is pro-American, particularly when his policies are compared with those of his predecessor Jacques Chirac. He has sent extra troops to join NATO's force in Afghanistan, and plans to return France to NATO's integrated military command when he co-hosts the alliance's sixtieth anniversary meeting in April 2009.

But with all good intentions kept in perspective, the fact remains that, terrorism aside, the themes which are in the minds of most nations are financial, economic and energy-related (Chapter 13) rather than territorial. A crucial problem is terrorism. Among other preoccupations, the world's leading industrialized states struggle to set up international bodies that will regulate everything:

- from Internet protocols

- to trade and genetic manipulation of food.

---

3    EIR, 26 December 2008.
4    *The Economist*, 20 December 2008.

There exists, furthermore, a plethora of memberships and loose alliances. The lists of nations who are members of the European Union and of NATO are very similar. The EU list reads: Austria, Belgium, Britain, Bulgaria, Cyprus, the Czech Republic, Denmark, Estonia, Finland, France, Germany, Greece, the Netherlands, Hungary, Ireland, Italy, Latvia, Lithuania, Luxembourg, Malta, Poland, Portugal, Romania, Slovakia, Slovenia, Spain, Sweden – 27 altogether.

Five of these – Austria, Finland, Ireland, Cyprus and Malta – are not NATO members. But Canada, Iceland, Norway and Turkey are, bringing NATO membership to 26 – a large number which is difficult to manage as it includes nations with quite diverse aims and independent policy-making. Even in the domain of military affairs, the 26 have:

- incompatible weapons systems;

- very different training methods;

- a plethora of languages;

- highly diverse cultures; and

- conflicting national interests.[5]

It does not take a genius to appreciate that because of these differences NATO is bound to be ineffectual. References made to 'common causes' are wrongly labelled, while internal divergences are real. An added fact is that *déclinisme* – the modern way of fading away brought to the reader's attention in Chapter 4 – is contagious and NATO caught it too.

The last two decades have reinforced the European nationalists ranks, while in the 1960s France was their only standard-bearer. Self-interest has taken the upper ground not only among the original EU members of the Alliance, but also in the new accession countries in Eastern Europe. The general trend now is towards self-interest even if this desire for national independence often parallels the desire for membership in larger groups. It is indeed ironic that, like the European Union,

- the more NATO expanded its list of member states,

---

5    Those characterizing Greece, Turkey and Bulgaria – as an example.

- the looser have become the bonds holding them together.

Increasingly, each NATO member looks after its own objectives, and the affinity which at early times used to bind them together is disappearing. The pros say that doomsayers who predicted that, with the demise of the Soviet Union, NATO would lose its *raison d'être* and vanish like the Warsaw Pact, and before it the Baghdad Pact, were wrong. As proof, they add that 18 years after the Berlin Wall came down, NATO is still alive. Yes, NATO is still alive, but it is not well.

Military misfortunes in Afghanistan (a project under United Nations mandate, section 4) documents this statement about NATO being in decline[6] – and so does the angry reaction of several of its members to the Iraq adventure. The late November 2006 meeting in Riga, Latvia, of the Alliance's top leaders and its cohorts, provided an irrefutable example of loose ties. That was a heads of state meeting which faced awkward questions about the future and plenty of recriminations over Iraq. The meeting ended with NATO leaders

- finding no unity of purpose and

- reaching no agreement on overcoming the weaknesses of the mission in Afghanistan.

As if to make the situation worse, a fortnight later (on 17 December 2006) the French defence minister flew to Kabul to announce that her government had unilaterally decided to end the participation of its special forces contingent to the NATO force in Afghanistan. Instead of bringing the personnel up to the level needed to win, its member states tore it down as if they supported the Taliban. (This was reversed by Sarkozy when he became president of the French Republic, but memories of it were not erased.)

Although they have 2.4 million men and women under arms, NATO's European members pretend to be unable to meet requests for meagre contingents of soldiers to make up a reserve for the Afghan mission – numbers so small that they mean nothing either way. This problem of personnel and

---

6    See also Lawrence S. Kaplan, *NATO Divided, NATO United: The Evolution of an Alliance*, Praeger, Westport, 2004; Carl Cavanagh Hodge, *Atlanticism for a New Century, The Rise, Triumph and Decline of NATO*, Prentice Hall, Upper Saddle River, 2004; Kenneth W. Thompson (ed.), *NATO Expansion*, University Press of America, Lanham, 1998; Jan Willem Honig, *NATO: An Institution under Threat*, Westview Press, Boulder, 1991.

firepower is made worse by the countless restrictions placed by governments on:

- what their contingents on the ground can do;

- where they can go to face the Taliban; and

- what equipment, such as helicopters and other gear, they may share.

The Americans, British and Dutch have put their troops in the forefront in southern Afghanistan, the Taliban's heartland. The Canadians, too, headed NATO's assault on entrenched insurgents outside Kandahar (section 4). But the French, Italians and Spanish, among others, chose to work in what used to be safer places – but because the fortunes of war have turned against NATO they are no longer safe. Bluntly stated:

- *if* forces under the NATO commander refuse to be deployed as he judges to be necessary;

- *then*, NATO is a label without substance; the Alliance may still be around in name but it is only a shadow of what it was in the past.

It does not need to be explained to heads of state that the commander of a military operation is the real decision-maker, however much he might consult others. Unwillingness to perform by different members means that the organization has lost its purpose and this is equally true whether we talk of NATO or of the European Union.

## 2. Atlantic Alliance and Institutional Crisis

The fact that NATO has lost its bearings is no surprise. Everything changes and we never face the same conditions twice, as Heraclitos, an old Greek sage, once suggested. The notion of a 'permanent security institution' modelled along the lines of World War II is not just obsolete, it is against any good sense. All alliances are dispensable.

- When their scope fades and their time is gone, they become impediments that inhibit creative strategic thinking.

- There is simply no logic for deploying troops and retaining a network of World War II model bases in countries that face a challenge totally different from the one NATO continues to provide.

The first institutional crisis came in 1958 when French President Charles de Gaulle, partly for nationalistic reasons and partly because of contesting the special relationship between America and Britain on top of NATO's political command structure, sent a memorandum to President Eisenhower and Prime Minister Macmillan in 1958. In it, he asked for the creation of a tripartite directorate that would put France on an equal footing with the United States and Britain. Dissatisfied with the answer:

- France first started building its own independent defence capability; and

- in 1959, de Gaulle withdrew the country's Mediterranean fleet from NATO command, banning the stationing of foreign nuclear weapons on its soil.

The US Sixth Fleet left Villefranche-sur-Mer for Naples (in 1962).[7] The weaponry was transferred to Germany, and France developed its own nuclear *force de frappe*. The French nuclear weapon was tested in 1960 in the desert of Algeria and it became operational in 1964.

- In 1966, the NATO headquarters moved from Paris to Brussels;[8] and

- the Supreme Headquarters of Allied Powers Europe (SHAPE) relocated to Casteau in Belgium.

A behind-the-scenes continuing disagreement is that of military budgets. Largely for political reasons, EU member states cannot have large increases in defence spending. There are other priorities, dictated by the welfare state, the unemployed and aging populations; there is, moreover, a lack of a visible military threat. From 2001 to 2007 Britain, France and Spain spent more than 3 per cent of their gross domestic product on defence. But Italy spent 1.5 per cent,

---

7   When all French armed forces were removed from NATO's integrated command and all non-French NATO troops were asked to leave French soil.

8   During the 1995 Balkan crisis, President Jacques Chirac renewed basic French coordination with NATO's Military Committee and agreed to 'insert' some French liaison officers into SHAPE.

and the defence budget of Germany declined. Besides that, it is not at all clear where the defence money should go.

- Taken together, the 27 EU countries have nearly 2 million people in their armed forces, of whom 400,000 are conscripts;

- but both within and outside NATO they have assumed many commitments, with the result that their capacity is overstretched.

To make matters worse, these commitments are of an old era when everyone knows that the revolution in military technology is, at heart, a revolution in the use of space. America's supremacy is made possible by this major switch, with technology playing a core role – a switch that no EU country is well positioned to match.

Operational costs have also been one of the handicaps, particularly for the smaller member countries. When he was NATO's commander, General James Jones[9] said that the policy that each national contingent should pay its own way – known as *costs lie where they fall* – was a big disincentive for many member countries. Jones correctly thought that several members:

- held back for fear that they would bear the cost of an expensive operation; and

- wanted many of the expenses to be paid jointly by all the allies.[10]

Even if the issue of 'who pays what' is left aside, there are other reasons for the *déclinisme* of NATO, their common ground being discord over policies and a sort of unusual care (for military operations) about casualties. Stalin once said that a single death is a tragedy; a million deaths is a statistic. What made the Riga meeting special is that, as distinct from Iraq, there should have been no quarrel about the mission in Afghanistan. NATO is in the country under UN mandate. At least theoretically:

- it is operating in defence and

- it is doing so at the behest of an elected government.

---

9   Currently chief of homeland security in the Obama administration.
10  *The Economist*, 25 November 2006.

In practice, there is little dispute about the fact that the stakes are high. Failure would encourage jihadists around the world; it would bring back to power the hardline Talibans and, with them, al-Qaeda, giving the message to radical Islamists that the West is weak and indecisive when challenged. The parallels are disquieting, because that's precisely what emboldened Hitler and the Nazis in 1938.

If NATO fails in its mission in Afghanistan, as becomes increasingly likely, the fundamentalists will have the proof that Western democracies, supposed to constitute the main body of NATO, are not serious about defending themselves and their freedoms. As an after-effect, the next step would be to deprive them of oil. Iran can do so permanently just by closing the Strait of Hormuz. Iran, however, is another cornerstone issue where the main NATO members don't see eye-to-eye.

Who says 'Iran' unavoidably also brings to mind its nuclear threat – a subject on which NATO's members are far from having the same views, let alone a common plan on how to meet that challenge. The impotence of NATO deciding what to do about Iran's nuclear weapon finds a parallel with the position of the International Atomic Energy Agency (IAEA) and the United Nations.

It is the IAEA's job to assure that countries abide by the Nuclear Non-Proliferation Treaty (NPR), with all five official nuclear weapons states now signed up to an Additional Protocol. A list of tough safeguards was agreed in 1997. Instead of just mandating checks on declared material, the new rules let inspectors go in at shorter notice, give them more access to information and let them search more widely, with better techniques. The trouble is:

- IAEA is not overeager to apply the freedoms of action which it got;

- the United Nations Security Council is totally disunited in deciding what to do with Iran; and

- NATO is simply looking the other way, as doubts persist among its members on the need for action, some disagreeing that Iran has replaced the Soviet Union as the Alliance's 'salient problem'.

Other institutional crises may have not hit the headlines, but their existence leaves no doubt that decade after decade NATO's impact has waned. An example of self-created damage has been its impact in the Balkans, where its unwarranted meddling in the collapse of former Yugoslavia moved the area backwards toward sectarian nationalism, flawed elections, lawless economics and politics corroded by corruption and cronyism.[11] At one time it might have been possible to leave the Balkan states to take care of their own problems, but now they spill over the region's borders to affect the whole continent of Europe. They also have global geopolitical consequences.

To make matters even worse, though they share a lot of the same member states (section 1), instead of coming together the EU and NATO are squabbling and putting their own ill-defined interests ahead of a common policy. This often happens when national governments disagree with each other. Moreover, the lack of common goals, like defence against Soviet threat in the 1940s and 1950s make convergence of opinion questionable at best.

Charles de Gaulle might have been the first to look at NATO as a broken model in need of restructuring. At that time he was in a minority of one, but today this view is becoming mainstream in Western Europe – in a wave fed by the not-so-brilliant NATO insistence eventually to place missiles with nuclear warheads on the European continent. Military reverses in Afghanistan have further damaged NATO's image.

There is, moreover, a difference between NATO placing missiles in Poland and the United States staying in South Korea, because the next big challenge will probably come from Asia, though not necessarily from North Korea (whose problem is famine rather than territorial hunger). This does not mean that China is the source of worry – by all evidence it is not. Quite the opposite; China, too, may eventually face a fundamentalist Moslem challenge from its western Moslem minority, which for the time being is tame but does not need to remain so in the future. An example of what might be in store is being provided by India.

---

11  A friend of mine, who had a look at this text, asked: 'Didn't the UN do more harm than NATO?' It is a thoughtful question revealing in 8 words the mass of hot air in both (by now obsolete) organizations, which still linger on.

## 3. NATO and the Next Challenge

Alert political analysts suggest that a glimpse at the origin of the next big challenge is being offered by the Mumbai bombings of 26 November 2008, which left 195 dead.[12] As with the case of North Korea, there is a reason for America to have a foothold in South Asia but not necessarily through NATO. A sprinkling of troops from the *Atlantic* Alliance has no business in Asia – even under UN mandate.[13] In addition, its excursion in Afghanistan is going very badly because of NATO's:

- inefficiency and

- inability to get results out of a patchwork of different small contingents, which should have been evident from Day One.

The whole strategic plan of the Western nations is flawed; it is as if the leaders of America and of the European states cannot understand that the challenges of the present and the future are increasingly transnational – and global – not 'Atlantic'. As globalization intensified, the export/import of terrorism[14] has increased. A key to success lies in convincing the leading governments of the gains from acting in cooperation, rather than in rubbing each other's feathers up the wrong way.

During his visit to France in the summer of 2008, the Dalai Lama made a most wise suggestion on how to ease Russia's fear of having been menaced by NATO's faltering forces. In an interview he gave to *Euronews* he said that: 'The best way to calm Russian fears that they are encircled by NATO is to invite them to join NATO. Then to move the NATO headquarters to Moscow.' The Dalai Lama has a point:

- The Chinese might have ideas to roll America's Pacific interests back to San Francisco.

- By contrast, the Russians look to America as a counterweight to China, which for centuries has been their friend and foe.

---

12  The Mumbai bombings were carried out by Laska-e-Talba, an internal Pakistani terrorist group and not by al-Qaeda. This gives a glimpse of who might be the entity which tries to take hold of Pakistan's nuclear arsenal.

13  While NATO is no UN outfit, unless the two have merged and I did not hear about it.

14  We have come a long way since the hijack of the Lufthansa plane 'Landshut' and its successful liberation by a special unit of the German GSG9 in Mogadishu. Since then, terrorism has taken on a different quality, which makes it so much more difficult to predict and prevent – requiring 'outside the box' ideas.

Asked during the World Economic Forum in Davos, Switzerland, about what is not negotiable, Vladimir Putin, the Russian Prime Minister and former President said: 'Any encroachment on our sovereignty is non-negotiable.' To press the point, a few days later, on 5 February 2009, Russia convinced Kyrzistan to close the local US military base at Manas – while at the same time offering collaboration against terrorism. That took place at the very moment a bridge linking Pakistan to Afghanistan was blown up by the Taliban.

It would be most reasonable for a new defensive framework, able to position itself against 2009–2020 realities, to replace NATO and include Russia as an important member of the alliance against terrorists, fundamentalists and all sorts of fanatics. China and India should also also be co-opted *not* under the NATO banner, but that of:

- a new structure and

- a well-focused defence goal.

America needs Russia in order to secure vital foreign-policy objectives of its own, such as preventing Iran from acquiring nuclear weapons (section 2), plus as a partner in energy resources (Chapter 13). America also needs China and India, because Pakistan (section 5) already uses the nuclear trigger as a banner. All three – Russia, China and India – should be allies.

Let's face it, old and rusty alliances like NATO, and loose old boys' outfits such as the Organization for Security and Cooperation in Europe (OSCE), do not fit the bill of twenty-first-century security. They are vertical, too limited in scope, too obsolete in their conception, as well as too narrow in membership that counts. In short, they are

- too old-fashioned in their scope and

- highly questionable regarding their effectiveness in the future.

The time has come to examine alternatives. Some experts say that a plan as outlined by Dmitry Medvedev, the Russian President, and presented by Dmitry Rogozin, his ambassador to NATO, is to have a big international conference of all NATO and EU countries, Russia and its ex-Soviet allies, as well as China and India. Its aim would be to set up a new security organization to deal with:

- terrorism;

- extremism; and

- illegal immigration.

Until now, however, the Western response has been muted, though European countries like the idea of a security structure that would rely on international law. It needs no explaining that it would be silly to dismiss that plan before hearing it in full and debating it. (The reader should notice that the concept of security organizations that span Europe and Asia is nothing new. Russia and China set one up in 1996 by treaty. In 2001 it became the six-member Shanghai Cooperation Organization, with India and three other countries as observers.)

A multipolar organization which rests on heavyweighters rather than on small fry could serve American interests well. As of mid-2008, under the management of Robert Gates, the Pentagon has taken a new look at Iraq, Afghanistan and campaigns against the likes of al-Qaeda. It now calls its ongoing business the 'long war' against violent extremist movements rather than the 'global war on terrorism' and by all evidence it considers that military force:

- is no longer the only way and

- it is not even the primary tool.

Indeed, the new US National Defense Strategy, released by the Pentagon in August 2008, states that the key point is not the fighting 'we do ourselves, but how well we help prepare *our partners*' to defend and govern themselves. That's a first-class principle for a multipolar defence solution, as presented in the preceding paragraphs. *If* twenty-first-century security is the objective, *then* it makes absolutely no sense to continue with America and the 25 dwarfs or, even worse, enlarge it with another microdwarf, Albania, as is currently under discussion.

In a multipolar solution national policies will evidently play a role. In mid-January 2008 France announced that it was going to open a military base in the United Arab Emirates, making a strategic shift in its defence policy. This will be France's first permanent base in the Gulf, coming on the heels of the country's first full defence review for 14 years – a radical rethinking of defence and security policy.

By drawing 400 troops from an existing base in Djibouti, France started withdrawing from its traditional African base (it currently has about 5,000 soldiers in three permanent locations in Africa – Senegal, Gabon and Djibouti – some 2,600 soldiers on a peacekeeping mission in Côte d'Ivoire and 1,100 on the ground in Chad plus 2,000 as part of a French-led European Union force (EUFOR[15])). As Nicolas Sarkozy aptly stated, his administration aims to construct the security and defence of tomorrow:

- according to needs and

- not conditioned by old habits.

There are cases where the Europeans prefer 'not to be there' militarily and the August/September 2008 events in Georgia are an example. The deal brokered by the European Union for the withdrawal of Russian troops from Georgia has been slammed by one of NATO's top brass as 'not acceptable' because it ceded 'too much ground to Moscow'. But to the majority of European nations, the accord brokered by Nicolas Sarkozy, while presiding over the EU, made sense – and it provided grounds for the revival of the EU–Russia relationship.

Sarkozy essentially said that if Russia abides by its commitment to withdraw from the buffer zones, the EU would reverse its decision to suspend discussions with Moscow on an economic partnership pact. Some experts also remarked that nether NATO nor the EU had a mandate to intervene in Georgia, recalling that NATO's air war on Kosovo and Serbia in 1999 was, like the Iraq War in 2003, conducted without the legal approval of the United Nations – while both wars were aimed in part at regime change.[16]

---

15  Like NATO, with whose aims it overlaps except that it is not under US leadership, the EUFOR initiative is not noted for brilliance. It is proof that Europe is a paper tiger, commented one critic; it is a ramshackle enterprise whose main aim was merely showing the EU flag, said another.

16  Under the UN Charter Article 103, Security Council resolutions generally take precedence over all other laws, domestic and international. Only in cases involving *jus cogens* (a fundamental principle of international law), such as the ban on torture or slavery, does this rule not apply.

(It needs no reminder that the Georgian affair split European governments into two camps. France, Germany and Italy were diametrically opposed to the position of Britain, Sweden and Eastern Europeans, the former Soviet satellites. Eager to preserve their Russian links, the French and Germans tried to be neutral, while the Italians blamed the entire war on Georgia's inflammable President. So much for a common EU foreign policy.)

Unfortunately, so far NATO has given no evidence that it is getting ready to restructure itself and face the next change. Instead, what goes on is cosmetic surgery. For instance, trying to redress the disparity between America and the rest, it has drawn up lists of capabilities that member countries 'must acquire'.

Another spinning of the wheels has been the push for the formation of a 20,000-strong deployable standing army, known as the NATO Response Force (NRF), with land, air and sea components. At least in terms of efficiency, more than anything else this is a pipedream. It is supposed to begin deploying in trouble spots around the world at five days' notice,

- making a forced entry if necessary and

- sustaining itself for up to two months before handing over to follow-on troops.

By all evidence, even the BRF's proponents doubt its military capabilities. Some elements of what might resemble the NRF have been used for humanitarian relief, but, as a 'force', this has too many gaps for it to be declared fully 'operational'. As an word of advice, it is better to abstain from making grandiose statements because in the last analysis it is better to lose one's eye than one's name.

## 4. NATO's Fiasco in Afghanistan

The year 2008 saw NATO troops engage in their deadliest fighting yet in support of the government of Hamid Karzai,[17] who was also known as the Mayor of Kabul because that's practically the real estate he controls (and even that is not sure). Not only are roadside bombings and suicide attacks – tactics the Taliban have picked up with increasingly lethal effect from al-Qaeda operatives in Iraq

---

17  As 2007 came to a close, the same was said for that elapsed year, and the situation continues to worsen.

– the order of the day, but the Taliban have also infiltrated formerly secure territories in the country's north.

As the toll among Western forces and ordinary Afghans mounts, the spectres of both military defeat and failure of political will haunt NATO. The job of stabilizing the country becomes more and more elusive while doubt is growing that the so-called International Security Assistance Force (ISAF) will ever complete its mission. To start with, the mission was uncertain. Theoretically, the NATO troops went to the country to:

- 'bring democracy';

- eliminate the bloody and retrograde Taliban regime; and

- teach al-Qaeda a lesson, whatever that might mean.

Practically, in the eight long years since 2001, when that operation started, none of the aforementioned goals has been achieved. By contrast, the opium traffickers have profited immensely, which was not one of NATO's goals. In exchange for their assistance in clearing their domain of the Taliban, the various warlords demanded and got a free hand in relaunching the hard drugs trade[18] and they turned against NATO when a new supply of oxygen for their opium business was denied to them.[19]

At its 9/10 October 2008 meeting in Budapest, under pressure from US Secretary of Defense Robert Gates and NATO Commander General Bantz Craddock, NATO made the decision to go after the drug traffickers. But while publicly supporting the NATO plan to take on drug traffickers in Afghanistan, the British government's military commanders have privately condemned the plan, according to the 8 November 2008 issue of the London *Independent*.[20]

---

18  According to some accounts, this is generating $1 billion in black market revenue inside the country.

19  Afghanistan produces more than 90 per cent of the world's opium and a growing share of its cannabis. If Karzai and his pals were not clients of the West, their country might well be classified as a narco-state. According to the United Nations Office on Drugs and Crime (UNODC), just one province, Helmand, produces more opium, and from it heroin and other illegal drugs, than the rest of Afghanistan put together – overshadowing the past decade's striking decline in the 'Golden Triangle' (the border region of Thailand, Myanmar and Laos) which UNODC says is now opium-free.

20  *EIR*, 21 November 2008.

Already by the end of 2007 a United Nations report showed that Afghanistan's opium production had climbed sharply, pouring into the market twice the amount it had just two years earlier and accounting for 93 per cent of heroin on a global basis. There is also increasing evidence of direct involvement in this opium business by the Taliban who have a double interest in it:

- money and

- the means to destabilize the West.

Not only has al-Qaeda not been taught a lesson by NATO's excursion into Afghanistan, but also the Taliban have become much bolder – thanks to neighbouring Pakistan (section 5). A dramatic proof of their resurrection was given in July 2007 when they abducted 19 South Koreans. Eventually, they agreed to their release on condition that South Korea:

- removed its soldiers from Afghanistan by the end of that year; and

- stopped missionary activities by South Korean citizens in Afghanistan.[21]

As for the advent of democracy in Afghanistan, its fate has striking parallels with the Iraqi experience of this 'exporting of democracy' as if it were potatoes. The Bush advisors had been selling hope, and the President himself lost his sense of realism. To cite just one case among many, a young Afghani was sentenced to prison for 20 years because he spoke out in favour of women's rights and similar issues.

- This makes a mockery of pronouncements that NATO troops were there expressly to chase away the Taliban and restore some kind of democracy to the country.

It needs no explaining that, despite the efforts of some of Pakistan's military and security apparatus, al-Qaeda still has a safe haven in Pakistan. In addition, the current government in Kabul is seen by some, rather ironically, as more corrupt than the unpleasant but deontologically driven Taliban.[22]

---

21  Rumour also had it that the Taliban asked for and got $20 million – over $1 million per head for the South Koreans' release. Other figures range from as low as $950,000 (around $50,000 per head) to at least $5,000,000 (*Newsweek*, 'For the Taliban, a crime that pays', September 2008).

22  Afghanistan's NATO-supported government has also ordered private television stations to remove popular Indian soap operas on the ground that 'they are immoral'. There is, as well,

In the meantime, Afghanistan's chronic problems – desperate poverty, fragile and corrupt government, and a drug-financed insurgency – continue unresolved and undisturbed, while various politicians sort out their differences and the clergy's heavy hand sees to it that nothing changes. Neighbouring Pakistan, theoretically a US ally, is in the grip of meltdown. It has a political crisis, an economic crisis, a jihadist insurgency, a coup-prone army and an intelligence service with (reportedly) links to the Taliban.[23]

'Taliban militants have struck terror into the container business that handles NATO supplies passing through Pakistan on their way to Afghanistan, and have virtually crippled the operation', stated an article in *EIR*, adding that: 'In December 2008 they destroyed some 400 containers carrying food, fuel and military vehicles, and NATO has begun paying tribes to get the supplies across. A recent Canadian report points out that NATO is paying the Taliban 'to guarantee the security of these supply routes'.[24]

What's the purpose of having 60,000 troops in Afghanistan in a war they cannot win? (Roughly 50 per cent are American; 13 per cent are British; a little over 10 per cent German, and about equal number French; next in number are Canadian, Dutch, Polish; and the remaining are from different other NATO countries including Italy, Spain, Turkey, Denmark, Hungary and Estonia.)

With so many different countries contributing rather small contingents to NATO troops, efficiency is bound to suffer. After all, numerically speaking, these are limited forces whose deliverables are battered by linguistic, training and weapons differences. The unwillingness of NATO members to increase the tiny contingent is another huge problem. Trained in Pakistan, the Taliban are growing in numbers but NATO forces aren't.

Even technical support seems to be wanting in spite of the Bush administration's Afghan Planning Group. Helicopters are a case in point. America has thousands of them but is already worried about its ballooning billion-dollar bills for wear and tear on its military equipment. European NATO

---

in Afghanistan wide use of the *burka*. Add to this the corrupt (s)elections (whose cost has been $400 million), and the conclusion is that NATO soldiers giving their lives in that country are surely not fighting for democracy and freedom.

23  Nothing is going to change unless the Pakistani government takes control of its North-West Frontier Province and the Federally Administered Tribal Areas (FATA) bordering Afghanistan – which it is both unwilling and unable to do. There is also the suspicion that some parties still think Pakistan's best Afghan friends are the fundamentalists.

24  *EIR*, 16 January 2009.

countries have more than 1,000 transport helicopters, but still rely heavily on American airlift in Afghanistan.[25] That reflects badly on NATO, underlining:

- the outdated design of Western armed forces;

- strategy still focused on territorial defence against a Soviet invasion; and

- military plans that assume a defined frontline with rear staging areas supplied by road.

By contrast, in Afghanistan, as in Iraq, there are no frontlines and road convoys everywhere are vulnerable targets. The resurgent Taliban are betting that the countries sending troops to the NATO-led ISAF do not have the stamina for it, as depressing news of casualties among their own soldiers and Afghan civilians is wearing away whatever support the troop deployment had.

In a way reminiscent of the French public opinion's reaction to the (losing) battle in Vietnam and the (winning) war in Algeria, in practically all countries that have sent troops Afghanistan is a huge political issue. This is true even when the troops are deployed in the north of the country, away from the fiercest fighting. Some critics say that it was a mistake from the start to create two separate forces, both under American officers:

- the international Security Assistance Force (ISAF), the NATO-led operation; and

- the combined Joint Task Force 82, which consists of special forces and elite infantry who hunt Taliban and al-Qaeda leaders under America's Operation Enduring Freedom (OEF).

Others, however, suggest that, though the lack of unity of command is regrettable, it is not the only reason for poor results. 'The era of easy foreign missions is over,' said France's Senior General, Jean-Louis Georgelin. 'We are witnessing a return of missions of war.' And he may well be right.

---

25  The way an article in the 15 January 2009 *Financial Times* had it, John Hutton, Britain's Defence Secretary, planned to attack the commitment of EU allies to the war in Afghanistan, saying that Europe could no longer continue 'freeloading' on the back of US military security and that NATO's Afghan campaign exposed 'a continued over-reliance from certain members on the US to do the heavy lifting'.

General Georgelin is not alone in this assessment. On the ground the mood is bleak. Foreign aid workers in Kabul feel under siege. Taking note that by mid-September 2008 violence in Afghanistan was at its highest level since the toppling of the Taliban in 2001, Admiral Mike Mullen has admitted he was 'not convinced we're winning it'.[26]

No wonder, therefore, that American and European defence officials seem to be nearly unanimous that the current course of action is failing and that the Afghan–Pakistani border region has become a new command-and-control hub for al-Qaeda and the Taliban. Pentagon and intelligence sources have reportedly estimated that a minimum of 100,000 combat troops, and a total of nearly 400,000 troops altogether, would be needed to stabilize Afghanistan militarily. For its part, however, history suggests that Afghanistan will never be tamed by foreign occupation. Just ask:

- the Russians about their expedition[27] and

- the British about their souvenirs from the days of the Raj.

Now, as then, Afghanistan looks unwinnable no matter what the toll it takes in lives. Critics also say that the Bush administration never had a Plan B, while at the same time it hoped for too much and demanded too little from the Karzai government, which has been a thorough disappointment. 'Great Britain's long association with Afghanistan has shown that we got ourselves into this country by forming tribal alliances. Equally we will get ourselves out, over time, by forming tribal alliances that support the government of Afghanistan,' Brigadier Andrew Mackay wrote in a report on 30 October 2007.[28]

According to London's *Daily Telegraph* of 29 November 2006, Khurshid Mahmud Kasuri, then Pakistan's Foreign Minister, advised NATO to include the Taliban in the Kabul government. In a private briefing to Foreign Ministers of some NATO member states, Karsuri said that the Taliban were winning the war in Afghanistan and NATO was bound to fail. One Western official commented: 'Kasuri is basically asking NATO to surrender and to negotiate with the Taliban.'[29]

---

26  *The Economist*, 30 August 2008.
27  When the Russians were in Afghanistan they had 100,000 and didn't win.
28  *EIR*, 4 January 2008.
29  *EIR*, 8 December 2006.

As 2007 came to a close, the news broke that the British had indeed been negotiating with friendly Talibans labelled as 'moderate'. This initiative rested on the ground that, with its superior firepower, NATO could win any battle, but it was losing the war – or at least not winning, which practically amounts to the same thing. By the end of 2008 the British were not the only ones losing heart in Afghanistan; the Americans, too, were rethinking their strategy and, while sending more forces, rumour has it that they were negotiating with the more moderate Taliban.

Nothing came out of those negotiations but a year later, on 14 July 2009, a different story hit the public eye: the day on which the bodies of eight servicemen were repatriated back to Britain, broadcast live on TV, with thousands of veterans of past wars and plenty of other people attending. 'They [the Afghans] thrashed the Russians, and they are going to thrash us again,' said a former soldier wearing campaign medals.[30]

There has been no river of blood. Nothing comparable by any measure to the 1944 Battle of Normandy which (including the D-Day landings) cost the lives of 83,000 British and Canadian soldiers, 126,000 American, 240,000 German and, including other contingents plus the aviators, approached altogether half a million lives.[31] But neither has there been the will to win in Afghanistan; just staying around and drifting.

The battle of Afghanistan started badly in 2001 when American forces overthrew the Taliban, but nothing has been accomplished over the elapsed decade to stabilize the situation. More recently, Operations Sword (Khanjar), which began on 2 July 2009, and Panther's Claw, a parallel operation, were the biggest actions by US and British forces. But critics say that, so far, the result is just hot air as the Taliban melted away.

Suddenly the original goal of clearing Helmand Province of the Taliban changed, and the objective became one of protecting the population. The Taliban answered that their own response, Operation Foladi Jal, would avoid frontal battles but 'would teach a lesson' through roadside bombs and ambushes.

Lives aside, that 'lesson' comes at high cost to the American taxpayers. Judging from appropriations the Obama administration asked Congress to authorize, in 2009 the cost of Afghanistan and Iraq will be $150 billion, or $411

---

30   *The Economist*, 18 July 2009.
31   Anthony Beevor, *D-Day – et la Bataille de Normandie*, Calman-Levy, Paris, 2009.

million per day which adds up to $17.1 million per hour in the night when the soldiers are sleeping.[32]

Worst of all, this is a protracted war that NATO cannot win in the way it is managing it, as it repeats the same mistakes the Russians did in 1970. There is also another bleaker precedent of which it would be wise to take notice. In April 1964 Charles de Gaulle warned Charles Bohlen, then US ambassador to France, that the US was repeating 'the experience that the French had earlier'.

According to an excellent analysis by H.R. McMaster, de Gaulle argued that in contrast to Hanoi's determination, the South Vietnamese 'had no stomach for war'. (It sounds a familiar note to that of the corrupt government in Kabul.) Therefore, he strongly recommended that the US pursue immediate neutralization. America, the French President said, had either to choose that path as an announced policy or 'demonstrate the willingness to really carry the war to the North and if necessary against China'.[33]

Today China should be an *equal rights* partner in finding a political solution in Afghanistan. The same is true of Russia and maybe of Iran. For the West this is a quagmire. NATO has no business in central Asia. Obama's wrong decision to intensify a mismanaged war would take more and more combat troops, and zooming casualty numbers without a realistic hope of ultimate victory. It is just another Vietnam.

## 5. The Dubious Role of Pakistan

Pakistan has its own problems and US policy is confused, as are relations between Pakistan and India - in respect of which there is a view that Pakistan is a potential aggressor.

In mid-January 2009, Yousuf Raza Gilani, Pakistan's Prime Minister, denied that a dossier handed over by India on the murderous attack of November 2008 in Mumbai constituted 'evidence' of Pakistan's involvement. Initially, his thesis was that Mumbai terrorists were 'stateless'. Later on, however,

---

32  *Le Canard Enchaîné*, 2 April 2009.
33  H.R. McMaster, *Dereliction of Duty*, Harper Perennial, New York, 1997.

Pakistan said that it had arrested more than 120 people allegedly linked to these attacks.[34]

Pakistan's dubious stance regarding the Taliban (and other murder specialists) correlates with its handling of relations with neighbouring India. Suggesting that India might be planning military reprisals, Pakistan moved troops from the Afghan border, trying to be in readiness to kill two birds with one well-placed stone:

- moving troops from an unpopular war on the Afghan border; and

- creating a diplomatic incident with India, but in a clumsy way which reasserted the dominant role of the army and intelligence service (ISI) over a fragile civilian government.

Political analysts these days are not quite sure whether Pakistan is heading for plain meltdown or Taliban takeover. Even Asif Zardari, the country's civilian president, has reportedly admitted that militants and fundamentalists hold huge amounts of land. 'The porous border between Britain and Pakistan is frequently abused,' said an article in *The Economist*.[35]

In April 2009, British police in Lancashire arrested a dozen students from Pakistan on suspicion of involvement with terrorist offences. Although in many such instances the authorities do not uncover suitable evidence to put before a court, there clearly seems to be plenty of worrying intelligence concerning the dubious activities of some people with links to Pakistan. They are visiting or resident in countries like Britain, but they don't respect the law of the land of the country providing them with residence or asylum.

In Pakistan itself, a Taliban takeover would go against the will of the people because most Pakistanis are moderate, but the militants hold the upper ground and the government is awfully weak. No administration has succeeded in eradicating militancy in Pakistan and doing away with some 40-odd jihadist groups with links to the army's Inter-Services Intelligence (ISI) agency. The ISI was beefed up by the US to fight the invading Russians in the 1970s, but then:

- it turned against the Americans and

---

34  *The Economist*, 17 January 2009.
35  *The Economist*, 18 April 2009.

- it has allegedly produced renowned figures from bin Laden to the rest of al-Qaeda's top brass.

Even if the Talibanization of all Pakistan is not for 2009 or 2010, the danger the Taliban represents should not be understated because the fundamentalists are strong not just in the Pushtun borderlands of Baluchistan, the Federally Administered Tribal Areas (FATA) and the North-West Frontier Province (NWFP), but also in other areas of Pakistan's jurisdiction. And as in the Swat Valley, they want to impose Sharia law all over Pakistan and in a European country if possible. Guess which one.[36]

The fact is that Pakistan has no control over its north-west tribal areas, and the ramifications of official policy in places like Bajour, Mohmad, Khyber,[37] Kurram, North Waziristan and South Waziristan are way beyond the notional central government's reach. These are the so-called Federally Administered Tribal Areas (FATA), but 'administered' is a big word that has little to do with reality.

- This is a rugged region, a hinge between Pakistan and Afghanistan;[38]

- the so-called FATA is also the home of 3.5 million Pashtun tribesmen who live there.

According to some accounts, in the vain hope of seeing some law and order in this north-west frontier, America so far has paid the Pakistani government some $12 billion to raise and sustain a frontier corps. That's not as bad as the $60 billion[39] it paid during and after World War II to Cash-my-Cheque (Chiang Kai-shek) to keep the communists from taking over China – except that in both cases it got no value for its money.[40]

Losing patience with the Pakistan government's uncertain handling of the fundamentalists' safe havens in the FATA, in late February 2007 the US Congress threatened to link further American financial and military assistance to a certification by George Bush that General Pervez Musharraf was actively

---

36  To help the reader in guessing, it's an imam (who, if I am not mistaken, is now in prison) who said that his dream was to apply Sharia law in the country which (unwisely) had given him hospitality.

37  Famous for its mountain pass.

38  Part of the North-West Frontier under the British Raj.

39  In today's value of 1940s dollars.

40  Sterling Seagrave, *The Soong Dynasty*, Corgi Books, London, 1996.

battling the Taliban and al-Qaeda. Congress did not lose sight of the fact that both had regrouped in Pakistan's tribal borderlands. In the law-makers' opinion:

- Pakistan had done very little in spite of the billions of dollars it had received since pledging support to the 'war against terror' in September 2001.

- Or, perhaps, because of it. Who would want to part with such a torrent of subsidies given for doing nothing by eliminating the reason for them?

One could only hope that this Congressional reaction will send a message. Apart from its massive aid of roughly $2 billion a year to Pakistan, since 11 September 2001 the United States had been paying about half that amount each year to reimburse Pakistan's military for 'fighting' Taliban and al-Qaeda forces along the Afghan border. But in mid-2006 Pervez Musharraf, the then Pakistani president, radically pared back the anti-al-Qaeda effort while the lavish payments by Washington continued.

Critics of this pay-for-nothing policy have been vocal, pointing out that Islamabad's military cutbacks make it easier for the Taliban and al-Qaeda to kill American, British and other NATO troops in Afghanistan.

In an effort to get things going again, Dick Cheney, then America's vice-president, visited Musharraf in late February 2007 and asked him to do more to tackle the Taliban and al-Qaeda fighters taking refuge in Pakistan's tribal borderlands, before an expected spring offensive by Taliban against NATO forces in Afghanistan. From there Cheney went on to Afghanistan, where a Taliban suicide-bomber attacked the entrance to the military base at Bagram, where Cheney was staying.

- Cheney survived.

- The bomber and 11 others did not; and

- the plea to do something to seal off the porous FATA fell on deaf ears.

Despite his go-slow policy, a short while later, in April 2007, Musharraf faced the fundamentalists' anger. Abdul Aziz, a mullah, gave the government a month to close the capital's brothels and music shops and tear down advertisements showing women. He also declared Sharia within the high walls of his mosque Lal Masjid, and the adjoining Qur'anic school (*madrassa*) – all of which eventually had to be cleared of insurgents by the Pakistani army.[41]

Many Pakistanis say that for a long time their country has had trouble coping with repercussions from the anti-Soviet jihad that the US sponsored in Afghanistan during the 1980s. They also add another unwanted consequence: Pakistan's military intelligence (ISI) first got into action in Afghanistan to support the anti-Soviet insurgence; then it started to bite the hand that fed it.

Some people add that the ISI's current involvement is engineered not just out of Pashtun solidarity but to give Pakistan 'strategic depth' in its contest with India, particularly over Kashmir. (The Indians answer that military intelligence is also active in suicide bombings, while other military experts add that it appears to be furnishing al-Qaeda with a new base of operations.)

Critics of successive Pakistani governments also recall that Abdul Qadeer Khan, whose fame still runs high in his country as the father of its nuclear bomb, turned Pakistan's illicit procurement network into a private and hugely profitable supply chain. Khan was allegedly ready to sell all sorts of nuclear secrets and devices in violation of the global anti-proliferation effort; Iran, North Korea and Libya are the evidence.

According to knowledgeable sources, Khan's speciality was the art of enriching uranium, though in Libya's case he allegedly threw in a nearly complete weapon design that had earlier been supplied to Pakistan by China. In fact, Khan was a metallurgist, not a nuclear scientist, who happened to find employment at a Dutch consortium where uranium was enriched for peaceful purposes in a tandem of linked centrifuges. At his leisure, Khan allegedly:

- copied the plans for centrifuges; and

- bought parts for them, mostly on the open market in Europe.

---

41  The mosque, which was staffed by thousands of army zealots and defied the government, was less than a mile from the country's Supreme Court and parliament buildings.

Then Khan set himself up as the mail order-style supplier of packaged bomb-programmes. All this happened under Bhutto's watch not Musharraf's (it was also under Bhutto that Pakistan openly backed the Taliban in Afghanistan). As an after-effect of a 2003 British American interception of a shipload of centrifuge parts bound for Libya, bearing the clear signature of his operations,

- A.Q. Khan came under benign house arrest in Islamabad;

- but experts say there is a high likelihood that much of the network he established remains alive and active worldwide.

Nor has anything changed with the post-Musharraf regime. Because of fears that a nuclear-armed Pakistan could fall to the jihadists, the West keeps on pouring good money after bad into the country. By 1 November 2008, with inflation hitting 30 per cent and the rupee devalued by about 25 per cent in just three months, the economy was close to freefall.

- The country's fiscal deficit reached 10 per cent of GDP; and

- foreign-exchange reserves cover just some weeks of imports.

Finding itself in dire straits (which happens with increasing frequency), Pakistan desperately appealed to America, China and Saudi Arabia for financial help. But America has severe problems of its own. The Chinese did their due diligence and concluded that they cannot advance billions to an increasingly dysfunctional state. And the Saudis have dragged their feet on a Pakistani request for $5.9 billion-worth of finance in the form of deferred oil payments.

In the aftermath, reluctantly, Pakistan had to turn to the International Monetary Fund (IMF) once again cap in hand, hoping to get a $10 billion loan to top itself up for a few months. The IMF granted a $6 billion loan for 20 months, then topped that with another $1.6 billion. It is most definitely the wrong policy to extend financial support and all sorts of loans to countries unwilling or unable to put their house in order.

## 6. The Eastern European Missile Adventure

The thesis of this chapter has been that NATO is in *déclinisme*, and to come up from under NATO or (better), its successor organization has to establish twenty-first-century goals. It also has to invent a new military doctrine that is appropriate for such goals rather than emulating WWII practices. The main goal must be the *salient problem*. Management theory teaches that a salient problem is the top subject to which chief executives must address themselves.

- Today troublespots abound around the world from Darfour to Iraq, Afghanistan and Iran – you name them.

- But surely the miserable missile story in Central–Eastern Europe is no salient problem; it is just a matter of George W. Bush's ego, which hardly merits the friction it has created.

Frank-Walter Steinmeier, the German foreign minister, exploded over the decision of the Czech and Polish governments to accept (respectively) US radars and missiles on their soil, saying that the two governments did so without consulting with their neighbour and the EU. With total lack of political union among member states, the Poles and Czechs felt free to decide as they pleased about their sovereignty. They have no obligation whatsoever to consult the Brussels executive or any other EU government – or do they?

Sensing that things might get out of control, in early March 2007 Germany called for talks on the proposed NATO missile defence shield for Central Europe, asking for wider consultations on the project (Ukraine had also complained that the US had not consulted it). The arguments surrounding the proposals appeared to be reminiscent of the past Cold War period, and the continent should not allow itself to be split into 'old' and 'new' Europe, Steinmeier wrote in the *Frankfurter Allgemeine Sontagszeitung*.

Most evidently, the Russians were even more critical of that initiative. In fact, as the reader is in all likelihood aware, not only the Germans and the Russians, but also others have denounced the possible arrival of missiles in the heart of Europe. Jean Asselborn, Luxembourg's foreign minister, labelled the US plans incomprehensible, telling a European Union foreign ministers' meeting: 'We'll have no stability in Europe if we force Russia into a corner.'[42]

Some military people, also critical of the radar and missile sites, said that these would be the wrong locations to defend against Russian or Iranian missiles, because of a lack of *battle space*. (That's the time needed to detect a missile launch, point a radar towards the incoming missile, lock on to it and

---

42  *Financial Times*, 7 March 2007.

pass the target information to the interceptor missile for launch.) For his part, Jacques Chirac, who was then the French President, warned that the US initiative risked returning Europe to the tensions of the Cold War.

Many Americans, too, were against this Bush administration effort to try to encircle Russia from Poland and Georgia. Said a former New York judge: 'Here is America chronically energy short and Russia the largest energy supplier in the world. And instead of working together we try to find reasons for friction in Georgia. Who cares about Georgia. We should be partners with Russia.'[43]

As the aired differences in opinion were wide, what seemed to be a strategic choice for partnership between Russia and America turned into a crumbling tactical alliance, which in no time started to fall apart. In return for what the Russians saw as concessions, as for instance tolerating America's military presence in Central Asia and swallowing NATO's expansion to Russia's Baltic border, they expected something back. Instead, what they got was:

- a bitter criticism of their domestic affairs;

- radars and missiles on their doorsteps;

- disdain for their views on Iraq and elsewhere; and

- resistance to the international ambitions of Russian companies.

At the time of the 'Orange Revolution', the Russians saw the regime change in Ukraine as evidence of perfidious American meddling in their sphere of influence. But what touched them more than anything else has been, by all likelihood, the missile adventure.

The reaction of some of the former Soviet satellites was exactly the opposite. 'What's good for Polish security is good for Lithuania's,' said the Lithuanian Deputy Foreign Minister. Others, however, gave the missile adventure a less-than-ringing endorsement by complaining that Russia had not been consulted while still others regretted that the EU lacked a coherent policy on what to do. Lithuania's Prime Minister declared: 'I can't imagine it will be possible for Europe to speak with one voice [on the missile shield].'[44]

---

43  From a personal conversation.
44  *The Economist*, 3 March 2007.

As the reader is aware from the previous discussions, not only the EU but also the 26-member NATO is split down the middle over policy. This is clearly seen in the differences in opinion which reflect a deep-seated division over how to deal with Russia:

- France, Germany and Italy want to do business with Russia;

- former Soviet satellites are suspicious or actively hostile;

- Britain and Sweden are among the elder EU members promoting a tougher line towards Russia.

An early 2008 Polish–Swedish plan suggests that the EU should develop closer ties with Ukraine, Moldova, Georgia, Armenia and Azerbaijan – not with Russia. As a start, its sponsors want to negotiate visa-free travel deals and free trade zones for services and agricultural products and also to promote unspecified regulatory overhauls.

That particular proposal came a short time before Nicolas Sarkozy, the French President, introduced his Union for the Mediterranean project at a summit meeting in Paris mid-July 2008 – as if to force his hand. With a less ambitious plan than Sarkozy's, the sponsors of the so-called Eastern Partnership say that it should be run by the European Commission (which, incidentally, is none of its business).

The Eastern Partnership initiative has reawakened a debate within the EU about how and where to deploy its influence and how to pay for expenses which expand right, left and centre for both civilian and military projects. After the fall of the Iron Curtain not enough thought was given to the cost and effectiveness of different projects, but this is changing, with both civilian plans and military equipment starting to come under scrutiny because the treasuries have run dry.

Indeed, one of the reasons against the US missile system advanced by those who criticized it has been its lack of cost-effectiveness. Among its other shortcomings, it is designed to shoot down a small number of missiles and would be overwhelmed by a large-scale strike. On the other hand, that system will cost more than $10 billion *a year* – while its effectiveness is highly in doubt and (egos aside) its aims are in 'Cloud Cuckoo Land'.

There is no issue in the present-day EU and NATO structure where the lack of open debate and of convergence of opinions is not part of the problem. There has been a discussion in Europe on missile defence, with controversy flaring up along every step of the way. To this has been added the fallout from the projected US installations. To critics:

- the feasibility of protecting Europe through a missile system is questionable at best; and

- the issues are both technical and political – therefore requiring a wider political discussion on the wisdom of such a system, as well as on who is going to pay what.

The arguments regarding political convergence have been going on for years and the only issue on which everyone seems to agree is that it would not be easy to achieve. As an article in *The Economist* had it back in 2007: '... the row over missile defences has made plain a broader challenge to America's moral sway over its old allies. Four years after the assault on Iraq, America can sound a warning about threats from rogue states – only to find many European voters would rather hear the opposite message from Russia.'[45]

## 7. Iran and North Korea are Closer to the Bomb

On 2 March 2009 the news was that, according to the Obama administration, Iran had amassed enough fissile material to build an atomic bomb. So said Admiral Mike Mullen, the chairman of the US Joint Chiefs of Staff. Mullen's comments came when he was asked to assess a report by the United Nations' International Atomic Energy Agency (IAEA), which found that Iran had enough nuclear material for a nuclear bomb.

'We think they do, quite frankly,' Mullen said on CNN, 'and Iran having a nuclear weapon – I've believed for a long time – is a very, very bad outcome for the region and for the world.' The IAEA had found that Iran had understated by a third how much uranium it had enriched. For the first time, the international watchdog declared that the amount of low-enriched uranium that Tehran had stockpiled, estimated at more than a ton, was sufficient to make an atomic bomb.

---

45  *The Economist*, 31 March 2007.

The case looks serious enough for a concerted action involving the United States, European Union, Russia, China and India – not the US and EU *alone*. Therefore the challenge falls well beyond NATO's Snow Whites and dwarfs. But weak and distracted US Presidents and three ladies who almost in tandem managed the State Department:

- did not seem capable of thinking outside the box and

- have not apparently been able to decide how they can fulfil their responsibilities.

Instead, they stick to the old line of opening up more radar and missile sites, which means focusing on the symptoms rather than trying to cure the illness at its roots. As if this was not enough, they also ruffle the feathers of those who should have been their *true allies* in a common policy towards Iran and North Korea.

The United States says that its planned missile sites in Poland and the Czech Republic are needed to defend against a potential Iranian nuclear attack. Russia contends that those missiles have been designed to threaten it, not to defend anybody. The policy is one of sharing discord, rather than sharing power and action.

The Obama administration seems to propose that *if* Russia wants the United States to rethink its plans for building missile sites in Eastern Europe, *then* Moscow must do more to help halt the Iranian nuclear weapons programme. The real issue, however, is the other way around:

- if the US wants Russia and China to help in controlling the Iranian nuclear menace;

- then it must engage in serious negotiation with Asia's two powerhouses – and in a negotiation one gives and takes, rather than take everything for oneself.

By acknowledging that no single power politically, economically, and militarily dominates the world today as it did at end of World War II,[46] Barack Obama's best strategy would have been that of a wily negotiator – who magisterially ends the strife between East and West, North and South, the US and Russia, as well as the US and China. Personal diplomacy with everything negotiable on the table and the eyes wide open is the key.

---

46 If it did, NATO would not be losing the war in Afghanistan – to mention just one example.

Instead, the current policy is one of steady provocation, like the planned 2009 NATO exercises in Georgia, a place where NATO has no business whatsoever to be. The irony of all this is that both Russia and China are alienated – yet they are most crucial partners to the solution not only of the Iranian puzzle, but also of the other current major weapons problem which has been drifting for over a decade: North Korea.

When George W. Bush, arguably the worst-ever President of the United States (at least so far), planned his invasion of Iraq, the Russian Foreign Minister had said that this was the wrong identification of the immediate challenge. The salient problem was not Iraq, but North Korea. Years down the line when, in early April 2009, the North Koreans tested a missile conceivably able to hit Alaska, they proved him right.

Ironically, North Korea's long-range missile adventure came shortly before Barack Obama outlined his 'nuclear-free dream' in Prague. Kim Jong Il, the baby-faced dictator of a starving nation, claimed that his rocket aimed to launch a satellite. Others, however, noted that this was a message-giver. The tested nuclear-capable missile flew about 3,200 km before dropping into the Pacific.

The Japanese and South Koreans, who depend on the US nuclear umbrella, were enraged. For America, this was an embarrassment, but China and Russia had no reason to come to the rescue of President Obama. As might have been expected, because of being left outside the Western power circle, they blocked all rebuke of Kim and his North Koreans at the UN Security Council, saying that:

- he had a right to a space programme and

- though a UN resolution supposedly bans his missile work, Kim had only good intentions.

Down to the bottom line, this was a huge failure of US diplomacy which, since Bill Clinton's time, has tried to be nice, friendly and loved by feeding the starving North Koreans and hoping, just hoping, that they would be nice too. Madeleine Albright had got it all wrong. The solution to the Kim Jong Il problem is in Beijing and in Moscow – not in Pyongyang.

The so-called Comprehensive Test-Ban Treaty, which was submitted to the US Senate for ratification and rejected in 1999, is dead in the water. President Obama's plans to jump-start long-stalled negotiations on a verifiable treaty to end the production of fissile material for military uses are also stillborn. This is no matter for the United Nations, which never had any real power on nuclear armaments.

Among the experts, those who are optimists suggest that China would probably ratify the ban if America does. But most sober-thinking experts say that Pakistan will not accept a test ban unless India does so, and even that is not sure. Moreover, without a belligerent North Korea changing its policy of taking everybody for a ride (as it has done for nearly two decades) and with Iran doing as it pleases, a test ban may be worse than nothing.

There is also an arresting implication in this whole business. Western defence planners would be well advised not to miss the fine print of who may be using North Korea as a whipping boy, to serve his own interests. In March 2009 China entertained a visit by North Korea's Kim Jong Il with all the usual honour-guard pomp. With fine hyperbole, President Hu Jintao told Kim that the two countries' friendship had become 'the common treasure of both nations'.[47] A treasure hunt indeed.

## Note to the Reader

If the war in Afghanistan has been against insurgency and for democracy, the funny (s)elections of September 2009 suggest that this may be smoke and mirrors. Nancy Pelosi, the speaker of the US House of Representatives, put it in this way: 'Do we have an able partner in President Karzai? Is the government capable of acting in a way that is not fraught with corruption?'[48]

As for the generals, their opinions are divided. Stanley McChrystal, the man on the ground in Afghanistan, wants 40,000 more US troops. But some twenty-five centuries ago, Sun TZU, the great Chinese general and statesman had said: 'In war numbers alone confer no advantage.' Quoting a senior American officer: 'Tactical battlefield successes are meaningless unless there is something to join up to.'[49] Barack Obama finds it difficult to decide. Stephen Biddle, of the US Council of Foreign Relations, is more forthcoming: 'What would it take to defeat the Taliban? No one knows.'[50]

---

47  *The Economist*, 11 April 2009.
48  *The Economist*, 17 October 2009.
49  *Financial Times*, 23 September 2009.
50  Idem.

# Energy Supplies and New Alliances

## 1. Energy Means Power

According to ancient Greek mythology, Prometheus was one of the seven Titans who foresaw the rebellion against Cronos[1] – the God of Gods – and chose to fight at Zeus' side. Athene, the goddess of wisdom, taught Prometheus architecture, astronomy, mathematics, navigation, medicine, metallurgy and the art of fire, which he passed on to humanity. Zeus grew angry at their increasing power and talents, punished Prometheus and withheld fire from humankind. Since remote antiquity:

- fire and therefore energy has meant power and

- from the beginning of all things, energy has set the universe in motion.

In more recent times – starting with the Industrial Revolution back in the eighteenth and nineteenth centuries – energy always meant power. Before the steam engine, it was difficult to cover long distances in a short time by using natural and manufactured energy sources, such as muscular power, wood, coal, water and wind. Even if wood and coal have been in abundance, the energy they released could not be used much beyond producing heat. In fact, in the physical sense of transferred motion, useful work could be done only by:

- wind and

- falling water.

---

1   More precisely *Chronos*, which in Greek means *time*; Chronos, according to ancient mythology, ate his children.

Both, however, are erratic and not always found where they are needed. Therefore, for millennia muscular power remained the main energy source in transport and in production, as well as being one of the basic reasons for slavery. 'The Northern States are jealous of our slaves and our prosperity; we owe them nothing,' said Ralph Waldo Emerson to Achille Murat, son of the ex-King of Naples, nephew of Napoleon, and landlord of Liponia in the US South.[2]

The steam engine changed all that, but also added to the need for developing energy sources further. A simple but ingenious device, James Watt's controller (developed 1782–1784), permitted the harnessing of the power of steam, opened new horizons and made it feasible to convert the heat energy of coal and wood into a form that could do productive work. This further boosted the need for more energy.

- Over time, harnessed energy became a pivot point in the Western way of life; and,

- as such, it made a major contribution to development and sustenance of higher standard of living.

It comes as no surprise, therefore, that as people became more affluent and more numerous, the uses of energy proliferated and new sources had to be found. The exponential growth in energy consumption had lasting implications, ranging from environmental pollution to power plays for control of energy sources as well as the search for new ones, as those already known and available are no longer sufficient or are becoming depleted. Taking *world* electricity generation as a reference to energy consumption, in 2008 the origin by source was approximately:

- 40 per cent coal;

- 19 per cent renewables (including hydroelectric);

- 16 per cent nuclear;

- 15 per cent gas; and

- 10 per cent oil.

---

2    Robert D. Richardson, Jr, *Emerson. The Mind on Fire*, University of California Press, Berkeley, 1995.

If oil's share in world electricity generation is in fifth position, it is way up at the top of the list in terms of mobility, born out of the internal combustion engine. With the minor exception of gas,[3] it is difficult to imagine a source of energy that has done more to change the nature of human existence.

- Transport is no longer a luxury, but the means for moving people and goods in a way that has become an economic necessity; and

- as transport based on the internal combustion engine became increasingly a commodity and assumed broader economic and social power, so too the role of oil increased.

Not only mobility itself but also access to mobility has become a crucial building block in a modern economy, all the way from civilian to military life. Moreover, advances in technology increased the demand for energy – and most particularly for oil. 'Communicate, don't commute' was a slogan of the 1970s, whose promises have not been fulfilled, and this is not going to change with cloud computing.

Take the US as an example of total energy consumption (not just electricity generation). Statistics show that in 1850 less than 10 per cent of energy was supplied by coal; the balance came from wood. Within a quarter of a century, however, coal provided almost 30 per cent of energy and this grew to about 73 per cent in 1900. By then, the share of wood had shrunk to 20 per cent while there were two newcomers:

- about 4 per cent of energy came from gas; and

- at the dawn of the twentieth century another 3 per cent was provided by oil.

In 1950, the distribution of American energy sources had again greatly changed: oil accounted for nearly 38 per cent of total energy production, gas for 14 per cent and coal for 35 per cent, with the balance shared between nuclear, hydroelectric and wood. By 2008 the share of oil and gas had zoomed, that of

---

3   Electric power for motor vehicles is still a product with flat tyres, having been invented in the nineteenth century and still having not played any important role. As Roger Bishop wrote in an article about hybrids, 'There are also some rather ludicrous excesses being engineered by our major automotive companies under the auspices of protection of the environment ... difficult to see how even a hybrid drivetrain can add much environmental credibility to a 2.3 tonne limo motivated by a 5 liter engine' (*European Automotive Design*, May 2008).

coal had come down to about 20 per cent, wood was making an insignificant contribution and on a percentage basis the part contributed by hydroelectric power had shrunk while nuclear power production had gained – with a smaller percentage going to new sorts of renewable energy.

Statistics on the pattern of change in energy types in the European Union are more loaded towards oil and gas than those just mentioned. In order of magnitude, oil accounts for about 42 per cent and gas for another 22 per cent; taken together the two represent nearly two thirds of energy supplies.[4] Britain, Norway (not an EU member) and Romania are black gold producers, but as a whole countries in the EU are far from being energy-independent. Eastern, Central and Western European countries use coal and buy a huge amount of energy from somebody else– and to do so they give their economies as collateral.

More to the point, the amount of energy consumed by the average European every year is enough to make a voyage by car one-and-a half times around the Earth. Spoilage of energy is unprecedented and no effort, official or individual, is made for conservation in spite of big words to the contrary and the fact that, of the total amount of energy consumed in the European Union:

- only 42 per cent is produced within its borders; and

- 58 per cent is imported, putting the old continent at the mercy of energy producers.

To understand America's and Europe's dependence on imported energy better the reader should know that spoilage is widespread and this happens in both a transparent and an opaque way.[5] An incandescent bulb made of a wire filament encased in glass emits as light only 5 per cent of the energy it consumes; the balance is wasted as heat. Fluorescent lamps, which consist of tubes filled with mercury vapour, are roughly four times more efficient, but they still waste 80 per cent of energy as heat.

- The Greens bet their political capital on environmental protection but, blah-blah-blah left aside, they have provided no roadmap for doing so.

---

4    With the exception of France where about 80 per cent of electricity production is nuclear.
5    Which is true worldwide.

- Of other political parties, too, the environmental zeal is smoke and mirrors, and this exacerbates the energy problem.

One of the hoaxes at the end of the twentieth century was that some countries abided by emission-reduction targets under the Kyoto Protocol, while others didn't. If they miss them, those who supposedly do abide can buy up offsetting pollution credits from countries that have cut their emissions. Or, they may outright flout the Kyoto obligations they solemnly undertook (which they do), and admit to voters that they were not really serious about curbing greenhouse gases (which they aren't).

Nor are $CO_2$ emissions the only challenge connected to pollution. Disposing of computers, monitors, printers and mobile phones is a large and growing environmental challenge. An estimated 20 million to 50 million tons of *e-waste* is produced each year, and according to experts e-waste has become the fastest-growing pollution source – eventually to be joined by solar panel and other alternative energy waste.

## 2. Energy Prizefighters and their Remit

It is indeed surprising that the European Union's prime ministers, heads of state, and Brussels-based EU Commission have one-track minds in terms of energy and pollution and, therefore, they don't understand how much can be achieved by reducing overall energy demand in an orderly, well-studied manner. In spite of all the rhetoric about $CO_2$ and the control of pollution, literally nobody seems to care about *energy savings* because telling the people to cut their energy appetite is political dynamite. Yet,

- conservation of energy should be at the top of everybody's agenda; and

- nobody should ever forget that, geopolitical reasons aside, the better-known energy sources are in finite supply.

Affordable and reliable energy is not God-given, even if it is seen as an indisputable right. Billions of times every day, the flip of a switch, turn of a key, push of a button, or some other command sees to it that energy is delivered instantly. Few people doubt that this energy is the economy's fuel, but even fewer ask, 'How long will the clean electric power last? Or the oil at the pump for my car?'

As the thrust for energy is not going to abate and spoilage continues, governments are obliged to guarantee by all means that there will be no disruptions in supply. Europe today imports from Russia 43 per cent of its gas, and projections bring that share to 60 per cent by 2030. Even a ten-day interruption in gas supply can have serious consequences, as documented by the events of January 2009 in the wake of the Russian–Ukrainian rift over the latter's delayed payment of Gazprom's bills. On this occasion:

- both companies and consumers found out the hard way what it means to be short of gas supplies; and

- this brought up another aspect of the energy crisis – the event of shortage, which added to the financial pain they had experienced at the filling stations when oil hit $145 per barrel.

If the market for energy is huge, this is not necessarily true of the supply. At present the world's population consumes some 15 terawatts ($10^{12}$ watts) of power. The price tag attached to it is an estimated $6 trillion ($10^{12}$ dollars) per year, nearly a third of global economic output. No wonder that a high priority in the US, EU, China, India and all other countries is to assure that energy supply will be on call.

There is also the challenge of energy transport and delivery. Proximity pays a crucial role, and Europe's nearest energy supply for oil and gas, particularly the latter, is Russia. Russia saved Europe from Napoleon nearly 200 years ago and from Hitler in the 1940s. It would be apt to welcome it back into the European fold. Russia, however, has its own problems and priorities as energy producer and distributor, which up to a point it has tried to solve with the assistance of Western oil firms.

But only up to a point. One of the many aspects of the disorder that Boris Yeltsin left behind when he retired has been the looting of the Russian economy by people in his inner circle, particularly of resources like energy that matter the most. Mikhail Khodorovsky, and his company, Yukos, is an example. In 1990–1993 he had entered the Yeltsin government, serving first as economic advisor to the Russian Prime Minister then as Deputy Minister of Fuel and Energy.[6] From there he became an oil billionaire – but not for long.

One of the Yeltsin legacies which interests us in this section was the Production-Sharing Agreements (PSAs) with foreign energy giants, which Vladimir Putin aimed to dismantle. They were signed in the 1990s by consortia led by Royal Dutch Shell and Exxon Mobil, to provide advanced oil exploration technology as well as assurance against unpredictable changes in oil demand and price.

The PSAs stipulated that the Russian state took a share of the profits only after the costs had been recouped, and this was one of the reasons the Putin government objected to them, the other being its desire to gain control over the country's natural resources. The downside of the renationalization of the PSA oil fields was the exposure the Russian government took to the oil market's volatility in terms of demand and pricing.

As should be recalled in this connection, the PSAs were invented in the mid-1990s when oil prices were low and Russia was struggling under the weak Yeltsin government to develop its energy supplies. Aimed at attracting foreign investors, they were designed to insulate them from legal and taxation surprises. But with oil prices reaching for the sky in 2006–2008, many Russian officials soured on the whole idea of PSAs.

Poor management of the PSA consortia, out-of-control budgets and the clause of first recovering the costs also contributed to that negative reaction. In the summer of 2006, Sakhalin Energy, a joint venture with Shell said its costs had almost doubled, which might have been due less to adverse environmental and other conditions and more to laxity in cost control.[7] Overruns probably gave the Russian government the idea of a double pressure:

- putting foreign firms under notice to do something about runaway expenditures; and

- prompting them to bring in as major partner Gazprom, Russia's state-controlled big gas firm.

---

6   Paul Klebnikov, *Boris Berezovsky. Godfather of the Kremlin*, Harcourt, New York, 2000.
7   Exxon and Total also saw at least part, if not all, of their investment in Russian energy go up in smoke, as did BP. Under the title 'Yukos Revisited?', *The Economist* reminded its readers that Sakhalin and the sea around it host two of the world's biggest energy projects.

Shell blinked and experts said that it's a safe bet that the others will follow. For Russia, that meant a windfall. Additionally, because energy is a geopolitical weapon (section 3) it has been using it as a tool in the arsenal of its international strategy. Russia is not only the world's biggest producer of oil and gas; as already noted, it is also next-door to Europe.[8]

A successful product strategy, however, must be balanced. Therefore, an important aim for Russia's economy should be to serve markets in North America, Japan and South Korea. (For this reason Shell and its partners Mitsui and Mitsubishi were building Russia's first liquefied natural gas (LNG) plant, which for some time was the only big energy scheme without a local partner.) Sakhalin was part of the master plan to recapture its geopolitical strength through the ingenious use of energy resources.

Political analysts link the resurgence of a self-assertive Russia to the Putin presidency not only because of his strong personality, but also because he knows what he wants and how to capitalize on the recent Germano-Russian friendship (section 4). Strategic analysis outfits say that Germany provides Russia with all the know-how and technological assistance it needs to confront the rest of the world.

Supported by many experts, this thesis has a rationale. With a European Union energy policy in shambles and the sources of supply uneven, some 80 per cent of Germany's energy is currently covered from Russia. This is a near-monopoly, which provides a good incentive for good relations. And *what if*, some political analysts ask, Russia sponsors a permanent seat for Germany in the UN Security Council[9] and the Chinese second it? France will raise a veto, but will it be alone in doing so? Or will America and Britain second it?

- *If* France is all alone in objecting to Germany's UN prestige, *then* we are back again to the 1910s, or worse.

- *If* America joins in vetoing Germany's seat in the Security Council, *then* the Russian–German energy alliance will become much stronger.

---

8   The Baltic Alliance (section 4) capitalizes on this by offering a country-independent channel for gas supplied – which is neither the case of those through the Ukraine and Belarus nor of the new ones being contemplated.

9   According to rumours, Sarkozy made a similar promise to Lula about a seat for Brazil in the UN Security Council.

Politics is a game of chance, and chances are that things are already moving in a way that would precipitate a very tough choice for Barack Obama, the new US president, to which George W. Bush gave no forethought and therefore left him no planning. In his political memoires published in late October 2006, Gerhard Schröder is caustic about Bush who, he says, gave the impression that he took his political decisions after discussing them with God. By contrast, Schröder is most appreciative of Putin's personal relations and national assets.

In a market economy, marking to market an alliance à la Schröder counts a great deal. Putin, he states, has lots of intelligence and an uncommon physical form. This permitted him to confront single-handedly the EU's lightweight heads of state who, during the late October 2006 meeting in Finland, pressed Putin to liberalize the energy market – but without offering concrete counterparts and therefore without any success.

## 3. Energy is a Geopolitical Weapon

In the course of 2008 relations between the US, EU and Russia were in an uneasy phase because of Georgia, the recognition of Kosovo and the issue of American missile defences in Eastern Europe (Chapter 12). Some analysts suggest that this has led to the postponement of a decision to set Georgia and Ukraine on a structured pathway to membership of NATO. Others say that this was never really on the cards, because it is far from achieving unanimity, and one should rather look at the background reasons – precisely at the energy policies.

If egos are kept out of the geopolitical equation, since they have no rightful place there and their contribution can only be negative, then Georgia and the Ukraine are leftovers. The central theme is energy exploration and neither country today qualifies as a potential producer. New finds are hugely more critical than secondary geographical outposts, particularly as:

* no major oil fields have been found since 1976 and

* experts suspect that there may be no more around, in any case.

Optimists on energy issues suggest that technological progress in exploitation might allow output to rise for another decade. Oil industry specialists, however, argue that world production is already at or near its peak.[10] New fields in deep water are extremely expensive to exploit and exploration is stretching the limits of available technology and knowhow.

To appreciate the importance of finding alternatives to depleted resources rather than beating around the bush, one must keep in mind that the world currently consumes the equivalent of about 230 million barrels of oil *per day*. Experts suggest that by 2030 the world's energy needs will require double that amount in oil-equivalent barrels per day, and even that may be an underestimate. Growth in oil demand will be driven by a long list of factors, among the most important being a big increase in transportation, especially in developing countries.

- As section 1 underlined, oil is uniquely suited as a transportation fuel; and

- in the short term there is practically no alternative to it on a global scale.

NATO or no NATO, decision-makers must pay attention to the fact that the West is particularly vulnerable in energy terms because its oil supplies are being depleted very rapidly. Up to the 1950s the US was a net exporter of oil. Since then America has become the largest importer worldwide. With oil imports at over 60 per cent of US needs and production on decline, there is no quick solution to the domestic energy dilemma.

For their part, domestic natural gas supplies are gradually falling, even with record drilling activity. Imported liquefied natural gas (LNG) is providing some relief, but the American, European and Asian markets are very hungry for energy, with the result that they aggressively compete among themselves in the global LNG supply chain. American experts say that:

- the global energy markets continue to endure tight supply while demand rapidly expands;

- phenomenal capital investments are required across the globe to search out and develop future production sources; and

---

10  Paul Roberts, *The End of Oil*, Bloomsbury, London, 2005.

- large-scale energy projects cost billions, or at least hundreds of millions of dollars, take years to build and may last for less than two decades.

*If* NATO were an energy exploration and defence alliance, *then*, in all likelihood its appeal would have been much greater than it is at present – and it would have also been fulfilling a most valuable mission. This, however, is not the case, and the 20 years that have elapsed since the Soviet Union dissolved have seen to it that the large majority of people have essentially forgotten all about the threat that used to be.

This has practical implications. During the Cold War's long decades, the European governments depended on, and deferred to, US decisions on where and how NATO should act. In the present globalized world, where military threats are dispersed, judgements differ about priorities as well as in regard to what to do and where. With each government wanting to have its own way, the command-and-control structure became dysfunctional. What remains unchanged is the fact that:

- *if* a union or an alliance is not able to speak with one voice to the challenges which it confronts,

- *then déclinisme* becomes the rule, the likelihood of being successful in what one does fades away, the lines dividing the union's or alliance's members get deeper and new problems override old concerns.

While energy is a geopolitical weapon, the might of classical military gear has lost a great deal of its weight as the Russian invasion of Afghanistan and more recent excursions into Iraq and (again) Afghanistan demonstrate. Real estate for real estate's sake is no longer the prize it used to be, by any stretch of the imagination.

The 2001 invasion of Iraq and the 2008 Georgian crisis have exposed not only gaping holes in opinions and dividing lines among NATO members, but also, and most significantly, a shift in the global balance of power. They have also confirmed Europe's sense of an America in relative decline. Not many years ago Jacques Chirac and Gerhard Schröder dreamt of a multipolar world, in which several powers would wield clout – and they found a partner in the Bush administration, which was compounding mistake upon mistake.

According to a growing body of political analysts and articles published in the American press, the invasion of Iraq had nothing really to do with weapons of mass destruction (WMDs), which were never found, but plenty to do with safeguarding and controlling energy supply sources. If so, even leaving aside the human cost, it has been utterly mismanaged and therefore a failure. The pros say that there was a rationale:

- at any time, the local dictator could take control of oil resources in Kuwait and Saudi Arabia using them for blackmail; and

- insurgents or terrorists could disrupt energy routes, set oil wells on fire and blow up refineries, depriving the US and the EU of Middle East oil supplies.

The pros, however, don't care to face the fact about why and how the whole operation turned into a nightmare. Critics say that, when he was appointed all-mighty American pro-consul in Iraq, Bob Bremer made three fatal mistakes overnight, which led to the mess: he disbanded the 300,000 strong Iraqi army, initiated a deep process of de-Baathization and did away with the representative assembly of Iraqi notables put together by his predecessor.[11]

The mismanaged Iraqi adventure has been counterproductive in many ways. Leaving the human consequences aside, one of the ironies is that its forces consumed 7.3 million litres of fuel per day in Iraq alone – accounting for 70 per cent by weight of all supplies delivered by the Department of Defense. The DoD also spent over $1 per kw on electric power in battle zone – an order of magnitude more than the civilian prize.[12]

As for purely military results, within the geopolitical perspective chosen by the Bush administration, with the notable exception of the British fighting force, whether we talk of Iraq or Afghanistan the multinational troops did not provide much assistance. They were made up of troops from different nations which had separate rules of engagement with the result that:

- coordinated action was a nightmare and

---

11   Allegedly blessed by George W. Bush, Bremer's hubris cost dearly in American lives – 5,000 dead and 95,000 wounded and mutilated – as well as in British lives, and a much greater tragedy among the Iraqis.

12   *The Economist*, 6 December 2008.

- at the end of the day they consumed more resources than their contribution could justify.

This is no reflection on the quality or bravery of these troops, but on the fact that schemes which involve a patchwork of troops don't really work. The many differences in fighting factors end by showing up in poor results, which essentially means that a great variety in military training, gear and line of command is counterproductive because an amalgamation delivers little or nothing in fighting capability – or in solving any problem, including energy problems.

All this is quite relevant when discussing about geopolitical forces because international relations are a matter of military and economic power, as Henry Kissinger wisely advised Dick Cheney.[13] Moreover, to the Iraq misfortunes and those in Afghanistan have been added the deep economic, banking and credit crisis of 2007–2009 (as well as the weak dollar), which saw to it that, with the interminable salvage operations of the banking industry, economic power, too, took leave of absence not only in America, but also in the EU.

## 4. NordStream and the German–Russian Energy Axis

While German relations with France have cooled significantly, a leaked memo by the German foreign ministry's think-tank triggered a heated debate because it exposed the foreign ministry's thinking and highlighted friction between foreign ministry (under a Schröder ally) and chancellery. Not without reason, the leaked paper argues that the EU should strengthen its economic and cultural links with Russia, an approach it calls 'growing closer by interweaving'.[14] This explains:

- why some have dubbed it 'a new Ostpolitik' and

- why Russia now feels more confident to assert its own foreign policy's independence.

Political analysts suggest that the Russian position toward the United States, the rest of Europe and China has been most significantly strengthened by the *Berlin–Moscow energy axis*. 'EU minus Germany' finds itself at a huge

---

13  Bob Woodward, *'State of Denial': Bush At War, Part III*, Simon & Schuster, New York, 2006.
14  *The Economist*, 18 November 2006.

disadvantage in negotiating an energy deal with the Russians provided Brussels has precise goals, in negotiations, which is not sure.

In the absence of goals, bureaucrats and heads of state use platitudes, threats and impertinence. In the mid-October 2006 summit of the (then) 25 EU members plus Russia, which took place in Helsinki, furious at being accused of violations of human rights, Putin turned the tables on Romano Prodi, the then Italian Prime Minister and former CEO of the EU, telling him: 'The word Mafia is Italian not Russian.'[15]

The German Chancellor, too, was treated in the most impertinent manner by the President of the EU Commission when she refused to pay for a €200 billion plan to relaunch the EU economy. Brussels and some EU heads of state seem unable to understand that something important changed in Germany when Helmut Kohl's defeat as chancellor in 1998 brought to power Gerhard Schröder, the Social Democratic Party and the Greens in a loose alliance.

A new epoch had started even if at the time nobody gave thought to what would be the cost of Germany's red and green coalition. The best guess was that the new government would do nothing other than keep the German economy in hibernation, as Kohl had done in his long years in power, for fear of public reaction to:

- structural labour changes and

- other urgently needed reforms to get the German economy moving again.

This prognostication about inertia was only partly valid, because Schröder and his socialists found the courage to move ahead with some mild restructuring of unemployment benefits and health care. Another Schröder initiative, however, proved to be more deep-rooted. By risking everything in a single throw, he set in motion a new foreign policy.

Schröder's government approved the Nord Stream gas pipeline from Russia under the Baltic Sea, bypassing Poland and the Baltic States and thereby providing a route free of different sovereignties (after quitting as chancellor,

---

15  *Libération*, 23 October 2006.

Schröder chaired and chairs the shareholders' committee of the consortium building it). Nord Stream competes with other gas conduits:

- Yamal, through Belarus and Poland;

- Brotherwood, through Ukraine and Hungary;

- Blue Stream (so far to Turkey, to be continued to Central Europe by Nabucco);

- South Stream, through Bulgaria, Greece and Albania (being planned).

For the Germans, the Nord Stream pipeline means greater security, but some of the other countries in the region (albeit a minority) see it as a threat. Former Soviet satellites in particular have suggested that Russia might use it (as well as the pumping stations) for espionage. That's far-fetched.

The 1998/1999 switch in Germany's post-World War II strategic goals has been a sort of Gaullism which started by insisting that the country's foreign policy be decided in Berlin. This partly explains German opposition to the Iraq War, which helped Schröder to get re-elected in 2002 but also badly damaged Atlantic relations. Schröder's nationalistic approach led to both close friendship with Russia and the pursuit of a permanent seat at the UN Security Council (section 3).

Critics say that the pipeline under the Baltic linking energy-rich Russia to energy-hungry Germany is only the visible tip of the iceberg. They also add that, as with any iceberg, the main part cannot be seen. For instance, even by removing the prime minister who originated this Baltic alliance, Germany did not abandon its new-found friendship with Russia. The pros answer that there is absolutely nothing wrong with that.

Well before the time of Otto von Bismarck, its nineteenth-century Iron Chancellor and builder of the German empire, Germany's different kingdoms and principalities had always cultivated relations with both Eastern and Western neighbours, and for good reason. The great northern central European plain has classically been a natural path for invaders from the East, while in the West stood France – which was then, in much of the seventeenth as well as eighteenth and early nineteenth centuries,

- Europe's most populous and

- most powerful nation state.

The first time Germany attached itself to the West practically without reservations was in the immediate post-World War II years. Konrad Adenauer gambled Germany's post-war future on the Atlantic Alliance, and saw his country's underwriting and membership of the European Union (then European Economic Community, EEC, see Chapter 1) as a commitment that would last. West Germany's leveraged buyout (LBO) of East Germany changed the rules of the game.

In a way emulating the policies followed by Britain, France and other EU members, the roots of the Russian–German Energy Axis were planted by Schröder without any consultation with the other states of the EU, but the energy alliance also got Angela Merkel's implicit blessing.

- This lone-wolf approach is no different from the policy followed by every other sovereign nation, including European Union members.

- Practically every government makes commitments in a totally unilateral way, *as if* the country is at the same time in and out of the EU. Why not Germany?

The after-effect is political, but not threatening. The fact that America wanted to ostracize Moscow after Russian troops pushed into Georgia in August 2008, capitalizing on a severe error in judgement by Tbilisi, was also political. But Germany appeared eager to return to business as usual – sceptical about toughening the EU's stance.

In a memorandum to Barack Obama, the American Institute for Contemporary German Studies, a think-rank, gave warning that differences over Russia could harm the relationship severely, while Germany and America may clash over Iran.[16] This is not impossible because the difference of opinion extends all the way to what to do about Iran's nuclear weapons menace.

---

16  *The Economist*, 1 November 2008.

Still a German–American split is rather far-fetched, for two reasons. First the crisis in Georgia was not enough to shock the EU into a common position on Russia, even if it was Frank-Walter Steinmeier, Germany's Foreign Minister, who demanded an inquiry into the causes and conduct of war – reckoning that Russia was unreasonably held responsible for a war that was started (and lost) by the hot-headed Georgians, probably (but not certainly) with US blessing.

The second reason is that the collapse of Soviet power, along with memories of World War II carnage left Russia allergic to militarism, rather than with a spirit of aggression. Why do the Russians need to scare Western Europe or America? Their interest is to benefit from a collaboration, not from a confrontation.

In fact, the Russian military budget in 2007 was at rock bottom at less than the equivalent of $50 billion while the American was 11 times higher.[17] This is also shown by the equipment used in Georgia: World War II crop tanks, no surveillance drones, no night vision equipment and age-old dumb bombs rather than modern smart ones. None of this poses a threat to European defences.

Two questions remain open, however. One is the likely move towards a Russian-led 'Gas OPEC'. Three nations today control among themselves over 50 per cent of proved gas reserves worldwide: Russia 27 per cent, Iran 15 per cent and Qatar 15 per cent – which means that the global supply of gas is concentrated in even fewer hands than oil is. Still, according to expert opinions, a gas shock akin to the oil shocks of the 1970s is unlikely, even if an Organization of Gas Exporting Countries gets off the ground.

- Long-term contracts also shield both buyer and seller from competition; and

- the way the international trade in gas works is another impediment to arm twisting.

Most of the gas supplies are sold in an opaque manner, not on the open market. There exist long-term contracts between a single producer and a single buyer, and there is little competition and almost no transparency in prices. Whether through pipelines or by ship in the form of liquefied natural gas (LNG),

- few firms are willing to invest the necessary billions without a guaranteed customer; and

---

17 *The Economist*, 20 September 2008.

- an enormous expense is associated to the infrastructure needed to transport gas.

A further question concerns the role a German–Russian technical alliance might play in oil and gas exploration in the Arctic. Russia has been beefing up its presence in the so-called High North. Between the main areas of Norway's and Russia's oil and gas platforms there is a grey zone which may hide plenty of wealth and, while Russia's training and upkeep of material support has improved, it is no less true that German technology and expertise might provide a quantum leap.

In mid-July 2009 the news media were dominated by some curious headlines, starting with the lavish coverage by *Euronews* – a European Union-funded television outfit – of heads of state signing the agreement for the Nabucco gas pipeline. This is the project that starts in Northern Iraq and zigzags through Asia Minor prior to landing near Istanbul with the intention of reaching central Europe.

With great uncertainty about Nabucco's rational and future, it is (to say the least) most surprising that *Euronews* stated in its 14 July 2009 late evening broadcast that, with Nabucco, Turkey reasserts itself as 'a great power ...'.[18] Hillary Clinton sent the same message like *Euronews* by calling Turkey a great power[19] (but with feet of clay and an empty pipeline in the middle).

Nabucco is and will remain far from a done deal as it is unclear where the gas will come from: Iraq, Iran and Turkmenistan have large reserves, but hardly qualify as riskless sources of supply. Azerbaijan can play Europe off against Russia, which is seeking supplies for its rival South Stream pipeline. Turkey angered the Azerbaijanis through its rapprochement with Armenia – an anger which led Erdogan to reverse this rapprochement policy.

There is, of course, little doubt that the European Union must diversify its energy supply and get out of its precarious dependence on Russian gas, which is presently by far its biggest source of energy. (This dependence was shattered by the winter of 2008–2009 gas feud between Russia and the Ukraine.) But pipedreams:

- based on pipelines empty of committed energy sources; and

---

18   Also, the TV camera focused on Erdogan but not on any of the other participants to the meeting – as if it were a paid advertisement.

19   *The Economist*, 28 July 2009.

- planned to be built sometime in the future, are no way to diversification.

Moreover, the EU should have no illusion that Turkey will try to extract a sky-high price for its empty conduit. Apart from using it to press for EU membership, it will be asking the EU's taxpayers for lots of money as Turkish economic activity tanked in the first half of 2009, while:

- consumer price index inflation (CPI) accelerated;

- industrial production caved in by a depressing 24 per cent; and

- gross domestic product (GDP) contracted by an unprecedented 13.8 per cent year-on-year.

In exchange for a pie in the sky, the EU will be asked to nurse all these wounds. The bill will be bigger than anybody currently guesses, and in all likelihood the hospitalization of the Turkish economy will be more lasting than that of the Baltic countries (and Iceland), which have required massive financial support to save themselves from falling off the cliff. Turkey knocked at the vault's door. The EU cannot continue to support economies in fringe countries which have a long record of mismanaging themselves.

## 5. Germany's Commercial Shift towards Eastern Europe

It is easier making alliances than changing people's minds, but in the immediate post-World War II years the North Atlantic Treaty Organization succeeded in doing both. It succeeded because it provided an American conventional and nuclear commitment to protect Western Europe, and this focused people's thinking on the need to group together to safeguard their personal freedoms. By contrast,

- today NATO is unable to stop theocratic Iran from becoming nuclear; and

- the United Nations is just as ineffectual, because it is divided, very timid and hence useless, in taking any action.

Ironically, as the Soviet nuclear threat waned, so did NATO's resolve, the UN's reach and the Treaty of Rome's after-effects. In its early years, the European Economic Community had strengthened the economic incentive of cooperation among its members and put a sort of seal of approval on a European integration. This worked for a decade or two, as France and Germany increased their commercial, industrial and capital links.

Roughly one-third of French exports went to Germany, and the flow of goods from Germany to France was just as strong. Beneath the surface, however, this has been a hollow friendship. Since the beginning of the 1990s, the German economy's other international capital connections increased sharply and, with globalization, trade between France and Germany waned. In the 2006–2008 timeframe Russia was the second fastest-growing export market among Germany's main trading partners.

Theoretically, since the completion of the single market in 1993 the commercial integration of the EU should have strengthened French–German intercourse. In practice, Germany's disenchantment with France and its fast-growing financial direct investments (FDIs) in Central and Eastern European economies (the EU's new member states), tilted the balance. A couple of other old EU members, too, have seen a fall in their share of German imports, while imports from the new EU members increased.

The pattern has been a regional shift which, experts suggest, is not solely the result of direct competition between foreign sellers in the global market. In large measure, it is attributed to a subtle government policy and the German companies' strategic decisions: shifts observed in the structure of German imports are partly due to German FDIs and partly to the search for new alliances in Eastern Europe. Since the second half of the 1990s:

- the import share of France, until then Germany's most important EU trading partner, and to a lesser extent of Italy and Spain, dived.

- By contrast, commercial and financial relations between Germany, the Czech Republic, Hungary, Poland, Slovakia and Slovenia have moved up.

A similar trend appeared with the amount of FDIs in the chemicals industry, the second most important industrial sector for German investors. Until the late 2008 global downturn which hit export trade like a hammer, Germany had a healthy current-account surplus and was a net exporter of capital. The high level of German FDIs was good for German companies, even if at the same time the export of jobs abroad encountered criticism from the German public. In this and other cases, offshoring has raised questions, two of which are general and one is specific to Germany's case:

1. how to be competitive in the global economy when at home the labour market is inflexible and labour costs are too high;

2. what kind of economic links exist at the macroeconomic level between big FDIs and at-home employment opportunities; and

3. how to judge the effects of large German investments in central and Eastern Europe, in view of the Russian–German energy axis.

In regard to issues 1 and 2, up to the 2008 deepening economic crisis, cost-driven FDIs had to be examined against the fact of increased global competitive pressures, particularly from China. This is true all over the EU and US. While domestic enterprises have specific qualities which make it possible for them to compete internationally, their advantages decrease in view of high labour costs, exorbitant social entitlements and unwarranted strikes in their home country (for instance, in Italy and France). Shifting production abroad has therefore become necessary to ensure:

• the home-based companies' global competitiveness; and

• their long-term survival in a global market which disdains and punishes nineteenth-century socialist labour practices.

These are issues which weigh most heavily not only on Germany, but also on France, Italy, Spain, Portugal and Greece (in Euroland), as well as Sweden and Denmark. By promising much more welfare than their economies can afford, most EU countries find themselves on the edge of an economic abyss. But as far as the future of the European Union is concerned, the greatest amount of disruptive power is embedded in politics.

There is little doubt that, after having been manipulated by France to serve its interests, in the immediate two post-WWII decades (which it accepted by necessity), Germany sought its own way. And given the total failure of political integration in the European Union, Germany now chooses the alliance(s) that serve it best – which are different from those it had in most of the second half of the twentieth century.

It is important, as well, to notice that while Germany is making this switch, France, Italy and Spain are losing the leverage they might have had in the EU. The silly economic nationalism Spain has shown with E.ON and Endesa (Chapter 10) is not making things better. In fact, it looks as if some EU governments specialize in self-destruction.

Political analysts suggest that there is one more geopolitical issue to consider: *what if* Germany assumes a neutral attitude towards Iran and its nuclear weapons? For over five years, the permanent members of the divided and largely impotent UN Security Council have been divided about imposing sanctions on Iran for failing to suspend its uranium-enrichment programme. From the EU, Britain, France and Germany have invested plenty of effort in tortuous negotiations that started in 2003. Precious time has been lost to Iranian indecision after Russia proposed to enrich uranium on the Iranians' behalf. They eventually said 'No'.

In 2006 Iranians swept past a Security Council resolution giving them until 31 August to suspend enrichment, by intimating that they might do so during a new round of negotiations. With that gambit, they emboldened Russia and China, two permanent members of the Council, to reiterate their long-standing opposition to UN sanctions.

Meeting after meeting involved the five permanent UN Security Council members *and* Germany in a fruitless search for a compromise solution. Germany offered its services as an intermediary between the diametrically opposed viewpoints of the US and Russia. Is this not the first step towards UN Security Council membership, starting with a *strapontin* (folding seat) in the nuclear armaments agenda?

Germany has a special relationship with Iran because it is one of its important trading customers within the shortlist of material Security Council resolutions permit to be imported. Indeed, as the biggest Western exporter to Iran, Germany has considerable leverage in the country. And *The Economist* quoted a senior Israeli official, whose country has more to fear from an Iranian atomic bomb than any other, as having said 'Germany is playing a responsible role on Iran.'[20]

---

20  *The Economist*, 1 November 2008.

## 6. The Need for Sound Governance is Overwhelming

John Foster Dulles, the former American Secretary of State, once said that only the strong can be productive and only the productive can be free. People, companies and countries would be well advised to keep in mind Dulles' dictum. Being productive is not just the better policy, it is the only one *if* one wants to survive.

A common market, and even more so a military alliance, are not just pieces of paper signed by politicians. To have any weight they must have deliverables, backed up by forces that are not only military, but also economic and industrial. In 2009, however, the West finds itself in a process of de-industrialization while other countries – particularly China – industrialize.

The knowledge society and the service economy may have merits, but we should never forget that World War II was won by America's incredible capacity to manufacture all sorts of goods and weapons, transport them coast to coast, then over the seas and deliver them where they were urgently needed in theatres of war. This does not underrate the human contribution; it underlines it.

It was George Marshall, US Chief of Staff in World War II, who aptly pointed out[21] that the value of the military lies in its ability to continue to deliver. The same is true of economic forces. Both will be paper tigers without a strong industry behind them. Even in this modern age, manufacturing and transport capacity remains a topmost pillar of any state, multinational trade organization or military alliance. Along with that, at the top of the list of priorities come:

- goals which have to be reached;

- timetables to be respected; and

- resources to be engaged, clearly stating by whom and how much.

Chapter 12 brought to the reader's attention old, worn-out objectives that are unable to motivate into action. Therefore, maintaining them definitely is the wrong policy, which is true both of the EU and of NATO. *If* NATO, or better the organization which succeeds it, is going to be successful in combating fundamentalism and terrorism, *then* it must clearly state both its aims and the

---

21  In a meeting with Manhattan Project scientists.

characteristics of insurgency it plans to combat. The terrorist acts in which a religiously motivated insurgency engages are based on four pillars:

- blind belief in a dogma;

- popular support for the movement;

- a sustained trend of sabotage and armed attacks; and

- the ability of insurgent groups to act autonomously, albeit with a certain coordination by an invisible hand.

In the case of plain malfeasance or gangsterism, the first bullet is replaced by lust and greed and the second by the mafia boss and the hierarchical structure he adopts. By contrast, the last two bullets remain practically unaltered, while a fifth one is added: inter-gang wars.

Combating an insurgency is much more challenging than facing a standing army. Moreover, terrorism has been internationalized and it often uses ammunition the West gives to some parties it considers to be its clients – but who in reality work for one of the insurgency's obscure branches. The explosives used in the 2005 London bombings, for example, where innocent people were murdered on the buses and on the Underground, were brought from Bosnia,[22] where NATO spread them lavishly to upstage the Bosnians against the Serbs.

Bosnia was one of the big blunders of the EU and NATO, decided on lightheartedly and built on previous mistakes. When in 1999 Bill Clinton came to the conclusion to confront Slobodan Milosevic, his advisors told him that bombing over 48 or 72 hours would make the Serbian dictator bend.[23] That proved to be a very lightweight assessment. It took not 72 hours but 78 days to complete the trick, and as so often happens at the top level of organizations:

- the US President's advisors were selling hope; and

- they were telling their boss what he wanted to hear, not the real situation (unless, of course, they were totally incompetent).

---

22  Bob Woodward, *'State of Denial': Bush At War, Part III*, Simon & Schuster, NY, 2006.
23  Idem.

In a way, Clinton's hand was forced by a policy of artificial states created in Europe in the twentieth century. Right after World War I there was Czechoslovakia, which broke up some years after World War II. Yugoslavia, too, was an artificial state and, when it fell apart, the 1995 Dayton Accord (in the US) created Bosnia composed of two halves: a Moslem–Croat federation and a Serb republic.

The peace agreement brokered by the Clinton administration ended the civil war, but the political system it engineered entrenched, rather than smoothed out, ethnic divisions. To keep itself alive and going, Bosnia has received more than €14 billion ($18 billion) in foreign aid since 1995 and has its security guaranteed by 2,000 European Union peacekeepers. 'It's time to pay attention to Bosnia again, if we don't want things to get nasty very quickly,' says Richard Holbrooke, the Clinton official who brokered the Dayton Accord. By late 2008 the artificial state had shown signs of breaking apart.[24]

Kosovo is another story where the US and the EU screwed things up. Rodolph Richard, a French diplomat based in Pristina and delegate to the United Nations mission, reported to Bernard Kouchner, the French foreign minister, that Kosovo was a microcosm of delinquents with connections to economic, criminal and political circles. Their activities ranged from the drug trade to money laundering. Richard also alerted his superior to the troubling role played by British and Americans who intervened to free the local drug bosses when they were arrested.[25]

One would be allowed to think that as far as the EU, US, and NATO action in the Balkans is concerned, the goals to be reached are muddy at best, while forecasting and planning have been alien words to the decision-makers. Yet, as President Eisenhower once said, 'The plan is nothing. *Planning* is everything.'

Another major ingredient of a successful political and military effort is organization. During World War II and in the immediate post-war years, America showed exceptional organizational and managerial skills, but by the 1990s these had waned.

To make matters worse, there is unprecedented mismanagement and lack of accountability, even in logistics. The following example comes from Iraq.

---

24  *International Herald Tribune*, 11 December 2008.
25  *Le Canard Enchaîné*, 18 July 2007. Under UN administration, Kosovo was kept alive by the presence of 17,000 blue berets and plenty of financial support. But, as Richard stated, the rule has been a well organized and generalized corruption – with the risk of being governed by criminals who would be in charge of political, economic and social affairs.

The way a 2008 Pentagon audit had it, a cool $8.2 billion of American taxpayers' money spent by the US army on contractors in Iraq has gone without leaving much of a trace. The audit found that:

- almost none of the payments followed federal rules; and

- in some cases contracts worth millions of dollars were paid despite little or no record of what was received.

The Pentagon audit discovered cases of a stunning lack of accountability in the way the US military spent about $1.8 billion in seized or frozen Iraqi assets, in the early phases of the conflict. According to documents displayed by Pentagon auditors at the hearing before the House Committee on Oversight and Government Reform, in one instance a cash payment of $320 million in Iraqi money was authorized on the basis of a single signature and the words 'Iraqi Salary Payment' on an invoice. In another, $11 million was paid to IAP, an American contractor, on the basis of a voucher with no indication of deliverables.

The Pentagon report, *Internal Controls Over Payments Made in Iraq, Kuwait and Egypt*, also notes that mysterious payments, whose total amounts had not been publicly disclosed, included $68 million to Britain, $45 million to Poland and $21 million to South Korea. Despite repeated requests, Pentagon auditors said they were unable to determine why these payments were made and what was delivered by those who received them.[26]

Nor are these the only incidents. Logistics, formerly a great strength of American management, is in a shambles. In 2008 Robert Gates, US Secretary of Defense, fired two top airforce officials after the service inadvertently shipped missile nose cones to Taiwan. A year earlier, in 2007, the airforce had to explain how a bomber mistakenly carried six nuclear missiles across America. *Déclinisme* has brought to the ground even the quality of management.

In another instance, a Pentagon audit into nuclear safeguards found that the airforce could not account for many components previously included in its inventory, with more than 1,000 items missing. A Pentagon spokesman conceded there was a weakness in record keeping.

- America used to be the world leader in security and logistics stewardship. No mistakes were permissible.

---

26  *International Herald Tribune*, 24 May 2008.

- But, as with banking regulation and supervision, under the Bush administration laxity and *déclinisme* were given the upper hand.

NATO or no NATO, what is happening and mis-happening around the globe teaches a valuable lesson about what can go wrong with opinionated and superficial decision-making. The aforementioned case of Kosovo provides an example of the nadir in quality of decisions and management skills. Kosovo has been 'recognized' by microstates like Nauru but not by China, India, Russia, Brazil, Spain, Egypt or even most Moslem countries – which leaves its intellectual parents, the US, EU and NATO – fully exposed.

That absence of recognition is interesting because since the end of the local war in 1999, Kosovo has come under the jurisdiction of the United Nations. However, it is not the UN but the US and the EU which set up the office of the international civilian representative (ICR), investing him with sweeping powers. Pieter Feith, its titleholder, is also the EU's special representative in Kosovo. 'He and his team are here as tourists. What are they doing? They can't take over the role they were assigned ...', said a quotation (and commentary) published in the daily press.[27] It looks as if NATO and the EU have invented a new mismanagement doctrine.

## 7. In the Land of the Blind, the One-Eyed Man is King[28]

While many people blame the US and the EU for inventing a country like Kosovo and destabilizing the Balkans, nobody can blame Germany for seeking its way in energy supplies; and the same is true of Britain, France and other EU members. The lack of political integration saw to it that there is no common policy and what is called 'European Union' is rather a disunion, with every member state following the policy that suits it best.

- A common strategy is nowhere to be seen; and

- organization and structure are quite unknown concepts, whose absence is leading to hilarious events.

---

27  *The Economist*, 31 May 2008.
28  'In regione caecorum rex est luscus', Desiderius Erasmus (circa 1510).

A recent example was Barack Obama's attendance at what was described as a US–EU 'summit' in Prague, right after the 2 April 2009 G-20 'summit' in London and the NATO 'summits' in France and Germany which followed it. Apart from welcoming Croatia and the megastate of Albania as the alliance's new members, that NATO 'summit' had to decide who would be its next secretary general.

Three men topped the list – Anders Fogh Rasmussen of Denmark, Radek Sikorski of Poland and Peter MacKay of Canada. The strongest candidate (who was finally confirmed) was Rasmussen, the Danish prime minister since 2001, but he faced the opposition and ire of radical Islamists over cartoons of the Prophet Muhammad in Danish newspapers published four years earlier, in 2005.

Recep Tayyip Erdogan, the Turkish Prime Minister, joined the Islamist chorus in opposing the nomination of Rasmussen, and as Turkey is a NATO member this represented headwinds. In 2005, as Prime Minister, Rasmussen had refused to meet Turkish and other Moslem diplomats to discuss the aforementioned cartoons in a Danish newspaper, correctly saying that free speech was non-negotiable.

However, on 6 April 2009 in Istanbul he took a soft line, speaking of the balance between free speech and a deep respect for personal religious convictions. The former Danish prime minister probably forgot that:

- selling one's soul for a job is an awfully wrong policy;

- we did not fight Hitler and his Nazis to fall under the yoke of the Islamists;

- cartooning, and the critique of ridicule which come with it, has been for centuries one of the characteristics of a free society;

- 'cartoons exercise a great deal of influence,' Churchill once wrote, 'they express ... all the antagonisms between nations or individuals'; and

- Euripides, the great philosopher poet and tragedian of ancient Athens wrote that 'A slave is he who cannot speak his thought.'

Or, as Plato put it: 'A life without criticism is not worth living.' Reportedly, Rasmussen's bending over brought smiles to Recep Tayyip Erdogan, but riled politicians in Copenhagen and in the rest of the free world – who judged it to be a severe mistake.

*If* NATO's policy is becoming synonymous with that of an agent of silence, and therefore of tyranny, *then* its existence is punishing rather than helping the free world. What is next is difficult to say. In Obama's April 2009 travails, 'next' has been the visit to Prague where he met three EU Presidents of a sort:

- the Czech Prime Minister, whose government fell, but whose country holds the six-monthly presidency of the EU;

- the Prime Minister of Sweden, who is next in line to become 'EU President'; and

- the President of the European Commission who is awaiting his renomination.

The way it has been reported in the press, Obama neither smiled nor spoke, his expression was unreadable, and he invited José Manuel Barroso, the third in the above EU Presidents list, to stand at the lone microphone. Barroso called the half-day US–EU summit 'a very important event', which it was not; then talked about strong transatlantic relationships while Obama gazed stoney-faced at his shoes.[29]

Next to the microphone came Sweden's Fredrik Reinfeldt, followed by the Czech Republic's Mirek Topolanek and by Obama himself, who spoke briefly, praising the 'leadership of the three gentlemen here' and talking a bit about North Korea (see Chapter 12). Neither on the side of the US nor on that of the EU was there any visible sense of leadership, and it would have been better for everybody if that Prague 'summit' had never taken place.

The 'leadership of the three gentlemen here' was particularly ludicrous, making fun of the EU – a fact of which the American President was fully aware as none of the 'EU Presidents' had anything to say (or could contribute a single thing) to the requests he had made during the early April 2009 tour, his first in the European continent as US President:

- more military help in Afghanistan;

---

29 *The Economist*, 11 April 2009.

- more fiscal stimulus in the EU economies; and

- 'buy more non-Russian gas', supposedly to assure more energy security.

Almost nothing was offered on the first Obama demand. Regarding the second, the G20 conclusions have been a non-event, with papered-over lingering transatlantic differences on financial regulation and stimulus plans (see the Epilogue). As for the 'buy more non-Russian gas', the request was hilarious as America has no alternative to offer.

Barack did, however, manage to earn a public rebuke from Nicolas Sarkozy, the French President, for strongly backing Turkish membership of the EU. This is something the French President opposes and he flatly stated that this is not the American President's business anyway (nor is it the business of out-of-office Tony Blair).

In the week of 18 April 2009 news broke of an account of a political meeting published in a French newspaper about Sarkozy's comments that he was not at all impressed by Obama's leadership, and that he regretted his lack of experience. A growing number of political pundits and commentators share the same impression, though they may not say so out loud.

At least one economist, however, had good advice to give to Obama just prior to the 2 April 2009 G20 meeting. Writing in the *Financial Times*, Martin Wolf suggested that Obama should say: 'My fellow leaders ... Let me get a big point out of the way: Yes, the US has messed up. We thought we knew about sophisticated modern finance. We were wrong. On behalf of my country I apologize . . . We must learn the lesson and look ahead, not backwards.'

It is a pity indeed that Obama did not follow Wolf's advice, and that he did not stand for banking regulation but instead espoused Orwellian 'New-Speak'. Had he taken leadership for global bank supervision (the global sheriff) and for righting the balances of the world's financial system, he would have been the one-eyed king in 'summit-land'.

# Epilogue: The 2010 Greek Financial Drama

*'Mine is a real battle against the forces of the shadow.'*

*Process and death of Socrates*

## 1. Spending Well Beyond One's Means

In early 2010 it has been exposed in a dramatic way that the euphoria with the euro, which prevailed as the global economy was in upswing, was largely based on smoke and mirrors. During the good years, instead of applying fiscal discipline to redress their balance sheets, the PIIGS: Portugal, Ireland, Italy, Greece and Spain accumulated debt, as if money grew on trees.

Year-on-year deficit budgets revealed a roadmap for fiscal catastrophe. The mismanagement of public affairs has been widespread and, to make matters worse, some of these countries faked their financial data. For their part, the EU's bureaucrats have been slow in sharpening their pencils and in watching carefully.

Things got out of hand in 2010 with the Greek financial drama. Only then did the European commission woke up and asked several member countries to explain how they would put their house in order. It was *as if* Euroland's chiefs of state and finance ministers have been taken aback and found it difficult to decide whether to bailout Greece or bring in the International Monetary Fund (IMF) as financier and policeman.

Increasingly, all this looked like the old-fashioned emerging markets debt crisis. Markets evidently drew their own conclusions from gaping deficits, government uncertainties and absence of fiscal discipline. The fact that the euro's interest rate is also fixed by the European Central Bank (ECB) makes it impossible for country-by-country devaluations.

To appreciate the background for this mess, as well as its possible aftereffects, the reader should know that since the launch of the euro as a single currency for a group of countries, there have been worries about profligacy. The absence of political union, or at least of a watchdog, saw to it that free spending jurisdiction borrowed excessively and passed on the bill to those sober – for instance, Germany.[1]

While this was most likely to happen was nobody's secret, nothing was done to install a euro sheriff. The Stability and Growth Pact signed by all of Euroland's members became a joke. No surprise therefore, that eleven years after the euro's birth, Greece hurtled towards disaster and those fears turned into an urgent question of policy.

It might have been Italy, Spain or Portugal playing Greece's role in the financial drama, as I wrote a couple of years ago in my book *Globalization's Limits*.[2] Let's face it, the euro is a currency without a country; a kid without a father.

In 2008/2009 it was looking like a national debt crisis spreading like brushfire in the European Union might have been launched by the East European ex-communist economies. Some of them, like Hungary and Latvia, were first in approaching the eye of the storm.

It did not happen that way. Eastern Europe still has to deal with its share of problems: an ageing workforce, poorly trained and autocratic officials, dilapidated infrastructure. But nobody has defaulted and nobody has rioted. By contrast rioting for 'no matter what' became current currency in Greece:

- greatly damaging its image,

- shaking its economy, and

- destabilizing its government.

---

1    For instance, Germany.
2    D.N. Chorafas, *Globalization's Limits. Conflicting National Interests in Trade and Finance*, Gower Publishing, Farnham, 2009.

The rebels without a cause, whose fight with police has become 'breaking news' for evening television, have been obstracting the functioning of the Greek state and shaking the confidence of the international community to it. But do they understand that they are also damaging themselves and their future, much more so than the fault they attribute to their country?

Greece has not been alone in this self-made descent into the abyss. Though the TV special of hooded hoodlums had not been seen in Portugal and Spain there, too, governments without a spine chose the easy way out, giving in to wages and subsidies pressures. As usual, they have been spending other people's money – but in this case the 'other people' are the taxpayers in Germany, France and the Netherlands.

Ireland is also near-bankruptcy, but for a different reason. When in the middle of the 2007–2010 economic crisis its government guaranteed the huge debts of overleveraged Irish (and some British) banks, it essentially took the euros out of the treasury of other Euroland member nations – just like that, without even asking.

This followed in the steps of the US and Britain, which had already given the bad example of coming to the rescue of their self-wounded banking industry by overleveraging and bankrupting the state. There is a good reason why Standard & Poor's and Moody's, the rating agencies, said that the AAA rating of the US and Britain has been put under review.

Smaller nations typically feel the consequences much earlier. The center-right Greek government had no business to imitate the US and Britain to the tune of a €28 billion (then $42 billion) injection to the treasury of private banks. This was public money going down the drain and Karamanlis, the then prime minister, knew very well that the Greek economy could not afford it because it was sinking into a sea of red ink.

- Swollen by mismanagement and years of budget overruns, the depth of Greek debt, has variable geometry between €300 billion (according to the optimists) and €405 billion (if the pessimists are right).

- As with any debt, this has to be serviced and the capital repaid when due. In 2010 alone Greece must finance its public debt to the tune of €55 billion – rolling over, if it may, a wholesome €25 billion in April and May 2010.

With a long and inexcusable delay of waking up to the facts, EU political leaders started to appreciate that a messy Greek default would harm almost everybody. Both markets and governments know only too well that behind Greece stand Portugal, Ireland, Spain and even Italy the world's second-biggest sovereign debtor (behind Japan, but ahead of Greece).

Theoretically, it looks like a case where Euroland countries should show solidarity and help. Practically, with the deep economic crisis of 2007–2010 every government is deep in the red. In addition, a hard question is how to assure that any help does not undermine urgently needed social reform in highly indebted jurisdictions. Also that it comes with conditions that promote sound policies, including:

- deep budget cuts;

- radical structural changes in the labour market;

- strict avoidance of budget deficits in the future; and

- facing up to the country's obligations, which unwisely have reached for the stars.

There has, as well, been trickery, not only of economic statistics but also (and more ominously) of official financial reporting. For this, those responsible should be brought to justice. Successive Greek governments who overspent also entered into derivative products with Goldman Sachs and other banks to lower their deficits. Swaps masked the numbers but the money is still due.[3]

Moreover, once again international banks have shown that their lending decisions are flawed. A swarm of them may go belly up if Greece defaults, which explains why different governments are on-and-off trying to find some sort of a solution. According to anecdotal evidence, the aforementioned wholesome amount of loans is concentrated to the banks of four nations with a huge share:

---

3    Angela Merkel aptly stated that, 'it would be a disgrace if it turned out that banks which already pushed us to the edge of the abyss were also party to falsifying Greek statistics.'

- French banks 25 per cent,

- German banks 18 per cent,

- American banks 15 per cent,

- Greek banks 10 to 12 per cent.

The balance comes from other credit institutions with British banks heading that second list. Getting out of the risk of this hallucinating financial drama requires leadership, resilience and level-headedness. This is a highwire balancing act which, if it fails, will have huge global consequences well beyond these €300–405 billion.

## 2. Politics, Politics and Politics

Politics have much to do with both the astronomical size of Greece's debt and with an orderly resolution of the crisis. In late 2009 the change in government from center-right to center-left intensified the Greek financial drama, as the socialists who came to power made wage increases for a large number of public servants, rather than wage control.

To finance this irresponsibility (which like Obama's healthcare was an electoral promise), since November 2009 the new government resorted to issuing short-term treasury bills with maturities of up to one year. Few takers were present for 5- or ten-year bonds, but for short-term financing the government:

- had to pay a sizeable premium, and

- it put Greek banks to the task, eventually taking them to the precipice.

Nothing has been learned from the Boris Yeltsin extravaganza of borrowing short-term at high interest rates from Russian banks, to make the government's ends meet. Russia defaulted in August 1998 and so did plenty of its banks, some of which went bust and others (like Sberbank) got nationalized.

Critics find no evidence that over the period of its first 3½ months in power George Papandreaou's socialist government understood the seriousness of the situation. Only on 14th January, 2010 did it unveil a poorly documented plan to cut the budget deficit:

- from 12.7 per cent to 8.7 per cent of GDP in the running year, and

- to below the 3 per cent ceiling for Euroland members by 2012.

Lack of detail, as well as the feeble and uncertain measures initially announced, were judged by the market as being unsatisfactory. As for the EU, reaction to the plan was lukewarm. In addition, economists questioned the plan's growth forecasts of 1.5 per cent in 2011 and 1.9 per cent for 2012 as utterly unrealistic.

The irony is that it had been Andreas Papandreou, the founder of the Socialist (Pasok) party,[4] who in the 1980s originated and presided over the origins of his country's crisis with a borrowing spree. This came over and above the lavish subsidies it extracted (at the time) from the EU.[5] Over the years, this infernal leveraging machine led to Greece's triple deficit:

- big budget imbalances,

- current account permanently in the red, and

- a soaring public debt leading to a humiliating last-ditch effort to escape sovereign default.

George Papandreou, a sociologist by training (which does not mean much) and also chairman of Socialist International, likes to blame speculators, including hedge funds, for the punishment that the country's bonds have taken in financial markets. Leaving aside the fact that it was Pasok who first signed up with Goldman Sachs to fake its financials through swaps, what Papandreou says has more than a grain of truth. But it does not solve Greece's problems.

It is good news, however, that the new prime minister accepts that Greece has made itself vulnerable by becoming Euroland's weakest link. For his part, George Papaconstantinou, the Finance Minister, has promised that the state

---

4   His son George inherited.
5   Spain continues extracting such lavish subsidies, in a totally unjustified manner. But this is the EU.

statistics office will be modernized and cut loose from political supervision (in reality: from political pressures).

It does not need explaining that whichever might be the solution to the crisis Greece will face tougher surveillance including regular monitoring by Eurostat, the EU's statistical agency. There is as well a long list of other necessary measures. This includes gaining credibility and selling the restructuring plan to the public.

- Happily, by a majority of about 53 per cent the Greek electorate supports the austerity measures.

- Unhappily, the pros are far from making unanimity in the ruling party. Senior Pasok members are objecting to austerity, which they claim will lead to social unrest.

It is quite likely that the restructuring of the economy will lead to more street riots, but there is no *deus ex machina*, and the global financial markets are unforgiving. The alternative is long suffering.

Credit rating agencies have cut the country's rating and still maintain a negative outlook. Compared to German Bunds spreads of credit default swaps zoomed from slightly over 100 basis points (bp) to nearly 350 bp.[6] While borrowing in euros, the cost of money for Greece is twice as high as that for Germany.

Critics say that as in socialist Spain and in socialist Portugal, the natural desire of some politicians for social cohesion is being abused to justify the protection of those in permanent jobs, in trade unions, in privileged professions, and in the bureaucracy. Structural changes are blocked by those who are 'in' the system, to the disadvantage of those who are 'out' of it. Critics also point out that in all these countries the public sector is, to say the least, bloated:

- With a population of just 11 million, Greece has a wholesome 1.5 million public employees.

---

6    At the height of its financial crisis in February 2008, because of the unqualified support it gave to its bankrupt banks, Ireland's CDOs spread hit 380 bp but by late 2009 the spread fell to roughly 150 bp.

- This number is roughly equal to that of German public employees, but Germany's population is 82 million.

Indeed, Greece, Portugal, Italy and Spain (and why not France) could learn from Germany's trick of reforming without strife. What all European governments must grasp, is that many policies adopted in the name of social cohesion do not promote compassion. Instead, they feed entrenched divisions and nurture *déclinisme*.

Following the Greek debacle and the uproar regarding Euroland's big spenders of other people's money, the Portuguese socialist prime minister announced some half-baked measures. It sounded *as if* the insignificance of his 'solution' could reduce the size of Portugal's problems – and of the deficits. In response, on 24 March 2010 credit rating agencies cut Portugal's rating, making money more expensive.

For his part, the Spanish socialist prime minister stayed aloof, probably trying in his own secretive way to fix-up with scotch tape the cracking dam of the economy's financial overleveraging. One is left wondering why all these politicians don't have the courage:

- to explain to the common people that the economy is in shatters, faring even worse than the derelict global economy, and

- that tough measures, including belt-tightening, are needed not because of any perverse pleasure in creating pain, but because without them the economy will go to hell – and those who will suffer most will, as usual, be the economically weaker.[7]

Why is it that Germany can manage both social cohesion and fiscal discipline, while the PIIGS cannot?[8] In terms of economic performance, from 1999 (when the exchange rates of the original eleven Euroland members were frozen), through 2006, Germany had a cumulative surplus in intra-EU trade of more than €800 billion. Per head, the Netherlands did even better with a cumulative surplus of €200 billion.

---

7   'We must tax the poor. They are the most numerous,' had said André Tardieu, a French socialist prime minister, in the early 1930s (That's exactly what the value added tax is doing).
8   Recently the PIIGS have been rechristened by analysts as the 'Club Med economies'.

By contrast, at that same period of time, Spain had a cumulative deficit of €300 billion; and so did France. Portugal had a cumulative deficit of €125 billion. Greece, which entered Euroland in 2001, had a cumulative deficit of €170 billion. These facts alone should have rung alarm bells. Politics, dirty politics, saw to it that they did not.

Not only do Germany and the Netherlands, but also the Indian state of Bihar – which used to be the country's most depressed and unruly member state for more than 15 years – provide an example on how to come up from under. Through leadership, in a few years Nitish Kumar changed the state's fortunes and altered its culture.

Kumar pulled off this transformation by first imposing law and order, restoring the state to its role as watchman rather than one of the rogue bodies around town. He put gangsters behind bars,[9] demanded speedy trials, and assured that convicted people no longer got lucrative licenses for liquor stores and ration shops, or subsidized food and fuel.

With law and order having gained the upper ground, Bihar citizens felt confident enough to engage in business. In the aftermath, the economy has grown at double-digit rates, though funds from Delhi also helped. Spain, Portugal and Greece too had lavish funding from the EU, but their economies have not been growing because they are utterly mismanaged by both center-right and center-left regimes.

'The huge imbalances from which the Greek economy is suffering are not sustainable in the long run,' said Joaquin Almunia, then EU monetary affairs commissioner on 3 February 2010. 'The markets are putting on pressure. This pressure cannot be ignored.'[10] The same is true of the economies of Portugal and Spain.

It does not take a genius to understand that when one is confronted with a fiscal catastrophe, there are only two options. Either taxes will have to rise and salaries be cut, or a very serious attempt must be made to rein in legally mandated entitlements and expensive chapters written for social purposes

---

9    In Athens shootouts by Albanians and other immigrants (legal and illegal) have become current currency. Demonstrators, including students, run wild and Molotov cocktails, are now a sort of a legacy. But the Karamanlis and Papandreou governments play impotent. Third age citizen simply don't feel confident to go out after dark.

10   *Financial Times*, 4 February 2010.

(including early retirement) – even if these have so far have been considered untouchable. There can be no sacred cows.

## 3. The Fiscal Challenge is Global, but in some Countries it is Much More Intense

Part of the irony with the PIIGS fiscal abyss is that scant attention has been paid to the destructive forces of huge budget deficits. At nearly 15 per cent, Ireland's is above Greece's 12.7 per cent; but Ireland has a national debt level of 'only' 65.8 per cent, hence it can better absorb the shock. Britain will also have a budget deficit of about 13 per cent, but it is no Euroland member (therefore it can devalue) and its national debt stands at 68.6 per cent of GDP.[11]

Italy has roughly a 5 per cent budget deficit, thought at 115 per cent its national debt is just a sliver worse than that of Greece.[12] For its part, Japan has so badly mismanaged itself during its last 'twenty lost years' that its national debt hit 200 per cent of GDP; the largest ever in the modern world. Judging from the fact that the Japanese economy continues to be in a coma, the reader should look at this statistic as an unmitigated disaster.

A news item published in the press on 10 February 2010, and attributed to a senior executive of the French Ministry of Finance, put it this way: 'If tomorrow, or the day after, speculation attacks Italy whose deficit is below 5.3 per cent but national debt is the highest in Europe with 115.1 per cent, France is the next one in the list.'[13]

The same news item states that the analysis which led to this statement has been shared (in the secrecy of her office) by Christine Lagarde, the French Finance Minister. There is more to this reference, all the way to the ECB. 'The European Central Bank continues to behave as if nothing happens,' that article stated, and 'The European governments are not able to coordinate their economic policies.'[14]

What the aforementioned quantitative information clearly shows is that in the end the degradation of national finances – from budget deficits, to current

---

11  Roughly similar statistics characterize the American economy.
12  *The Economist*, 6 February 2010.
13  *Le Canard Enchaîné*, 10 February 2010.
14  Idem.

account balances and debt as percent of GDP – comes home to roost. In fact while widely used, the figures regarding to national debt are very partial because they don't account for:

- the huge deficits of social security: pensions and health care,

- other occult commitments made by the state, like the silly salvage of bankrupt big banks at any cost, and

- the great indebtedness of families which in countries like France, Britain and the US is beyond 100 per cent of GDP.[15]

Where all these references lead to is that the Greek financial drama cannot be measured by the relatively small size of the country's economy in respect to that of Euroland. It has been frequently said that the first €20–25 billion immediately needed for salvaging Greece only represent 1 per cent of Euroland's GDP. This does not make sense, not for one but for three reasons:

- For Greece, the €25 billion is only a first installment and, as such, it is going to solve nothing.

- Hat in hand behind Greece stand Spain, Portugal, Ireland, Italy and more.

- German and Dutch taxpayers will violently object to throwing their savings in a firebrigade approach to rescue big spenders, while their own national budgets are under stress.

Moreover, the Greek financial drama has both a deeper and broader global perspective. Quite unsettling is its similitude to the 2007 American subprime crisis, which brought the world's financial system all the way to hell (it is still there). The common ground between the two disastrous events can be expressed as:

- very high leverage,

- abysmal credit standards, and

---

15 To its credit, the French government is now taking stern measures to protect consumers from the folly of over-indebtedness.

- lack of responsibility by the principal actors.

To this explosive mix is added the morphing of big and unjustified banker's bonuses into something even more sinister. In Greece, and in some other countries, salaries of the public sector add up to 51 per cent of the nation's budget. There is a swarm of bureaucrats and the government pays a 13th and 14th month salary.

To complement this financial suicide, nearly half the citizens declare a revenue below €12,000, and another 44 per cent of less than €30,000. The black economy thrives and there are as well the *fakelakia*, little envelopes with corruption money passed under the table.[16]

The fact that rampant corruption has become a sub-culture can have dire consequences. In other EU countries, too, from social security abuses to everything else (you name it) the looting of public wealth has turned into a national sport, joining superleveraging and spending beyond one's means.

The salient problem presently facing the governments of Greece, Portugal and Spain (to mention a few) is that of restructuring the whole society, reestablishing law and order and bringing leadership into politics. On paper that sounds reasonable, but the leaders are missing. Theoretically, but only theoretically, in the absence of leadership the way out is through one of five scenarios. Taking Greece as an example:

- The country muddles through on its own.

- There is a last-minute bailout by Euroland.

- The International Monetary Fund takes over, and establishes a new framework.

- An orderly default takes place, and shakes the markets.

- There is disorderly default, market panic and exit from Euroland (rather unlikely).

---

16  I have an aunt in Athens who had to be operated, and the doctor asked for a *fakelaki of €7,000*, over and above what the social security would have paid.

Greece could muddle through *if* it found the money to do so, which is not the way to bet. Still, this would be a bumpy ride. It will take time for the Greek fiscal data to improve, and for markets to trust the data. European institutions are likely to keep strong public pressure on Greece to adjust, instead of sounding the all-clear. In the mean time, the euro would remain weak.

The likelihood of a Euroland salvage plan (read: a German-Dutch loan) has considerably diminished as this would probably not pass the German Constitutional Court. Anyway Merkel is cool on throwing good money after bad money, as she sees that this is political dynamite – and an invitation to the PIIGS to continue spending other taxpayers' money.

More likely is an IMF rescue with IMF-style conditions for redressing a disastrous financial situation. But the ECB is against an IMF intervention, and other 'solutions' like a European Monetary Fund have little chance of getting through apart of requiring many years of difficult negotiations.

There is quite likely a reason why on 23 March 2010 it was announced that France and Germany agreed on IMF's role in the Greek crisis. Two days later on 25 March Euroland's finance ministers met, but nothing definite has emerged. In the meantime the April/May deadline for the billions of euros approaches, and economists raise biting questions:

- Would delays trigger a CDS event?

- How could contagion play out in various asset markets?

The way to bet is that these questions weighted on the thinking of European Council members, the 27 chiefs of state of the EU, who on 26 March 2010 gave themselves sweeping new powers to coordinate all EU economies. Agreement on a plan promoted by Angel Merkel and Nicolas Sarkozy includes a landmark €30 billion ($40 billion) bailout package for Greece to be used as last resort.

Though at the time these lines are written details are still missing, the official announcement states that such fund will be provided by the EU and International Monetary Fund to a ratio of 2 to 1. Money aside, the IMF's contribution includes its significant knowhow on how to put back on the rails economies in distress. The European Central Bank also chipped in, through its decision to keep the minimum credit threshold in the collateral framework at BBB-investment level, beyond the end of 2010.

The salvage plan puts Herman van Rompuy, the recently elected European Council president, in charge of the economic governance of Europe – including economic planning and fiscal scrutiny.[17] Sarkozy and Merkel wanted to see written the term 'economic governance', but Gordon Brown objected and it was watered down. The business of Europe is politics.

In its way, the Greek financial drama took an interesting and rather positive twist, though it is still far from an ending. It needs no explaining that from the list of the preceding two pages the most extreme cases are the default scenarios. If either of them materializes, it will have the most severe consequences for sovereigns and for markets.

Both an orderly and a disorderly default will greatly impact on equities, credits, interest rates, commodities and foreign exchange – as well as on globalization and on the international banking system. This is precisely why (as it has been already brought to the reader's attention) the 2010 Greek financial drama resembles so much of the American subprimes debacle of 2007 and Lehman Brothers bankruptcy of September 2008 in one go.

The risk is mounting that not only the PIIGS economies but also the world's financial system can become damaged goods. A timely warning on the precarious state of the global economy has been given on 21 March 2010 by John Lipsky, the second in command of the International Monetary Fund.

In a speech at the China Development Forum in Beijing, Lipsky offered a clear and grim prognosis for the world's wealthiest countries, which are at a level of indebtedness not seen since the end of World War II. For the United States, he said, 'a higher public savings rate will be required to ensure long-term fiscal sustainability.'

Who would have thought a couple of decades ago that America's economy will be in the sick list. In addition, the IMF's deputy managing director stated that the average ratio of debt to gross domestic product (GDP) in advanced economies is expected to reach in 2010 the level that prevailed in 1950. Even assuming that fiscal stimulus programs are withdrawn in the next few years,

---

17  Van Rompuy will lead a task force of member states and the ECB to look at all options of economic governance. The report is due before 2010's end.

the ratio of public debt in major industrial countries is projected to rise to 110 per cent of GDP by the end of 2014.

According to the IMF, the public debt of Britain, France and the United States will by 2014 surpass the 100 per cent level of GDP. That's very bad news for the 'blue ribbon' G7 and its members. (Italy and Japan already suffer from an unaffordable and unsustainable national debt. John Lipsky said that only Canada and Germany will escape that fate.

'Addressing this fiscal challenge is a key near-term priority, as concerns about fiscal sustainability could undermine confidence in the economic recovery,' said John Lipsky,[18] also warning governments not to try to inflate their way out of their debts. To his words:

- a moderate increase in inflation would have only a limited impact on real debt burdens,

- while accelerating inflation would impose major economic costs and create significant risks to a sustained expansion.

In conclusion, the challenges which come by staying at the edge of the fiscal abyss will be around for longer than many people think. To reduce debt ratios to the pre-crisis average of 60 per cent of GDP by 2030 would require an 8 percentage points swing, according to Lipsky. This means to a surplus of about 4 per cent of GDP in 2020, from a structural deficit of about 4 per cent of GDP.

The IMF estimates that advanced economies would also have to take other steps, like changes in pensions and health care programs, as well as cutbacks in spending and higher tax revenues. Does it sound like a dismal future? It is so. The real crime has not been the now and then mismanagement of the economy, but the fact that this continued over several decades in an unconscious and irresponsible way.

---

18  Fiscal policy is expected to be a top item on the agenda when in June 2010 leaders of the G20 nations gather for a summit in Toronto.

# Index